TRANS-PACIFIC RACISMS

AND THE U.S. OCCUPATION OF JAPAN

D0685309

A STUDY OF THE EAST ASIAN INSTITUTE

COLUMBIA UNIVERSITY

THE UNITED STATES AND PACIFIC ASIA:

STUDIES IN SOCIAL, ECONOMIC, AND POLITICAL INTERACTION

CAROL GLUCK AND MICHAEL HUNT, GENERAL EDITORS

STUDIES OF THE EAST ASIAN INSTITUTE

COLUMBIA UNIVERSITY

The East Asian Institute is Columbia University's center for research, publication, and teaching on modern East Asia. The Studies of the East Asian Institute were inaugurated in 1962 to bring to a wider public the results of significant new research on modern and contemporary East Asia.

A STUDY OF THE EAST ASIAN INSTITUTE

TRANS-PACIFIC RACISMS

AND THE U.S. OCCUPATION OF JAPAN

Yukiko Koshiro

COLUMBIA UNIVERSITY PRESS

NEW YORK

Columbia University Press
Publishers Since 1893
New York   Chichester, West Sussex
Copyright © 1999 by Columbia University Press

Library of Congress Cataloging-in-Publication Data
Koshiro, Yukiko.
Trans-Pacific racisms and the U.S. occupation of Japan / Yukiko Koshiro.
  p.   cm. — (A study of the East Asian Institute, Columbia University)
Includes index.
ISBN 0–231–11348–X (cloth). — ISBN 0-231-11349-8 (paper : alk. paper)
    1. United States—Foreign relations—Japan. 2. Japan—Foreign
relations—United States. 3. Racism—Political aspects—United
States—History—20th century. 4. United States—Foreign
relations—1945–1989 5. Japan—History—Allied occupation,
1945–1952.   I. Title. II. Series: Studies of the East Asian Institute.
                E183.8.J3K67   1999
             327.73052—dc21   98–39912

Casebound editions of Columbia University Press books are
printed on permanent and durable acid-free paper.
Printed in the United States of America
c 10 9 8 7 6 5 4 3 2 1
p 10 9 8 7 6 5 4 3 2 1

For Carol Gluck

THE UNITED STATES AND PACIFIC ASIA:

STUDIES IN SOCIAL, ECONOMIC, AND POLITICAL INTERACTION

CAROL GLUCK AND MICHAEL HUNT, GENERAL EDITORS

ALSO IN THIS SERIES

The Great Powers in East Asia, 1953–1960
Warren I. Cohen and Akira Iriye

To the People: James Yen and Village China
Charles W. Hayford

CONTENTS

ACKNOWLEDGMENTS
ix
A NOTE ON THE ORIGIN OF MODERN RACISM
xi

Introduction: Race in U.S.–Japanese Relations
1

1. The International Framework for Postwar Japanese-American Racism
15

2. Race and Culture: Person to Person
49

3. Racial Equality, Minorities, and the Japanese Constitution
89

4. Japanese Overseas Emigration
123

5. The Problem of Miscegenation
159

Epilogue: The Aftermath—The Lesson of the Occupation
201

A NOTE ON THE SOURCE CITATIONS
221
NOTES
223
INDEX
285

ACKNOWLEDGMENTS

My early studies on U.S. immigration history and policy and their impact on the international community started under the instruction of Professor Konami Takashi of the Tokyo University for Foreign Studies. They continued in my graduate work in international relations at the University of Tokyo, especially with Professor Hirano Ken'ichirō, who introduced his students to the new field of cultural analysis of international relations.

I am very thankful to Professors James Shenton, Alden Vaughan, and Hollis Lynch of the History Department at Columbia University for enhancing my understanding of the issue of American racism. Also, I would like to thank all my friends in my days at Columbia who read and commented on my dissertation, upon which this work is based. Debbie Rosen, André Schmid, and Ken Ruoff deserve special mention for their critical help at an early stage of writing.

In the process of improving the book, Professor John Dower, History Department at the Massachusetts Institute of Technology, read an early version of the manuscript and offered invaluable comments. Professors Marc Gallichio, History Department at Villanova University, and Warren Cohen, History Department of the University of Maryland, Baltimore, also read the manuscript and encouraged me. Professor Michael Hunt, History Department at the University of North Carolina at Chapel Hill, went out of his way to help me sharpen my arguments and analysis. My colleagues in the History Department at the University of Notre Dame also offered references, suggestions, and critical comments. I am grateful especially to Professor Gary Hamberg for his mentorship and friendship. My greatest debt, both academic and personal, goes to my adviser Professor Carol Gluck of Columbia University, who not only encouraged me to do a synthesis of American and Japanese histories but also helped me launch my career in the United States.

ACKNOWLEDGMENTS

Both Madge Huntington of Columbia University's East Asian Institute and Kate Wittenberg of Columbia University Press encouraged me to move forward with the manuscript, and Roy Thomas of Columbia University Press provided the best editorial help one could ever hope for. The institute for Scholarship in the Liberal Arts at the University of Notre Dame awarded me a generous publication grant.

Special thanks should also go to my Notre Dame students, who discussed my work with professional acumen, and to Sergei V. Tikhonov for his inspiration and help of one sort or another on Morningside Heights. For the rest of my friends in Japan, the United States, and elsewhere, I hope to have a chance to thank you in person soon.

Finally, I wish to express gratitude to my mother Koshiro Mitoko and sister Koshiro Noriko and to close relatives in Japan and the United States for their support. My mother and sister especially deserve credit for their superb research assistance on this project: to Noriko, who shared my interest in the subject and helped me with archival research in Japan, and to Mom, who sent me newspaper clippings on the Occupation and kept me up to date with the latest news. On completion of this project, I cherish fond memories of my father Koshiro Yoshio, my grandmother Ogawa Aki, and of course Picky.

A NOTE ON JAPANESE NAMES

In this volume, Japanese names, unless otherwise indicated, are given in traditional form—that is, the family name precedes the given name. For individuals who follow (or are better known by) the Western form of family name last, the family name appears in capital letters (e.g., Akira KUROSAWA).

A NOTE ON THE ORIGIN OF MODERN RACISM

Arthur de Gobineau (1816–1882), a French diplomat by profession and the author of various writings in the fields of philosophy, history, Oriental studies, and archaeology, is often considered a founder of the belief in racial inequality. His work, *Essai sur l'Inégalité des Races Humaines*, published in parts from 1853 to 1855, proposed a thesis on racial inequality explained by different degrees of capacity to originate a great civilization. Though he accepted the opinion that all mankind had a single origin, he justified and further promoted the concept of dividing the races into three—the white, the black, and the yellow. Gobineau differentiated these three races in terms of beauty, intellectual capacity, physical strength, fertility, and other traits and placed them in a hierarchical order with the negroid variety at the lowest, the yellow races slightly higher, and the distinctly superior white people at the top. Gobineau's works influenced both the Germans and the British in developing their separate racial views and became well established in the last decade of the nineteenth century.

TRANS-PACIFIC RACISMS

AND THE U.S. OCCUPATION OF JAPAN

Race in U.S.-Japanese Relations

The U.S. occupation of Japan after World War II transformed a brutal war charged with overt racism into an amicable peace in which the race issue seemed to have vanished. How did this happen and what were the domestic and international racist threads that intertwined to produce such a result? This is the question that defines this study.

During the war, each side demonized the other. The United States portrayed the conflict as a battle for the preservation of Anglo-Saxon civilization against Japanese aggression and depicted the Japanese as inferior imitators of the white races (sometimes even characterizing them as "apes"). Japan claimed to be the sole champion of civilization in Asia and railed against white supremacy, portraying the Anglo-Saxon foe as "demonic and beastly Americans and British" (*kichiku Bei-Ei*). Both sides indulged in heated racist rhetoric, criticized each other's racist attitudes, and proclaimed their own superiority.

Once the war was over and U.S. occupation of Japan began, the overwrought propaganda subsided and both Americans and Japanese quickly moved to collaborate in the remaking of Japan. In April 1952, under the terms of the San Francisco Peace Treaty, Japan reemerged as an independent and permanently unarmed nation with the United States as its designated guardian. The success of the Occupation and the subsequent formation of an alliance spawned the myth that the two nations had learned a lesson from the Pacific War and had forever removed the race question from U.S.-Japanese discourse. Under the spell of this myth, racism became a mutual taboo, something both countries avoided discussing altogether for the sake of postwar friendship. Thus racism itself, albeit hidden though it was tacitly practiced on both sides, provided the basis for a new relationship.

The relative harmony of the Occupation should not be surprising, since prewar Japan and the United States shared, in terms of basic values and attitudes, more areas of agreement than disagreement. Much of the mutual wartime animosity was forged and intensified by morale-bolstering propaganda. When hostilities ceased, each country learned to adopt more "rational" perceptions of the other for the sake of a mutually beneficial normalization of their relations, and they abandoned wartime hatreds.[1] Furthermore, as Akira IRIYE has pointed out, even at the height of the war there had been a parallel development on both sides of the Pacific. Prominent figures in Japan and the United States sought postwar political and economic cooperation within a Wilsonian framework of world politics. These Wilsonian aspirations subsequently eased the tasks of the Occupation.[2] In the process of reconciliation, racist propaganda was no longer useful, and indeed was downright pointless and destructive.

For many years after the war, disputes based on racism were muted or disappeared. In the 1980s, however, the world witnessed a sudden revival of the rhetoric of U.S.-Japanese racial confrontation. When Japan dramatically increased its investment in the American market and closed the financial and industrial gap that had existed since after the war with the United States, a racist rhetorical confrontation occurred again, as it had in the prewar period. The Western world, as well as Japan's Asian neighbors, suspected that Japan was becoming increasingly ambitious, aiming to replace the United States as the foremost economic superpower. The United States interpreted Japan's challenge as an Asian threat to Western superiority. Japan, in turn, saw a white peril in Western economic domination and condemned the United States for denying Japan a fair share of the world market because of its race.[3] The revival of the old yellow-versus-white peril surfaced again in both countries' competition for world control, exposing the myth that racism had disappeared. Despite a miraculously smooth collaboration during the Occupation, the fundamental rhetoric of race had lain hidden and intact, resurfacing as a destructive force only some two and a half decades later, when the political situation changed. What had happened in the meantime? This study argues that the race issue was transformed from an instrument of wartime hatred into a negotiable part of a broader Japanese-American arrangement during the Occupation. Racism did not evaporate; it merely moved from the battlefield to the bargaining table.

A key to understanding the persistence of a strong substratum of racist thinking in U.S-Japan relations lies in the ambiguity of the nature of race. Race is a taxonomy invented to define one group's inherent identity as embodied in physical characteristics and consolidated by common sociocultural and historical ties. It is a ubiquitous concept demarcating groups at various levels—social, national, and international. In modern times rabid nationalisms have institutionalized racism into the behavioral and attitudinal features of an entire nation, in order to justify that nation's actions against inferior "others" through an ideology of superiority. Racial discourse has thus transformed conceptions of class, culture, religion, and nation into matters of social subjectivity, and has lifted ideology, hierarchy, and domination from the communal level to the global level.[4] Thus, in the context of U.S.-Japanese relations, the term *race* came to represent two separate ideas— that is, race as manifested by physical appearance, and race as an explanation of national power and status in the world. This double meaning of race has evolved into ever-widening ramifications of use, depending on the varying social and diplomatic circumstances between the two peoples.

On the one hand, the race issue in the prewar period triggered a dispute involving anti-Japanese immigration (into the United States) and eventually helped to draw the two nations into a collision over each other's claim of preeminence as a leader of Asia. On the other, there were yet occasions when the United States and Japan nurtured a common racial ideology, extolling each other's fitness for world leadership. When this was the case, race promoted U.S.-Japanese collaboration. Throughout the twentieth century, this two-edged issue has been a significant force, at times bringing about friendly cooperation, at other times hostile confrontation. The experience in the U.S. occupation of Japan was no exception.

The role of race has not received its due in the voluminous work written since the Occupation period on the political, economic, and diplomatic relations of the United States and Japan. Both American and Japanese scholars have hesitated to acknowledge or analyze the racial aspect as an independent variable in U.S.-Japanese relations.[5] The dismissal of race from scholarly discourse may be related to the immediate postwar tendency among scholars to deny the existence of race altogether for the sake of promoting a fundamental belief in the biological equality of human beings. After having seen the virulence of pseudoscientific racism that spurred on the genocide of World War II, most notably the Holocaust, these scholars may have felt the urgent need to battle the mythologies of racism by presenting a less provocative— perhaps more rational—view of the perceived differences in human beings. Thus, in 1950, UNESCO (United Nations Educational, Scientific, and Cultural Organization) issued a denial of racism from a scientific point of view:

"Scientists have reached general agreement in recognizing that mankind is one; that all men belong to the same species, *Homo sapiens*."[6] Henceforth, scholars became wary about using the term "race." References to race without objective and theoretical definition were all but eliminated.

Apart from the world of science, however, race as a concept persisted and eventually included sociological and anthropological definitions of culture that embraced almost every human activity. Arguments for the sociological existence of races continued independent of the biological claims. Regardless of whether or not there was a scientific basis for race as a determinant of innate human traits, scholars conceded that in the world at large ideological constructs of racism persisted.

From this early postwar search for an acceptable definition of race (and racism) scholars found a way to approach race in the cultural context. Racism was now seen as a form of discrimination against differences in culture and lifestyle, not against physical differences per se, and considered a clash of the sociocultural constructs between groups. This so-called "culturally determinist orthodoxy" interpretation had emerged as early as the 1920s in an attempt to replace theories of racism based on biology: culture, not biology, was now offered as the central paradigm of human behavior. Cultural anthropologists Claude Lévi-Strauss, Franz Boas, and his renowned students Ruth Benedict and Margaret Mead contended that compared to the influence of the cultural environment in which a "racial" group lived, the biological influences on the formation of personality were altogether irrelevant. Darwinian laws of evolution and natural selection and the "survival of the fittest" should in no way legitimize racism. Discrimination, these anthropologists argued, occurs because of differences in culture, not because of a dynamic between the innately superior and the innately inferior. More important, these anthropologists also emphasized cultural relativism and environmental determinism—that all cultures are equal and no culture is destined to produce either superior or inferior individuals.[7] The postwar culturalist approach might be regarded as a resurgence of this prewar attempt to negate physical racism.

In keeping with this trend in scholarship, culture became a favorite tool for the analysis of postwar U.S.-Japan relations. In fact, as long as race—or racism—was merely one mode of thinking, ideologically or otherwise, and existed only as an image in the minds of the two peoples, then it could be examined in a framework of intercultural analysis, as pioneered by Akira IRIYE. His early multiarchival works (e.g., the use of various archives in more than one nation for an analysis of a certain international event with an aim to establish a multilateral view of it), for example, demonstrated how Japanese and American mutual racism was a result of misconceptions of each other's society and culture, which in turn led to unwarranted fear and distrust and resulted in a tragic confrontation.[8] Proponents of the cultural approach, or cultural relativists, hope to achieve a better understanding of the ideological and intellectual underpinnings of international behavior. They treat racism as transnational interactions of the cultural visions, self-images, and prejudices of one society toward another. They anticipate that racism can be cured through the two cultures' mutual understanding.

In a way, this approach has validity. The Americanization of Japan and the Japanization of America are possible to a certain extent. Dynamic cultural interactions are indeed capable of creating a global culture. Various cultural aspects—conventionally embodied in ideas, activities, and even goods—can be experienced, shared, exchanged, and transferred among peoples. American goods, ideas, and ways of life can spread to and influence Asian societies and thus enhance mutual understanding between American and Asian peoples. The reverse flow may bring the same result and together stimulate and even create a new hybrid culture.

This promising outlook enticed scholarly attention to the U.S. occupation of Japan because the Occupation offered an unprecedented level of cross-cultural interactions. The Japanese experienced the Americanization of their society in such areas as education, literature, music, entertainment, sports, diet, housing, family relationships, marriage, dating, and sexual mores. To the Japanese generation that grew up during the Occupation, baseball, jazz, Wrigley's, Hershey's, and a few English phrases picked up on the street from GIs bring bittersweet memories of their wondrous encounter with America. At the same time, thousands of Americans, GIs and civilians alike, discovered Japanese society and popular culture and were instrumental in bringing *sushi*, *tempura*, *kabuki*, *sumo*, and *haiku* to American society, along with many Japanese songs as well as other words, phrases, and ideas. These Americans remember with nostalgia their Occupation transit in an exotic culture wherein they had felt privileged to witness the ancient Orient.

Beneath the relatively smooth surface of this reciprocal exposure, however, lurks an insidious racism, a racism that cannot be laid to rest through an examination of cultural differences. Despite the common perception that, during the Occupation, cultural and intellectual distances across the Pacific narrowed at great speed, perceived racial differences between Japanese (and other Asians) and white Americans remained intact, ultimately hampering the fullest range of interactions between the two sides. The sociocultural transformation of Japan into an Americanized nation did not remove this wall. In Japanese-American interactions, racism was implacable. Race was an uneradicable idea—a construct based on physical traits—within each side's national identity and, as such, presented an immovable barrier between the Japanese and the Americans. It was easy enough for the Japanese to adopt Western-style clothing or for Americans to wear kimonos, but in each case it was always clear who was Japanese and who was American. A simple look at facial features and skin color kept the lines clear. Race as an ideology constructed on the basis of physical traits is not as fluid or fungible as culture is.[9]

In American society itself, race, as a physical rather than a cultural construct, is a distinct issue. Historically, American society required a color separation in order to preserve the melting pot exclusively for the white peoples of European origin. The "melting pot" rhetoric—America's power to amalgamate people of different origins and create a new population for American democracy—served as a powerful ideology for national cohesion and growth, but such Americanization applied only to European races, never to the Asian or African races. Only when the immigrant became physically indistinguishable from the mythical creation of the "average American" had assimilation taken place. Until the 1940s and 1950s, social assimilation did not count toward full Americanization. Let us suppose that, sometime in the 1930s, Mr. Fujimoto, a Nisei, was the deacon of a Methodist church in Los Angeles as well as a lawyer, pleading many court cases in excellent English, with a wife who was engaged in volunteer work in the community and two children in public school. None of this would have made him or his family thoroughly assimilated Americans at that time.[10] What is critical is not a person's physical appearance per se, but the significance attached to this appearance. This has always been true in racist thinking.

Even today, in spite of the absence of a statutory definition of race, an ongoing institutionalization of physical differences continues to shape various facets of American life. Note that the U.S. government in its own census categorizes Americans into five major groups—American Indian or Alaskan Native, Asian or Pacific Islander, Black, White, and Hispanic—and gauges the level of racial interactions as well as integration in society. With a goal to combat racism, America needs to remain racist—and as a result typifies the obvious contradictions inherent in modernist racial ideology.[11] Race and racism continue to prevail.

The force of race, or racism, during the Occupation and afterward cannot be overestimated. Ironically, in fact, it was the race factor that was the positive element in the dynamics between the two nations during the postwar years. Pseudoscientific racism survived the destructive war: notions of innate superiority and inferiority, both intellectual and physical, not only determined uncompromising American attitudes toward the Japanese but shaped the two peoples' views of each other and of the other peoples in the world. On their part, the Americans maintained racially segregated units within their own military, continued the anti-Oriental immigration and naturalization policy until 1953, and retained the immigration quota system unfavorable to Asians until 1965. Moreover, racial discrimination was officially sanctioned in the United States, especially in the southern states, until the mid-1960s, and continues to affect many aspects of social and political life. The Japanese, too, retained the same prewar racist thinking that had justified their imperialism and colonialism. They were just as unenthusiastic about racial interaction with the Americans.

Racism and discrimination had developed in East Asia along the same lines as the West, relying on myths of origin, descent, and the supposed blood ties that exist among peoples. East Asian racism targets and discriminates against outsiders, or the "others," with ideologies of racial hierarchy, just as white racism does.[12] Japan's twentieth-century racial discourse closely resembled that of any Western imperialist nation, in that a myth of Japan as a racially homogeneous and pure nation began to form within a quasi-scientific pretext. When Japan expanded its colonial empire, growing to become a multiethnic and multiracial empire, racial superiority became an ideological force to legitimate Japan's rule over non-Japanese peoples in Asia. Scholars of biology, physiology, eugenics, cultural anthropology, sociology, history, theology, and linguistics argued for the racial origin of the Japanese and the desirability of preserving racial purity. Racial proximity seemed to indicate racial unity between Japanese and other Asians, but assimilation into Japanese culture never established relations of equality. The Japanization of colonial peoples in terms of appearances and lifestyle was a benevolent administrative device in Taiwan, Korea, and other areas. At the same time, the Japanese evoked the moral right and duty of the advanced race to rule over lesser races in their colonies, because of their belief that innate racial differences made it impossible for colonial peoples to rise to a higher level of civilization.[13]

American and Japanese racism ran along parallel lines when it came to interracial marriage. In American society, since the time of the introduction of black slaves into the original colonies, a taboo on miscegenation had been institutionalized through state laws banning marriage between a white and a colored—including an Asian—person, leaving the latter group permanently unassimilable.[14]

Japanese society, though it did not codify such mores into law, developed a similar ideology on the importance of preserving racial purity. A loose taboo existed against miscegenation, punishable by latent to blatant ostracism. While Japanese officials were establishing a Greater East Asian Co-Prosperity Sphere, they were avoiding racial mixing with other Asians.[15]

Despite the enthusiasm for cultural exchanges during the Occupation, there was no desire for nor encouragement of racial mixing between the Japanese and the Americans. Each society refused to accept the offspring of interracial marriages—a half-Japanese and half-American generation—as part of their respective national identities. Japan disdained America as a mongrel nation of immigrants, and America scorned Japan for its ancestral origin as a hodgepodge of Asian races. In their mutual perceptions lay the belief in their own racial purity—a peculiar symmetry of their racist thinking that clearly survived the war. It is this belief and practice on both sides that continues to complicate interactions between Japan and the United States.

A taboo against miscegenation has, in this case, an interesting contradictory effect. In a nation-state, such a taboo is part of the desire for so-called racial purity, which in turn is a source of national pride and solidarity. For Japan and the United States, this taboo provided a crucial element in their identities as nation-states and, from the beginning to the twentieth century, as world powers. Remarkably, while this mutual racism kept Japanese and Americans apart as individuals, it also lured the two nations into a collaborative acceptance of the existing racial hierarchies of world politics.

As Michael Hunt has pointed out, an ideology based on the racial classification of "other" peoples has shaped American diplomatic history along with a conception of national mission and a hostility toward social revolutions. When the United States became the dominant power, its domestic racism engulfed the world.[16] Since Matthew Perry's fateful expedition, which opened up Japan in the mid-nineteenth century, the United States and Japan were keenly aware of the disparity in power between a superior West and an inferior non-West. But the United States adopted a flexible attitude toward Japan and did not immediately apply the negative label of nonwhite. Japan, on the other hand, developed for itself a dualistic racial identity—a unique by-product of its successful Westernization attempt— and entered the Western-dominated racial hierarchy to share world power. After the Russo-Japanese War (1904–1905), U.S. political and military figures were inclined to let the qualities of the Japanese as a race be an aspect of their acceptance of Japan as a world power. In this unique arrangement, race symbolized the power of a nation-state and became an elastic concept, almost like a cultural construct.

Since the success of Commodore Perry's expedition, there had been an innocent belief among Americans that the Japanese had more of an aptitude for acquiring the civilization of the West than any other Oriental peoples, and the U.S. government bestowed an honorable racial label on the Japanese through diplomatic protocols. Alfred Thayer Mahan, naval historian and strategist, who steadfastly advocated Anglo-American cooperation based on a belief in shared racial superiority, respected only the Japanese among Orientals because they were "repeating the experience of our Teutonic ancestors." Theodore Roosevelt, who justified the Chinese exclusion laws because he perceived the Chinese as weak and passive, distinguished between Chinese and Japanese. The Japanese earned his admiration especially after their victory against the Russians. In his annual message in December 1905, he placed the Japanese in the same rank as "Englishman or Irishman, Frenchman or German, Italian, Scandinavian, Slav, or Magyar," and warned that discrimination against them was not in the good old American tradition.[17]

For its part, Japan made it easier for a mutual U.S.-Japan racist accommodation when it adopted the "Western" notion of race as an ideology and rapidly transformed itself into a modern nation and a colonial empire. Like the United States, it established a racial ideology to legitimize its diplomatic goals. In the age of imperialism, when competition with the West was perceived as a vital condition for survival, Japan adopted a Western sense of racial awareness, especially regarding its mission in the world. It was this close resemblance to Western rhetoric that enabled Japanese and Western— and American—racial ideologies to mesh.

The Japanese leaders of the modernization process, while aware of racial differences among Europeans and Asians, developed an optimistic belief that their efforts to modernize could easily duplicate Western entrepreneurship. They did not consider themselves inferior to the West. Thus, in accepting Western racial theory, they had no trouble exempting themselves from the category of colored races. The Japanese government taught school children in an 1874 textbook that "what makes the difference between the wise and the unintelligent among human beings is the good act of learning or the lack of it" (my translation).[18] The government hoped to instill in the minds of Japanese children that any racial differences between them and highly civilized Westerners were not innate and could be overcome by their constant effort at learning.

This early disregard of the theory of innate racial superiority and inferiority based on skin color was also expressed in the official record of the Iwakura Mission of 1871–1873. The Iwakura report argued that, since Asia, and especially East Asia, had developed its own high civilization independent of the West, Asians were not inferior to Europeans in intelligence or ingenuity, only different in temperament. The white race was emotional, zealously religious, uninhibited, and greedy—all quite opposite to the stoicism, asceticism, and self-restraint of the yellow race. The Iwakura report thereupon advised the two races to combine their complementary characteristics and work together. To sum up, categorizing the Japanese as a yellow race—and subsequently Japan as a yellow nation—was a variable subject to the sociological environment, not a deterministic biological barrier against certain achievements.[19]

A combination of the ideology of racial superiority and the myth of racial purity—both developed during the modernization process—propelled the Japanese toward becoming an imperialist power. In the process of modernizing, the Japanese lessened their physiological identity as an Asian race and heightened their psychological identity as a European race.[20] They saw themselves as the only Asians who could progress to a higher level of civilization along with white Westerners. This identity was extremely important in legitimizing Japan's status as a colonial power in the eyes of Asians as well as Westerners.[21]

If there was room for accommodation in the international arena, however, it was constantly offset by unreconcilable differences in the respective domestic settings. During the 1890s and 1900s, the United States had already faced the contradiction in the split racial identity of Japan—that is, its view of the Japanese nation as an "honorary" white race in the international community and that of the individual Japanese immigrant as a member of a colored race. Japan's symbolic Westernized identity as a nation did not alter the skin color of the Japanese immigrant. Treating a Japanese individual in America as an honorary white became impossible in a country where human interactions across color lines were controlled by rigidly constructed antimiscegenation, immigration, and naturalization laws.

Sensitive to all these implications, the Japanese government requested and then demanded that the Western nations acknowledge Japan as a nation and its people as honorary whites, at least through diplomatic protocols. Only thus could Japan accept U.S.-Japanese relations as amicable. For Japan, the Western treatment of Japan as just another Asian nation was not only inappropriate but humiliating to a rising colonial power. Japan's demand for respect culminated in the government's effort to insert a racial equality clause in the preamble to the Covenant of the League of Nations at the Paris Peace Conference in 1919.

Ultimately, after the trial-and-error period of racial accommodation, Japanese immigrants were denied the dualistic identity that characterized the U.S. appeasement with Japan as a nation. The anti-Japanese agitation that erupted in West Coast society and politics culminated in new federal law. In 1922, in the so-called Ozawa case, the Supreme Court ruled that Japanese were ineligible for citizenship because of race. The passage of the 1924 Immigration Act, with its Japanese exclusion clause (*Hai-Nichi Hō*), branded Japanese immigrants undesirable as members of a nonwhite race— a designation the Japanese government had attempted to avoid at all costs since the late nineteenth century.[22]

Some authors have claimed that the psychological origin for U.S.-Japanese conflict in World War II could be found in this law which was so damaging to Japan's prestige.[23] The Japanese public increasingly called for a separate racial order in which they could collaborate with their fellow races in Asia. Thus, America's final refusal to recognize Japan's dual racial identity prompted Japanese nationalists to justify severing the country's psychological affinity with the United States and other Western nations and gradually drove Japan down the road of Pan-Asianism.

The actual Japanese wartime view of future relations with the whites, however, was neither as monolithic nor as hostile as the Japanese propaganda. Under the slogan *hakkō ichiu* (eight directions under one roof), no official plan emerged to specify exactly what would be a proper place for the white race. Nowhere in the rhetoric of the Greater East Asian Co-Prosperity Sphere did Japan propose a framework for a future relationship with the white race, either on an equal or a superior basis. Neither did it rank the white race on the same plateau as the Koreans and Formosans, who were described as being suitable for carrying out the heavy physical work of a protracted war. Most wartime planning by the Japanese simply suggested the wisdom of coexistence or interdependence with the white Western world. Even during the clashing rhetoric of the war, Japan upheld the basic notion of a racial hierarchy similar to that of America.[24]

Given the nature of such historical interactions, the relationship of the two trans-Pacific racisms was more one of codependence rather than of mere coexistence (i.e., it was codependence within the Western hierarchical order). The Western attitude of elevating the Japanese to the status of honorary Westerners was arrogant. The West saw Japan as a unique exception in Asia but not quite equal to the West. When the Japanese claimed equality to Westerners, they appeared arrogant for presuming to cross the color line and violating the American sanctuary. However, their claim of racial equality with white Americans might be interpreted as proof of the Japanese belief in American superiority. The Japanese, in accepting the West's designation, appeared servile. The Japanese yearning for any sort of equality with the Americans appeared to be rooted in an inferiority complex toward whites—a proof of their willingness to survive in the Western racial hierarchy.

Japan's Pan-Asianism was, in a sense, a desperate attempt to escape from the cul-de-sac of a Japanese modernization bound to a Western paradigm of racial hierarchy. However, to deny the racial hierarchy was equivalent to a denial of the racial rhetoric that justified Japan's Pan-Asiansim. Japan's Pan-Asianism was well nested within the Western version of a worldwide racial hierarchy. Modern Japan's dualistic racism needed American racism to reinforce the validity of white supremacy, upon which Japan built its own superiority in Asia. Japanese racism also reinforced American racism.

A good chance for friendship after World War II emerged with this fine line of mutual dependency on each other's racism. Both the United States and Japan knew by then that a congruence of American and Japanese racial attitudes would generate a positive as well as a negative dynamic for their relations. As the prospect of the Cold War's spillover was looming in Asia, the United States, in order to keep Japan as a strategic and ideological ally, quickly moved to endorse and even praise Japan's new racial identity. This was done through various political gestures, including an improved immigration policy.

The United States could at this point render a final verdict on Japan's assimilability into Western civilization and its racial compatibility with whites, thus setting a pattern of intimacy with Japan. Postwar Japan needed to cultivate such an ideology as a base for reestablishing itself as a world power. In doing so, Japan also accepted a subtle yet convincing logic of American supremacy in Asia. When the United States defined Japan's identity as an honorary white nation, a designation conventionally preserved for European nations, and Japan accepted this as a purely symbolic gesture without expecting similar privileges within the American domestic context, the two countries reached an equilibrium. In this manner, based on their mutual lesson from the past, Japan and the United States finally reached a firm racial accommodation for the first time in their relations, one that seemed to promise a stable alliance in the years to come.

Then came the bitter confrontation in the 1980s. "Japan-bashing" was the new popular attitude in the United States. The happy surface of racial accommodation which had characterized the Occupation was ripped open, releasing the fumes of a still smoldering—and still mutual—racism. This renewed racial animosity between the two countries revealed a serious defect of the postwar friendship. In launching the reconstruction of Japan during the Occupation, Japan and the United States had ignored the consequences of dovetailing their mutual racial ideologies in a world attempting to remove racist ideologies from international politics. The success of the U.S. occupation of Japan was a short-term victory for the two nations' racial ideologies, allowing them to use a myth of superiority as a sanction for their vested interests in world affairs. In the long term, however, the unresolved racisms inherent in U.S.-Japan relations has proven to be a stumbling block in the progress toward mutual understanding within each society as well as within the international community.

CHAPTER 1

The International Framework for Postwar Japanese–American Racism

"The United Nations shall promote . . . universal respect for, and observance of, human rights and fundamental freedoms for all without distinction as to race, sex, language, or religion." With these words, in June 1945, Article 55 of the United Nations Charter heralded an era of human rights. World War II had ended with the devastation of Germany and the unconditional surrender of Japan. The world, suffering from the horrors of the Holocaust and other genocides, was weary of racial strife. The new United Nations took the lead with its ringing proclamation in the charter. Three years later, in the "Universal Declaration of Human Rights," the UN reinforced its strong stand against discrimination. And on July 18, 1950, UNESCO issued the aforementioned statement characterizing racism as a defective pseudoscientific concept. The world had had enough of the destructive power of racial war.

Despite these brave and hopeful pronouncements, in the framework of postwar American planning for Asia, the Americans were able to readjust Japan's racial status in a way that not only legitimized American ascendancy to superpower status in charge of a new order in Asia but transformed Japan into a useful satellite nation. To change an official interpretation of race relations from a hostile to an amicable one proved a remarkably smooth task because the change took place in the continuity of (rather than in an eradication of) mutual racism. The restoration of a shared racial hierarchy was manageable because of empirical knowledge from the past. In this process, race functioned as a maneuverable factor in the easy engineering of the new friendship between the two nations. And yet, neither the United States nor Japan noticed—or cared to notice—the dangers lurking within the positive power of race.

In the U.S. occupation of Japan, a mutual racism that had existed before the war was thus maintained within a new equation that involved the two peoples' tacit consent and paved a path for their quick reconciliation. For U.S.-Japanese diplomatic relations, mutual racism had always served as a political variable in determining the pattern of intimacy of alliance, ranging from check and humiliation to cooperation and appeasement. The experience in the Occupation was no exception: race defined a wide range of power relations and also convinced the two peoples of its legitimacy with remarkable ease. In the early stage of the Occupation (1945–1948), race functioned as a punitive tool used to instill among the Japanese people a proper sense of relations between the white conqueror and the colored vanquished. In the second stage (1949–1952), along the line of the so-called Reverse Course, race expedited the radical change in their relations by upgrading the Japanese status to that of honorary whites and an ally of strategic value. Mutual racism displayed extraordinary maneuvering power in restoring proper U.S.-Japanese relations. As a result, the postwar friendship between the two nations was restored within the same racial hierarchy as in the prewar period.

How did the tacit agreement on race emerge, when the Supreme Commander for the Allied Powers (SCAP) never issued a directive to, nor did it convene a meeting with, the Japanese government concerning the preservation of racism? It almost looks as if they had been playing a game of charades in conveying each one's purpose and desire to the other. Except for the early period in the Occupation, the two nations managed to agree upon the same rule and the same game of race through subtle, indirect, and even nonverbal communication. They understood each other's sensitivity, desire, and intention and accommodated one another's racism as a gesture of reconciliation. With their empirical knowledge from the prewar period, they rediscovered that modern Japan's dual racial identity fit comfortably within the Western-centered racial hierarchy.

In the American wartime planning for the Occupation of Japan, racial consideration was indispensable for establishing American leadership in the eyes of the Japanese. Race, however, was far from being a catalyst for improving U.S.-Japanese relations. On the contrary, for the United States it was a medium to carry out stern justice against Japan, the defeated enemy: impose the concept of white supremacy and make the Japanese comply with the American victors in the remaking of Japan and Asia. SCAP and the U.S. government expected the Japanese to accept a "proper" sense of relations between the white victor and the colored vanquished and legitimize new American (white) leadership in Asia, replacing Japan. The reeducation of the

Japanese concerning right relations between themselves and the whites became an early prop of the Occupation.

The United States, while intent on reasserting its leadership role in Asia, was simultaneously championing the ideal of international racial equality. At the conference held in San Francisco in the spring of 1945 to launch the United Nations, President Truman, in support of the UN Charter, endorsed racial equality as the principle of this new international organization. He also pledged his support for a UN commission on human rights that would work to end racial discrimination on a global basis. Despite opposition from southerners in the U.S. Congress, the commission held its first meeting in January 1947, chaired by America's former first lady Eleanor Roosevelt.[1]

Even with Truman's official approval of the principle of racial equality, American racial attitudes toward Asia remained much as they had been before. Racial awareness, sharpened in the war with Japan in the Pacific, guided basic American policy planning in Asia. The Atlantic Charter of August 9, 1941, endorsed objectives in the Anglo-American alliance for the restoration of the world order that Woodrow Wilson had stated after World War I (i.e., that the principle of equality among nations would apply only to nations in Europe, thus preserving the Western colonial empires and rejecting the principle of self-determination for nonwhites). The charter respected the doctrines of sovereign rights and self-determination in Europe, but restored these rights only to the countries that had been forcibly deprived of them by Axis aggression. In a compromise with British imperialism, the charter did not include colonial subjects who had had no sovereign rights or self-government at the outbreak of World War II.

Implicit in this Anglo-Saxon partnership of the United States and Britain was a belief in the superiority of Western civilization and the race that created it.[2] In Asia and the Pacific, after the demise of Japan's colonial empire, the United States not only backed the return of the European allies to colonial rule but increasingly assumed more responsibility over the regional order, taking on the "White Man's Burden"—the Victorian concept of the duty of the white races to bring their civilization to backward (i.e., nonwhite) peoples. A strong racial awareness was deemed necessary as the United States battled what it thought was the legacy of Japan's racial conspiracy against whites. To American eyes, the worst Japanese war crime was the attempt to cripple the white man's prestige by sowing the seeds of racial pride under the banner of Pan-Asianism. Now it was up to the United States to salvage that prestige.

The fruits of Japan's Pan-Asianism were clear to the Western colonial nations when revolts against the "white colonial masters" increased in the Dutch East Indies and in French Indochina.[3] Brig. Gen. Elliot R. Thorpe, head of SCAP's counterintelligence section, said in November 1945 that the Japanese in the last period of the war operated schools of treason for Asian nationals with the purpose of creating antipathy to the white race throughout the Far East. These Japanese-trained Asians were now creating trouble for Allied troops. Chinese, French Indochinese, British Malayans, Burmese and Indians, Koreans, Filipinos—all now constituted a barrier to a peaceful settlement of disputes between the native peoples and the former white colonists.[4]

An editorial in the *New York Times* on February 18, 1946, stated that although Japan had lost the war, its slogan "Asia for the Asiatics" (later changed to "Asia for the Asians" and "Asia for Asians") appeared to have won: "What is happening in the Far East is a warning that the oriental peoples, instead of being subdued by the victories of the western powers, are more stirred up than before against occidental domination." The editorial speculated that "white rule" and Western administration were beneficent and obviated any need for independence. Once the Japanese—"Oriental invaders," as the editorial put it—disturbed this pattern, the Asians "conspired to rebel for the first time." As a result, the editorial continued, antiwhite feeling cropped up in all parts of Asia and "Americans have lost most of the popularity they once enjoyed."[5]

In the Philippines, despite a honeymoon period following the defeat of the Japanese in the islands in 1944, anti-American feeling among the Filipino people began to take over. To Americans, this new Filipino attitude was unmistakable evidence that Japan's conspiracy had worked and the power and prestige of white people in the Far East had waned. One *New York Times* article lamented: "Respect for the white man's attainments remains, but in the eyes of the Asiatics he is no longer a master who is invincible."[6]

The United States and the other Allied nations ascribed Japan's ambition to eradicate the white presence in Asia to Japan's own ideology of racial superiority. The International Military Tribunal for the Far East, which presided over the Tokyo War Crimes Trial (1946–1948) held in the former War Ministry building in Ichigaya, Tokyo, accused Japan of, among other things, "racial arrogance" in challenging the stability of the status quo that existed under Western rule. The Tokyo War Crimes Trial was marked by Eurocentrism in its legal ideas, its personnel, its historical thinking, and, as some observers have commented, by its racism. With the exception of Mei Ju-an, a prominent attorney representing China, the original members of the bench—representatives of Australia, Canada, New Zealand, Britain, the United States, France, the Netherlands, and the Soviet Union—were all European, or predominantly Anglo-Saxon. There was no representative from the colonial peoples. The initial absence of Asian representation suggests that the tribunal itself symbolized the last phase of the traditional international legal system that had supported Western colonialism. Only the independent nations, the sovereign nations that had been at war with Japan, had representatives on the bench. Moreover, the initial membership reflected white paternalism, justified by pseudoscientific racial theories, wherein colonial subjects were not deemed competent to be judges.

In February 1946, the British government informed Washington in confidence that India was sensitive to its lack of representation on the bench and that it wished to receive recognition in the appointment of a judge and prosecutor. In fact, India, which defended such British holdings as Hong Kong, Malaya, Singapore, and Burma during the war, also had troops in southern Japan as part of the British Commonwealth Occupation Force. Gen. Douglas MacArthur acted promptly to amend this imbalance for the Philippines as well. MacArthur sympathized with the Filipino people in particular because his army had also suffered during the Japanese invasion of their islands. At the time of the Tokyo trial, the Philippines was already self-governing and scheduled to acquire full independence on July 4, 1946. A few months after the Tokyo trial started, Justices Radhabinod Pal of India and Delfin Jaranilla of the Philippines arrived in Japan as new members of the bench.[7]

From the beginning, the Tokyo War Crimes Trial was criticized even by members of the Allied nations as a forum for vengeance, vindication, and propaganda. As early as October 5, 1946, only five months after the tribunal opened, U.S. Senator Robert Taft commented on its "spirit of vengeance," which he pointed out was "seldom justice." From a legal perspective, the trial was in no way a part of any established judicial system. As president of the tribunal and also its official spokesman, Sir William Webb, then chief justice of the Supreme Court of Queensland, Australia, himself inevitably put forward the attitude of the other members of the court, thus bound by prejudgment. In fact, Webb had been chief of the Australian group investigating Japanese atrocities against Australian troops. Nonetheless, he did not hesitate to openly express his opinion that the trial should serve as a kind of propaganda: "It is the purpose of the Supreme Commander, and indeed of the Allied Powers, that this trial should get the widest publicity, and it is getting it."[8]

The Tokyo Trial successfully administered and publicized the "white man's" justice in the Pacific War. This was the only time during the Occupation when the crime of Japan's racial conspiracy was officially and openly brought up. The prosecutors blamed Japan's ideology of racial superiority as the main force behind a stratagem to drive the whites from Asia and a subsequent attempt at world conquest. They placed this racial conspiracy in the period between January 1, 1928, and September 2, 1945.[9]

Although in the end the prosecutors concluded that the Japanese conspirators never seriously attempted to conquer North and South America and subsequently removed the allegation of attempted world conquest, the disturbing fear of a Japanese plot against the white race and its possible recurrence in the future haunted Americans for some time. For this reason, at the Tokyo War Crimes Trial, Japanese cruelty toward white prisoners of war evoked strong emotions. Americans interpreted Japan's so-called sadism as its revenge for Western imperialism, combined with some deeper pattern of innate behavior characteristic of the Japanese. Gen. Jonathan M. Wainwright, a former prisoner of war in Japan, explained on a national radio broadcast that Japanese wartime atrocities toward the white race were a result of their particular desire to demonstrate Japanese superiority over the "Anglo-Saxon races." One Australian Air Force officer, who was detained at Macassar Camp, Celebes, testified in 1943 that the Japanese went out of their way to humiliate the Europeans and that they had no regard for the welfare of prisoners or even for the sanctity of life.[10]

Meanwhile, policymakers in Washington, D.C., more savvy than the military officers in understanding U.S.-Japanese relations, preferred that the vulgar expression of a crude racist feeling against the Japanese be avoided in the Occupation. From prewar experiences they knew how such an expression—the 1924 Japanese exclusion clause is the best example—might aggravate Japanese fury, driving them to be not only resentful and uncooperative but even rebellious against the American authority, thereby making the Occupation more difficult than necessary. Fully aware of the importance of the racial dimension in postwar American policy in Japan and Asia, they prepared for a more sensitive racial scenario in postsurrender Japan.

Before launching the Occupation, the Americans had expected to confront serious Japanese resentment against white rule and sought to mitigate it with an occupying force that was racially mixed. In early 1944 a discussion of the racial composition of forces in the event of the occupation of Japan had already begun in Washington. A memorandum prepared by the Inter-

Divisional Area Committee on the Far East, dated March 13, 1944, cited a British recommendation on the use of Malayan regiments and Chinese eagerness to participate, stating that the presence of Asiatic units among the allied occupation forces and military government might be better for American interests than if they were "exclusively American or Caucasian."[11]

On August 13, 1945, a few days before the surrender, the Department of State issued a top secret memorandum regarding the racial composition of occupying forces. Both the State-War-Navy Coordinating Committee (SWNCC) and the Joint Chiefs of Staff recommended the participation of "Orientals" in the Occupation forces and in the Occupation authority in Japan. Such measures, they believed, would serve the interests of the United States in making the ruling structure appear less like one of white victors and Oriental vanquished.[12]

Once the Occupation began, however, there was no attempt to rectify what the International Military Tribunal for the Far East had called Japan's racial arrogance. Had there been, the Occupation forces would have had a triple-sided problem. First, what would be an appropriate way to punish the Japanese for racial arrogance? Stripping them of their sense of superiority might be one answer. But, second, educating them on the democratic principle of racial equality would not be appropriate since the United States regarded the Japanese as racially unequal to Americans in both American domestic and diplomatic contexts. Finally, teaching the Japanese that they were inferior to whites did not exactly fit into the process of education for democracy.

Thus, SCAP launched the Occupation of Japan with no concrete racial policy, depending on symbolic gestures to convey necessary messages on the issue of race. American policies highlighted the racial schism between white Americans and yellow Japanese as a punitive measure to insinuate, if not openly declare, the power and prestige of the conqueror. Fraternization between Americans and Japanese was prohibited for almost four years, although in occupied Germany the ban had lasted less than five months. The nonfraternization policy permeated Japanese society like a kind of racial segregation, discouraging any interaction. As if disturbed by their inconsistency, Occupation censors, from late 1945, prohibited all mention of race in the Japanese mass media. Japanese remarks on racial superiority or inferiority, relations between whites and colored, and racial discrimination in American society were strictly censored without explanation. Any mention of fraternization was also subject to deletion. As a result of this policy, in the early phase of the Occupation the public's awareness of the status of race disappeared, while racial segregation remained a reality in Japanese life.

While SCAP carried out a toned-down policy of white supremacy in the Occupation, the Japanese on the other hand rapidly set out on their own racial reconciliation plan, along with their acceptance of defeat and the new American leadership in their country. This Japanese healing process was ironic in that they interpreted the war's result as a draw and took it upon themselves to continue their mission as the leader of Asia to correct American racism. It was also ironic that, because of their continuing belief in their own racial superiority over other Asians, they failed to detect American contempt for their own race. However, precisely because of that continuing sense of superiority and mission in Asia, the Japanese became ready to reconcile with the Americans and rebuild a new Asia as equal friends—the two superior races together.

Although Americans had worried about a series of "racial conspiracies" and a determination on the part of the Japanese to prove their racial superiority in the quest to control the world, none of these fears were warranted.[13] There was ambiguity in the wartime development of Japanese thought about racial relations. In fact, even during the harshest anti-Western propaganda in the war, the Japanese could not define their current and future relations with the whites.

Through the 1930s to the Pacific War, when the Japanese increasingly demanded an Asian racial and cultural bloc as a new world order, they did not attempt to refute the modern Western theory of racial superiority in the capacity to modernize. In creating a colonial empire with the claim of a superior level of civilization, the Japanese did attempt to lead their fellow Asians without Western intervention. Yet in the fervent exercise of Pan-Asian racial rhetoric, Japanese dualistic identity continued, and as a result they remained dependent on Western racism for their very raison d'être as the leader of Asia.

The most frequent argument made during the Pacific War was that the Japanese were so successful in amalgamating the best of East and West that they were never inferior to the whites, but they were never certain that they could lead the Western world, let alone the entire world. Among senior officials who had reached the junior level of their career in the 1920s, during the period of the so-called Taisho democracy movement and cosmopolitanism, the desire for restoration of peace with the West remained. When Pan-Asianism seemed doomed by the fall of 1944 after a series of costly defeats in the Pacific, some Japanese bureaucrats had already revived a hope for postwar U.S.-Japanese cooperation and interdependence as a more desirable framework than rivalry in developing the Asian economy.[14]

The principle of racial equality reemerged as an important component of Japan's postwar diplomacy with the West. The collapse of Japan's colonial empire freed Japanese liberals—intellectuals and bureaucrats alike—from their dilemma of a moral obligation to the cause of Pan-Asianism. Contrary to what Americans had feared, the Japanese proposal for postwar racial relations made no claim of superiority over the whites nor carried any trace of a racial plot or revenge. They discussed the ideal of racial equality between Japan and the West in a matter-of-fact way and desired a quick restoration of Wilsonian-style cooperation in world affairs. There was a determination to "ascend" to the level of the Western nations. In reverse proportion to the rising hope for friendship with the West, the theme of friendship and leadership across Asia quickly disappeared.

Kase Toshikazu—then Japanese Foreign Office spokesman and veteran diplomat, who had served in the United States, Britain, and Germany, and who was engaged in a task of ending the war with the United States through diplomatic channels—openly expressed his desire to reestablish cordial relations with the West, especially with Britain. In an interview with the *New York Times* in late October 1945, he explained that the Japanese people had always looked on Britain as one of their best friends and felt that in their royal families the two peoples had something most precious in common. In his statement, he even said that the Japanese liked to believe that Britain's participation in the Pacific War had been merely to fulfill its obligation to the United States.[15] Britain was, after all, the first Western nation to abrogate the unequal treaty with Japan and recognize Japan as a first-rate power by signing the Anglo-Japanese military alliance of 1902. To a pro-Western diplomat like Kase, there was no reason why Britain should not resume its traditional support in the reconstruction of Japan.

When pro-Western planners such as Kase set out to chart a postwar diplomatic agenda for Japan, they naturally turned to Wilsonian ideals as the framework for cooperation with the Western powers on world development. These diplomatic efforts began within the Ministry of Foreign Affairs. For a short period following the acceptance of the Potsdam Declaration, the Japanese government continued diplomatic relations with Switzerland, Portugal, and four other nations, all of which had maintained a neutral status toward

Japan during the war. Although the Japanese government initially insisted that it could technically retain diplomatic relations with these nations even through the Occupation, SCAP rejected such an interpretation and terminated Japan's diplomatic rights.

On October 25, 1945, SCAP instructed the Japanese government to cease relations with foreign governments. By December 10, the Japanese government discontinued all communication between itself and former diplomatic and consular representatives abroad.[16] The Ministry of Foreign Affairs thus lost its justification for existence, and most of its staff was transferred to a liaison office between SCAP and Japanese governmental institutes for general administrative work. Deprived of its original function in diplomatic administration and greatly reduced in size, the ministry was left with just one main task: to begin preliminary research for the peace treaty negotiations. For this purpose, the Executive Research Committee on Problems Concerning a Peace Treaty (Heiwa Jōyaku Mondai Kenkyū Kanji-kai) was conceived.

According to Shimoda Takezō, who served as the committee's regular secretary, both Shigemitsu Mamoru and Ashida Hitoshi, his senior staff members, originally suggested a plan to establish this committee.[17] Shigemitsu was a diplomat with an antimilitary stance, having served as an ambassador to the USSR (1936–1938), to Britain (1938–1941), and, during the year 1942, to Wang Ching-wei's Chinese regime, the pro-Japanese puppet regime in Nanjing, installed by the Japanese government in March 1940. At the war's end, he also signed the surrender document as foreign minister. Ashida, who resigned the Foreign Ministry in 1931 because of his opposition to militarist policies in the Manchurian Incident, subsequently served on the Diet nine consecutive times before the war and became welfare minister in the first postwar cabinet headed by Shidehara Kijūrō. These two veteran politicians with liberal tendencies advised Shimoda and his colleagues to prepare for a peace conference with the Allied nations as early as possible so that Japan would not be devastated as Germany was by the Versailles Treaty after World War I.

The Committee on Problems Concerning a Peace Treaty was organized on November 21, 1945, with twenty-one members. The first meeting took place in mid-January 1946, at which time basic principles for a peace treaty were discussed.[18] A classified paper, "Basic Principles Regarding Some Problems in Concluding a Peace Treaty," prepared on January 31, 1946, confirmed Japan's resolve to conclude a peace treaty on a fair basis as soon as possible. It advised the Japanese people, both inside and outside the government, to endeavor to carry out the duties imposed on them by the Potsdam Declaration. This action would display to the whole world the organizational power, the capacity for independence, and the peace-loving nature of the Japanese people. It would also eliminate the outside world's suspicion, misunderstanding, prejudice, and hatred of Japan. The paper set a timetable for the negotiation and conclusion of a peace treaty by mid-1947.[19]

Another paper prepared on January 31, 1946, proposed five indispensable provisions for a peace treaty. Article 1 dealt with a resolution to set up a definite date for the recovery of Japan's national sovereignty. Article 2 requested nonintervention in issues regarding the institution of the emperor. Article 3 demanded economic sufficiency suitable for a democratic and peaceful nation. Article 4 called for territorial integrity based on international justice. Finally, Article 5 called for an affirmation of the principle of racial equality. In relation to the last article, another paper, "Problems Regarding Provisions on Economic Conditions," devoted a whole chapter to discussing the possibility of an emigration and immigration clause in the peace treaty.[20]

Historians, American and Japanese alike, have virtually ignored the significance of this committee's early blueprint for Japan's postwar diplomacy with its strong remnant of prewar racial diplomacy. In his article on the Foreign Ministry's effort to draft a peace treaty, Watanabe Akio, a Japanese political scientist, said that the mention of the principle of racial equality, which "seems very strange to current diplomatic sensibilities," was made as a mundane agenda merely to comply with routine prewar style.[21] Watanabe argues that since the committee's staff quickly realized the peripheral nature of the principle of racial equality for postwar Japan, they gave less consideration to the issues of racial equality, emigration, and immigration and eventually erased them completely from the peace treaty agenda.

Contrary to such an interpretation, further analysis of the draft peace treaty of the Foreign Ministry's committee, which was completed in the first nine months in the Occupation, indicates the committee's devotion to the issue of racial equality with the West. The issue received special attention not only for the sake of Japan's national pride but because of a more pragmatic need for Japan's economic and industrial recovery in the postwar world. For example, the committee regarded the removal of racial restrictions such as the anti-Japanese Immigration Act of 1924 as one of the most crucial elements in securing Japan's access to overseas lands and markets both in emigration and commercial activities. Although defeated Germany and other former Axis nations had already resumed emigration and immigration activities with no opposition from the Allied nations, the Japanese government was fully aware of the difficulties facing Japan's future. Therefore, the committee proposed, in yet another paper dated January 31, 1946, that in any agreement between Japan and the Allied nations, no signatory should be allowed to impose discriminatory restrictions or prohibitions on any other signatories' nationals regarding their engagement in business, commerce, or industry. That is, Japan and the Allied nations would expressly agree that the signatories would not discriminate against people based on their birth, nationality, language, race (*shuzoku*), or religion.[22]

Another paper, "The Problem of Nationality [*kokuseki*] and a Peace Treaty," also completed on January 31, 1946, was more straightforward in stating the committee's aim in establishing the principle of racial equality in nationality and naturalization laws. It advocated that no signatory nation in the peace treaty should discriminate against people based on differences of race (*jinshu*), religion, language, or social or cultural customs (*fūzoku*) in exercising their individual rights in daily social life.[23] Here the committee perhaps aimed at solving the problem of 70,000 foreign-born Japanese immigrants residing in the United States, who, because they were ineligible for U.S. citizenship, were left with no choice but to retain their Japanese citizenship.

The committee also pointed out several flaws in prewar Japan's nationality law, which was responsible for the Japanese immigrants' dual nationality—a cause of American suspicion. When the Nationality Law (Kokuseki Hō; Law No. 66), promulgated in 1899, established criteria for the eligibility of Japanese nationals, it adopted the rule of jus sanguinis ("right of blood"), whereby one acquires nationality by virtue of one's descent or parentage through the father only. The United States, on the other hand, adopted the principle of jus soli ("right of soil"), whereby one acquires nationality according to place of birth. To accommodate the need of persons of Japanese parentage born in the United States and adhering to the principle of jus soli, the Japanese government amended its nationality law in 1916 and 1924 so these people could renounce Japanese nationality and avoid dual citizenship. However, conditions for renouncing Japanese nationality were difficult. For example, a Japanese male was not allowed to renounce Japanese nationality until he had fulfilled an obligation to serve in the armed forces.[24] The committee thus recommended that in peace treaty talks Japan and the Allied nations should collaborate to solve the problem of conflicting nationality and naturalization laws.

The committee did not ignore Japan's postwar responsibility toward its former colonial subjects. Indeed, it seemed interested in experimenting with the unfinished project of Japan's Pan-Asianism. The committee was influenced by precedents in international politics for establishing the nationality of Japan's former colonial subjects through a peace treaty. The Versailles Treaty of 1919 regulated the postwar status of former colonial subjects of the defeated nation, Germany. Under the terms of Article 22, Germany's former colonies in Central Africa, South-West Africa, and the South Pacific were to be administered under the laws of the Mandatory on behalf of the League of Nations because these peoples were "not yet able to stand by themselves under the strenuous conditions of the modern world." On Germany's frontiers (such as the Saar territory bordering on France and the Schleswig area bordering on Denmark), the League itself took charge of determining the inhabitants' nationality.[25]

Based on such precedents, the committee expected the status of Japan's former colonial subjects to be determined by a peace treaty. The committee proposed that the peace treaty grant peoples in Japan's former colonies (such as the Korean and the Taiwanese) the right to choose, under certain conditions, between their home country's nationality and their previously forced Japanese nationality. It also advocated that the peace treaty permit Korean and Taiwanese peoples currently residing in their home countries to acquire Japanese nationality on request.[26] In a paper dated February 1, 1946, the committee recommended the enumeration of six basic principles to achieve regional stability in the aftermath of decolonization in Asia. The principles of "racial equality" and the "advancement of the Asian people and their peaceful cooperation with one another" were listed side by side, followed by other principles of "military cutback," "freedom of trade and commerce," "improvement of labor and social conditions," and "cultural exchange."[27]

The emphasis on a close and friendly relationship with other Asian nations, however, disappeared rather quickly. On February 21, 1946, only three weeks later, the committee issued another paper with major revisions regarding relations with Asia, canceling its previous proposal on the right of Japan's former colonial subjects to choose their nationalities. In this paper's original draft, provisions regarding peace and cultural exchange in the Far East were also crossed out, while the provision on racial equality with the West remained intact, supplemented by the right of freedom of emigration and immigration.[28] These alterations suggest that the focus of the committee vacillated between the West and Asia, and that the committee had perhaps decided to give diplomatic priority to the United States and other Western nations at the expense of the Asian theater.

The explanation for Japan's shifting priorities in postwar diplomacy was not long in coming. A paper issued the same day contained the following: "Considering the future status of the United States in the Far East, it is imperative for Japan to maintain a close tie with it." For Japan's security, the committee subsequently recommended that a peace treaty be so concluded as to remove any disruptive elements that had existed between the United States and Japan.[29] Improving its relationship with the United States, especially by removing the latter's racial barriers, was a more important first step in Japan's postwar recovery than the possibility of better relations with Asian nations.

By the time the Tokyo War Crimes Trial opened, the committee had issued its first investigative report based on preliminary research conducted from January to May 1946. The paper listed four demands that Japan would make in a peace treaty in spite of possible opposition from the Allied nations.[30] The principle of racial equality was at the top of the list. The phrase "insert the principle of racial equality either in the preamble of the peace treaty or within the treaty provisions" remained intact. While the second point demanded the guarantee of Japan's national security either through a bilateral treaty with each Allied nation or through a collective treaty with all Allied nations, the remaining two points again referred to the guarantee of the freedom of international movement of people and goods, with the implication of removal of the racial barrier. The third point requested a guaranteed freedom of commerce and navigation among the signatories by removing trade barriers. The fourth point demanded freedom of overseas emigration and equal treatment of Japanese immigrants in the receiving nations. The last point was further emphasized by an additional explanation that overseas emigration was vital to solving the population problem of a small country with scarce raw materials.

In this May 1946 report, the committee made additional efforts to ensure the principle of racial equality in the peace treaty with the Allied nations. When recommending that an international court of justice be established in the spirit of Wilsonianism, the committee enumerated five important actions to accompany the establishment of such a world court. They were: (1) the establishment of a world government, (2) world disarmament, (3) the repeal of racial discrimination, (4) the granting of independence to colonies in Asia, and (5) the granting of freedom of the seas, the repeal of discrimination in commerce and trade, and encouragement of the exploration of un-developed regions in the world. As for the third point concerning the repeal of racial discrimination, the paper demanded that each nation work on spe-cific measures to realize this principle in the different domestic contexts.[31]

Thus, as the Foreign Ministry's committee expressed it, the Japanese gov-ernment's early postwar desire was to win a racial status equal to the West, secure the sphere of overseas activities, compete with Westerners on an equal basis, and share with the United States and other Western nations the re-sponsibility for the welfare of the world. The government believed these ac-tions were crucial to a quick national recovery, and would place Japan on an equal footing with other world powers.

This desire for improvement in U.S.-Japanese relations along the lines of the Wilsonian vision was reflected in an interesting, individual case. In June 1946 one Inagaki Yūjirō, former ocean-liner captain living in a small village in Aichi Prefecture, wrote to MacArthur himself with proposals for his own vision of a better world for postwar Japan, proposals surprisingly similar to those of the Foreign Ministry committee in its peace treaty planning. Inaga-ki, introducing himself as a veteran of a peace movement in the 1930s, said he had founded a new organization, the World Peace Organization (Sekai Heiwa Kai) with a hope that it would spread a spirit of universal love and mutual aid (*hakuai gojo*) for the entire world. This organization planned to sponsor research promoting world peace, a series of lectures and film show-ings, a petition drive, and to publish a journal (*Wakō* [Peaceful Light]) and other related pamphlets. Inagaki attached two different printed brochures to his letter. A list of slogans emphasized "universal love, friendship, and help, sincerity, wisdom, justice, and internationalism over nationalism [*kokka yori sekai e*]." Another brochure enumerated five principles for his organization and movement. These were a unified world government (*sekai tōitsu seifu*), complete world disarmament, no tariff barriers in the world market, an open-door policy for all the world, and complete eradication of racial dis-crimination (*jinshu sabetsu o teppai*). Another attached flyer—handwritten with brush and ink—announced a special lecture (to be given by Inagaki), along with performances by a troupe of magicians, comics, and acrobats.[32]

This local project was perhaps a mere farce, because Inagaki proudly claimed that the event was sponsored by both the Japanese cabinet and SCAP—an unlikely arrangement in the Occupation. However, the fact that both an obscure individual in the countryside and the Foreign Ministry's committee endorsed the same principle of racial equality as a prerequisite for Japan's better future indicates the nation's quick reversion to the days of Wilsonian idealism, Japanese style.

Throughout 1946 the Foreign Ministry's Executive Research Committee kept working on a peace treaty draft independent of SCAP's supervision. The Foreign Ministry's committee, however, gradually understood how subtly persistent the Americans were in skirting the topic of race. They also realized that Americans would regard a Japanese discussion of the principle of racial equality with them as an act of impudence on their part. To bring up the race issue as an official topic in the peace treaty agenda with the United States appeared to be not only inappropriate but might endanger Japan's chances for a better peace treaty. After the report of May 1946, the committee toned down its claim for a desirable peace treaty and completely withdrew the principle of racial equality from the treaty's agenda.[33]

On June 3, 1947, the committee decided to file with SCAP for the first time its rather low-key proposal for a peace treaty. In the paper "Loci of Problems on a Peace Treaty and Japan's Stance on Them (Part I)," the committee requested the recognition of such rights as industrial development and participation in world trade as essential to Japan's survival in the postwar era. The paper also asked the signatories to recognize Japan's freedom of emigration and immigration. In these proposals, however, the committee no longer used the phrase "racial equality."[34]

On July 26 and 28, 1947, Ashida Hitoshi, now minister of foreign affairs in the Katayama cabinet, handed the memorandum to political adviser George Atcheson, Jr., and Gen. Courtney Whitney of SCAP, Government Section, on a visit to their offices. Both of them accepted copies of the memorandum. However, shortly afterward they returned them to Ashida, explaining that such a memorandum would only serve to stimulate anti-Japanese sentiments in some nations. They pointed out that Australia, in particular, would think such a Japanese initiative arrogant.[35] The American rejection of the committee's draft thus ended the Japanese government's attempt to include the principle of racial equality in a peace treaty or to initiate a peace treaty.

With this stalemate, the Japanese government dropped the issue of racial equality with the West. The Occupation had produced remarkable changes and success in democratization so the Japanese government realized that silence on this sensitive issue was the best course. Japan's racial equality with the West became a quiescent desire—not an aggressive claim. So ended Japan's racial diplomacy, not with a demand but with a hope. Such a hope, however, was totally dependent upon America's decision-making, for as the dominant power during the Occupation, the United States took the lead in drawing a map of racial relations.

Why was there so little dissatisfaction on the part of the Japanese when they gradually realized that America's attitude of white supremacy would not accept Japan's request for racial equality? A crucial factor lay in the shrewd American tactic of utilizing modern Japan's double vision—that the Japanese saw themselves as superior to other Asians and colored races but inferior to the white race—as a tool for educating the Japanese about their proper place vis-à-vis the whites. In choosing this course, the United States was able to maneuver the Japanese with much more subtlety than if it had imposed a blunt white supremacy on the colored Japanese. Since the Japanese posture of having a double-sided racial identity had evolved within the Western-centered racial hierarchy, it naturally followed that the Japanese supported both white supremacy and American leadership. In sum, American endorsement of the dual racial identity of the Japanese smoothed the way for instilling and legitimizing the concept of white supremacy among the Japanese.

From the beginning of the Occupation, U.S. authorities had shrewdly observed and studied Japanese racial attitudes as they planned the appropriate psychological policies. There was some questioning among U.S. authorities at Japan's paradoxical racial position. On the one hand, the Americans were alert to Japan's "racial conspiracy" to remove the white presence in Asia, while on the other they observed that the Japanese were prone to flatter Westerners. The fact of this paradox was evident in an address delivered by Dr. Wilson Compton, president of the State College of Washington, Seattle, at the annual University of Washington Honors Convocation on May 15, 1946. Dr. Compton commended MacArthur's leadership in Japan as a crucial key to trans-Pacific relations in the next century, especially for the Pacific Northwest. But he also referred to the general spirit among the Japanese of "cheerful and willing cooperation with the Americans," which he had observed a few weeks before in a visit with MacArthur. He said; "It did not seem . . . to be the attitude to be expected of a vanquished people toward a victor. I described it as 'extraordinary'; said I was puzzled. General MacArthur replied that it was extraordinary and that he, too, had been puzzled."[36]

Some Americans had advised SCAP that Japanese friendliness toward the Americans should not be dismissed simply as a sign of their racial arrogance—the shameless belief in their equality with the Anglo-Saxon race—

nor should it be repressed. Rather, they suggested it be interpreted as a sign of their continuing belief in and psychological and emotional vulnerability to the superior quality of the Anglo-Saxon race, and should thus be carefully promoted. They advocated making use of the Japanese desire to mimic the Anglo-Saxon race; first, to establish a teacher-pupil relationship and, second, to facilitate the democratization process. They thereby urged the Occupation authorities to stimulate both Japan's racial pride and Japan's inferiority complex in regard to the Anglo-Saxon race.

George Atcheson, the acting political adviser in Japan, was among those who noticed the importance of exploiting both outlooks in order to cultivate a desirable attitude toward democratization. Only a month after the Occupation started, in late September 1945, he submitted a memorandum to the Secretary of State on his initial impressions of occupied Japan. He wrote about the general attitude of the Japanese toward the Occupation, including their racial attitude. There was an almost universal acceptance of the fact of defeat. However, this acceptance was not accompanied in most cases by a sense of guilt or shame. On the contrary, "Pride in Japanese race, mores, and culture remains widespread." Although he admitted that such Japanese racial pride was unacceptable to the Anglo-Saxon race, he did not consider it particularly problematic from the viewpoint of Japan's modernization. Atcheson suggested that Japanese racial pride represented their determination to show that they were as good as the Anglo-Saxon race as well as their desire to adopt Anglo-Saxon democracy. Such pride, he argued, if properly stimulated in the Occupation, might be valuable in advancing U.S. policies and would serve as a catalyst for rapid democratization.[37]

SWNCC 162/2, "Reorientation of the Japanese," a secret report issued on January 8, 1946, by SWNCC also stated that Japanese racial consciousness might be valuable to American strategy. Although the report recommended that extreme racial consciousness be weeded out in the course of democratization, it nonetheless hesitated to advise its complete eradication. The report pointed out that in Japanese psychology an antiforeign complex—not mere xenophobia but in fact an anti–white race feeling—was combined with great admiration for the superb achievements and learning of Western civilization. The report analyzed the feeling as not hatred per se but rather a jealousy or envy of the white race. Therefore, it continued, such racial feeling is not necessarily an obstacle to Japan's democratization; on the contrary, so long as the racial consciousness of the Japanese people contained the element of an inferiority complex toward Westerners, it could be so guided as to maximize their desire to emulate Western civilization. The interests and hopes of thinking Japanese therefore lay in imitating things American as far as possible. In this respect, the report concluded, the strong racial pride of the Japanese would not necessarily pose a problem for the Occupation. If properly handled by SCAP, Japan's pride—best exemplified in the dualistic identity— would be an asset for U.S. policy in Asia.[38]

The impetus for improved race relations came, however, not from the Foreign Ministry's efforts nor from the general success of the Occupation. It came from the Cold War. To secure the alliance, the United States began a calculated effort to move the status of the Japanese race closer to that of the white race, giving recognition to and praising their closeness to whites based on the success of postwar democratization efforts. There were specific mutual benefits to be gained in negotiating the upgrading of Japan's racial status: the United States secured an Asian ally against communism, and the Japanese acquired "pride and status," the diplomatic goal much sought after in the prewar period.

The fight against communism was a strong motive behind the U.S. proposal to improve race relations in general, both at home and abroad. Dean Acheson, the undersecretary of state, warned in 1946 that the charge of American racism would be a destructive tool in the hands of Communist propagandists in Asia. Discrimination against minority groups in the United States would have an adverse effect on relations with other countries, especially in Asia and Africa. By ending "Jim Crow," the United States would improve its image in the world.[39] In October 1947, seven months after the enunciation of the Truman Doctrine, the President's Commission on Civil Rights launched an assault on racial segregation. Implementing racial equality within American society was one expedient way to conduct the Cold War, Truman argued, because depriving people of basic rights was "an invitation to communism."[40]

In line with Acheson and Truman's position, a crusade to eliminate legislation encoding Japanese exclusion gained momentum in Washington. The Japanese attack on Pearl Harbor had led many Americans to think that the Japanese were taking costly revenge for American racism. And during the war an effort to accommodate melting pot rhetoric to shifting international relations had already begun. In an experiment with the Chinese people, the United States had moved to give certain nations in Asia a nominal privilege in the national quota system without imperiling the fundamental ideology of racial inequality between whites and Asians. In December 1944 the United States passed a law, purely as a wartime measure, which granted China a symbolic token of a maximum 105 immigrants per annum.[41] The act was intended to refute Japan's incessant propaganda against American racism toward Asians. It was also a symbolic gesture of American gratitude for China's heroic fight against Japanese aggression. In addition to these diplomatic signals, the act assured American society that it was not going to make any great changes in its basic racial ideology.

A bill to repeal exclusion of the people of India, introduced unsuccessfully by Rep. Emanuel Celler of New York in 1944 and 1945, was passed favorably by voice vote in both houses in early 1946. Four days after the proclamation of Philippine independence on July 4, 1946, President Truman also established a quota of one hundred for the new nation, a measure that both houses had approved in the previous year with no debate. In July 1947 a delegate from the Territory of Hawaii, Joseph Farrington, introduced a bill, H.R. 857, to remove racial restrictions on naturalization.[42] This bill, if enacted, would have granted to all people, the Japanese included, a quota of one hundred and would have extended the right of naturalization to citizens of those countries already legally resident within the United States.

Only four years after the war, the Chinese under Mao Zedong's Communist government were emerging as the new enemy in Asia, and national sentiment was growing increasingly favorable to the bill's privileged treatment of the Japanese. The image of Communist China attempting to conquer the whole of Asia now created a new yellow peril in the minds of Americans.[43] The theory of Japan's Pan-Asian conspiracy in postwar Asia quickly waned, perhaps due to Japanese cooperation with the Occupation. The image of the collaborating Japanese spread. But to embrace the Japanese as equals was still too radical a concept for American society at large. The appropriate solution seemed to be to treat Japan as an exceptional nonwhite nation and to give the Japanese a psychological edge among the rest of the Asian peoples. The solution sounded all the more reasonable now that the Chinese and the North Koreans were allied in the Communist bloc and becoming America's enemies.

On August 6, 1947, Congressman Bertrand Gearhart of California sent a letter to MacArthur, asking for his personal consideration of the abolition of the Oriental exclusion laws. The letter opened by saying that in light of the rapidly deteriorating world situation and the rising importance of cementing international friendships, it might be possible to assuage a sense of unfair discrimination through the elimination of the remaining Oriental exclusion legislation. Gearhart argued that in the event of confrontation with "that country the name of which is constantly a part of our daily thinking," America's position would be improved in Japan if the Japanese were extended "equal treatment with the Chinese, the Filipinos and Hindus who had been recently freed from the Immigration and Naturalization discrimination." Such token quotas were hardly the measure to free them from discrimination, but Gearhart nonetheless continued (with some fulsome praise of MacArthur's administration of the Occupation), noting that Japan would be a useful ally, and asked him to recommend that the Congress remove such legal discrimination, grant a quota to the Japanese, and authorize their naturalization.[44]

Walter Judd, a congressman from Minnesota and the architect of the repeal of the Chinese exclusion law, had introduced a series of similar bills to revise the Oriental exclusion laws and to extend the quota system to all of Asia. In 1947, Judd first introduced H.R. 4824 and in 1948, upon the advice and suggestion of the departments of State and Justice, a tighter and more expanded version (H.R. 5004) was developed. Following comprehensive open hearings held in April 1948, the House Judiciary Committee on Immigration and Naturalization further worked on H.R. 5004 and perfected it into H.R. 6809.[45]

A new aspect of Judd's proposal was to set up an Asian-Pacific triangle, a geographical boundary that encompassed all the countries inhabited by Asian peoples. It provided an annual quota of one hundred immigrants for each country within that triangle and an additional quota of one hundred for the entire region to cover racially mixed individuals (e.g., half-Asian half-white individuals)—people whose race could not be strictly defined as Asians—as well as inhabitants of colonial dependencies. Most importantly, under the proposed plan for the Asian-Pacific triangle, Japan would be the biggest beneficiary. Only Japan's quota was raised from the current 100 (a defunct quota reserved for emergency use only) to 185, due to national origins computations under the provisions of the present bill, which used the number of inhabitants as of 1920. (Note that in 1920 Japan was the only Asian nation that continued to send its immigrants to the states.) China's quota would remain the same as the current 105, which had been provided by the 1943 act, yet the figure would be the second largest in Asia. Meanwhile, the rest of Asia—countries such as Afghanistan, India, the Philippine islands, Bhutan, Nepal, New Guinea, Samoa and other Pacific islands, Burma, Ceylon, Indonesia, Korea, Pakistan, and so on—would receive a maximum of one hundred per each country.[46] Judd explained that the purpose of the bill was to remove the stigma attached to certain races that were denied immigration rights. Judd stressed that he did not favor throwing open the gates to unlimited immigration from the Far East or from any other part of the world. Nonetheless, he expressed his support for a small immigration quota for the Far East based on his belief that the issue was one of principle, of recognition of the innate equality of peoples, and of giving force to America's own democratic beliefs, saying: "It seems to me to be the height of folly to ask the support of democratic elements in these countries, yet at the very point where our democracy comes to test, to back away."

Judd pointed out the special importance of this bill to Japan, where a new democratic leadership was emerging under American tutelage. He criticized passage of the Japanese exclusion clause in the Immigration Act of 1924, which he interpreted as a major contribution to the final crisis between the two nations by classifying the Japanese as an inferior race. He insisted on a repeal of the discriminatory provisions and a recognition of Japan as an equal. The American occupation of Japan had been a great success thus far, and the Japanese proved that their sense of loyalty lay very deep. However, there was no way to forecast how long this spirit would continue. In the event that all American troops were withdrawn, the final outcome would depend upon Japanese leadership, which the United States could assist by solidifying the present trend of friendship. Judd concluded by insisting that Japan would become a valuable friend only if mutual confidence were built between the two nations: "There are realities in the world situation today which should impel us to strengthen by all means our bonds with nations whose friendship can be ours."[47]

This argument by the renowned expert on Asia was convincing enough to override opponents of the Judd bill. The State Department strongly endorsed the bill, stressing the need to win Asian friendship in the struggle to contain Communist expansion.[48] Subsequently, on March 1, 1949, the Judd bill was introduced again in exactly the same form as H.R. 6809 (i.e., with the Asian-Pacific triangle), this time as H.R. 199, and was promptly passed by the House by a vote of 336 to 39.

In June 1949 the Committee for Equality in Naturalization conducted research on more than forty editorials published in fifteen states and the District of Columbia. No unfavorable editorial had been written on the Judd bill, and sentiment on the West Coast favored enactment of this legislation. All editorials emphasized the importance of giving favorable treatment to the Japanese in order to strengthen their faith in democracy in a troubled world. Also, they all insisted that skin color could no longer be the test of human merit. "The darker races," "a yellow person," "a darker skinned Polynesian," or "human beings who happen to have brown or yellow skins" should all be allowed to come to the United States, the editorials unanimously argued. According to a letter to the Senate Judiciary Committee by a citizen in the state of Washington, "Anything that will improve our laws in regard to Orientals and do away with an attitude of superiority toward them *IS* important." The letter concluded that "it should make no difference *WHAT* race is involved. Adjusting these situations could do as much as dollars to win Asian friends for the American way of life."[49]

Senate hearings on the Judd bill began on July 19, 1949, focusing on its effect on Japan. Walter Judd insisted that Asian peoples wanted to believe in the United States and in democracy. Yet the current U.S. immigration laws officially stigmatized people of brown and yellow races as biologically inferior human beings. Under such circumstances, it would be very difficult for them to maintain that belief.[50]

Gen. Robert Eichelberger, commanding general of the Eighth Army in Japan from 1944 to 1948, testified to the effect that enacting such a measure as the Judd bill would have on occupied Japan from the viewpoint of SCAP. He began his statement by saying that the B-29 and the two atomic bombs had worked effectively to add to the prestige of the United States before MacArthur arrived in Japan on August 30, 1945. Since then, that prestige had been enhanced by "the discipline in the Eighth Army, the courtesy and generosity and heart of the American soldiers"; as a result, the United States had found a place in the hearts of the Japanese. He stated that the Japanese were "bright" enough to realize that the Russians would have acted in quite the opposite manner if they had occupied Japan. In the past three years, as his duties brought him into contact with many types of Japanese people, he realized that much of the hatred which had motivated the militarists to launch the Pacific War grew out of the fact that "the Japanese were not treated as a great power in so far as the Asiatic exclusion act was concerned." He concluded that in postwar Japan there was still a great deal of resentment over the exclusion clause and that passing the Judd bill would have a very good effect upon the Japanese people.[51]

Among the many letters Judd introduced into the record was one from William Castle, a former special assistant and chief of the Division of West European Affairs at the State Department, and a special ambassador to Japan under the Hoover administration during the London Naval Arms Conference in 1929 and 1930. Castle explained that the Japanese exclusion clause of 1924 was his greatest handicap during the time he served as ambassador to Japan. He endorsed the Judd bill in every respect: "I believe that fewer than 200 Japanese would be admitted annually if Japan were put on the quota, but, in Japan, it would be felt immediately that the United States was rectifying a wrong, that it was showing a spirit of fair play." Castle insisted that this reversal of America's former position would do more than anything else to give the Japanese confidence in the United States at an important time.[52]

Thus, the United States, too, resolved on returning to the familiar prewar racial diplomacy with Japan. Just as Theodore Roosevelt had praised the superior racial character of the Japanese, so did MacArthur. The relaxation of Occupation controls was already in progress. MacArthur's 1949 New Year's message to the Japanese people highly commended their hard work, which had laid "imperishable foundation stones in the political mold of freedom and dignity and peace." By then, Japanese nationalism was no longer an obstacle to democratization or a threat to world peace. On the contrary, U.S. authorities saw a growing need to encourage it as a buffer against Communist revolution. On May 3, 1949, on the second anniversary of the new constitution, MacArthur again praised the Japanese for honoring their commitments as enunciated in the Potsdam Declaration and assured them that the character of the Occupation had now changed from the stern rigidity of a military operation to the friendly guidance of a protective force. He announced his intention to carry out a revised Occupation policy while urging the Japanese to maintain a ceaseless vigilance against the "destructive inroads of concepts incredulous of human wisdom," his reference to communism.[53]

About this time, the U.S. Department of State was discussing with MacArthur a reduction in the size of the U.S. military government in Japan as well as the timing of a peace treaty with Japan. As early as March 5, 1948, George Kennan, U.S. political adviser for Japan, wrote a memorandum to MacArthur recommending a new Occupation policy, one that would prepare Japanese society for self-reliance with maximum stability when the protecting hand was withdrawn.[54] Kennan suggested a firm U.S. security policy for this area, one designed to give the Japanese adequate assurance against future military pressure from the Communist nations. He recommended an intensive program of economic recovery and a relaxation in occupational control to stimulate a sense of direct responsibility among the Japanese.

On July 16, 1949, in a conversation with Cloyce K. Huston, the chargé in Japan, MacArthur stated his belief that the Japanese people welcomed the

Occupation because it had been so "kind and helpful." Huston suggested that no people could welcome the presence of foreign troops over so long a period, even under the best of conditions. In a top secret cable to the Office of Far Eastern Affairs dated July 26, 1949, William Sebald, the acting political adviser in Japan, reported a discussion in which he said to MacArthur that it was high time for the Occupation to be placed solely on a policy level with a radical reduction in the number of personnel. It was Sebald's impression that MacArthur seemed prepared to go along with the State Department's policies.[55]

On July 28, 1949, MacArthur virtually ended the U.S. military government of Japan. The order disbanded the military government section of the U.S. Eighth Army (which controlled all American and Allied ground forces in Japan), another military government section of the army's First and Ninth Corps, and forty-five civil affairs teams which had operated in all Japanese prefectures. Only eight district and regional U.S. military government headquarters were to remain, and they would be largely staffed by civilians.[56]

By September 1949 the U.S. Department of State began discussions with President Truman on the subject of a peace treaty with Japan. On September 20, William Sebald had an informal conversation with MacArthur. MacArthur said that in view of the changing world situation and developments in Japan, the substantive provisions of the peace treaty should be as simple as possible and should be designed solely to bring about a state of peace with Japan in order to strengthen Japan's sovereignty.[57]

On the American political scene, pro-Japanese sentiments continued to grow, overriding even the remnants of wartime animosity. In January 1950 a group of ten Japanese Diet members and four of the Diet's secretaries started an official tour of American cities. The tour was authorized by Congress with State Department cooperation and sponsored by SCAP to show the Japanese lawmakers democratic processes at work. In California and South Carolina, they were received cordially by city and state officials.

Their arrival in Boston, however, was less cordial. On January 30, shortly before the Japanese group arrived at City Hall to observe a City Council meeting, Councilman James Coffe, a disabled World War I veteran whose son had served in Germany during World War II, claimed that they were spies. He proposed a motion to ban the Japanese visitors from council chambers, intimating that "they are probably here taking pictures of fortresses and trying to learn all they can about the A-bombs. We are feeding them and clothing them. But don't educate them so that they can start another war in a few years." Councilman Milton Cook, a former army officer who had served in the Pacific, made a motion for reconsideration of the order. But the council vote was eleven to eight to ban the Japanese. The Japanese group had to leave City Hall, escorted by Col. George Lynch, their U.S. Army guide. Although the Japanese refused to comment on the council's action, high authorities in SCAP in Tokyo immediately expressed a concern and fear that the "unfortunate incident" in Boston might be used by Japanese Communists to whip up anti-American feelings.[58] Although Coffe said he had received about 180 phone calls within a day congratulating him, national sentiment was strongly against his action.

The day after the incident at Boston City Hall, the Japanese group was enthusiastically welcomed at the Massachusetts State House. When the Japanese filed into the House Speaker's gallery to watch the state's legislature at work, all but one of the members of the House stood and applauded. During the tour of the Capitol, on February 20, the U.S. Senate gave the Japanese group the unusual privilege of coming onto the Senate floor. Sen. Charles Tobey of New Hampshire condemned the Boston Council's action as "un-Christian and un-American." Sen. Olin Johnson of South Carolina promised the good old-fashioned Southern hospitality his state later showed the visitors. The fiercely anti-Communist Sen. Joseph McCarthy of Wisconsin was also among those who offered an individual welcome during a twenty-minute recess. The following day, the Japanese group received a standing ovation from the House, after Rep. George Miller of California praised the Japanese as "hard-working people who have changed their ways and now seek democracy."[59]

It was imperative for the U.S. government to make the Japanese not only pro-American and anti-Communist but also "non-Asian" in the Asian geopolitical arena. From the point of view of the United States, Japan's Asian identity had to be carefully stripped off through its new relations with the United States so that Japan would feel no psychological or emotional attachment to an Asian nationalism directed against the West. The U.S. government needed to make the Japanese into "honorary whites" while at the same time alienating them in Asia—a traditional tactic since the early twentieth century whenever the United States sought Japan's collaboration in its Asian-Pacific strategy. So American policymakers went through an elaborate examination of cultural and racial dimensions in U.S.-Japanese relations and moved to upgrade Japan's status among the Asian peoples, almost exactly what the Japanese Foreign Ministry had tried to achieve. American reasons for elevating Japan's racial stature in Asia were, however, quite different from those of the Japanese.

John Foster Dulles, assigned primary responsibility for fashioning a peace treaty with Japan, was among those who had considered the sensitive task of maneuvering Japan's cultural and racial awareness into the pro-Western camp in support of American strategy in Asia. A veteran expert on international law and a delegate to numerous international conferences including the Paris Peace Conference in 1919 as an adviser to President Wilson, he noted the advantage of maximizing the pro-Western inclination manifest in modern Japan's dualistic identity. In his opinion, the long-range objective of the peace treaty for the Japanese people was to make them "able by their conduct and example to exhibit to the peoples of Asia and the Pacific Islands the advantages of the free way of life and thereby help in the effort to resist and throw back communism in this part of the world."[60]

Dulles was concerned about the inherent racial problem between Japan and the Western nations. "There is a certain barrier with the West in the face of the assumed Western sense of white superiority," Dulles had cautioned the Secretary of State in a secret memorandum dated June 7, 1950. He also noticed that the Japanese people felt themselves superior to the Chinese and wanted to be treated as social equals by the West. In dealing with this frame of mind Dulles suggested that the United States needed to do more to break down the barriers that it had created by its attitude toward the yellow race. He also pointed out the importance of permitting Japanese immigration to the United States at least on a par with the Chinese and Indians. Dulles then recommended trying to get Australia and New Zealand to change their approach to this problem.[61]

Dulles's view on the need to fully nurture Japan's dualistic identity—to align it with the West and alienate it from Asia—was best exemplified in his conversation with Sir Alvary Gascoigne, political representative of the British Liaison Mission to SCAP. On January 29, 1951, the two discussed on a "purely personal basis" the tentative views of the two countries concerning the Japanese peace treaty. In their discussion of a new accord between Japan and the West—which would include ideological as well as racial and cultural relations—they agreed upon a new racial identity for Japan. Dulles said he thought that despite their admiration for the ancient culture of the Chinese, the Japanese felt a certain superiority toward them. On the other hand, he argued, they felt that Western civilization—represented by Britain and more recently by the United States—had achieved a triumph which gave the Westerners a better social standing in the world than that achieved by the "human masses of Asia." Dulles thus laid out the strategy: The Japanese think that they have achieved mental superiority over the Asian masses and like to feel that they belong to and are accepted by the Western nations. Anything Westerners could do to encourage this feeling would bind the Japanese closer to them. An American effort to encourage the cultural relationship between Japan and the United States conveyed a certain social prestige to the Japanese. Therefore, Dulles concluded, not only the U.S. government but other Western governments such as Britain, France, and the Scandinavian countries should take an active part in this project. By establishing cultural relations between Japan and the West, Dulles argued, the Western world would allow Japan "access to an elite Anglo-Saxon club."[62]

A smooth and successful racial reconciliation during the Occupation was, however, a mirage. While there was an increase in the U.S. immigration quota for the Japanese, and while it was the biggest for an Asian nation, it was never as big as that offered to any one European nation. Miscegenation laws, applied to Japanese-American marriages, persisted (and are discussed in a later chapter). Within the United States, the Japanese, as a colored race, had no legal recourse against discrimination until 1965, when the Johnson administration introduced the Civil Rights Act. Rather, the underlying psychology of new U.S.-Japanese relations played on the Japanese sense of fear, insecurity, and nervousness toward the Anglo-Saxon presence and the American fear, disrespect, and distrust of the Japanese. That both sides complied to this deceptive truce speaks also to a mutual guilt. Mutual trust and a sincere sense of affinity never existed and failed to take root in the post-Occupation era.

On September 4, 1951, the San Francisco Peace Conference opened at the San Francisco Opera House, attended by fifty-two nations. On September 8 the San Francisco Peace Treaty was opened for signature by forty-nine nations. Under the terms of the treaty, Japan gained independence, effective on April 28, 1952, when the U.S. occupation would also formally terminate. As had been discussed in various wartime agreements among the Allied nations, Japan lost all of its territories seized after the Sino-Japanese war of 1894–95. Japan's territory was confined to the four main islands. The Ryukyu Islands (including Okinawa), the chain of islands southwest of Kyushu, and the Bonin (Ogasawara) Islands, a small group of mountainous islands located some six hundred miles south of Tokyo, were placed under American trusteeship for an indefinite period of time. Japan also renounced all claims to property in its former colonies and occupied territories, and agreed to pay reparations for war damage.

In the legal sense, the San Francisco Peace Treaty ended the state of war between Japan and most of the Allied nations and symbolized Japan's reentry into the international community. Such an international community, however, was only half of a world now divided by Cold War antagonisms, the half under American influence. Because of each nation's ideological split, neither China nor Korea—the two countries most ravaged by Japan's aggression—was invited to the conference. The Soviet Union, Poland, and Czechoslovakia refused to sign the treaty because of the absence of the People's Republic of China. India, Burma, and Yugoslavia declined to attend the conference because of their opposition to the terms of the treaty.

Only two hours after the peace treaty was signed, the United States and Japan signed the U.S.-Japan Security Treaty, which defined Japan's subordination to the United States in the larger network of the American global security alliance. The ostensible American strategy was to build and integrate the noncommunist countries in the region to forestall further expansion by communist economies, now that the Wilsonian "one-world system" had become an impossible formula to achieve. The treaty gave the United States the exclusive right to station military troops in Japan for the purpose of protecting Japan and maintaining order in East Asia, as well as quelling internal disturbances in Japan.

Yoshida Shigeru, Japan's prime minister from October 1948 through December 1954 and known in the prewar period as a leading pro-Anglo-American politician, had objected to the idea of a neutral Japan in the process of peace treaty negotiations, but was "willing to accept whatever practical arrangements the United States might consider necessary" in order to assist in the maintenance of Japan's security after concluding the peace treaty. He confirmed his belief to Cloyce Huston, American Embassy counselor in Tokyo, that Japan would have to remain dependent on American protection after the Occupation ended. In response to the people's concern that Japan would become a colony of the United States in the post-treaty period, he explained Japan's relations with the United States to be like that of the American colonies with Britain in the eighteenth century. Just as the Americans eventually won dominance in the Atlantic, Japan would start as a colony of the United States, develop its national power while fully protected by the latter, and eventually become stronger.[63]

Yoshida often expressed his satisfaction that Japan did better as a loser at the San Francisco Peace Conference than as a victor at Versailles in 1919.[64] In a strategic sense, Yoshida's shrewd observation proved accurate. In terms of race relations—the focal subject for Japan at Versailles—the San Francisco Peace Treaty concluded with no principle of racial equality written in. However, at least as a result of the enactment of the McCarran-Walter Act in June 1952, Japan as the vanquished received the immigration quota that prewar Japan as the victorious allied power had failed to obtain. Japan's new racial identity as defined and approved by the United States under the San Francisco System was as an honorary Western nation of Asia.[65]

By then, the Chinese Communists themselves were using the old Japanese war slogan of "Asia for the Asians" and attempting to rally other Asian nations to rise against all Western influence. Shortly after the San Francisco Peace Conference, John Foster Dulles, as consultant to the Secretary of State, cautioned Dean Rusk, assistant secretary of state for Far Eastern affairs, that India's refusal to attend the peace conference should be understood in the context of its historic distrust of the white man's motivation and interest in Asia. Dulles explained that India rejected the terms of the U.S.-Japan Security Treaty because it was skeptical that the United States could move toward mutual goals "with a defeated nation of alien race." In Dulles's view, if Westerners (as represented by the United States) could not deal with Orientals as equals, there would be grave repercussions. If all Asia united under Communist leadership against the West—not motivated by Communist ideology itself but by antiwhite racial animosity—the situation would be more dangerous to the United States than Japan's wartime attempt at a Greater East Asian Co-Prosperity Sphere, he concluded. Dulles thus emphasized the need for the West to keep Japan on its side at all costs.[66]

Was Japan better off as an associate member of the Western nations in the age of the Cold War? The great ideological clash of the Cold War seems to have wiped out little by little the racial line between Japan and the West and to have brought Japan into the circle of the Western alliance as a full member. The reality was that the racial line of Western nations in world politics continued to mark Japan as a somewhat unpredictable factor. Japan's racial reliability as a Western ally remained suspect despite its newly acquired quasi-Western status.

American military forces in Japan, for example, now stood in a position not only to project U.S. power in Asia but also to contain the potential threat of post-Occupation Japan—that of growing into an anti-Western power in racial and cultural terms. In official circles, policymakers in Washington acknowledged confidentially that America's military presence in Japan not only integrated Japan into their anticommunist world strategy but simultaneously created a permanent structure of U.S. control over Japan.[67] With approximately 200,000 U.S. servicemen and 630 U.S. military installations in Japan (excluding Okinawa), containing bases, training areas, depots, warehouses, and communication facilities, the U.S. military presence established an on-site deterrent against hostile remilitarization by Japan itself, which the United States and other Western nations suspected would result in a direct threat to their own global interests.

In fact, encompassing the U.S.-Japanese security pact was a larger framework of protection for traditional European interests, formerly represented by the British colonial empire in Asia and the Pacific. On the eve of World War I, in March 1914, Winston Churchill, as First Lord of the Admiralty, had asked the United States to protect the "white men" in the Pacific.[68] In the postwar era it was Australia and New Zealand, two British Commonwealth nations, that raised concerns for the fate of Western civilization in the Pacific and requested American protection against Japan's threat. Britain followed suit. In February 1951 the British Embassy in Washington, D.C., sent a top secret memorandum to the U.S. Department of State, calling for a "white man's pact" to protect Australia and New Zealand from the potential aggressor—either the Soviet Union or Japan.[69]

As fear of the Soviet Union loomed, a concern grew among the Anglo-Saxon nations in the Pacific Basin—Australia, New Zealand, and the United States—that Japan might suddenly betray them, switching sides and becoming a pro-Communist power. But more unsettling to these nations was the prospect of Japan's reincarnation into an anti-Western power on cultural and racial terms and the creation of a Pan-Asian bloc that would exclude white Australia and New Zealand. The Western allies therefore saw in the Soviet Union an ideological threat and in Japan a racial threat.

The U.S. government agreed to secure a tripartite treaty of alliance with Australia and New Zealand, in which the United States officially assumed a leadership role in providing security for the two British Commonwealth members. The ANZUS Pact, concluded on September 1, 1951, in San Francisco, only three days before the opening of the peace conference, was designed to safeguard the security of their sphere of influence in the Pacific area, ideologically, culturally, and racially. The pact assuaged their fears of both Communist aggression and the traditional yellow peril coming from Japan.

Great Britain had originally claimed its place in this Pacific pact, keeping the region under traditional Western influence, despite the fact that it no longer had sufficient resources to protect its own Commonwealth members. The United States had to decline the British request for fear of creating an Asian-Pacific alliance under exclusive Western leadership—suspecting that in the event of British participation, the French, Dutch, and even Portuguese would also request admittance to the pact. If the pact consisted of these Western nations, it "thereupon acquires colonial nature which wld [sic] make it anathema to Asian nations and destroy its realism as genuine security arrangement among powers with primary Pacific interests," wrote Secretary of State Acheson to Sebald, the U.S. political adviser to SCAP, in a secret telegram.[70] The United States launched a solo mission to represent and protect Western interests on ideological, cultural, and racial terms in Asia and the Pacific. American Cold War strategy thus reinforced Japan's subordination to traditional Western prestige and leadership in Asia.

In Cold War terminology, the division of the West versus the Oriental East shifted to a new ideological demarcation of the capitalist and democratic West versus the Communist East. The West meant countries west of the "Iron Curtain." East Germany and Poland were no longer the West. However, it did not automatically categorize Japan as a Western nation with legitimacy. In fact, in the ideologically divided world the same "West versus non-West" thesis existed, leaving Japan out of the full circle of the "elite industrialized Western nations."[71]

In keeping with the new multiple interpretations of the old duality of East versus West, a third denomination was added to global economic and political terminology. The French demographer Alfred Sauvy first proposed his theory of three worlds in 1952 in an attempt to explain the rising U.S.-Soviet conflict as these competitors divided between them the postcolonial world. Sauvy proposed a threefold conceptual division of the world, or *tiers monde*. This offered a new way of understanding the U.S.-Soviet rivalry over spheres of influence. The three-world concept was also used to understand conflicts between the first and second worlds based on modernization theory, so fashionable in the 1950s and 1960s. The first world consisted of the advanced capitalist nations in North America and Western Europe. The second world consisted of socialist nations in Eastern Europe. The first two worlds represented modes of modernization. The underdeveloped countries constituting the third world were unaligned objects of the ideological competition of the first two worlds. Since it was presupposed that the second world countries must inevitably "modernize," a concept equivalent to "Westernize," third-world leaders had to choose to follow one of the two worlds. As a result, the third world was at the very core of the problems of coexistence between the first two worlds.[72]

Beneath its conspicuous ideological tone of the three-world division lay the traditional racial divisions of the globe. The first, or capitalist, world was efficient, democratic, and free—the most natural form guided by the invisible hand of universal Reason. The second, or Communist, world was modernized and partially rational, yet repressed by socialist ideology. If the second world emulated the first world through a common heritage of Western civilization, it could avoid permanent stagnation. In contrast, the third world was primitive and underdeveloped. It was the world ruled by tradition and irrationality, i.e., by disorder and chaos.

The theory defines the first and second worlds as culturally European, whether capitalist or Communist, or geographically located in the West or the East. Their populations are termed Europeans, (North) Americans, and more generally Westerners or East Europeans, located in the moderate climate of the Northern Hemisphere. More characteristically, their inhabitants are white. Thus, Australia and New Zealand are included in the first-world designation, though they are the least European in geographical terms. South Africa could also be included in the West insofar as that governmental entity represented white or non-African people who considered themselves part of Europe, not Africa. In comparison, the third world, encompassing Africa and Latin America—largely located in a tropical climate—and all of Asia except for Japan and the Soviet Union, is non-European and nonwhite. Korea, Singapore, Taiwan, Kuwait, and Saudi Arabia belong to the third world.[73] Sauvy thus maintained the prewar, hierarchical view of the world based on racial, cultural, and geographical categorization, with the notion of Western superiority still in place.

This then-current ideological cartography of the world encouraged the United States to invite Japan to its side in a common guardianship of Asia against Moscow's threat to conquer the world. American sponsorship gave other leading Western nations a guarantee of Japan's transformation into a quasi-Western nation.[74] In the post-Occupation period, Japan played the same dualist identity game, advancing its own cause with a remarkable range of flexibility in a turbulent global arena. Japan could exert its superiority in

Asia in a manner the Western nations found nonthreatening. Japan could also pose as a racially neutral nation in a rebuttal of the Communist campaign of "Asia for Asians."

However, the "fact" that Japan was not racially Western was never in question in the eyes of the West. Japan's place in the first world was never fully legitimate. Japan's cultural, not racial, difference as a non-Western nation was much celebrated through various cultural exchange programs, not just with the United States but with most Western nations.[75] Japanese culture, celebrated as distinctly different from other non-Western cultures for its compatibility with modernization, became highly acclaimed by the West as a contributing factor in Japan's miraculous economic growth. Yet despite its successful industrialization and democratization, Japan was not part of the West except in the official Cold War diplomatic category. In contrast, despite the geographical distance or isolation, the Australians and New Zealanders were part of the West. Even with the ideological split, the Slavs were much closer to the West than the Japanese. The three-world theory reinforced the common game of race between the Japanese and the Americans.

The tacit racism that had characterized the Occupation held fast for decades to come. The persistence of this silence on the subject of U.S.-Japanese racism at the international level was more than supported by the repression— even forgetting—of the mutual racism that developed at the street level, as will become apparent in the next chapter.

CHAPTER 2

Race and Culture: Person to Person

In the official record of the Occupation, as we have noted, the Japanese were given diplomatic recognition, were restored to their prewar racial status, and became eligible for immigration and naturalization in the United States. However, the disparity between official and actual day-to-day personal relations between the Americans and the Japanese during the Occupation were enormous. In the public memory, there is very little on record from either American or Japanese sources of their individual racial experiences. Of course, there were friendly interactions between the former enemies. But when they are asked about a color barrier between them—or their awareness of it—they do not remember. There is a kind of amnesia regarding their mutual racial experiences in occupied Japan.

Why the absence of a mutual public memory of race? One reason was SCAP's deliberate nonrecognition of the subject. Despite its efficacy, racist thinking itself was a fearful prospect because of its negative force. And the subject of white supremacy was too embarrassing to discuss openly or to even acknowledge. Throughout the Occupation, despite the elaborate politics of race, SCAP adopted a so-called color-blind approach with the Japanese people while censorship of the press supposedly erased racial differences. The Japanese quickly noticed the Achilles heel of their new ruler and complied with SCAP's careful neglect of the subject. Besides, on their part, the reality of their submission to white supremacy was also too embarrassing to acknowledge or protest. Thus, together they conspired to pursue a covert mutual racism. The subject of race submerged into a subconscious level, never marking its presence in the vivid memory of the two peoples.

Another, and more fundamental, reason for the absence of racism in a mutual public memory is the fuzzy nature of the Japanese dual racial identity which was subject to SCAP policies. Even at a conscious level it was extremely difficult for the two peoples to conceptualize the precise nature of the Japanese race, or racial identity, applicable to their relations. In the history of U.S.-Japanese relations, Japanese racial identity was both a national identity—a cultural construct accountable for a level of civilization—and a matter of the physical characteristics of the members of Japanese society—characteristics that made them unfit for coexistence with the white Americans. In the Occupation, definitions of race vacillated and even overlapped between such cultural and physical constructs, making the boundary between the two peoples either malleable (temporary) or unchangeable (permanent), thus confusing them as to the nature of the differences that set them apart.

Early policies relied on race as visible physical characteristics and drew a permanent line between the conqueror and the conquered. SCAP carried out a series of measures such as the antifraternization order which effectively segregated the Japanese and established American superiority. In the second phase of the Occupation, as the international political climate deteriorated, SCAP quickly abandoned a physical concept of race and substituted culture. The Japanese adjusted to this drastic change well. They understood the implicit message of the Occupation to be that democratization could improve their racial quality to a level close to that of civilized Westerners. The hope for such transformation eroded much of the Japanese fatalistic notion of a permanent color barrier. There was even optimism among the Japanese that the racial barrier was temporary, removable upon the completion of the Occupation. SCAP implemented various cultural programs that put an official stamp on America's growing respect for Japanese culture, which in turn satisfied such Japanese hopes.

After all, Japan's dual racial identity was like a mirage—a sensory illusion consisting of a superior culture and an inferior skin color. The maneuverable race in U.S.-Japanese relations was always that of a cultural construct.[1] Diplomatic recognition of the Japanese would henceforth focus on abstract qualities such as the ability to democratize and to attain a higher civilization. Only in the realm of cultural activities, where individual contacts were not necessary and the concept of interaction remained purely abstract, did the Occupation allow the distance to narrow between the two peoples. Crossing the color line, meanwhile, remained forbidden. Both Japanese and American peoples perhaps felt that an improvement in purely abstract cultural relations would serve and shelved the problem of physical race.

It was after Japan gained independence and received no more guidance from SCAP that the troubling problem of physical, not cultural, interaction of races became worse. When the Japanese realized that democratization and other successes in the Occupation did not metamorphose them into a white people in the American perception, this rude awakening left an increasingly awkward situation with the Americans.

By recalling the memory of race, both repressed and obscure, we can explore the story of how physical race kept the distance between white ruler and colored subject and how the Japanese themselves collaborated, making the Occupation a great U.S.-Japanese success. And we can begin to understand why, in spite of Japan's improved status in the world, racial barriers— or the color line—between Americans and Japanese did not come down.

The initial Japanese encounter with American GIs was exceptional in the story of their street-level racial experience. It reflected a multitude of emotions enveloping the racial war that had just finished. The different physical appearance of the former enemy—and now the new ruler in their land— caused the Japanese a sense of uneasiness and fear mixed with some odd curiosity. On the morning of August 25, 1945, sixteen American planes landed at Atsugi Naval Air Base, carrying 150 signal corps men to prepare for the August 30 arrival of Gen. Douglas MacArthur. Outside the Atsugi Air Base, public traces of Japan's wartime propaganda remained everywhere—on telephone poles, billboards, or buildings, the words *teki* (enemy) or *shōri* (victory) persisted where posters had been hastily torn down. Incidents had already occurred in Tokyo in protest against Japan's surrender, including several coup d'état attempts and the staging of ritualistic suicides.[2]

The American arrival caused some panic among the Japanese. In Yokohama, the city MacArthur chose as headquarters for the 8,000 men of the First Cavalry Division for the first three weeks of the Occupation, people fled the central part of the city like refugees. Local governments across the country issued directives and briefed residents on how to avoid problems with foreign soldiers. According to the Kanagawa Prefecture's "Preparatory Guide to the Residents" (*Jūmin kokoroe*) issued on August 29, the local government encouraged every citizen to remain calm and dignified in the face of danger. Women were given special advice for self-protection: they were warned against walking alone, being out at night, wearing provocative clothes, or using cosmetics.[3] But confrontations were inevitable. Within the first month, in Yokohama alone, there were four homicides, twenty-one rapes, forty bodily injuries, and 872 robberies and lootings. In every case the victims were Japanese.[4]

As the Occupation progressed in an orderly manner, with no sign of any fearful and much-rumored atrocity, the wartime image of Americans as *kichiku* (beastly and demonic) quickly waned, replaced by a positive reappraisal of Americans as equal human beings. Perhaps the euphoria accounted for a naive optimism that with the war's end the issue of racism had also gone out of sight.

The confrontations that characterized the arrival of American troops in Yokohama faded away and, by the fall of 1945, the Japanese had begun to accept the presence of the Occupation army. Friendly gestures gradually developed into sociability. Japanese people invited American GIs to their homes for supper, and the latter gave them American souvenirs.[5] Interactions between black Americans and the Japanese also began, as hundreds of Japanese stevedores worked under the supervision of black noncommissioned officers on the Yokohama docks. According to the *Pittsburgh Courier*, a leading black newspaper, black troops in Japan were impressed at how rapidly the Japanese were getting accustomed to them and said that "their initial awe and unconcealed curiosity is being replaced by friendly overtures." One black private, comparing this friendly atmosphere in Japan to the Jim Crow situation back home, was quoted as saying: "We have encountered not the slightest sign that the Japanese regard us as anything but Americans."[6]

Although Japanese newspapers had warned against fraternization, they now began to demonstrate a warmer feeling toward Occupation soldiers and a desire to develop better relations with the Western nations, especially the United States. Various newspapers carried interviews with American soldiers, who expressed their desire for friendship with the Japanese. After the surrender Japanese newspapers remained under imperial censorship for some time; the Japanese government perhaps encouraged the newspapers to create a friendly atmosphere toward American soldiers. In contrast to the usual praise of Pan-Asianism, these pro-American articles by the Japanese media conveyed a curious mixture of Japanese pride and hope for mutual friendship.

While the Japanese press went further and conveyed an impression of American goodwill toward Japan, the American press did not initially follow suit. An interview with two American military correspondents—Frank Kluckhohn of the *New York Times*, who would soon become the first foreigner to interview Emperor Hirohito, and Gordon Walker of the *Christian*

Science Monitor—appeared in the August 31 issue of the Japanese newspaper *Asahi*. The two Americans were reported to have expressed their genuine respect for the Japanese and their sincere hope that the Japanese would again become friends with the United States. Another *Asahi* interview with a female United Press (UP) correspondent assured Japanese readers of the sincere desire of American women to renew their friendship with Japanese women. But in their articles published in American newspapers, these same American journalists offered a very different slant on their interviews with the Japanese reporters. Their views of the Japanese more or less constituted a continuation of U.S. wartime views of Japan and its people.[7]

According to the Japanese press, however, the relationship between the Japanese and the soldiers of the Occupation was made into one of old friends. The Hollywood image of a light-hearted all-American boy—youthful, innocent, carefree, down-to-earth, cheerful, curious, easygoing—quickly captured the Japanese, who could never resist the alluring symbol of American culture even during the war. Nowhere in the Japanese press were Americans portrayed as aloof or condescending. An interview with American soldiers in the September 12 issue of *Asahi* conveys a casual and relaxed atmosphere between American and Japanese people and their mutual hope for a better future. When an American soldier and a Japanese reporter discuss the use of atomic bombs, the Japanese confesses to having bitter feelings about it. The American agrees, saying that the use of the atomic bomb had provoked serious criticism in the States, too. The Japanese reporter follows up: "But now we think very well of you [because] we can clearly see you are sincerely cooperating with us." The American soldier suggests that from now on we determine things through talks, not by a Pearl Harbor attack or atomic bombs, and recommends that the newspaper company sponsor events to promote mutual friendship, such as baseball games, or even football games, between Occupation forces and Japanese teams.[8]

The Japanese desire for friendship with Americans was carried to an extreme in some cases. This is apparent in a collection of letters from Japanese citizens to General MacArthur. Although many of these letters were written in a tone of supplication to an omnipotent—godlike—MacArthur, there were also those written with criticism, advice, personal opinions, and requests regarding the U.S. occupation. They expressed their belief that MacArthur stood side by side with them in working together toward Japan's reconstruction and democratization, striking a note of confidence in the equality of the Japanese race.

The original suggestion for letter writing is believed to have come from Prime Minister Prince Higashikuni Naruhiko, who on the day of MacArthur's arrival at Atsugi solicited advice from the people about shaping a new policy for Japan. Soon after his statement appeared in the major newspapers on August 31, an average of forty to fifty letters flooded the prime minister's residency each day. SCAP also encouraged the Japanese to write to MacArthur as part of a democratization program. Although letters ceased to flow into Higashikuni's office when his cabinet collapsed on October 5, they continued to pour into MacArthur's headquarters. During MacArthur's tutelage, an estimated total of 500,000 letters reached his office, about one in every 150 Japanese writing at least once. Every letter was read, translated, and summarized by the Allied Translation and Interpreting Service (ATIS), and a few of the positive ones were published in newspapers both in English and Japanese.[9]

These letters to MacArthur, written with a mixture of supplication and self-confidence, represent both sides of Japan's contradictory racial attitudes discussed in the preceding chapter. Those who wrote asking MacArthur to solve Japan's national problems exemplify the belief that Americans are superior not only in might but in intelligence, political sophistication, and ingenuity; those who wrote to MacArthur as a partner in the rebuilding of Japan represent the view that the Japanese are on a par with Americans, and even that the Japanese might teach them something. A letter written in October 1945 from one Asai Takashi, who claimed to be affiliated with Waseda University, begins: "I am writing this piece with an aim to give you some advice." Asai requested America's help in encouraging the growth of the truly liberal Japanese who never gave up their faith in democracy even during wartime so Japan would someday emerge as a Switzerland in Asia, able to contribute greatly to world peace and welfare. In doing so, he argued, the great racial quality of the Japanese would be a certain advantage. "The Japanese are indeed an interesting race worth studying," he continued. "Our race should be the best in Asia in terms of anthropological capacity. If such a talented race was intellectually guided toward a peace-loving nature in a proper manner by the American Occupation, the whole world would benefit from this outcome to an immeasurable degree." He concluded his letter by saying that he remained thoroughly optimistic about MacArthur's democratization program and the outcome of this Occupation.[10]

There were also those letter writers who expressed disappointment in their nation and people and requested a serious rescue effort by the United

States. A letter from Kyoto, dated February 15, 1946, called for the American annexation of Japan (*Bei-Nichi gappei*) as the only way to save it from collapse. Another letter from a sixty-two-year-old man in Okayama also asked the Americans to make Japan a protectorate (*zokkoku*), since Japanese leadership was no longer trustworthy. A letter from Kōchi, on February 18, stated: "My request to you [General MacArthur] is to add one more star to the Stars and Stripes and make Japan a new state of your country. Then you will hopefully introduce a drastic birth control program for the Japanese race [*Nihon-jinshu*] and rectify the entire people. I believe this is a request in need of urgent consideration."[11]

As convenient as it was for the Occupation procedure, the Japanese turnabout in their view of relations was unacceptable to SCAP. Having accepted unconditional surrender to the Allied powers, Japan as a nation was in no position to expect equal status from the United States. Nor could the people of Japan expect equal standing. The Potsdam Declaration, the so-called "terms for Japanese surrender," proclaimed the Allies' intention not to rape or enslave the Japanese as a race. But in no way did it afford the Japanese ground for expecting racial equality between the Americans and the Japanese. After all, in the American domestic context, the principle of racial inequality between whites and colored citizens was a norm, and the Occupation brought in segregation for the white and colored soldiers in quite a matter-of-fact way. The American view of the Japanese as an inferior race was openly expressed in the early phase of the Occupation and was further justified by the fact of their nation's unconditional surrender and loss of sovereignty.

The principle of racial equality had been declared the American creed from the beginning of the Occupation. In *Our Job in Japan*, a War Department film shown to the Occupation forces in Japan in November 1945, that principle was proudly promoted as the American way. The movie's narrator states: "We can prove that most Americans don't believe in pushing people around, even when we happen to be on top. We can prove that most Americans do believe in a fair break for everybody regardless of race, or creed, or color."[12]

The reality for Americans in occupied Japan—a reality that the Japanese were quick to identify as discriminatory—was the policy of racial segregation between white and nonwhite soldiers. The black units serving in the Occupation forces in Japan rose rapidly due to high recruitment and low discharge rates among black soldiers. In these units, inequities in assignments and promotions, frequent discrimination in housing and recreational facilities, and problems of crime and punishment were evident. MacArthur, an honorary member of the Southern Society in New York, showed little interest in racial desegregation within the army. In July 1948, President Truman issued an executive order declaring a new policy of "equality of treatment and opportunity" in the military services. MacArthur refused to conform, denying the integration of black troops into white units.[13] Black soldiers in occupied Japan, undergoing the same sort of discrimination as in the United States, were often frustrated by this irony of the democratization program. In an article published in the leading black newspaper, the *Pittsburgh Courier*, in the fall of 1945, a correspondent reported from Tokyo that a new Jim Crowism had been introduced into occupied Japan. Colored soldiers were now barred from recreational facilities reserved for whites, such as clubs, snack bars, and swimming pools, although the white soldiers freely used the colored facilities. "Here is the first lesson in 'democracy' and we may be sure that the Japanese, apt as usual, are learning it," deplored the reporter. Once they learn this typical American democratic practice, he lamented, the Japanese will soon be qualified to enter the democratic fold.[14]

Nisei, or second-generation Japanese-Americans, also remained second-class American citizens in the Occupation. After the outbreak of the war, the Army discharged approximately 3,500 Nisei from the ranks of the National Guard and assigned them to army engineers as common laborers. The Navy's color line kept them out of naval uniform, while the Army Air Corps accepted only a few. Nisei men petitioned federal officials, requesting that they be allowed to join the armed forces. After the enactment of Executive Order 9066 on February 19, 1942, the government reinstated former National Guardsmen and organized the "all-Nisei"—euphemism for "racially segregated"—100th Infantry Battalion, which, along with the famed 442nd Regimental Combat Team, proved to be among America's most highly decorated and heroic military units during World War II. Although the military service of Japanese-American soldiers during the war led some Americans to insist on repealing the discriminatory laws against the Japanese and other Asian peoples, the atmosphere remained hostile to Japanese-American returnees, especially on the West Coast. In occupied Japan, most Japanese-Americans worked in the ATIS in low-ranking positions. Racism hampered promotions, and the highest-ranking Japanese-American soldier in occupied Japan was Lt. Col. John Aiso, an aide to Brig. Gen. Charles Willoughby.[15]

Americans in the Occupation were ready to establish themselves as white conquerors. First of all, in the minds of the Americans, the Japanese remained far from being equal partners. Their wartime stereotypes of the Japanese did not vanish as quickly as the Japanese presumed. According to a September 2 *New York Times* article, "Japan is a strange mixture of Oriental and Occidental. Ancient and modern are side by side.... A grotesque melange of Japanese and American clothes lends a touch of incongruity to the scene."[16] The War Department film *Our Job in Japan* (November 1945)—the final film produced by Frank Capra's Special Service Unit intended to familiarize American soldiers with the enemies' characteristics—portrayed the "Japs" as being still dangerous and not to be trusted. Although top SCAP officers ordered that all showings be halted lest they disturb Occupation policies, the film returned to Japan in March 1946, readied for restricted military release in Japan, Korea, and Okinawa. *Our Job in Japan* begins with the animation of a Japanese brain which had been warped by evil influences. The narrator declares that Japanese brains are the same as others; they are good or bad depending on the ideas that are put into them.[17] While the point that there is nothing inherently warlike in the Japanese psyche seems a more lenient interpretation than that presented in the earlier film *Know Your Enemy—Japan*, its visual insinuations, through an animated collage of human brains, was less than acceptable even to Occupation officials because of its distasteful effects.

Contemporary books and articles on occupied Japan were full of animosity. *The Conqueror Comes to Tea: Japan Under MacArthur* (published in 1946), by the journalist John LaCerda, frequently used terms like "the Japs" in the early part of the book. The author rejected the idea that the Japanese were strange, unfathomable creatures. He claimed they had a national inferiority complex that showed up in various ways, and that they were sneaky and animal-like. He questioned "whether a Japanese is being an obstructionist or just plain dumb." Brig. Gen. Sherman V. Hasbrouck was said to be inclined to feel that "in most instances it's dumbness."[18]

There were cases of mistreatment of Japanese, especially women, by Occupation personnel. A GI standing in a movie line threw a cigarette down in front of a Japanese woman. When she stooped and reached for it, he ground his foot into her hand. In some cases, innocent women who were mistaken for prostitutes were forcibly taken to a hospital for a VD checkup. A controversial incident took place when Occupation officials halted a train at a station in a Tokyo suburb and sent all the female passengers to a prophylactic station. It was thought that Japanese women did not deserve the same kind of respectful treatment American women did. Even American women in the

Occupation shared that feeling as well. Japanese maids were readily available to almost every Occupation family for an affordable price and, according to one observer, "The American enjoyed the full privileges of the clean-cut master-servant relationship between themselves and their Japanese maids." At Red Cross billets, the American women ordered tea or sandwiches or a dress pressed or any other service at any hour of the day or night from the Japanese staff. One sergeant's wife trained her Japanese maid to follow her around with cigarettes and an ashtray. Another woman from a country town in Arkansas had one Japanese servant, whom she named "Mary." Since "Mary" did not understand English, this woman often waved her hands when she ordered her about, as she would to a pet animal.[19]

The most telling evidence that the Japanese desire for friendship was not reflected by American attitudes toward the Japanese was that MacArthur himself, except for his sense of a messianic mission to revolutionize the un-civilized nation of the Orient, took very little interest in Japan or its culture. He stayed aloof from the Japanese public, calculating that Orientals pre-ferred an autocratic leader, and successfully established himself as a new ruler of the land—"*Aoi me no Shōgun* [blue-eyed Shogun]," euphemistically meaning a Caucasion/white Shogun in Japan, not literally meaning a Shogun with blue eyes—among both Americans and Japanese in occupied Japan. The American media soon circulated an exaggerated story for its readers that the Japanese believed in MacArthur's divinity and looked up to him as Japan's new god.[20]

Americans were increasingly annoyed at Japanese willingness to frater-nize with their troops. The Japanese were seen as presumptuous, like ser-vants presuming friendship with their masters. In spite of American "gentle-ness and good nature," an American reporter complained, GIs would lose their tempers when the Japanese approached them as if they were old friends, because "a conquering army cannot and does not desire to bridge the spiritual gap between the people and themselves."[21]

Only a few weeks into the Occupation, SCAP had concluded that the friendliness of the Japanese was a dangerous sign that they remained arro-gant despite unconditional surrender. On September 5, 1945, SCAP an-nounced that its relations with Japan did not rest on a contractual basis but on an unconditional surrender. Subsequently, MacArthur assured the American public of the lines drawn in the Occupation. No fraternization was developing between American troops and the Japanese civilian popula-tion, he testified, because "the general aloofness of the American soldier, based upon his innate self-respect, is one of the most noticeable character-istics of the occupation."[22] Fleet Adm. Chester Nimitz believed that Japanese friendliness was a calculated act to deceive the Americans into ending the Occupation as soon as possible and, even worse, that the Japanese were not conceding their inferiority to Americans. In his own words, the friendly Japanese did not seem to have learned the "lesson" yet. Worse than mere friendliness was the Japanese expectation that Americans would apologize in a quest for mutual reconciliation.[23]

To draw a sharp line between the conqueror and the conquered and cre-ate a military aloofness, SCAP moved on to consider a drastic measure of physical segregation by introducing a policy of nonfraternization. Nonfrat-ernization policy—a military ban on cordial association with members of the former enemy in the war—took on a drastically different outlook in oc-cupied Germany and Japan. In Germany, with the absence of a color line, the policy fizzled away quickly. In Japan the same policy assumed a racist con-notation and proved stunningly effective. It accentuated the racial cleavage between the white master and the colored subject, thus helping to make vis-ible the racial hierarchy and shoring up the prestige of Americans in Japa-nese eyes. Thus the calculated race factor entered the Occupation scene for the first time.

In Germany the Allied occupation began with a nonfraternization policy as early as September 12, 1944, the day after American troops entered Ger-many. Although the policy was originally intended to prevent leakage of in-formation, as well as to protect the lives of individual soldiers, it also aimed at creating more respect for U.S. troops among the Germans.[24] Under the policy of nonfraternization, soldiers were forbidden to entertain Germans, to visit German homes, to shake hands with Germans, to play games or en-gage in sports with Germans, to give or accept gifts, or to attend German dances or other social events. In German church services, Allied troops would be seated separately.

Though the punishments for violation of the nonfraternization rules were severe, Germany's experiment in segregation was doomed to failure from V-E Day forward. For one thing, Americans at home did not unani-mously support the policy of nonfraternization in Germany. A June 1945 Gallup poll asked American women: "Do you think American soldiers in Germany should be allowed to have dates with German girls?" Sixty-seven percent answered no, while 22 percent answered yes. American men were much more tolerant toward the idea and almost equally divided over the issue. Although 48 percent of them answered no, 41 percent answered that they should be allowed to date German girls.[25] The policy also collapsed as American soldiers began to seek out relatives. By October 1, 1945, less than five months after its implementation, the Allied Control Council, acting on American recommendations, removed practically all restrictions on fraternization except for marriage and billeting.[26]

In Japan, although no nationwide antifraternization regulation had yet been issued, some local Occupation troop units announced harsh directives intended to stamp out any wartime defiance to Anglo-American authority. An order was issued on September 4, 1945, by the twelfth division of the First Cavalry of the U.S. Army, stationed in the Tachikawa area in Tokyo and made public on September 6, through major newspapers including the *Asahi* and the *Yomiuri shimbun*. According to the directive, the Japanese were banned from wearing American clothes, possessing American foods or cigarettes, or from using American furniture, utensils, or automobiles. Anyone who purchased goods from or exchanged goods with an American soldier would be punished either with imprisonment for up to thirty years or with the death penalty. Although the order was, in part, issued to stop black market activities, the overall intention was more insidious: the directive stipulated that "the Japanese must respect 'America.' Any car, train, or horse carriage that carries a Japanese person on board must not pass an American automobile. A violator may be shot to death."[27]

On April 2, 1946, almost seven months into the Occupation, MacArthur finally introduced formal antifraternization regulations in Japan primarily as a measure to ban sexual liaisons between "Japanese women of immoral character" and American GIs. The antifraternization order quickly evolved to regulate a wide range of social relationships between Americans and Japanese—male and female. Within two months, on June 7, 1946, all Japanese women except employees—prostitutes or not—were ordered to stay out of army billets. Subsequently, Japanese, both male and female, were barred from the mess hall. In contrast, in occupied Germany, Germans working for the army who claimed that they were anti-Nazis were permitted to eat army food at the same low rate that officers paid.[28]

By the summer of 1946, American GIs and the Japanese were completely segregated. Special first-class cars appeared on trains, with accommodations restricted to Allied Occupation personnel. American troops rode in spacious comfort, while the Japanese were jammed into unheated coaches, usually with no windows. The Japanese were forbidden to take taxicabs marked

"Foreigners' Cab." Other public transportation such as streetcars, subways, ferries, and boats were all segregated. Restaurants, cafes, bars, and hotels that were reserved for GI use were placed off-limits to the Japanese, whereas by then nothing was off-limits to the public in occupied Germany. The GIs were prohibited from using Japanese hotels, inns, and theaters. In the interest of sanitation no American servicemen could legally drink "indigenous" (Japanese) water nor eat "indigenous" food. Even if they bought their own food, they could not have it cooked in a Japanese kitchen. GIs could no longer legally give away American food and other goods to the Japanese. They could not visit any Japanese private house that was surrounded by a fence. If a GI entered other types of houses, he must leave before eleven o'clock at night. They were even prohibited from playing sports with Japanese people, or from inviting Japanese people to attend and participate in social activities.[29] All recreational facilities for GIs had warning signs such as "Allied Personnel Only," or "Japanese Keep Out [Nihon-jin tachiiri kinshi]." In the doors of public office buildings appeared signs such as "Allied Entrance" and "Japanese Entrance." Edward Seidensticker, later an authority on Japanese literature, thus depicted racial segregation in the scenes he witnessed at Tokyo bars and cafes in those days.[30]

The former War Ministry building at Ichigaya, where the Tokyo War Crimes Trial took place, was also segregated. The main entrance to the building was reserved for Westerners—judges, prosecutors, and American defense lawyers. Japanese, defendants and lawyers alike, had to use the rear entrance and get to the courtroom on the second floor via the basement. If a Japanese tried to enter the main entrance, one Japanese defense lawyer recalled, the Military Police would halt him and deny entry even when he was a lawyer with a permanent pass. American and Japanese defense counsels used separate lounges—one on the second floor for the Americans and another on the first floor for the Japanese. Inside the courtroom, American and Japanese counsels sat separately. The gallery for press and visitors was also divided into separate sections for the Japanese and the "gaijin"—a Japanese euphemism for Westerners or foreign whites (e.g., people of the victorious Allied nations). Bathrooms on the first floor and up were for the exclusive use of Westerners. The Japanese, including the lawyers, had to go down to the basement to share the dark bathroom with service and maintenance people.[31]

Although these regulations were not intentionally racist in origin, the strict dividing line between the ruler and the ruled looked like a racial line, not dissimilar to scenes in the American South. Some Americans feared that the Japanese saw all these special privileges accorded to the Americans in railway and bus transportation as implying American racism against inferior Orientals. Two American college professors, a sociologist and an economist, recognized the dangers of "inhumane, thoughtless, and insulting army regulations." As experts on social relations, they feared that undesirable psychological reactions would ensue. They cautioned that Occupation indifference to Japan's national pride might ignite the feeling that the United States was treating Japan as a subject race and would create problems in the future.[32]

Ironically, the Japanese were slow to notice the racial dimension of the new policy of segregation. At least in the beginning, they did not see it as particularly offensive; after all, it was customary for the ruler to maintain aloofness. Besides, it seemed that the physical distance allowed the Japanese some breathing room in assimilating their status as a defeated nation. Nonetheless, SCAP was increasingly sensitive to possible Japanese condemnation of the nonfraternization policy as racist. It was the Americans, not the Japanese, who became much concerned about and disturbed by the inconsistency between the democratization program and the ostensible practice of racism. Subsequently, SCAP launched an elaborate policy throughout 1946 to censor any discussion of race and racism in the Japanese media. Under this guideline, any mention of race, regardless of circumstances or intentions, was prohibited. Japanese criticism of American racism was subject to censorship because, according to SCAP, it questioned America's moral position and amounted to a defiance of American prestige. Japanese self-criticism of their own racism and Pan-Asianism could be considered good democratic training, but since the Japanese discussion of Pan-Asianism included references to American and Western racism against the colored peoples, SCAP began to censor every comment on race or racism on either side in all media—newspapers, journals, and even films.

A general censorship policy had started at the beginning of the Occupation. On September 10, 1945, SCAP issued a directive that ordered the Japanese government to stop the dissemination of propaganda through newspapers, radio broadcasting, or other means of publication which disturbed the public tranquillity. Any story that portrayed Japan as equal to the Allied powers was subject to severe censorship. Subsequently, on September 19, SCAP issued SCAPIN 33, "Press Code for Japan" (a comprehensive directive that encompassed earlier directives) and on November 25 a follow-up directive.[33] The censors at the Civil Censorship Detachment (CCD), which operated under the Civil Intelligence Section (CIS), read everything that was to be published, from weather reports to sports news, from *go* and *shōgi* (Japanese chesslike games) columns to fiction. Material that had to be deleted was marked in red ink by an examiner and returned to editors, who were then usually summoned to the CCD.

Owing to a lack of instructions from the Civil Information and Education Section, inexperience in newspaper work on the part of the personnel at the censorship detachment, and the language barrier between American officers and Japanese examiners, application of the censorship rules became so confusing that censors often put the broadest possible interpretation on the press code, going far beyond its original intent.[34] Censorship in radio and films led to the November 19, 1945, directive that prohibited themes that were militaristic, feudalistic, nationalistic, chauvinistic, antiforeign, or that discriminated in the areas of race or religion.[35]

In the print media, though SCAP did not adopt similar directives prohibiting racism per se, it moved to erase any mention of race, racism, or the mere suggestion of it. SCAP prohibited any discussion of interracial interaction between American GIs and Japanese women that could be interpreted as having sexual connotations since such liaisons could both provoke Japanese racial hatred against whites and ridicule American authority. Under the November 25, 1946, directive, SCAP began censoring any mention of fraternization between Japanese and Americans.[36] An examination of galley proofs of Japanese materials rejected by SCAP censorship reveals SCAP's growing intolerance of mentions of race and racism in Japanese print through 1946 and beyond. All mention of fraternization or American racism were now taboo. Although no directive specified American racism as subject to censorship, any mention of it was considered tantamount to a criticism of the United States and was therefore prohibited. References to the racial makeup of Americans either white or black and reporting on their negative (especially criminal) behavior in Japan were deleted because these supposedly stirred up Japanese racial hatred. Even the phrase "yellow race" disappeared from the press, since such a label was believed to arouse Japanese racial awareness and might lead them to rebel.

One of the earliest examples of the censorship of American racism toward blacks, Indians, or Asians was the suppression of an article written from the leftist viewpoint and due to be published in October 1945 in *Shinsei* (New Life), a magazine founded by members of a constitutional study group. Because of one paragraph that equated U.S. democracy with ancient democracy, calling both systems of slavery, the entire article was excised [37].

Another article, "Amerika senji seikatsu no taiken (My experience during the war in America)," scheduled to be published in the November 1946 issue of *Chūō kōron* (the Central Review), Japan's leading intellectual journal, had several portions deleted because of criticism of American racism. An example is provided by the italicized part in the following sentence: "Regarding racist feelings [*jinshu-teki kanjō*] *which was the cancer and defect of American society* and actions that went further beyond their limit, the American public applied rather severe criticism during World War II." The censor ordered the entire portion to be deleted, with the comment "critical of the United States."[38]

The scholastic journal *Amerika bunka* (The American Culture), published by the Institute of American Studies, then located on the campus of Japan's leading Christian school, Rikkyō University, had several articles censored in its initial volume (December 1946) because of observations about American racism. For example, the article "Minshu-shugi-sha no denki—Furankurin (Franklin—Biography of a Democrat)," by American historian Hayashi Fumio, met the CCD's order of deletion where it touched upon Benjamin Franklin's discriminatory attitudes toward American Indians.[39]

Different censors applied different criteria. For instance, the following entire paragraph from the article "Amerika-jin no seikatsu (The Livelihood of the American People)," by Sakanishi Shiho, scheduled for the same December 1946 *Amerika bunka*, received two opposite verdicts from two censors.

> Not a few American have prejudice, too, and their racial antipathies are deep-seated. Racial discrimination against the colored people is one of the big obstacles in society, however, which varies in different districts and the intelligent classes have been making efforts to eradicate such a wrong idea, to say the least of it. Many Jews of New York and Japanese of the Western Coast had once fallen victim to this racial antipathies *and they will probably experience the similar hardships in future*, but both American officials and people are striving for rooting up of this prejudice.
>
> (In the CCD's original translation)

Although the first examiner suggested a deletion of the entire paragraph above, the second censor reversed his judgment and approved the entire paragraph except for the italicized portion. His handwritten explanation reads: "I should like to pass the rest, as it is true and every intelligent Japanese knows it and has read about it. Nobody expects the U.S. to be perfect, there is no such country in the world. Nothing should be more dangerous than to cover up the truth and show the Jap only the [illegible] side of the picture!" He recommended the deletion of only the italicized part, as "this is nothing [more] than pure speculation on the part of the author."[40]

Occupation sensitivity to Japanese racial consciousness against the whites also led the CCD to censor any mention of the Japanese as the "colored race." Two entire paragraphs were deleted from "Heiwa kokka no kensetsu (The Construction of a Peaceful Nation)," an article by Morito Tatsuo due to appear in the January 1946 Kaizō, another leading Japanese intellectual journal. The first portion was censored because Morito mentioned that the Japanese belonged to a group of colored races, and added that this fact would unite them with other colored groups. The second portion was deleted because he insinuated that American racism would prevent the formation of a peaceful international society.[41]

Interactions were possible when it was an occasion for the GIs to teach Japanese various "lessons" in public. In such cases, the mood was far from amicable. Herbert Passin, then an officer in the Occupation and later to become a leading sociologist on Japan, witnessed four drunken Australian soldiers forcing the Japanese to show them respect. They lined up the Japanese, male and female, young and old, on the train platform, and ordered them to remain standing as the Australians walked back and forth. The Japanese were forced to bow every time the Australians passed in front of them.[42]

If such scenes were depicted "properly" to enhance American dignity, they could be published. The practice of "treating ladies with respect"—one that GIs frequently were happy to demonstrate in public toward Japanese women despite the antifraternization regulation—was in many cases ridiculous to the Japanese, not only because of cultural differences but also because of its flirtatious nature. Quite a few Japanese passages in the press did mention such experiences in a rather contemptuous tone and were subsequently deleted. On the other hand, "Lady First," which was to appear in the May 1, 1946, issue of Modan Nippon (Modern Japan), related an incident between GIs and a Japanese crowd and was approved in its entirety with only a few words deleted. A big, formidable American soldier had stopped a train and, waving a pistol above his head, told the passengers to get off, then ordered only women to return to the cars. The bewildered passengers, male and female, were all frozen with terror. But when he strode through the train shouting "Ladies first!" it became clear that he was only making the point that male passengers should give up their seats to women, and everyone laughed with relief.[43] Only the statement that he carried a gun was deleted, possibly to avoid an impression of American coercion. As long as the Japanese were portrayed as subservient pupils and the Americans as triumphant heroes, interaction was acceptable and sometimes even funny and friendly.

Stories of romance between Japanese women and American men were entirely suppressed. For example, a story of the romantic encounter of Mizunoe Takiko, Japan's foremost popular singer and actress, with a Japanese-American man, an Occupation soldier whom she had dated before the war, was censored even when, in this case, the fraternization had taken place between a Japanese-American man and a Japanese woman. Another story, reporting a happy engagement between a Japanese woman and a GI, due to appear in the entertainment magazine *Amerika* (America) in May 1946, was rejected. Even a letter to a magazine supposedly from an American GI, which admonished Japanese girls against fraternization with the Americans, was suppressed. The letter explained that interracial relations were not possible because "we American men can never be serious about Japanese girls." He warned: "It is impossible for us to love Japanese girls in the strict sense of the English word love. So please be realistic before you believe that American GIs are seriously in love with you. . . . Please be virtuous and lead a happy life."[44]

Equal relationships or friendship between Americans and Japanese were unacceptable even in fiction. A distinct example appears as an incident in *Niji no kobako* (A Small Rainbow Box), a novel that came out as a series in a monthly juvenile magazine *Shōnen kurabu* (Boys' Club). The entire story, scheduled for the May 1946 issue, was suppressed because in this episode an American Occupation officer apologizes to two Japanese boys (this novel's protagonists) for having mistaken them as thieves, and even entrusts them with the future task of developing a love for the people of the whole world regardless of nationality or religion.[45] To SCAP, this story would apparently give young readers not only the wrong idea about the prestige of the Occupation forces but also an illusion of equality between the Japanese and the Americans. SCAP censors found this unacceptable even in juvenile fiction.

How did the Japanese come to understand this segregation and its eventual removal? How did they feel about the changing American measures? An *Asahi* newspaper editorial, appearing a few days after the signing of the San Francisco Peace Treaty, described how the Japanese had lived under the psychological burden of the antifraternization regulation but had not been allowed to express their feelings publicly until then. At a train station, the "cold-hearted border segregated the same human beings just like a farm fence" into victor and loser. During rush hours, when a warning was whistled, the crowd jostling each other along the stairway would halt immediately and wait until the Occupation officers passed by. Almost every morning, the editorial confessed, the Japanese had to go through this ritual and experience a moment of abasement. Japanese also patiently observed the deference to foreign soldiers (the so-called "street etiquette for foreigners" [gaijin ni taisuru gaitō sahō]). Surprisingly, the Japanese rarely caused trouble with foreigners. The above editorial writer suspected that it was because the Japanese rationalized these forced customs as a temporary consequence of their nation's defeat in the war and expected relations to improve when the Occupation ended. In fact, for some time the Japanese remained optimistic about the prospect of improving relations with the Americans. Anti-Americanism was hardly the mood among them even after the introduction of segregation. On the contrary, the Japanese saw in these self-segregating Americans an aura of prestige, just as SCAP had intended, and began noticing their physical characteristics as a source of superiority. Primitive as it sounds, this might well be an inevitable consequence of human psychology of the time. When there was such a tremendous inequality between the two groups of people in terms of power, authority, and material wealth, the Japanese should naturally look for symbols of innate (or intrinsic) difference—and race was one way to rationalize how and why such inequality originated.

The Americans' physical appearance now symbolized their superiority for Japanese to adore. Amid the cultural and intellectual impoverishment of the Occupation and their weakening sense of esteem for the nation, the Japanese were desperately turning to the United States for cultural and intellectual stimuli. The lavish lifestyle enjoyed by American GIs in contrast to impoverished Japanese life led to an earnest admiration of the American way of living and for anything American—from baseball to jazz and blues, not to mention the English language. The United States and its people were transformed into a kind of forbidden fruit craved by the Japanese people.

At the same time, the Japanese developed a feeling that they were somehow physically inferior to Americans. Both conquerors and conquered had always been aware of physical differences. The American mass media continued to use expressions such as "docile, meek, little Japanese" and reported that the Japanese believed that Americans were physically superior.[46]

Caucasian facial features were admired by the many Japanese who felt that all white people looked like Hollywood actors and actresses. American GIs were easily flattered and liked to believe that Japanese women pictured American men as tall and handsome Clark Gables.[47]

The contrast between robust GIs and emaciated Japanese prompted a search for the reason for these physical differences. In fact, Japanese people in the Occupation were slightly smaller in build than in the prewar period because of chronic wartime food shortages and subsequent undernourishment.[48] Food shortages continued, and even worsened, in the Occupation. The awareness of physical differences between the Japanese and Americans, however, sometimes saved some Japanese from a sense of shame about Japan's loss in the war. Nosaka Akiyuki, the Naoki prize-winning novelist dubbing himself a "Yakeato-ha" (a generation growing out of the ruins of the war), tells in various semiautobiographical writings that the realization of Japanese physical inferiority to Americans helped him rationalize Japan's loss. Before the Occupation began, Nosaka believed Japan lost the war only because it lacked the resources to fight; in terms of spirituality, Japan should have won. However, once he observed the magnificent physical build of the Americans, Nosaka believed that it was this inherent physical difference that decided the outcome. Recognizing that nothing could be done about racial characteristics, he felt liberated from the emotional burden of his country's loss and accepted Japan's loss as inevitable.[49]

There were those who, like the intellectuals in the Meiji period, insisted on the need for the physical improvement of the Japanese in order to catch up with the Americans. Some, including scientists, argued that the Japanese should change their traditional diet and lifestyle to be like the Americans. In an article, "Japan's Future Seen from Scientists' Eyes—What Will Happen to Our Physical Structures," published in the educational journal *Kokumin no kagaku* (Peoples' Science) in the fall of 1947 (which somehow evaded SCAP censorship), Mizuno Kon, author of the article and a physician, estimated that it would take the Japanese a whole century to even reach an average height of 170 centimeters (5 feet, 7 inches)—the contemporary average height among Westerners (*Ōshū-jin*). Mizuno concluded that only with an improvement in living standards could the Japanese hope to look at least like Japanese-Americans, who were superior to the Japanese in physical structure.[50] To eat and live like Americans, to increase the intake of animal protein, especially milk, was the key to the physical improvement of the Japanese.

Thus the Japanese pondered how improvement of not only their national strength and status but also their physical characteristics would bring them to the level of Westerners. To reform the nation into one of Western-style civilization was an ongoing task under SCAP leadership. But what about the difference in physical appearance? Could the Japanese become as civilized, democratized, and "human" as Westerners, while physically remaining non-Western? SCAP obviously provided no answer to that.

Curiously, there was a peculiar irony about the Japanese idolization of the physical appearance of Westerners. The Japanese had a confused notion of the cultural and racial perspectives of Western people's identity. Their admiration existed within an abstract idea of Western contributions to world civilization—from the Greek and Roman civilizations through the Renaissance to the modern era. The Japanese admired the white people's physical appearance as an icon of their cultural achievement, embodied especially in the classical works of art. Yet it was not contradictory for the Japanese to hesitate and even abhor physical contact or interaction with individual Westerners. Admiration for Western culture and civilization was one thing, intimate social interaction another.

Despite the popularity of American culture, a rising interest in American lifestyles, and even a scientific interest in physical improvement, Japanese society attached a stigma to those, especially women, who fraternized with GIs. It was not because they violated Occupation regulations but because they crossed the prohibited social and racial boundaries. Interracial fraternization was unacceptable, whether in the form of dating, marriage, or childbearing.

The Japanese government, too, initiated an antifraternization project before the arrival of Occupation soldiers by creating segregated comfort facilities exclusively for foreign Occupation soldiers (*gaikoku chūton-gun ian shisetsu*). The plan was intended to "appease and comfort" Occupation soldiers in regard to their sexual appetite and make the Occupation a success. A larger scheme, however, was to protect the virtue of Japanese women and the purity of the Yamato race. Ikeda Hayato, then chief of the Tax Bureau, Ministry of Finance, is said to have remarkered, "[The budget of] 100 million yen [to prepare such comfort facilities] is nothing if it can be used to protect the pure blood of the Yamato race," and he approved a generous budget to start the project.[51] On August 18, 1945, the Home Ministry issued a memorandum authorizing prefectural police to designate a specific quarter in their jurisdictions for carrying out the project, regardless of prewar regulation standards. The memorandum also instructed them to give hiring priority at the facilities to hostesses, prostitutes, waitresses, barmaids, and women with frequent criminal records in smuggling and sexual misconduct.[52]

On August 26, the Special Comfort Facilities Association (Tokushu Ian Shisetsu Kyōkai) started. Within a month it was renamed the Recreation and Amusement Association (RAA), and was supervised by a coordinating committee representing the ministries of Home Affairs, Foreign Affairs, Finance, Transportation, and the Metropolitan Police. Women were recruited through government advertisements calling for "new Japanese women." By August 27, the day before the arrival of the Occupation forces, the RAA had recruited enough women to work at all the facilities in Tokyo.[53] The RAA appealed to many women from ordinary farms or village homes near a military base because it gave them access to special foods and luxuries as well as psychological rewards—from the women's point of view—of being able to associate with the victorious Americans. These women enjoyed a better self-image because of their special access to "American life," which was off-limits to most Japanese.

In this self-imposed segregation, Japanese who fraternized with Americans were often repudiated. A Japanese maid reported to an army wife she worked for that she had been slapped by a Japanese when she accompanied a GI to a Japanese theater. A typist in the SCAP office in Tokyo said that whenever she wore clothes handed down to her by her American boss, the Japanese in the train made insulting comments about her service to the Yankees.[54]

Perhaps a key to the success of SCAP's antifraternization policy was that it correlated with a preexisting Japanese aversion to physical contact with American GIs. The Japanese enjoyed contact with Western culture—books, music, art—but face-to-face contact, let alone sexual contact, with Westerners was another matter altogether. If it had been otherwise, as American sociologists suggested earlier, the Japanese would have expressed some kind of dissatisfaction with the segregation imposed by SCAP. But there was no such voice.

Toward the end of 1948, when the growing emphasis on the danger of Communism altered the relationship between the Americans and the Japanese, a series of programs quickly emerged which removed the previous antifraternization policies and instead furthered a symbolic friendship.

The SCAP program to improve U.S.-Japanese relations took place exclusively in the realm of media images, mostly through staged public events—particularly sports events—and movies. The underlying message was the rising American appreciation of the quality of Japanese culture and America's readiness to embrace Japan as an old friend. Despite such cultural propaganda and the lifting of segregation, the color line remained, challenged by neither of the two peoples. Behind the enthusiasm for cultural exchange and interactions lay the unwritten rule of nonphysical contact. To a certain degree, SCAP was blatant about its resolution to maintain the obstinate fine line between race and culture concerning Japanese identity. Compromise was possible with their cultural identity but not with the racial one. SCAP was in fact mirroring the Japanese position: that admiration for foreign (in this case Japanese) culture was acceptable in print or film, stage or sports events, but face-to-face, body-to-body contact was not. Needless to say, amicable feeling was never genuine. Various American official documents, both classified and declassified, demonstrate a profound ambivalence—along with a sense of anxiety, guilt, and fear—concerning American racist attitudes toward the Japanese. Some of these documents deny any injustice or wrongdoing on the part of the Americans toward the Japanese; others speculate about an impending Japanese revolt against American racism.

In fact, just as the cultural programs were successfully implemented, the Japanese gradually and finally came to notice the nature of American racism, the treacherous line between culture and race, and, above all, their growing inferiority complex toward the whites. However, the prospect of a clash with SCAP over the issue of race seemed both futile and harmful, damaging all the other successful outcomes in the Occupation. The Japanese simply opted to collaborate with SCAP in celebrating a new friendship, self-censoring the racial matter and satisfying themselves with a cultural solution only.

In the spring of 1949, the army newspaper *Pacific Stars and Stripes* printed a memorandum issued by SCAP's Civil Information and Education Section, instructing all American soldiers in Japan on how to deal with the Japanese people. They were told to treat them with respect and never to look upon them as an inferior race. The memorandum warned the GIs against a sense of superiority as victors and instead encouraged them to make new friends with the conquered. It also encouraged them to respect the different customs, habits, and traditions of the Japanese instead of antagonizing them.[55]

On September 20, 1949, the day MacArthur discussed the subject of a peace treaty with William Sebald, the acting political adviser in Japan, MacArthur announced a pro-fraternization regulation, reversing his earlier policies in Japan. The purpose of this announcement was to "permit an attitude of friendly interest and guidance toward the Japanese people, which is reflective of democratic ideals and to avoid unnecessary military control."[56] Under this new regulation, SCAP announced its intention to establish the same relationship between Occupation personnel and the "indigenous population of Japan" as existed between U.S. troops stationed in the United States and the local population.

Occupation personnel were now allowed to use all Japanese hotels, inns, and theaters not specifically posted off-limits, provided that food and drink was obtained from authorized sources. They were also permitted to travel anywhere in Japan. If Occupation force billets and rail facilities were not to be used, their identification cards or similar identifying documents could serve as authorization for such travel. Competition and participation with or against the Japanese in all sports on an individual or organized basis was now permitted when specifically approved by local commanders. Only when such activities would interfere with regularly scheduled sports programs, or co-opt sports equipment or facilities, were they disapproved. Occupation personnel were allowed to invite Japanese nationals to participate in organized social activities, such as service club activities, when authorized by local commanders. But the Japanese were to be invited on an individual basis; they would have to conform to club regulations; and they were not to interfere with normal participation by other Occupation personnel. Giving bona fide gifts to their domestic help or Japanese acquaintances was now permitted, provided that existing regulations pertaining to the sale, trade, and barter of goods or the use of foreign exchange and yen currency were not violated.[57]

Official athletic games between American and Japanese teams had already started shortly before the pro-fraternization announcement. Six Japanese swimmers, including Furuhashi Hironoshin, the world record holder, were invited to compete in the U.S. National Championship in Los Angeles between August 16 and 20. Furuhashi, internationally known as "the Flying Fish of Mt. Fuji" (Fujiyama no tobiuo), set four world records in the 400-meter, 800-meter, and 1,500-meter freestyle. His teammate Hashizume Shirō also set a world record in the 1,500-meter freestyle, only to have it broken by Furuhashi on the same day. MacArthur praised the Japanese team's victory, calling it an appropriate accomplishment for the democratic nation it represented, and remarked that true national characteristics could be most eloquently demonstrated at international athletic competitions.[58]

The spirit of fraternization was also embodied in the first postwar professional baseball games between the two nations. In the early days of the Occupation, Frank "Lefty" O'Doul had asked SCAP to give his team, the San Francisco Seals, permission to visit Japan. Having visited Japan as a big leaguer in 1931 and again in 1934 with Babe Ruth, O'Doul thought well of the Japanese fans' enthusiasm and insisted to SCAP that his team's visit would help to resume friendship between the two nations. On October 12, 1949, the San Francisco Seals arrived at the Tokyo Haneda International Airport, to be greeted by a host of Japanese actresses. The team's twenty-seven players paraded in twenty-two open cars on Ginza Street through the cheering crowds with "Welcome Seals" banners and confetti. On October 15, in the first game against the Tokyo Giants, the Seals, who had finished seventh in the Triple A League that season, won the game by 13 to 4. The remaining five games against All-Japan teams also turned into easy victories for the Seals. Nonetheless, the first game alone attracted 45,000 spectators to Kōrakuen Stadium.[59]

A change took place even in a children's book. "Anmitsu Hime (Princess Anmitsu)," a serialized cartoon that appeared in *Shōjo* (Little Girls), a monthly magazine for girls, started to portray a U.S.-Japanese friendship shortly after the issuance of the pro-fraternization policy. Princess Anmitsu (named for a Japanese sweet dessert), a spunky tomboy and seemingly a character of the Edo period (1600–1867), makes friends with Miss Kasutera (sponge cake), her English tutor, and an American woman with a Pinocchio-like nose, and together they concoct mischievous pranks involving all the people in the castle and even in the whole town. This comic book became immensely popular among both girls and boys.[60]

In regard to censorship, SCAP had announced to sixteen major newspaper companies and three news agencies on July 15, 1948, that it would change prepublication censorship to postpublication censorship. On October 24, 1949, the postpublication censorship was lifted as well.[61] Now the Japanese press had relative freedom to portray the theme of U.S.-Japanese friendship if it so desired. During the Occupation, the leading newspapers had to print the American comic strip series "Blondie" every day as a showcase of American democracy. Now, just like the children's comic strip "Anmitsu Hime," a warm comradeship could bloom between Japanese and Americans in fiction. The Japanese, however, did not quickly jump on the bandwagon. Rather, they adopted self-censorship, basically observing the original SCAP press code, and remained cautious about covering race and racism at least until the end of the Occupation.

As we have seen, it was John Foster Dulles, a central figure in charge of fashioning the peace treaty with Japan, who favored cultural exchanges to secure Japan's cooperation with Western interests. After World War II, cultural exchange programs were actively pursued as part of the propaganda effort to promote the American way of life to the world. Following the passage of the United States Information and Educational Exchange Act of 1948, under the auspices of the Department of State, the International Educational Exchange Program began to promote "a better spirit of cooperation and understanding" among students, teachers, scholars, and civic leaders between the United States and other countries. While the Occupation was still in effect, educational exchange activities in Japan were assigned to the Department of the Army with the assistance of other government agencies and private organizations. By 1950, various plans had been offered to make the Japanese pro-American: the teaching of English; the opening of U.S. Information Centers; book exhibits; the distribution of periodicals; translation programs; aid to schools; exchanges of students, teachers, professors, and research scholars as well as scientific and technical activities; and numerous other educational projects.[62]

In January 1951, on his second trip to Japan concerning the Japanese peace treaty, Dulles invited John D. Rockefeller III to join the mission. Dulles explained that he wanted the Japanese to understand that Americans were not thinking entirely in military and economic terms, but also hoped to strengthen long-range cultural relations between the two peoples. Rockefeller, an appropriate figure because of his family's historic role in promoting cultural relations between the two nations, accepted the invitation.

On another occasion, Dulles explained that the U.S. government could make the Japanese feel that they had something of value to contribute to Westerners through an exchange of scientific and medical knowledge. For example, in 1949, Yukawa Hideki became the first Japanese to receive the Nobel Prize for his numerous pioneering works in particle physics, including the meson theory and the theory of nonlocal fields. This international recognition bolstered Japanese morale. Noticing this new mood, Dulles suggested that the United States initiate scholastic exchange programs and develop goodwill in a nonmaterial way, which should be invaluable in keeping Japan as America's ally over a longer period.[63]

Policymakers in Washington, D.C., considered America's most critical problem with Japan to be cultural, not military or economic. The United States now recognized that Japan, not easily classified as West or East, was different from other countries, and it would be careful to enhance this uniqueness in cultural exchange programs in order to gain Japan's help in resisting Communist pressures. Japan could also become a valuable ally in dealing with underdeveloped countries.

Prime Minister Yoshida Shigeru sought a similar cultural program in his separate effort to revive Japan's great role in the international community in close cooperation with the Allied Western nations. Yoshida had requested through the U.S. government that a peace treaty guarantee the promotion of cultural relations between the two nations. "The strength of cultural ties between Japan and the United States is a fundamental question that concerns the Japanese-American friendship," wrote Yoshida in a memorandum handed to a member of the Dulles Mission in January 1951. He emphasized Japan's fervent wish to be "allowed to take a positive part in the cultural interchange between nations" and to "take all possible measures to promote cultural cooperation between the two countries."[64]

Between the years 1949 and 1956, under the international educational exchange program signed with ninety-nine nations under the sponsorship of the State Department, a total of 33,365 foreign nationals were invited to study and lecture at a university level, or to conduct advanced research and other training in the United States. In the same period, a total of 13,625 Americans were sent abroad as university students, lecturers, teachers, researchers, and advisers.[65]

Hollywood did its part to encourage U.S.-Japanese friendship by making an effort to produce so-called international films. In May 1953, Fleur Cowles, associate editor of *Look* and *Quick* magazines, gave a speech at a Chamber of Commerce luncheon criticizing America's propaganda failures in Asia where, according to her observations during her recent world tour, the Communists were doing much better. Showing American-made films and comic books would never work in Asiatic settings, she claimed. Talking about the distant golden wheat fields of Kansas to the Asians was like trying to sell the great new American life to Martians, she told the audience. None of "this mass of people living in dirty shacks in Asia" would care about American skyscrapers or giant tractors, cars, and telephones. Therefore, "We should employ native films with native actors who speak the language of the most illiterate primitive localities and look disarmingly familiar to their audiences."[66]

Hollywood had adopted somewhat different tactics toward Japan by producing "pro-fraternization" movies featuring Japanese and American actors and actresses as congenial equals. The first such movie, *Tokyo File 212*, released in January 1951,[67] tells about Matsudo Tarō, a survivor of the suicidal

Kamikaze pilot unit who cannot accept defeat and plots a coup with Communists to destroy Japan's system, and his college friend, a journalist from the United States who comes to Japan with a secret mission to stop the plot. After a series of complex incidents, Tarō realizes the folly of his working for Communism and eventually commits heroic suicide to save his Japanese fiancée and his American friend.

Japanese War Bride (Japanese title: *Higashi wa higashi*), directed and produced solely by Americans and released in January 1952 in New York and in May in Tokyo, is a romantic movie, or a soap opera, about a marriage between an American soldier and a Japanese woman and her troubles as his wife in America.[68] It ends with a melodramatic touch. In despair because she has been falsely accused of infidelity, she is about to throw herself over a cliff when her American husband saves her. *Itsu-itsu made mo* (Forever), released in October 1952, was written, directed, and produced in Japan by an American staff employed by a Japanese film company. The story is again about an interracial romance between an American soldier and a Japanese woman from a respectable family. The plot is full of obstacles such as her family's opposition and his service in the Korean War, and ends with her tragic death in an earthquake. *Futari no hitomi* (Eyes of the Two Girls), also released in October 1952, featured Margaret O'Brien, Hollywood's prewar child star, as a compassionate American girl who accompanies her father to Japan on business, and Misora Hibari, Japan's foremost popular teen singer of the time, as a spunky orphan. From their first encounter, the girls build a solid friendship, despite the language barrier, and together help build an orphanage and finally make their dream come true.[69]

Partly because of the great success of Akira KUROSAWA's 1951 film *Rashomon*, a winner of the 1951 Oscar for Best Foreign Film and also a Grand Prix winner at the 1951 Venice Film Festival, Hollywood continued to foster Japanese-American joint productions in stories about the fortitude of a Japanese farm wife, a strange encounter between an American soldier and a Japanese scholar in post-Occupation Japan, and so on. Even an American-made Japanese sword opera (*chanbara geki*), set in the Edo period, was considered. In one scene, for example, while Kenne Duncan, a Hollywood cowboy actor, corrals a band of toughs, all in kimonos and knotted/topknot hairdos, Kasagi Shizuko, singer of the hit song "Tokyo Boogie," winds her way through a Betty Hutton version of "Ol' Man River" aboard a river junk. The *New York Times* also cheerfully reported that Japanese film star Yamaguchi Yoshiko (alias Li Hsiang-lan in the wartime movies portraying Sino-Japanese friendship and now Shirley YAMAGUCHI in her postwar American debut in *Japanese War Bride*) recently advertised for a "Caucasian foreigner aged between 35 and 50 to play opposite her in the thriller 'Port of Shadows'—a story of a triangle love affair in which a rich foreigner, a poor Japanese girl and an attractive Japanese youth were involved." Japan had become a "happy hunting ground for amateur American actors and actresses," the article reported; "The mysterious Orient will no longer be mysterious if American producers continue using *Shinto* shrines and *geisha* girls as backdrops for their films and Japanese directors enlarge their search for Western faces."[70]

The State Department also intervened in Hollywood's release of anti-Japanese films on the Pacific War. The U.S. Embassy in Tokyo pressed the Secretary of State to discourage the Motion Picture Association of America (MPAA) from releasing in Japan movies made during or shortly after the war, movies such as *Bataan* (1943), a big box office film; *Thirty Seconds Over Tokyo* (1944), a film about the first American attack on Japan, featuring Spencer Tracy; *They Were Expendable* (1945), a film about life in and around motor torpedo boats in the Pacific, featuring John Wayne and Robert Montgomery; *Task Force* (1949), a film about a retiring general recalling his struggles in the Air Force, featuring Gary Cooper; *An American Guerrilla in the Philippines* (1950), an adventure story featuring Tyrone Power; *Flying Leathernecks* (1951), an action film about two marine officers fighting the Japanese on Guadalcanal, featuring John Wayne; *Above and Beyond* (1952), a film about the training of Col. Paul Tibbets, pilot of the *Enola Gay*, the plane that dropped the first atomic bomb on Japan, featuring Robert Taylor and Eleanor Parker. In the fall of 1954 the State Department wrote to Eric Johnston, president of the MPAA, requesting self-restraint on film distribution in Japan. The most damaging films, according to the State Department memorandum, would be likely to cause unfavorable reactions among the Japanese audience because these showed scenes of individual conflicts between American and Japanese military personnel; related Japanese cruelties both to other Japanese and to foreigners; contained open or veiled criticisms of Japanese culture, traditions, and institutions; or reflected the strong wartime animosities between the two peoples.[71]

The U.S. government took further precautions to insure the image of mutual friendship in a much larger historical context—in the time of Commodore Matthew Perry. The year 1953 was the centennial of Perry's expedition to Japan, and "Black Ship Festivals" were held on July 14 at Tokyo and Kurihama, the landing place in the Miura Peninsula, to celebrate the occasion. Since preparations for these events were under way in Japan, the State Department contemplated using them as a springboard to promote U.S.-Japanese relations. However, it determined that participation in the Japanese festival by a former American military leader or leaders representing the U.S. government was unwise. In view of the circumstances of Perry's "gunboat diplomacy" approach and the vast influence the United States had exerted in Japan since the end of the Pacific War, the Japanese, not the United States, should take the initiative in celebrating the festival, argued Navy Adm. Richard Herndon. He warned that America's official presence at the centennial festival might backfire badly in view of the delicate political climate in post-Occupation Japan.[72]

The United States took an even smaller part in the 1954 centennial celebration of the signing of the Kanagawa Treaty, the first U.S.-Japanese treaty. An early proposal to send a presidential representative to attend the festival was suspended by John Allison, U.S. ambassador to Japan. "I am fearful that if the suggestion comes from us, the Japanese would become suspicious as to our motives," wrote Allison. He thought that the dispatch of a military or naval emissary to the festival would produce additional strains on American-Japanese relations.[73]

Beneath the glossy Hollywood-style amity and extreme governmental sensitivity, neither the Japanese nor the American people were ready to actually interact with each other in the intimate manner portrayed in these Hollywood movies and imagined by the U.S. government. The exchange of high culture and technology between Japan and the United States was easy, just as it had been successful even before the war. The portrayal of friendship in films or fiction was even easier (indeed, these movies portrayed the two peoples' interactions as if the racial barrier never existed). However, there was no definite plan for actual interactions between American and Japanese people in postoccupied Japan, especially after they had gone through six years of variable segregation under the Occupation. Now that American military troops were to be stationed in Japan for an indefinite period after the Occupation ended, neither Japanese nor Americans knew what the appropriate attitudes should be between the two, in the name of mutual friendship.

Ironically, while promoting the image of friendship in the cultural realm, policymakers in Washington grew highly concerned about the possible prospect of racial tension between American troops and the Japanese populace in the post-Occupation arrangement. Many American experts on Japan, including Robert Scalapino, then professor of political science at the University of California, feared that the lessened admiration for America and the recovery of pride might lead to the resurgence of "super-racialism" and "super-culturalism" in Japan, which would eventually erupt as a racial war.[74] The British government shared a similar concern about a Japanese insurgency. Shortly after the San Francisco Peace Conference, the American ambassador in London telegraphed the Secretary of State, telling of British concern over the current "Jap psychology." A British diplomat was quoted as saying "since San Francisco Japs have been construing their status as already semi-independent," they "are beginning to feel 'uppish' and will likely react strongly to strong-arm methods."[75]

If pro-Japanese cultural programs and the efforts of Hollywood did not work, policymakers did not know how to deal with supposed Japanese racial anger, which had been suppressed relatively well thus far. Even the use of Occupation forces against extremist Japanese—an action stipulated in the U.S.-Japanese security treaty—would raise the "ugly prospect of a racial conflict," John Allison, then director of the Office of Northeastern Asian Affairs, warned the Army in 1950.[76]

Dulles, as consultant to the Secretary of State, admitted that the fundamental problem with a new relation with Japan was the immense difficulty in advising Americans to treat the Japanese as their white equals. He said: "It will be peculiarly difficult to carry out our treaty resolve 'as sovereign equals' [to] cooperate in friendly association to . . . maintain international peace and security." Dulles was aware that the post-Occupation period needed a new relationship very different from that between the Japanese people and MacArthur, in which the general had simply played God. Dulles noted that it would be difficult for American soldiers in Japan, who had gotten into the "habit of treating the Japanese as inferiors," to develop an equal relationship with them. Worse, he suspected that Japan's new status of equal sovereignty with the United States would not alter the attitude of Americans in general.[77]

On September 11, 1951, with its status of sovereignty restored, the Japanese government ordered the removal of signs posted by SCAP which were discriminatory and offensive to the Japanese—such as "Allied Personnel Only," "Allied Entrance," "Japanese Entrance," or "Japanese Keep Out." Gen. Matthew B. Ridgeway, the head of SCAP after MacArthur's recall in April 1951, also ordered all military units in Japan to avoid using designations offensive to the Japanese people. Some Americans speculated that such discriminatory measures had a long-term effect on the Japanese psyche and that they would resort to violent retaliation against Americans once the segregation signs were removed. A letter to the *New York Times* confessed that some Americans had recommended that "foreign whites" stay off the streets for a week or more after Japanese independence was reestablished so they could avoid possible Japanese violence motivated by racial revenge. The letter also reported the actual aftermath of the sign removals with relief: "There was no slaughter either."[78]

A year later, in April 1952, hotels, office buildings, golf courses, dockyards, apartment houses, and other facilities were restored to the Japanese. Although high-ranking U.S. army officers would no longer have two to six free Japanese servants, the Americans were not being forced to give up all perquisites since, under the separate U.S.-Japanese Security Treaty allowing U.S. forces to remain in Japan, they would continue to enjoy many extraterritorial privileges.[79] The U.S. government concentrated American garrisons in self-sufficient camps partly as a prevention against unnecessary confrontations with Japanese civilians. The most developed camps provided almost all the services of a fair-sized American town, including schools and churches, stores and movie theaters, libraries and newspapers, radio stations, gymnasiums and sports fields, post offices, and other social amenities such as dance clubs and bars for adults, and Boy and Girl Scout troops for children. Such amenities made it possible for an American soldier's family to spend an entire tour of duty in Japan without leaving the American community. It also made their interchange with the Japanese completely unnecessary. Besides, in building such large-scale American camps, the U.S. government dislocated thousands of Japanese families and their houses.[80]

Some Americans raised doubts about the wisdom of containing American soldiers and their families in such isolated conditions in Japan. One journalist pointed out in the summer of 1952 that the handful of white residents, a good reminder of the legacy of the Occupation, looked like an indirect source of growing anti-Americanism in Japan. Even though the Japanese had become masters in their own country again, the superior attitude of the Americans remained unchanged.[81] These Westerners enjoyed extraterritorial status until 1952 and still demanded preferred treatment as their right. They maintained a much higher standard of living than the Japanese people around them, taking for granted the same foods to which they had been accustomed at home, overheated houses, smoothly paved streets, and so on. American observers in Japan argued that these Europeans and Americans, drawing a sharp line between themselves and the Japanese, often ended up antagonizing Japanese who believed that all whites regarded Orientals as inferior. Yet, at the same time, these American critics unwittingly called such Japanese "supersensitive," suggesting something of an overreaction, thus blind to the fact that there were certain grounds for complaint on the part of the Japanese.[82] Meanwhile, other Americans feared that such a segregated atmosphere in Japan might remind other Asian peoples of the legacy of Western colonialism and eventually lead them to the conclusion that the new American imperialism had finally turned Japan into its colonial appendage.

On the part of the Japanese, it was only when the Occupation was drawing to its conclusion that they came to a realization of American racism toward them and cautiously expressed some unpleasant reactions. They did not unconditionally endorse the SCAP version of U.S.-Japanese friendship. Neither were they led to believe in a new Japanese equality with the United States as advertised by SCAP. After having been "forced to keep their mouths shut during our military occupation," as a *Saturday Evening Post* article put it in spring 1953, some Japanese finally opened up and criticized American arrogance in Japan, even expressing contempt for it. This came as a surprise to the American public, which had assumed that the Japanese, like any Oriental people, would unconditionally obey authority. The article even argued that, for the first time in the history of American-Japanese relations, Americans were finding out what the Japanese really thought of them.[83]

Notwithstanding, the concept of race and racism had been so artfully deleted, obscured, and disguised throughout the Occupation that the Japanese, even when they came to sense the core of American racism against them, could not crystalize it into a concept and then make it an object of protest. Instead, the Japanese simply opted for collective nonresponsiveness. Perhaps to publicly admit American racism against them would be too humiliating. Only by pretending not to have noticed it could the Japanese manage to maintain their poise. It was the deliberate Japanese public denial of American racism that continued to obscure their memory of it.

As the San Francisco Peace Conference drew near, the Japanese were increasingly coping with their own growing sense of inferiority. The Japanese press frequently discussed proper interactions with *gaijin* (a euphemism for whites) after Japan gained independence. An *Asahi* newspaper editorial, appearing a few days after the signing of the San Francisco Peace Treaty, confessed that no one seemed to know what would be an appropriate Japanese attitude toward Americans, especially after the forced street etiquette was abolished. It would be absurd if the Japanese were to suddenly behave as if they had become superior to Americans upon gaining independence. The editorial suggested: "We shall become citizens of the world [*sekai shimin*], and start associating with foreigners [*gaikoku-jin*] in a sophisticated manner." This time, this would not be done by order but as "a voluntary act of an independent people."[84] Such a suggestion, of course, was simply too vague to be of much use.

A year later, shortly before Japan's independence went into effect on April 28, 1952, various articles in *Asahi* again discussed how to begin interacting with *gaijin* as equals. The special ticket windows and the white-striped railroad cars reserved for Occupation personnel had been abolished, and Japanese passengers were mixing with *gaijin* in trains. The article said that the Japanese were timid and awkward in this new situation because of their feelings of inferiority as a conquered people. However, now that Japan and the United States had become equal sovereigns, the two peoples would become equal as well. The article suggested that "once the people learn to feel this way, we can mingle with foreign passengers on quite a casual and friendly basis so we do not have to feel uncomfortable."[85]

The Japanese had to solve many issues before they could be casual about their interactions with Americans. The controversy over the nature of the U.S.-Japanese military alliance was growing, and anti-Americanism also entered the picture as a result of the Japanese sense of inferiority. The Japanese feared that Japan might soon become an American military colony and would therefore be in perpetual danger of being drawn into major wars against other Asians, be they Koreans, Chinese, or Vietnamese. Under the terms of the U.S.-Japan Security Treaty, a 75,000-man "National Police Reserve," which had been authorized by General MacArthur after the outbreak of the Korean War, had become the National Self-Defense Force. Considerable opposition was raised to the ever-growing Self-Defense Force; the Japanese public felt it was violating Article 9 of the new constitution, known as the "No War Clause."

Opposition to Japan's rearmament and fear of involvement in U.S. military activity culminated in a storm of violent anti-American protests throughout Japan. On May 1, 1952, just three days after Japan regained independence, some twenty thousand demonstrators, mainly union members and university students under Communist leadership, clashed with three thousand Japanese policemen armed with pistols and tear gas in front of the Imperial Palace. In a rock-throwing melee two civilians were killed and more than two thousand were injured. The demonstrators then turned their attention to some U.S. military vehicles parked by the palace and burned at least a dozen of them. Three American GIs out on the street despite the official warning were assaulted by the mob, tossed into the moat surrounding the palace, and peppered with stones until they were rescued by other Japanese. Sporadic rioting continued throughout the month of May. On May 31, riots broke out in Tokyo, Osaka, Nagoya, and Kobe, killing three persons and injuring eighty. In Tokyo a Molotov cocktail was tossed into the U.S. Occupation residential compound though the resulting fire did no damage.[86]

Japanese society on the whole remained rather passive about the continuous show of American racism. MacArthur's view of the Japanese as an inferior race had become widely known to the Japanese public after his testimony at the May 1951 Senate hearings in Washington, regarding his mission in the Far East. His paternalistic attitude toward the Japanese was reflected in his assessment of the impact of the American Occupation on an isolated and backward Japan. He likened it to a forty-five-year-old adult guiding a boy of twelve, unlike the occupation of a mature Germany. When they realized that the United States of America would administer a decent and just form of government, he said, the Japanese were "so astonished and so grateful that their inclinations were to follow us, and to copy what we did." Because "like all Orientals," they had a tendency "to adulate a winner, and to have the most supreme contempt for a loser," he believed they would continue to follow the Americans, although "it does not mean that the Japanese character has undergone a great moral reformation."[87]

Japanese attention quickly focused on MacArthur's equating of their collective intellectual level to that of a twelve-year-old child. They were not particularly offended by it, however, since they justified his comment as typical of the victorious conqueror toward the vanquished. Instead, it simply provided a source of jokes about MacArthur's pompousness.[88] Notwithstanding, after MacArthur's statement became known, cynicism mounted and optimism waned in the Japanese perception of their relations with Americans, a distinct difference from the early days of the Occupation, when the Japanese expressed an innocent belief in equality and friendship with the United States. Despite Hollywood's goodwill, Japanese movie critics and the general audience were not necessarily honored by the pro-fraternization movies. *Tokyo File 212*, for example, was severely criticized in Japan because of its stereotypical portrayal of Japanese objects—clothing, housing, social customs, and so on—out of context. One Japanese critic argued that this kind of movie was another indication of how the United States, even with good intentions, never made an effort to understand Japan as it is. *Japanese War Bride*, which received a lukewarm review in the *New York Times*, was introduced to Japanese audiences as a story of "international love" or of "true love despite the racial differences." The public was curious as to how well a Japanese actress (Yamaguchi Yoshiko/aka Shirley YAMAGUCHI) could perform a leading role with Hollywood actors and actresses. The plot itself meant hardly anything at all to the Japanese.[89]

Japanese movie critics were generally embarrassed at the poor quality of these movies, especially the trite plots and strange depictions of Japan, and called them "Amerika-san sābisu eiga" (movies made just to flatter Mr. and Mrs. America).[90] One critic cynically commented that the happy ending of *Japanese War Bride* was an "extraordinary exception—say, as generous as the San Francisco Peace Treaty" in the history of Hollywood, because "interracial love portrayed in Hollywood movies always ends in tragedy." He explained to readers that "to the good citizens of the United States, miscegenation is as shocking as incest—something that should not exist—and as such has been a taboo for a long time." He cautioned that such a shallow veneering of "international or interracial romance," so enthusiastically depicted in recent Hollywood films, was misleading and dangerous, and that the Japanese had to delve into their own racism against Chinese, Korean, Indian, and other Asian peoples and see if they were open-minded enough to accept interactions with the outside world so lightheartedly.[91]

These anti-American sentiments rarely grew to more than a simple criticism of American arrogance. They did not go so far as to express superiority over Americans nor even equality with them. In a self-deprecating manner, the Japanese accepted their sense of inferiority to Americans, and the American attitude of superiority to the Japanese. It seemed that they had learned it was the only way the Japanese could survive in a turbulent world, over which Japan no longer had any control.

Writer Ishikawa Tatsuzō wrote in *Chūō kōron*, in the fall of 1953, on why anti-American sentiments were on the rise after Japan's independence. He admitted that America had tried its best to produce pro-American leaders in Japan in various ways. But many conscientious Japanese could not help but feel indignant about the Americans in Japan, citing their poor taste, attitude and behavior, manners and morals. They saw Americans as powerful, arrogant, and self-centered. They seemed to have a natural instinct to despise the colored races. Violent behavior, shameless conduct with prostitutes, and even reckless driving in Japanese streets all derived from this arrogance. Ishikawa was convinced that the Americans despised the Japanese, as they always did any colored race. Although he censured the Americans for their wrongdoing, he lacked the foresight to propose a constructive plan for improvement. He did not know how the Japanese could avoid becoming victims. Despite his vocal anti-American stance, he remained a passive victim himself of American discrimination.[92]

A journal *Jidō shinri* (*Child Study*) held a roundtable discussion by educators on the impact of the American military presence on Japanese children. They focused their discussion on the wide gap between the concept of American democracy as preached to the Japanese since the Occupation and the reality of Americans' behavior in Japan. In the beginning of the Occupation, they noted, all Americans looked intelligent, sophisticated, and superior to the Japanese, even when they were just plain folks back in America. Now that the Japanese were disillusioned with things American, they should try to liberate themselves from such illusions and understand the true nature of America, both good and bad.[93] But what their true nature was vis-à-vis the Japanese and how to cope with it—no one could tell.

After independence, even children, especially those living around U.S. military bases, held a negative image of American GIs as lawless, bullying, rude, and promiscuous. In the fall of 1952 a publishing company announced plans to put out a book of children's essays on how they viewed their lives surrounded by U.S. military bases (there were some six hundred U.S. bases located all across Japan). About seventy elementary and junior high schools responded to this project, sending 1,325 essays by students ranging from the first to the ninth grades. The publisher selected two hundred and in April 1953 issued an anthology, *Kichi no ko* (Children Around the Base).[94]

Most of these essays discussed violent behavior by American GIs. A sixth-grade girl in Nishi Tama, a western suburb of Tokyo, wrote in a poem of her indignant feeling about three American soldiers. The soldiers tried to sit a little boy on a bridge girder so they could take pictures. When the scared boy cried, a Japanese woman walked up to take him down from the girder. Offended at her meddling, one American soldier struck her on the head with his fist. Another sixth-grade boy wrote about drunken American soldiers boating at a lake in Inogashira Park in Tokyo. They approached some craft with Japanese aboard and rocked the boats, throwing the Japanese into the water. When some managed to swim back to the pier, other GIs kicked them back into the lake.[95]

Stories of friends, parents, brothers and sisters, and even pets being kicked and hit by American GIs were abundant in the children's essays. A composition by a fifth-grade girl told of her experiences visiting an American residential area adjacent to the military base. She and her friend wanted to befriend American children, so they tried to play with them near the base for a while. Then, a small boy came out and urinated on her leg. Though she wanted to cry out in shame, she could not say or do anything. She wrote that she could not understand why the adults who happened to be nearby just laughed at this incident and did nothing to reprimand the boy.[96]

Japanese critics lamented that children living near the U.S. military base innocently wished to become prostitutes catering only to American GIs. These children said that that was the only way they could dress well, speak English, and make friends with Americans.[97] In the anthology of children's poems, a fourth-grade girl in Yokosuka, where there was a large U.S. navy base, wrote that she did not understand why a beautiful Japanese woman would do these things with blond American soldiers. A first-grade boy living in the same city wrote that he liked *panpan* women (postwar slang for Japanese prostitutes catering only to American GIs) because they were rich and beautiful. A second-grade girl in Nara, ancient capital of Japan, deplored that three little girls in her neighborhood—one four-year-old and two five-year-olds—often played "*panpan*." A sixth-grade girl in Sasebo also wrote about two little children "playing *panpan*." One child said to the other, "I'm *panpan*, and you're Ame-san [Mr. America]," and then they held hands and walked away.[98]

More realistic children in the higher grades saw prostitutes as a mark of Japan's humiliation and understood the imbalance of power between Japan and the United States reflected in the way Japanese interacted with American GIs. A third-grade boy in Yokosuka wrote that the reason for so many *panpan* in Japan was Japan's defeat in the war. A sixth-grade girl in Fukuoka wrote about a quarrel between an American GI and a Japanese woman in front of a sweet shop. The American soldier yanked her hair, beat her neck, pinched her cheek, and eventually dragged her away, while she screamed and tried to escape. The crowd just watched, doing nothing. The girl argued that the cause of such misery was the war: "No matter if it's an American soldier or a dark-skinned foreigner [*iro no kuroi gaikoku-jin*], whenever I see them, I cannot but feel that the world should be united into one nation."[99]

Japanese adults, too, suffered from the dangerous pranks of GIs. One critic remembered seeing them firing small pistols at Japanese who were fishing by the river. The GIs laughed as they ran pell-mell. Another GI threw stones at other Japanese for no reason. Even if these were meant to be typical American practical jokes, the critic wrote, "anyone who threatens others' lives for fun has no right to say that the Japanese people's mental age is below twelve years of age." He wished such American "pranks," which showed no common sense, would disappear for the sake of U.S.-Japanese friendship.[100] Another American "prank" that took place shortly after Christmas of 1953 became a national headline. In the middle of the busy Ginza district in Tokyo, several American GIs randomly grabbed Japanese pedestrians and threw them over the bridge railing into the river.[101] A similar incident had occurred in the May Day demonstration of the previous year, in which three American GIs were tossed into the moat by an angry mob. However, many Japanese felt that such things happened to Japanese because Americans thought nothing of Japanese human rights. They believed that Americans would not do such things in the European countries where they were stationed, even in Germany. But the Japanese did not or could not confront Americans because they felt that challenging them would be useless.

Japan was subdued both militarily and in terms of an economy wholly dependent on the United States. In the mid-1950s the United States had spent about $4 billion in Japan for "special procurement," that is, the purchase of supplies, equipment, services, and recreation and entertainment for American troops. The Japanese economy also received a strong impetus from the Korean War boom. In an effort to keep Japanese goods out of the American market, the U.S. government mediated trade arrangements in Asia among nations occupied by Japan before the war. The United States also sponsored Japan's participation in the international economic system amid European opposition. Because European policymakers were reluctant to accord special privileges on account of Japan's strategic position in East Asia, they did not allow Japan to enter the General Agreement on Tariffs and Trade (GATT). On September 10, 1955, the United States pushed through Japanese membership despite European opposition.

By the mid-1950s, with improvements in living standards, a mood of relative contentment and stability had settled in in Japanese society. But beneath the surface, a gnawing sense of inferiority and guilt continued. This feeling of inferiority became a leading topic among the postwar literary generation. Kenzaburō ŌE, recipient of the Nobel Prize for literature in 1994, wrote about the sense of fragmentation expressed in the racial context vis-à-vis the West, especially the United States. Nobuo KOJIMA in *Amerikan Sukūru* (The American school), published in 1954, Kenzaburō ŌE in a series of works that focus on the theme of occupied Japan and the United States, and Shūsaku ENDŌ in his works on the strictures of Catholicism—the inability of European and Japanese Catholics to understand each other as equals because of their skin color—all explored Japan's postwar burden of racial inferiority toward the superior white Westerners.[102] In their works, the voice of protest and a call for racial justice was curiously absent. Japanese society was presented as being almost impotent, and any feeling of contentment was hollow. Despite racial humiliation, however, things seemed to be going well.

Within the cocooned world of post-Occupation Japan, more fundamental problems in the abrasive encounters of Americans and Japanese gradually surfaced in spite of cultural propaganda. Yet the presence of these sensitivities were largely perceived by both peoples and governments as irrelevant. Disturbing racial experiences were sanitized, which suggests complicity in pursuing common political interests in the world with as little friction as possible. The absence of racial experiences in public memory explains how much both the Americans and Japanese were confused about Japanese dual identity but simply left the obscurity as it was for the mutual good. Besides, the absence of memory also explains how they feared the destructive power of race in their interactions in society, in spite of the rapid healing of their diplomatic relations.

CHAPTER 3

Racial Equality, Minorities, and the Japanese Constitution

When Japan's new constitution, the so-called MacArthur Constitution, was promulgated on November 3, 1946, the public concentrated its attention on the radical provisions of popular sovereignty, equal rights for men and women, and the renunciation of war. But Article 14 contained another significant principle—a guarantee of racial equality as a basic human right for every Japanese citizen. This article, known as the "equality before the law" clause, declares: "All of the people are equal under the law and there shall be no discrimination in political, economic, or social relations because of race, creed, sex, social status, or family origin."

The inclusion of "race" in Article 14 was, and still is, the least-known and most puzzling fact about the SCAP-sponsored constitution. When the Occupation deliberately ignored the issue of race and made it a taboo, why did SCAP allow the concept to appear in the nation's sovereign law? Why did SCAP approve the language of racial equality, while the American practice of racial segregation was not considered a violation of the U.S. Constitution? Moreover, how did the Japanese, while becoming accustomed to racial inequality as the postwar reality, perceive the constitutional guarantee? Above all, what is the significance of this provision in the light of intriguing racial politics in the Occupation?

A group of Japanese scholars and journalists took the initiative in drafting a new constitution with the racial provision and submitted it to SCAP. As the aforementioned research group at the Ministry of Foreign Affairs also drafted a peace treaty with a racial equality clause inserted, such a principle continued to inspire Japanese leaders with a lingering momentum from wartime. After all, during the war Japan had claimed in its propaganda that it fought for the cause of racial equality. In fact, these Japanese liberals continued to interpret the language of racial equality in the style of Pan-Asianism or Wilsonianism, both plagued by colonialist paternalism toward other Asians. They perhaps felt no dilemma in maintaining their support for the same creed, with considerable self-righteousness, at least until SCAP imposed a restraint on the issue of race.

SCAP for its part had little trouble endorsing the principle of racial equality in the new Japanese constitution. Of course, equality between the yellow Japanese and the white Americans was both unacceptable and not part of the Japanese domestic constitutional question. However, in terms of relations between the Japanese and other Asians—the minorities in Japanese society—SCAP could uphold the principle in the name of Japan's democratization and pacifism. To educate the Japanese about the crime of racial arrogance—the presumed assumption of their superiority in the world—SCAP needed to convey the message that they were "no superior" to any other Asians (but altogether inferior to Westerners). This way, SCAP could maintain the basic framework of American superiority while teaching the Japanese the lesson of racial equality (with other Asians). Universal applicability of the concept was never a consideration for SCAP.

Just as American and Japanese wartime slogans—the fight for democracy and equality—served merely as propaganda, the principle of racial equality in the SCAP-sponsored Japanese constitution was merely the mutual recitation of a wartime goodwill, ultimately destined to become a dead letter. Besides, there was no discussion or agreement between the Japanese and SCAP on the interpretation of the clause. Neither of the two sides was willing to take a radical step toward realizing racial equality in actual practice. Discriminatory policies toward the racial and ethnic minorities—the most likely beneficiaries of the clause, such as the Ainu, Ryukyuans, Chinese, and Koreans—continued.

It was in this mutual racism against other Asians—in this case, Japan's minorities—that the Americans and Japanese found a confluence of their political interest. As SCAP gradually upgraded the racial status of the Japanese, the two nations naturally endorsed the shared perception of other Asians as inferior to the Japanese. Under SCAP's auspices, the same racial hierarchy upheld by Japan's Pan-Asianism slowly revived in Japan's domestic context as well. Moreover, for the purpose of praising Japan's unique racial and cultural quality in the common fight against communism, SCAP moved to approve the view of homogeneous Japanese society at the cost of the minorities, to which measure the Japanese had no objection.

The story surrounding the least-known provision in the SCAP-sponsored constitution—its origin, intention, and impact—offers further evidence of mutual U.S.-Japanese racism against other Asians, much to the advantage of the U.S.-Japanese alliance. Although the two nations had difficulty from time to time in reconciling the principle of racial equality, the United States and Japan shared a long history of mutual perception of Asians as inferior— people in need of care, guidance, and protection. This historic background paved the way for their approval on that constitutional principle, with much skewed altruism on both sides.

The attempt to establish an international principle of racial equality began after World War I. At the Paris Peace Conference in January 1919, the Japanese delegate became highly vocal about the issue of racism in world politics, fearing that Japan's gains in China during World War I would be revoked by the Western allies' discriminatory attitude. Japan, as the only nonwhite nation recognized as a first-class power, proposed an amendment to the Covenant of the League of Nations guaranteeing "to all alien nationals of state members of the League, equal and just treatment in every respect, making no distinctions, either in law or in fact, on account of their race or nationality."

This proposal, known as the "racial equality clause," was consistent with new principles for the post–World War I world: peace, justice, and humanity, as ardently advocated by the chairman of the conference, President Woodrow Wilson. But the Wilsonian principle of equality among nations was applied exclusively to nations in Europe. Britain and the United States, facing the problems of "Oriental" immigration into North America and Australia, as well as the problems of colonial administration, maintained their hierarchical attitude toward non-Western nations. In April, in the last session of the League of Nations Commission, the final vote was cast and, except for the United States, Britain, and Australia, all representatives voted for the principle. Nonetheless, President Wilson concluded that the racial equality clause simply caused "too serious objections on the part of some of us" to have it inserted in the Covenant and announced that the clause was not adopted.[1]

But during the Pacific War the United States came to endorse the principle of racial equality for Asia because it needed friends in the war against Japan. In fact, although the war was a clash of mutual racial hatreds between the United States and Japan, it was also a great contest to prove which was the favored champion of racial justice in Asia. The liberation of the oppressed peoples of Asia was an essential part of the propaganda of both nations.

Japanese propaganda pointed out the inconsistency between the American mission in Asia and its racism against Asians. It criticized U.S. immigration and naturalization laws as evidence of America's insistence on racial superiority. "The United States has always looked down on Chungking [Chiang Kai-shek's Guomindang regime]," a Japanese-controlled radio commentator often pointed out; the shortwave broadcast emphasized racial unity between the Japanese and Chinese.

> The United States abolished extraterritorial rights because she wished to ingratiate East Asia. She is not doing it because she wants to liberate China. From her immigration laws, you could see her real intention. The United States loves Britain more than Chungking because they are of the same race.... Since Chungking is a different race, an East Asian race, how could the United States be true in helping Chungking? ... Thus we call for the slogan of "Asia for the Asiatics."[2]

Japan's criticism impelled American lawmakers to reconsider the "moral inconsistency" expressed in U.S. immigration and naturalization laws. As a counteracting measure, some Americans advocated the elimination of *all* racial discrimination from the U.S. immigration and naturalization laws. Others, concerned about the disturbing effect of Japanese propaganda, emphasized the repeal of the Chinese exclusion laws so that America could at least save face with its wartime ally by awarding China an honorary annual maximum quota of 105 immigrants.[3]

Although the rhetoric of both sides was plagued by colonial paternalism and there was little or no planning for the liberation of Asian nations, both Americans and Japanese believed that they fought for the good of the Asians. They vehemently upheld the ideal of racial equality for all and promised to support postwar independence for all Asian nations.[4]

As such a wartime symmetry indicates, the United States and Japan shared a similar view regarding the secondary status of non-Japanese Asians, which was reflected in a series of diplomatic agreements in the early twentieth century. At the turn of the century, the United States had designated Japan as a kind of junior police force overseeing the stability of the Far East. Under the terms of the Taft-Katsura Agreement of 1905, for example, the United States recognized Japan's authority in Korea in exchange for Japan's recognition of American predominance in the Philippines. Japan and the United States acknowledged mutual responsibilities for elevating the level of civilization in Korea and the Philippines under their separate tutelage. Japan's responsibility toward Korea and America's "White Man's Burden" toward the Philippines coexisted in Asia and the Pacific.

Various international expositions also demonstrated the two nations' shared perception of Asia's backwardness. The Columbian World Exposition of 1893 in Chicago placed the Japanese pavilion on a man-made island prudently located halfway between the Western and non-Western sections; expositions held in Japan kept the Asian exhibitions away from the Japanese exhibition. At the Fifth Trade and Industrial Exposition of Japan held in Osaka in the spring of 1903, Western pavilions were laid out according to the level of each nation's industrialization, starting with the British, American, German, and French pavilions, continuing with those of other European nations, and finishing with the Turkish pavilion. Near the main gate to the 1903 exposition was a large space for the Pavilion of Races of Man, which exhibited the primitive civilizations of seven races in Asia: the Ainu, indigenous population of Hokkaido (Japan's northernmost island) and sole surviving non-Mongoloid natives of Japan; the Ryukyuans or Okinawans, the regional population on the chain of islands southwest of Kyushu, whose religion and language showed distinctive cultural characteristics; the Kaoshan, descendants of Taiwan's pre-Chinese population and a physically distinct aboriginal people; then the Koreans, Chinese, Hindu, and Javanese.

Although the purpose of the Asian exhibit was to promote trade, the Chinese legation in Japan, infuriated at the public display of humiliating stereotypes, protested and the Chinese exhibits were immediately canceled. Korea and Ryukyu also objected, and the entire exhibit was finally canceled by the end of April.[5] In the United States, however, Asians continued to be treated in a similar fashion. At the St. Louis Exposition in 1904, an anthropological display entitled "Races of Man" no longer included the Japanese in the non-Western category. Instead, the Ainu were selected to demonstrate their primitive lifestyle side by side with native American and Canadian Indians, Pygmies, and the indigenous people of Patagonia, among others.[6]

These parallel views of Asian inferiority had a curious side effect. The Japanese could condone American racism against Asians by comparing it with their own attitude toward other Asian peoples. During the anti-Japanese movement in the United States in the 1920s, Japan's leading Christian socialist, Abe Isoo, had criticized the Japanese right wing's excessive indignation at the American measure and called for a better understanding of the complex issue of racist feelings. He argued that the Japanese section in San

Francisco posed the same problem to Americans as would a "village of filthy Chinese of the lowest class with a different language and customs in the middle of Tokyo." Just as it is not good for Japan to allow Chinese laborers to stay in their country indefinitely, the Japanese should not do the same in the United States. In addition, argued Abe, any further increase in Korean migration to Japan should be avoided at all costs, because it might eventually create trouble for Japan like the Negro problem did in the United States. He thus recommended that the best measure for guaranteeing both the welfare of the Japanese and peaceful relations with the United States would be to call back the Japanese from the United States and to turn the Chinese and Koreans away from Japan.[7]

As noted above, the clause on the issue of racial equality had originated in an earlier constitutional draft written by a liberal Japanese group. This citizens' draft, unlike any of the drafts prepared by the Japanese government, strongly influenced SCAP planning. However, an analysis of this version of the constitution reveals an almost complete absence of consensus on the matter among the Japanese drafters themselves. Some understood the language in the sense of a Wilsonian anticolonialist framework, while others approached it from a socialist ideal. There was a remnant of Pan-Asianism which upheld the principle from the viewpoint of Japanese noblesse oblige, while there was also the voice of self-criticism reprimanding Japanese arrogance and encouraging a true view of egalitarian democracy. Either way, the group never considered the issue of racial equality as a focal point of the new constitution. Aside from there being little possibility of broad universal applicability, there is no knowing what specific ideal the original drafters had in mind in discussing racial equality.

In October 1945, completely independent of SCAP supervision, a private citizens' group, Kempō Kenkyūkai (the Constitutional Investigation Association, hereafter cited as the CIA—as it appeared in SCAP documents), emerged to discuss and promote various reconstruction plans for Japan. Initially formed under the name Nippon Bunka-jin Renmei (Japanese League of Men of Culture), they had their first organizational meeting in Tokyo on October 27, 1945, and adopted a plan to publish a journal to be called *Shinsei* (New Life) as a means of disseminating progressive ideas. The members included philosophers, journalists, scholars, and politicians (the latter ranging from left to moderate right-wing). Most of them had been liberals in the prewar years.[8]

94

More important, during the high tide of the Taisho democracy movement, all the current CIA members had been quite active in support of socialism, social liberalism, Wilsonian internationalism, and other progressive principles. As young liberals in the 1920s, they believed in cooperation with the West as well as cosmopolitanism itself as the best path for Japan's future. After having spent the 1930s and the war witnessing the failure of Japan's Pan-Asianism and ultranationalism, they now saw a great opportunity to revive their prewar idealism and lead Japan to a place in the new world.

At the October 29 meeting Takano Iwasaburō, a legal scholar, suggested the formation of a study group to draft a new constitution. After the defeat in the war, Takano had publicly expressed the need to abolish the Meiji Constitution and draft a new one, a movement he thought should be initiated by a nongovernmental group. The group voted unanimously to put this plan into action, even though other versions by the Japanese government had already been initiated under SCAP's supervision.[9]

The draft constitution aimed to destroy those elements the members believed most responsible for Japan's path to war; they included the institution of the Emperor, limited popular rights, the unfair distribution of land and wealth, and restrictions on the labor movement. Takano invited Suzuki Yasuzō and Imanaka Tsugumaro, both legal scholars, to subsequent meetings. It was an appropriate move since Suzuki had insisted even during the war that the country's whole system needed a complete overhaul if it aimed to exercise leadership in reconstructing the whole of Asia. Since the end of the war, Suzuki had continued to publicly advocate the need for fundamental constitutional reform.[10]

On November 5, only a week after the first meeting of the league, the CIA held its first session to draft a constitution. The drafting committee of the CIA consisted of seven core members and other occasional participants. According to a SCAP memorandum on the CIA's activities, the seven members were Takano Iwasaburō, adviser to and intellectual leader of the Social Democratic Party; Baba Tsunego, president of the daily newspaper *Yomiuri-Hōchi* and adviser to the Social Democratic Party; Sugimori Kōjirō, professor of philosophy at Waseda University, writer on cultural topics, and supporter of the Social Democratic Party; Morito Tatsuo, writer on social and economic topics and member of the Executive Committee of the Social Democratic Party; Iwabuchi Tetsuo, political writer and supporter of the Social Democratic Party; Murobuse Takanobu, editor of *Shinsei* and Communist sympathizer; and Suzuki Yasuzō, writer, scholar, and socialist sympathizer, whose views were highly respected by the Social Democratic Party.[11]

Between the fifth and twenty-first of November 1945, the CIA held a total of three voluntary meetings to discuss fundamental problems in drafting a new constitution. At the top of the agenda was the problem of *kokutai*—national polity—and the locus of national sovereignty. After Suzuki drafted the first constitutional outline, the second draft developed from further discussion of the first plan. On November 29 the second draft received general approval from the committee members. The CIA sent the second draft (in the joint names of Takano, Morito, Murobuse, Sugimori, Iwabuchi, and Suzuki) to a total of twenty-five people in various fields for their opinions and comments. In early December they began the third draft, based on comments received from these readers, with the intention of sending the final draft to major newspapers for publication and to various political parties for their comments. On December 28 the third draft in its entirety appeared on the front pages of major national newspapers.[12] Its radical departure from the prewar constitution attracted nationwide attention and support.

Popular sovereignty was a major theme in the CIA's final draft, but what distinguished it from all other drafts was its constitutional guarantee of racial equality, which had not been endorsed by the interim Japanese government's drafts or even suggested by SCAP. The first article in a chapter on the rights and duties of the people declared: "The people shall be equal before the law, and all discrimination by birth and status shall be abolished." In the same chapter, one article stated: "Men and women shall be perfectly equal in public and private life"; and another article continued: "No discrimination shall be executed by race or nationality."[13]

What did the draft mean by the word "race," or *jinshu* in Japanese? It is important to understand that the Japanese terminology of race is as fluid in concept as the English word *race*. Just as the English word can mean either a color characteristic or feature, a common sociocultural trait or ancestral origin, or even a national group (e.g., the yellow race, the Jewish race, the German race, and so on), Japanese words such as *jinshu*, *shuzoku*, and *minzoku* interchangeably cover an equally wide range of meanings. For example, *Nihon ruigo dai-jiten*, a Japanese thesaurus published in 1910, provides no difference in definition for the terms *jinshu* and *minzoku*.[14] In the case of the Foreign Ministry's draft peace treaty, the word "race" ostensibly targeted a relationship between the Japanese and the Westerners. The CIA draft, however, had no such palpable designation for the word.

Amid such linguistic confusion, the most likely beneficiaries of the constitutional guarantee of "racial" equality would be the minorities in Japan, the Ainu and Okinawan people as well as former colonial subjects—the Koreans and Formosans—who opted to remain in postwar Japan. Radical as it sounded, however, the interpretation of the concept of equality among races and nationalities was neither defined, discussed, nor understood by the drafters themselves, who left no clue as to its applicability to the Japanese legal system.

The idea of racial equality seems to have originated with Suzuki, since his first draft of the CIA's constitutional plan already included such a guarantee. Suzuki admitted that he had drawn inspiration from the constitutions of various nations and that he had modeled the nondiscrimination clause on several articles of the Soviet Constitution.[15] The chapters on human rights were based not only on the Soviet but also on the U.S. and Weimar constitutions. The U.S. Constitution contributed its provision on habeas corpus in the First Amendment. The Weimar Constitution, often regarded by contemporary Japanese liberals as a preeminent human rights document, was quoted six times in the chapter on human rights.

The Soviet Constitution was cited five times for its provisions on human rights such as the right to work, rest, and pensions as well as equality of the sexes and races. Article 123 of the Soviet Constitution seems to be the direct source of inspiration for Suzuki's idea of a constitutional guarantee on racial equality. It states: "Equality of rights of citizens of the USSR, irrespective of their nationality or race, in all spheres of economic, state, cultural, social, and political life, is an indefeasible law." Actual conditions in the Soviet Union were quite different. Racial minorities had been oppressed in the name of Lenin's Russification program, and anti-Semitism within the Soviet Union was notorious.[16] With such realities perhaps unknown to them, Suzuki and the other CIA members who had long been inclined toward socialism may have been strongly attracted to Communist egalitarianism.

But there were other ideas. Takano, for example, wrote a separate draft. His main proposal was to set up a republican government by abolishing the emperor system and replacing it with a presidency. In his chapter on the rights and duties of the people, he made no mention of race or nationality.[17]

At times, Suzuki also interpreted the ideal of abolishing racial discrimination within a Japanese context, apart from Soviet ideology. In his writing, he quoted the words of a certain Western diplomat whom he had met: "As long as the Japanese hope to retain the national polity, the people will never be able to renounce their groundless pride that the Japanese are the most advanced race in the world [*bankoku ni hirui naki yūshū minzoku*]. As a result, they inevitably fail to make a fresh start as a modest member of international society."[18] Although Suzuki did not specify in his writing how he responded to the diplomat, he later denounced the excessive racial consciousness of the Japanese, especially the notion of racial superiority, in much the same way. In *Nihon no minshu-shugi* (Japan's Democracy), a book published in 1947, Suzuki criticized the narrow-minded parochialism of the Japanese which led to the exclusion of peoples of different races and nations, and attributed these attitudes to the remnants of Japanese feudalism.[19]

Wilsonian self-rule was the guiding principle for Imanaka Tsugimaro. At the crest of the Taisho democracy movement in the 1920s, Imanaka had written about the significance of Wilsonian nationalism, claiming it to be a key to good relations between the Japanese and other peoples in Asia. In 1919, shortly after the March First movement (nationwide mass demonstrations in Korea calling for national independence) was violently crushed by Japanese forces, he wrote an article in support of self-rule by a race (*minzoku*) as a foundation of international democracy (*kokusai minpon-shugi*).[20] If democracy is founded on the awakening of each individual, he argued, racial self-rule (*minzoku jiketsu*) should be founded on each race as well. He interpreted the Korean movement for independence as a sign of racial awakening (*minzoku no jikaku*). Therefore, he insisted that the Japanese must accord them the treatment due to any group that has developed such a consciousness.

Another CIA member, Sugimori Kōjirō, adopted a paternalistic tone similar to the wartime ideology of racial harmony. Sugimori had articulated his view of Japan as a leader of the weaker races in his wartime writing *Sekai seiji-gaku no hitsuzen* (Due principles of world politics), published in 1943. In his theory of the globalization of politics he discussed the role of race in the following terms: on the eve of the modern era, one race represented one nation; in the age of imperialism, self-rule by the victorious race became a norm; in the Pacific War, the time had arrived to shift toward the age of a "multiracial nation [*ta-minzoku ichi-kokka*]"—where a stronger race took charge of the welfare of weaker races and together they cooperated for the welfare of society.[21]

Another article by Sugimori published in June 1946 emphasized the importance of "sincere love" adopted by the stronger race in dealing with the weaker racial group.[22] Only with the presence of such an emotional tie would a special relationship develop between the two, and their raison d'être be mutually reinforced. He assigned the League of Nations or its equivalent as the proper forum to nurture such a tendency. Logically, in his perception, the League of Nations should consist of stronger national and racial groups properly supervising the weaker ones—a concept not radically different from the idea of UN trusteeship over former colonies such as Korea, which Franklin Roosevelt had suggested during World War II. In sum, for Sugimori, Japan's benevolent paternalism toward weaker races was part and parcel of his idea of abolishing callous racial discrimination and realizing equality.

It was much more difficult for the Japanese to explore the abolition of racism at home than it was for them to criticize Western racism toward the Japanese. Though Japan did leave the work of correcting Western racism against the Japanese in the hands of SCAP and opted for a passive path of reform toward a peace, this does not justify or explain Japan's similarly passive attitude regarding the task of correcting Japanese racism toward other Asians. However, the Japanese simply lacked the strength to pursue such a task by themselves. Worse, men like Sugimori continued to believe in the righteous cause of Pan-Asianism, remaining totally blind to the severe flaws of that view of Japan's relations with Asia. A curious question arises as to what would have happened had SCAP instructed the Japanese on how to pursue the task.

Although SCAP, during the first few months of the Occupation, issued directives to protect Koreans from "racial" discrimination, it did not include the principle of racial equality in its first thoughts on a Japanese constitution. The Potsdam Declaration had stated only that the Allies were fully empowered to demand that Japan's basic law should be altered to bring about the eventual establishment of a peaceful and responsible government. An interim imperial cabinet was formed on August 17, 1945, with Prince Higashikuni Naruhiko as its head to sign the surrender instrument and to initiate Japan's disarmament and other matters relating to the Occupation. Prince Konoe Fumimaro, Japanese prime minister between June 1937 and January 1939, and between July 1940 and July 1941, was the Minister without Portfolio until October 9 in Prince Higashikuni's cabinet. MacArthur suggested to Konoe that there was a need to reform the Japanese constitution.

On October 10, Konoe called on George Atcheson Jr. for advice and suggestions. Lacking any formal directive on this subject at that time, Atcheson offered unofficial comments on the general character of the Meiji Constitution. According to the summary Atcheson cabled to the Secretary of State on the same day, he mentioned seven undemocratic features of the constitu-tion, including the lack of popular representatives in the government and the absence of a people's right to impeachment. Atcheson also mentioned that each right enumerated in the "Bill of Rights" in the Meiji Constitution was emasculated by the restrictive phrase "within the limits of the law." At the end of the meeting, Konoe was reported to have indicated that the em-peror was in favor of revision and that Konoe himself would actively work toward it.[23]

Konoe believed that MacArthur had assigned him the job of drafting a new constitution, so he proceeded with the assistance of his chief adviser Sasaki Sōichi, legal expert at Kyoto Imperial University. Konoe and Sasaki thus produced drafts, although the Americans took a dim view of Konoe as the architect of a new Japan while being prosecuted as a war criminal.[24] After SCAP forced the Higashikuni cabinet to resign on October 9, 1945, on the grounds that its members included war criminals, both Konoe and Sasaki continued their work and transmitted their drafts to the emperor in late November, shortly before the Japanese government voluntarily abol-ished Konoe's office, the office of the Lord Keeper of the Privy Seal, on the twenty-fourth.

Meanwhile, to replace the Higashikuni cabinet, Shidehara Kijūrō, a lead-ing liberal politician active in the 1910s and 1920s, was recalled to serve as prime minister, as of October 9. During a formal courtesy call by Shidehara on October 11, MacArthur again suggested constitutional reform. The Shide-hara cabinet also acted promptly on MacArthur's request, and on October 27 appointed the Constitutional Problem Investigation Committee (Naikaku Kempō Mondai Chōsa Iinkai), under the chairmanship of State Minister Matsumoto Jōji and known as the Matsumoto Committee. From October to December the Matsumoto Committee met thirteen times, and at each ses-sion each committeeman submitted his own plan for the revision of the con-stitution. By December 26 the committee had come up with two different drafts for a revised constitution, one with only minor revisions to the Meiji Constitution and another with what the committee called wide-ranging re-visions. As it turned out, both drafts, Plans A and B, made only slight alter-ations to the Meiji Constitution. As Matsumoto later explained in his recol-lections, he and other members thought that they could handle the matter as they pleased, since the Allies said they would leave constitutional reform to Japan; they even considered leaving the constitution as it was. A tendency to maintain the status quo was conspicuous in each revision. Although the two drafts strengthened the position of the legislative branch, particularly the lower house of the Diet, both were negligent in their treatment of human rights. In the more conservative Plan A draft, Article 19 of Chapter Two, on rights and duties of subjects, remained unchanged from the Meiji Constitution, while Article 19 in Plan B simply said: "Japanese subjects are equal before the law. Japanese subjects may, according to qualifications determined in laws and ordinances, be appointed to civil or any other public office without discrimination."[25]

The neglect of human rights can be accounted for by the nature of Japanese constitutional scholarship under the Meiji Constitution. Prewar constitutional scholars, who made up the Matsumoto Committee, were mainly preoccupied with the study of a German-style theory of state structure, the national polity, and the organization of government, and paid little attention to human rights and their protection within such a political entity. Minobe Tatsukichi, the foremost liberal interpreter of the Meiji Constitution, is said to have commented at the committee's first plenary session that it would be sufficient if the constitution included one article regarding human rights stating that the rights and duties of Japanese subjects would be specified by law.[26]

The lack of concern for human rights was again reflected in the drafts prepared by Konoe and Sasaki. One item in both drafts which did differ from the Meiji Constitution was a provision for the equal treatment of foreigners. Konoe's draft stated: "The impression that subjects' fundamental freedom can be abrogated by the law shall be removed," and "it should be specified that as a principle foreigners, too, are to be treated equally as Japanese citizens."[27] Sasaki's draft contained the same provision regarding foreigners in the chapters on Japanese subjects. There was, however, no specific indication of whether the term "foreigners" covered anyone without Japanese nationality, or only former colonial subjects such as the Korean and Chinese residents in Japan.

It was a comment from George Atcheson that influenced the constitutional provision on the treatment of foreigners in Japan. On October 17, 1945, Atcheson received from Secretary of State James Byrnes a directive regarding an outline of fundamental provisions essential for a revised Japanese Constitution. This directive was later approved by SWNCC (State-War-Navy Coordinating Committee) and incorporated into a top secret document, SWNCC 228, "Reform of the Japanese Governmental System."[28] SWNCC 228, known for its outline of the emperor system in postwar Japan, also enumerated seven general objectives for the Japanese authorities to accomplish in order to reform the Japanese governmental system. Among these primary objectives was one referring to the equal treatment of non-Japanese, guaranteeing "fundamental civil rights to Japanese subjects and to all persons within Japanese jurisdiction." Atcheson perhaps conveyed these objectives to Konoe before the latter started his draft, which may account for Konoe's decision to incorporate the specific provision on equal treatment of foreigners without elaboration.

In spite of this possible influence from Atcheson, SCAP did not elucidate whether the constitutional protection of foreigners in Japan simply accorded with international laws or aimed at emancipating the second-class citizens of Japan's former colonies. Occupation authorities had not produced a consistent policy nor had they established a single agency with responsibility for the Chinese and Korean peoples in Japan; problems such as repatriation were handled by separate offices. For example, at an early stage of the Occupation, SCAP issued a series of directives which were rather sympathetic to the welfare of these non-Japanese peoples. One of these, issued on October 4, 1945, was to "abrogate and immediately suspend the operation of all provisions of all laws, decrees, ordinances, and regulations which . . . by the terms of their application, operate unequally in favor of or against any person by reason of race, nationality, creed, or political opinion."[29] In late November, SCAP also directed the Japanese government to insure that there would be no discrimination in employment policies.[30]

In spite of this encouragement from SCAP, the new election law, issued on December 17, 1945, which adopted universal adult suffrage for both men and women, ruled out former colonial subjects on the grounds that, upon Japan's acceptance of the Potsdam Declaration, their countries were no longer part of the Japanese empire.[31] Minister of Home Affairs Horikiri Zenjirō explained: "It is inappropriate to allow Korean and Taiwanese residents in Japan to participate in elections, since in principle they are supposed to have lost Japanese nationality upon Japan's acceptance of the Potsdam Declaration. However, since they will retain Japanese nationality until a peace treaty is concluded, the Japanese government would like to regard this matter as a temporary suspension of their suffrage rather than an immediate prohibition of it." In the special Diet session on the new election law, he even speculated that (based on principles of international law) Korean residents in Japan would eventually be allowed to choose whether or not they wanted to retain Japanese nationality.[32] For the moment, however, the status of Japan's former colonial subjects in Japan was unsettled.

It was the CIA's draft constitution that directed SCAP's attention to the significance of the issue of race in Japan's new supreme law. Once the draft was submitted to the hands of SCAP officials, there occurred no discussion between the original Japanese drafters and SCAP officials concerning the language's interpretation. It was solely up to SCAP, quite independent of the CIA's original intentions, to interpret the language. SCAP refused to translate the word "race" into the white-and-color American paradigm and instead made an attempt to define its applicability in an exclusive Japanese context. At one point, SCAP adopted an interpretation that the language would serve as an important educational tool for uprooting Japanese racial arrogance from the national psychology. However, SCAP must have felt a slight uneasiness when it chose to dictate that the Japanese shed their attitude of racial superiority, rather than letting the Japanese assume this task spontaneously. Some such uneasiness among SCAP officials inevitably and almost unconsciously blurred the language's meaning to the degree that it no longer meant much at all.

While working on the drafts, however, some members of the CIA did have contact with SCAP authorities. Suzuki met with Canadian diplomat and renowned historian of modern Japan E. H. Norman, who then served on the Allied staff. Norman and Suzuki discussed the possibility of establishing a constitutional monarchy in Japan, though Norman is said to have rejected the idea. Morito also met several times with George Atcheson to supply the latter with information on the socialist movement in Japan. There is no written evidence to indicate that these Western officials mentioned in their discussions the desirability of inserting the principle of racial equality in the new constitution.[33] When the final draft was ready and the CIA decided to submit it to SCAP for its opinion, Sugimori served as a liaison to SCAP because of his fluency in English. However, no member of the CIA was informed of the details of how he submitted the draft to SCAP, or whether it was translated into English by the time he brought it to SCAP.[34]

There is no official record from SCAP describing how the CIA draft was submitted. According to the personal account of Lt. Col. Milo E. Rowell, government section special assistant, the CIA draft was submitted to SCAP in mid-December of 1945 and translated by two different offices—the office of the Allied Translator and Interpreter Section of SCAP and the office of the

Political Adviser to the Secretary of State. On January 3, 1946, Rowell received both translations for his comments and took notice of the article on racial equality in the CIA draft. In his January 11 memorandum—an overall summary of the CIA draft—which Rowell submitted to the Chief of Staff, he concluded that "the provisions *included* [emphasis in original] in the proposed constitution are democratic and acceptable." Rowell officially praised the CIA for raising the issue of race as an appropriate subject for inclusion in a new constitution.[35]

In this memorandum, Rowell pointed out eight provisions in the draft as being "outstanding[ly] liberal": the sovereignty of the people; prohibition of discrimination by birth, status, sex, race, and nationality; worker benefits such as an eight-hour day, holidays with pay, free hospitalization, and old age pensions; a popular referendum; control of all finances by the Diet; the limit on the right to possess property in the light of the public welfare; land use for the best public interest; and the required enactment of the constitution in ten years. Rowell then recommended nine additional and revised principles for incorporation into the constitution before approval. Indeed, in this recommendation was the earliest SCAP reference to a clause on racial equality in the new constitution. Just as the diversity of opinion among the CIA members implies, Rowell's own perception of the meaning of the racial equality clause remains unknown—but there is one clue to a possible interpretation.

On January 1, 1946, the emperor issued the Imperial Rescript, publicly renouncing his divinity. In this rescript he denied the wartime propaganda of Japanese racial superiority deriving from the emperor's divine origin. This declaration was the first and only SCAP-supervised public statement that touched on the issue of Japanese racism as part of democratization.

> I stand by my people. I am ready to share in their joys and sorrows. The ties between me and my people have always been formed by mutual trust and affection. They do not depend upon mere legends or myths. Nor are they predicated on the false conception that the Emperor is divine, and the Japanese are superior to other races and destined to rule the world.[36]

Rowell received the translations of the CIA draft constitution only two days after the issuance of the Imperial Rescript. The timing may suggest that the drafts meant to him the liquidation of Japanese racial pride.

SWNCC 162/2, a secret report issued on January 8, 1946, by SWNCC's Subcommittee for the Far East, also reiterated the need to eradicate the extreme racial consciousness of the Japanese, which it connected with the cult of emperor-worship. It was essential to change Japan's prewar ways of thinking, such as class stratification, the glorification of the military, and a habit of subservience to authority, in order to attain the ultimate objectives of the Allied powers. Racial pride, the report claimed, was considered a problem since it was closely associated with a bid for world leadership. The report proposed the development of new attitudes more in line with the basic principles of democracy.[37]

In the SCAP draft, however, the applicability of the English word *race* to Japanese reality was unclear—just as the CIA had no definition of nondiscrimination in their draft constitution. But it was clear that the SCAP draft did not indicate a category based on skin color; it did not signify the racial difference between the Japanese and the whites. Instead, SCAP designated a specific group as racially oppressed—when it was in fact socioeconomically oppressed. SCAP too had no desire to introduce the egalitarian principle to Japanese soil.

On February 1, 1946, when the so-called Matsumoto draft prepared under the Shidehara cabinet was revealed in the newspaper *Mainichi*, MacArthur decided to have SCAP's Government Section prepare a draft constitution as a model for the Japanese government. At a meeting of the Government Section on February 4, 1946, Gen. Courtney Whitney stated that the section would sit as a Constitutional Convention the following week and should have a draft completed and approved by MacArthur by February 12. MacArthur had specified this date (Abraham Lincoln's birthday) because he would be meeting then with the Foreign Minister and Japanese government officials for an off-the-record discussion.[38] Twenty-one persons were assigned the task of writing a model draft. They were divided into nine small committees, with one to four members each, to write various parts of the constitution.

The so-called MacArthur draft was submitted to the Japanese government for approval on February 13 (February 12, American time), 1946. Article 6 in the several early drafts read: "All (natural [this word added here in handwriting to the typewritten texts]) persons are equal before the law. No discrimination shall be authorized or tolerated in political, economic, educational, and domestic relations on account of race, creed, sex, caste, or national origin."[39] In the final draft, Article 13, rendered with small revisions to former Article 6, appeared as follows: "All natural persons are equal before the law. No discrimination shall be authorized or tolerated in political, economic, or social relations on account of race, creed, sex, social status, caste, or national origin."[40]

The Civil Rights Committee, one of the nine small committees formed on February 4, 1946, acting on its own, drafted a chapter (Chapter III) on the rights and duties of the people. No record in the whole draft process indicates any extended discussion on the importance of racial equality, although provisions referring to it had been included ever since the first SCAP draft.[41]

Article 13 sparked an all-night session with the Japanese government on March 4 and 5, 1946. The Steering Committee disliked the term "caste," changing it to "social status."[42] The committee also shifted "national origins" (which might imply Koreans or Chinese living in Japan) to "family origin,"[43] thereby limiting the coverage intended by Article 13's "no discrimination" guarantee. Article 16 in the MacArthur draft guaranteed the equal protection of law to aliens. The Japanese did not oppose it. But the Far Eastern Commission in Washington, D.C. (the supreme organ of allied policy formulation toward occupied Japan, consisting of representatives of eleven—later thirteen—countries at war with Japan and charged with scrutiny of SCAP activities), intervened in the process and inquired of SCAP as to which people were to enjoy such rights. SCAP responded by including aliens in the final concept of "all of the people."

The MacArthur draft went through the Japanese Diet and the Far Eastern Commission and was given its final form in late October 1946. The final draft of the constitution included several provisions that made reference to equal treatment regardless of race and nationality. For example, Article 42 in Chapter Four in the February 13, 1946, MacArthur draft specified that "the qualifications of electors and of candidates for election to the Diet shall be determined by law, and in determining such qualification there shall be no discrimination because of sex, race, creed, color or social status." Though there is no record of debate regarding the presence of the term "race" in this clause, or of its meaning, in the final form, this provision reappeared as Article 44 with a few revisions that read that the qualifications of members of both houses and their electors should be fixed by law, but without "discrimination because of race, creed, sex, social status, family origin, education, property, or income."[44] Article 14 in the final draft (Article 13 in the February 13 MacArthur draft), with the changes in wording described above and a few other minor revisions, now read as follows: "All of the people are equal under the law and there shall be no discrimination in political, economic, or social relations because of race, creed, sex, social status, or family origin."[45]

No SCAP staff member ever questioned what was guaranteed here. In the process of the CIA's drafting, several members of that association vaguely interpreted the principle of racial equality as supporting either Wilsonian idealism with some socialist spirit or the supposed glorious legacy of Pan-Asian benevolent egalitarianism. The concept as applied to Japanese society became even more obscure to Americans.

Article 14's nondiscrimination provision based on sex improved women's legal status considerably, but the "race [*jinshu*]" provision changed virtually nothing since there was no clue as to *whose* racial status was being protected, in what ways, and by what means.[46] The place of ethnic minorities and former colonial subjects in Japanese society was never discussed by either the CIA or SCAP, except for the *burakumin*, or what SCAP understood as the "outcasts" in Japanese society. Instead, the Japanese and the Americans collaborated to restore the kind of racial hierarchy that had existed in the days of Japan's colonialism. As the Cold War in Asia loomed, this common American-Japanese attitude toward the Asian minorities did not change. On the contrary, with the establishment of the North Korean government and the People's Republic of China, Japanese racist attitudes toward these Communist Asian neighbors were openly condoned and even encouraged by SCAP.

If SCAP's objection to Japan's racism against other Asian peoples was diluted in the Cold War environment, it was also further impaired by its own misreading of age-old discriminatory patterns in Japanese society. Beate Sirota, a member of SCAP's Civil Rights Committee, was quoted in an article in a Japanese journal as saying that the nonracial discrimination clause in the draft constitution originated neither in a denunciation of Japanese racial pride nor in a more universal ideal, but in the context of the particular Japanese problem of the *burakumin*, or social outcasts. This presentation of Japanese racism was misleading.

The origins of the *burakumin* go back to ancient times; they inherited occupations that were designated in Shinto and Buddhist concepts as being filthy and degrading (e.g., butchering, leather work, and so on). During the Tokugawa period, the government made the status of the *burakumin* hereditary and imposed discriminatory measures on them, such as residential segregation and a restriction against intermarriage with other classes—condemning them, in short, as social pariahs. It is important to note that the *burakumin* were never racially or ethnically different from other Japanese; this was socioeconomic discrimination. The outcast designation was officially abolished in 1871 and the *burakumin* given legal equality with other such groups as the samurai, peasants, and artisans. But in practice, social discrimination continued in the workplace, in housing, and in the institution of marriage. In March 1922 a group known as the Suiheisha (Leveling Society) was established with some two thousand members. The aim of this group was to abolish all discrimination in political, economic, and social aspects through the *burakumin*'s own efforts, rather than through government directives. The Suiheisha gradually linked their movement with the Marxist, proletarian class struggle, but with limited success. In 1936, Matsumoto Jiichirō, leader of the Suiheisha and himself *burakumin*, was elected to the Imperial Diet.[47]

Even during the war, Americans had focused on the phenomenon of the *burakumin* as an example of Japanese racism, ignoring—or turning a blind eye to—the racism inherent in Japan's colonialist attitude toward Koreans. This myopia led to at least one instance of downright confusion. The Psychological Division of the U.S. State Department mistakenly portrayed the *burakumin* in a 1942 State Department report, "The *Eta*: A Persecuted Group in Japan," as a special racial group of Korean origin which formed a weak point in Japanese social solidarity. The report claimed that because prejudice against the *burakumin* took many forms, such as a taboo on intermarriage, limitation of occupations, name calling, and so on, "[The] *Eta* develop certain personality traits, especially that of carrying a chip on the shoulder, in regard to possible discrimination."

The report carried its mistaken case even further. In Section XII ("Notes to Anyone Using This Material"), the report suggested that this persecuted group could be used to prove that the Japanese did not regard all Asiatics as brothers, especially considering the "fact" that "all *Eta* are of Korean origin." The treatment of the people of Korea, part of the Japanese empire, was just as inconsistent with Japan's Pan-Asian idea of brotherhood as was the persecution of the Japanese *Eta*. The report recommended using the ostracism of this group as an effective propaganda weapon to offset Japan's war propaganda on American racism. The report also made the following argument on the congruent conditions for minority groups in both societies: The Japanese government does not officially recognize any distinction between *Eta* and non-*Eta*; therefore, these people, not the Japanese government, should be held responsible for their own disadvantageous conditions to a certain extent. This reasoning should also be applied to conditions in the United

States, where the U.S. government makes no legal distinction between citizens of different racial or social backgrounds. This fact subsequently proves, concluded the report, that "the Japanese need throw no stones at the United States in regard to 'racial' and social prejudices."[48] The report thus drew a parallel in Japanese and American societies: it did not condemn Japanese racism but rather Japan's hypocrisy in condemning American racism.

Just as this 1942 State Department report was erroneous in using the term "racial" in regard to this problem, it is probably the case that the Civil Rights Committee chose to single out the status of the *burakumin* as the only example of Japan's racism. Further confusion stems from the use of the term "caste" (which would have been appropriate to the *burakumin*) in an early draft. Such attention within SCAP did not, of course, improve the status of the *burakumin* in the Occupation.

Matsumoto Jiichirō, the *burakumin* who was first elected to the Diet in 1936, continued his antidiscrimination movement during the war, officially questioning Japan's ideology of racial superiority, be it over the *burakumin*, the Ainu people, or the Chinese, as an obvious contradiction to the true spirit of Pan-Asianism. In November 1945 he joined the newly founded Japan Socialist Party, and in February 1946 he founded the National Committee for Burakumin Emancipation (Burakumin Kaihō Zenkoku Iinkai) and became chairman of the group. In April 1947, in Japan's first postwar election, he was again elected to the Diet, winning nationwide support for his democratic creed; he was subsequently appointed vice chairman of the Upper House. In his speech of acceptance, Matsumoto expressed his hope that a new Japan would stand for the principle of equality under the law, as guaranteed in Article 14 of the new constitution.

His vehement antidiscrimination campaign, his protest against the institution of the emperor as the source of Japan's ultranationalism, and especially his left-wing ideology increasingly disturbed SCAP. Based on Matsumoto's alleged wartime affiliation with the Headquarters for the Yamato Patriotic Movement (Yamato Hōkoku Undō Honbu), the ultranationalist organization, SCAP attempted to place him on a purge list. When Matsumoto denied a connection, SCAP withdrew his name for lack of evidence. But Prime Minister Yoshida Shigeru persuaded SCAP to reverse its decision and to purge Matsumoto anyway. In January 1949, Matsumoto was officially dismissed from public office. Only in May 1953, after the Occupation was officially over, was Matsumoto again elected to the Diet, where once more he continued to press the Upper House for the emancipation of the oppressed.[49]

The democratization program in the Occupation was equally disappointing for the Ainu people. In January 1946, Takahashi Makoto, an Ainu, started the Institute of Ainu Problems (Ainu Mondai Kenkyūjo) and Ainu Shimbun Sha (the Ainu Newspaper Company) and asked for SCAP's help in improving the status of the Ainu people. A group of other leaders in Hokkaido formed the Association of the Hokkaido Ainu (Hokkaidō Ainu Kyōkai) in February 1946 to heighten racial consciousness and to struggle against discrimination. In the spring 1946 election, three Ainu candidates also ran unsuccessfully for the national Diet. Takahashi himself submitted a petition to one Officer Bruce, a commander of the 77th Division, for the return of lands in Hokkaido confiscated by the Meiji government in the late nineteenth century for the purpose of colonization. Contrary to Takahashi's request for SCAP support in retrieving confiscated land, the land reform program forced the Ainu to part with 34 percent of their remaining lands in Hokkaido. A SCAP memo on October 23, 1947, described a visit to SCAP by Miyamoto Inosuke, chief of Shiraoi village, the largest Ainu community in Hokkaido, who asked for improvements in his community. His request did not receive serious consideration from SCAP at all.[50] Occupation programs had little effect on their welfare.

The only incident that shows an interest by SCAP in the cause of Ainu independence had an odd twist. In the spring of 1947, a Col. Joseph M. Swing asked the Ainu leaders to consider independence from Japan as indigenous natives of Hokkaido. When the leaders saw no immediate benefit in doing so and subsequently turned down the plan, he advised them never to attempt to do so in the future, nor to act in any way that was not in the Japanese government's interest, and donated some hundred thousand yen to their association. The Ainu leaders later suspected that the American proposal for their secession from Japan was a plan to gain control over their new land and to utilize it as a U.S. strategic base in Hokkaido against the Soviet Union.[51]

The situation for Okinawans was different from that of other minorities because the islands fell to U.S. forces in June 1945 and after Japan's defeat were placed under U.S. military jurisdiction. A wartime study prepared by Dr. John W. Masland Jr. for the U.S. Department of State between April and July 1943 had suggested several plans for the postwar disposition of Okinawa based on the racial affinity between the Japanese and the Okinawans. On the other hand, another paper presented by the Navy in October 1944 pointed out that the Japanese did not consider the Okinawans as racially equal—and therefore the United States might use this attitude to justify its control of the island in the eyes of the Japanese. Another paper, *Civil Affairs Handbook*, prepared by three cultural anthropologists at the Institute of Human Relations at Yale University and issued in November 1944, laid out a plan to rule the 450,000 "uncivilized" Okinawans under U.S. control, but separately from its rule over Japan proper.[52] It recommended that the military government place the Okinawans under strict colonial administration while the Japanese were given a more enlightened and democratic military occupation. The Americans saw Okinawans as racially inferior to Japanese, a view that was used to justify the separate American rule in Okinawa, which continued until the early 1970s.[53]

The defeated Japanese, for their part, reinforced the view of the Okinawans as non-Japanese outsiders and were ready to dispense with them. But the Okinawans living in Japan protested when the newspaper *Asahi* reported in the summer of 1946 that the repatriation program for Okinawans was almost complete along with those for the Korean and Chinese peoples. They demanded an explanation of when and how they had become non-Japanese and why they had to repatriate like the people of Japan's former colonies.

One letter from an Okinawan who worked at Japan's Ministry of Transportation in Tokyo demanded a definition of "non-Japanese." Was the term legal or racial (*minzoku-teki*)? The letter pointed out that although the Okinawan people may not be *naichi-jin* (the people of Japan proper), they were not very different either. Then he protested, "We have been made non-Japanese." The letter reminded Japanese readers that Japan lost Saipan and saved its four main islands at Okinawa's expense. If the Okinawans are forgotten, the letter continued, Japan's democratization cannot be completed.[54]

Another letter from an Okinawan living in Kyushu also pointed out the Japanese government's continuing hypocrisy toward Okinawa. The Okinawans suffered the worst sacrifice in waging the war, yet were proud of being Japanese. Now the Japanese government was attempting to expel the Okinawans as outsiders, terminate its responsibility to Okinawa's war casualties, and unload its material and psychological burden. "I am simply appalled," the writer continued, "wondering how we will ever reconcile our great sacrifice in the war with such humiliation."[55] Neither the peace treaty draft nor the constitutional draft seemed to be capable of answering such letters, though both attempted to deal with the issue of racial discrimination.

The Koreans—who made up 93.1 percent of all foreigners in Japan—suffered a complex and multiple discrimination under the Occupation as a result of the combined racist attitudes of the Japanese and Americans and the political turmoil in their country, especially in North Korea. In fact, both the United States and Japan found it to their mutual interest to squeeze this largest minority group out of the Japanese legal system while enhancing the concept of Japan's homogeneity for the sake of tightening national security. The presence of racial, ethnic, and cultural minorities with heterogeneous ideas, ideologies, and value systems became harmful to the integrity of a nation joined with the United States in the Cold War. SCAP's priority was for a racially and culturally "pure" Japan, where its much-prized dualistic identity, upon which its affiliation with the West was awarded, was expected to flourish.

Koreans in Japan were the worst victims of such "racial and ethnic purification" policies, which culminated in the new immigration and naturalization laws depriving them of the right to become Japanese citizens. By the time the Occupation reached its conclusion, the Koreans had become "permanent resident aliens," removed from the legal protection accorded to only Japanese nationals. Having therefore lost most of its potential beneficiaries, the language of racial equality in the new Japanese constitution was now totally hollow.

Japan's annexation of Korea in 1910 gave quasi-Japanese citizenship to the Koreans as well as the right to vote in Japanese elections. However, colonial subjects were never accorded the same status as Japanese citizens, since the Imperial government maintained a separate family registry (*koseki*) system for those of Japanese ancestry (*naichi-jin*) and the nationals of colonial origins (*gaichi-jin*). The place where a family registry was initially recorded was a person's permanent address, which also identified his or her national origin. Thus, social discrimination continued.[56] By 1925 the Korean population in Japan rose to 129,870, including approximately 106,000 laborers, 2,600 students, and 200 intellectuals. In official Japanese documents they were described as "lazy, who use their extra money for gambling and sake, and make no effort to improve themselves."[57]

In occupied Japan, Korean and Chinese residents continued to face harsh realities while in principle protected by the series of SCAP decrees. In April

1945 about 135,000 Koreans were working in Japanese coal mines as forced laborers. At the end of the war, the Japanese government estimated that, in addition to 30,000 Taiwanese Chinese and 30,000 mainland Chinese, there were about two million Koreans in Japan. The Korean community in Tokyo moved quickly to realize their emancipation and on August 18 organized the Committee for Korean Community Affairs, a liaison office which would negotiate with both the Japanese authorities and SCAP over issues such as reparation arrangements and the welfare of Koreans in Japan during the transitional period.[58] These Koreans, together with Chinese forced laborers, demanded improved working conditions as well as passage home. In view of the urgent need to maintain Japanese coal production at a high level, SCAP kept Korean forced laborers on the job until they could be replaced by Japanese. In response to the growing discontent of Korean laborers, in late October 1945 SCAP directed the Japanese government to make emergency arrangements for easy remittance of their savings to Korea and their deposit into a special account with the Bank of Japan. However, Korean and Chinese laborers refused to continue working, leaving the coal fields either for repatriation or for other parts of Japan.[59]

The legal status of those Koreans who remained in occupied Japan was confusing. Well over one-fifth of the Koreans in Japan chose to remain rather than attempt to start a new life in Korea, which had been divided and administered separately by the Soviet Union and the United States since August 11, 1945. In the October 31, 1945, order (SCAPIN 217), China was defined as a nation in the United Nations category along with other Allied nations. The name Korea did not appear in any category of nations—United Nations, neutral, or enemy—nor in "nations whose status has changed as a result of the war." Koreans immediately protested and demanded that they be included in the category of the most-privileged United Nations nationals living in the occupied country, which would mean that they could enjoy supplementary rations, tax exemption, and other perks like any of the Western allied nations. In response, SCAP explained that creating a form of extraterritoriality for Koreans in Japan was against occupational policy. SCAP subsequently gave them the same legal treatment that was accorded to the Japanese—"defeated nationals."[60]

Although the Koreans were allowed to retain Japanese nationality until Japan regained sovereignty, the Japanese of course did not treat them as equals. Under the December 17, 1945, election law, as we have seen, former colonial subjects lost the suffrage accorded to them during colonial times.[61]

In the Japanese perception, such a loss did not place them in the category of *gaijin*, or foreigner, either. Since the Japanese word *gaijin* was the euphemism reserved exclusively for Caucasians, or Westerners, but never indicated other Asians or other non-Westerners, *gaijin* in the Occupation meant only the Westerners who enjoyed privileges within the Occupation. Thus the Koreans were dubbed *dai-sangoku-jin* (the third national), neither Japanese nor *gaijin*.[62]

A series of contradictory SCAP decrees defined the temporary legal status of the Koreans who remained unrepatriated, but Japanese attitudes toward the Koreans became worse than they had been in the prewar years. Now Koreans were no longer colonial subjects but foreigners who opted to stay in troubled Japan. Japanese government officials as well as the mass media saw them as a societal burden, adding to food shortages, unemployment, housing problems, and other ills. The Japanese feeling about Koreans was expressed in an editorial in the newspaper *Tokyo Mainichi* for July 13, 1946: "The way the Koreans assume that they are liberated nationals, and therefore conquerors, frankly disgusts the Japanese."[63]

The Cold War quickened American support for the revival of Japanese dual identity, but it adversely affected the status of Koreans in Japan. Many Korean Communists were active in the new nationalistic movement, which caused a security problem, especially after the establishment of the North Korean government in the fall of 1948. Their alleged ties with the Japan Communist Party, which had in the prewar period advocated the liberation of Korea from the yoke of Japanese imperialism, led both SCAP and the Japanese government to suppress their activities as subversive mob actions. The Japanese hatred of Koreans was condoned and even justified in the name of security.

In the crackdown on the Korean community, education became a political weapon and Korean children were the most vulnerable victims. By the spring of 1946, Zai-Nichi Chōsen-jin Renmei (Chōren), or the Korean Resident League in Japan, under the "de-Japanization program," developed an overall educational program, which included not only the Korean language but history, geography, and other subjects, all taught in Korean. By the end of 1946 there were 525 schools, 62,000 students, and 1,500 teachers under this autonomous Korean educational system. In some instances, Japanese local school authorities permitted the part-time use of public school buildings for Korean education on the grounds that they were taxpayers.[64] However, the

Korean autonomous education system faced gradual regulation starting May 2, 1947, the day before the new constitution went into effect, when the Japanese government, upon a suggestion from SCAP, issued an Alien Registration Order for "administration and control purposes." It required all foreigners except Occupation personnel to register as alien and to carry an identification card at all times.

On October 13, 1947, SCAP issued another order to integrate the Korean schools into the overall Japanese education system. SCAP empowered the Japanese government to make sure that Korean schools met legal standards set by the Japanese Ministry of Education. Because of its opposition to a SCAP-approved history textbook *Kuni no ayumi* (Our Nation's Progress), which euphemistically explained Japan's colonialism in Korea as a cooperation between Japan and Korea and failed to criticize the institution of the Emperor, the Chōren demanded a separate history education for Korean children and refused to register its schools with Japan's Ministry of Education.[65]

Five days before the official deadline for closing the Korean schools that refused to comply with the new governmental regulation, violence broke out in the city of Kobe, where the Japanese police dispersed Korean protesters and some Japanese sympathizers who had gathered at the prefectural governor's headquarters for negotiations. After this incident, the local U.S. military commander, suspecting a Communist link to the protest, proclaimed a state of limited emergency. The Kobe police were deputized under the direction of the U.S. marshal and at midnight on April 24, a sweeping "Korean hunt [*Chōsen-jin gari*]" began. Military police arrested everyone who looked Korean in that region and threw them into the basement of a building adjacent to the downtown department store. The following day, children in the Korean elementary school were forced out of the building in the middle of class and the school entrance was nailed shut.[66]

Other violent protests spread to various cities in Japan. An incident in Osaka on April 28, in which SCAP authorized a "shoot-and-kill" policy in case of disobedience to the authorities, resulted in bloodshed. Forty-one protesters were arrested and ten severely wounded; a sixteen-year-old Korean boy was shot to death and a fourteen-year-old Korean girl was assaulted by a policeman, fell into a coma, and later died.[67]

No newspaper published these facts about the deaths of two Korean youths because of SCAP's strict censorship. Articles discussing Korean rights were routinely censored, in part because of an alleged Moscow-oriented

Communist plot. An article written by Kaji Wataru, a Communist critic, on Japan's colonialism in Korea and the aftermath of the Kobe and Osaka incidents received a SCAP order to delete the following paragraph:

> Why does the Japanese government create such a problem? [Because] the Koreans should not be Korean [in Japan]. . . . Korean, taught in the Korean language, is harmful to the national security. Indeed, in the days of Japan's imperialism, Koreans were slaves who were forced to forget their mother country. . . . Their national identity was certainly regarded as harmful to the security of the Empire. The recent incidents revealed that such a mode of thinking is completely preserved by postwar bureaucrats as well as by the conservative ruling class in Japan.[68]

Chang Du-sik, a Korean writer and journalist who had lived in Japan since he was seven years old, wrote an article which appeared in the same magazine. The following paragraph was deleted:

> [The proliferation of Korean schools in Japan] indicates our deep and passionate concerns for education for our own children as well as the amount of effort we put to realize them. How could the Japanese authorities close down our schools with a single order [without consulting our opinions]. . . . Why are we Koreans not allowed to educate our children in our own language? Why could the self-righteous action by the Japanese authorities determine our future unilaterally? Someday, we shall wipe away this Japanese sense of superiority.[69]

In the aftermath of the Kobe and Osaka incidents, during the special inquiry session at the Lower House, Prime Minister Ashida Hitoshi blamed those Koreans who opted to remain in Japan for their criminal tendencies and reiterated that there was a need to crack down on them. He also asserted his cabinet's determination to punish any violent mob acts in full cooperation with SCAP.[70]

Morito Tatsuo, an original member of the CIA and now minister of education, sympathized with the desire of the Koreans to have their own educational system, but he believed they should follow Japanese laws. Pacifism and democracy were the goals of Japan's education, he said, as manifested in the Basic Law of Education of 1947. Therefore, "our neighboring race [*rinpō no minzoku*]" should benefit from it. Morito advised Japanese schools to welcome their neighboring youths (*rinpō no shitei*) so they would face no racial discrimination (*minzoku-teki sabetsu*). He concluded by saying that if East Asia was to develop as a peaceful region, it was imperative for neighboring countries to cooperate with one another. Morito promised that the Ministry of Education would do its best to see that the children of both countries moved hand in hand toward the goals of peace and democracy.[71]

Japanese governmental control over the Koreans' "autonomous education" became especially harsh after the establishment of the North Korean government in September 1948. There was no public debate over the peaceful coexistence of Korean and Japanese children, and there was little inclination to encourage them to join together. Instead, the Japanese displayed marked hostility toward Korean children. Korean children in Korean schools in Japan were portrayed as rebellious and lagging far behind Japanese students in every subject, especially science, as well as making no effort to get along with the Japanese. One article that appeared in the newspaper *Yomiuri* in the summer of 1952 even ridiculed the way the children pronounced each other's names in Korean and portrayed a certain accredited Korean school in Tokyo as being a hotbed of "Red" indoctrination.[72]

SCAP recognized the problem and began (between May and July 1949) to consider a change in policy concerning Koreans in Japan. Two SCAP sections submitted separate recommendations to the Chief of Staff. The recommendation submitted by the Legal Section on June 9, 1949, proposed two alternatives for the "elimination" in Japan of the Korean minority as a group—repatriation or assimilation.

Japanese sentiment was definitely against assimilation.[73] In a Lower House session held on May 1, 1948, Attorney General Suzuki Yoshio accused the Koreans of starting systematic riots, despite the generous governmental policy. Suzuki emphasized the Japanese government's humanitarian policy in assisting those who wanted to return to Korea. He even went so far as to praise Japan for its generosity in allowing them to remain in Japan. Therefore, should they choose to do so, they would have to observe Japanese laws and perform their duties. Suzuki angrily concluded: "Only on that condition will the Japanese government allow them to lead a healthy life in Japan."[74]

Both the U.S. and Japanese governments, having no illusions about Japan's unwillingness to assimilate minorities, considered sending the Koreans back to South Korea as the only way to solve the problem. The idea of deportation was not new. When Lt. Gen. Robert Eichelberger, commanding general of the Eighth Army, took charge during the state of emergency in the

Kobe incident, he deplored the "uncivilized" mob violence of the Koreans and said, "I wish I had the *Queen Elizabeth* here to ship the whole lot of them to Korea."[75] By this time the United States and Japan had become close enough to make a joke about their mutual disdain for Koreans.

Prime Minister Yoshida wrote a letter to MacArthur, in late August or early September of 1949, suggesting a massive deportation of all Koreans in Japan as the most efficient approach to the problem. Yoshida argued that approximately a million Koreans, of whom about one half were illegal entrants, were a burden on Japan's economic growth. Their presence added extra pressure to Japan's population problem and worsened the food situation. Furthermore, a great majority of them were not contributing at all to the economic reconstruction of Japan, and many were Communists, "prone to commit political offenses of the most vicious kind."

Citing an alleged total number of 71,059 Korean criminal cases with 91,235 Koreans involved in the period between August 15, 1945, and May 31, 1948, Yoshida suggested that, in principle, all Koreans should be repatriated at the expense of the Japanese government. Those who wished to stay in Japan could do so only with permission from the Japanese government. Permission, however, would be granted only to those who were capable of contributing to Japan's economic reconstruction. In conclusion, he stated that upon receiving SCAP approval, he would submit to SCAP the budgetary appropriation and other measures to carry out his plan.[76]

SCAP approved Yoshida's plan. By September 9, 1949, a staff study at the Diplomatic Section, headed by William Sebald, submitted a recommendation on the repatriation of all Koreans as a solution to their problem in Japan. In a draft letter to Yoshida, Sebald reconfirmed SCAP's encouragement on the large-scale repatriation of Koreans to their own country because the excessively large number of Koreans represented a burden on the Japanese economy. While suggesting a negotiation between Japan and South Korea for a general settlement, Sebald promised Yoshida that any proposals concerning repatriation would be given full consideration.[77]

At about this time, the Japanese government began to prepare the enactment of new immigration and naturalization laws under the auspices of SCAP. The early peace treaty draft by the Foreign Ministry's special committee, made between late 1945 and early 1946, intended to allow former Japanese colonial subjects an option to retain Japanese nationality. However, unlike the Versailles Treaty, which regulated the postwar status of former colonial subjects of the defeated nations, the San Francisco Peace Treaty did not refer to the postwar legal status of its former colonial subjects. After the San Francisco peace conference, SCAP arranged diplomatic negotiations for Japan to sign a separate treaty with South Korea for the settlement of issues, including the status of Korean residents.

There was little consensus at the Japanese official level on this matter. On October 29, 1951, Diet member Sone Eki (Japan Socialist Party, Right faction) made an inquiry at the Upper House Special Committee on the governmental principle involved in the Korean minority issue. He said independent Japan should avoid a minority problem—the problem of people who do not assimilate. Sone argued that the desirable course would be to give the Koreans and other former colonial subjects a choice of nationality. For those who did not choose Japanese nationality, he suggested repatriation.

Prime Minister Yoshida was reluctant to allow Koreans to choose to become Japanese nationals and stay permanently. The prewar policy of assimilation—including the adoption of Japanese names for colonial subjects—made some Koreans look like Japan's "aboriginals [dochaku-ka shite iru]" and some, Yoshida admitted, were completely Japanized. However, selectivity in allowing their naturalization was important lest those who were unassimilable caused Japan to suffer. Yoshida continued: "We have to be especially careful in avoiding the creation of a minority problem which so many other countries are having difficulty with. . . . So I would like to remain cautious about this issue."[78]

Negotiations for a Korean-Japanese Treaty of Friendship began in Tokyo on February 15, 1952, with SCAP acting as observer. Items on the agenda included the status of Korean residents in Japan. The negotiations became deadlocked owing to disagreements on the issues of fishing rights off the Korean coast and Japanese property claims. On April 25, three days before the San Francisco Peace Treaty went into effect, the negotiations broke off and were suspended until April 1953.[79]

Koreans in Japan were now doomed to become stateless aliens—foreigners eligible for neither Japanese nationality nor immigration status. They were allowed national health insurance and unemployment compensation but were denied access to public housing, child welfare, and other social benefits. On April 19, the attorney general of Japan had issued an ordinance stating that all former colonial subjects would lose Japanese nationality upon enactment of the San Francisco Peace Treaty on April 28 and thereafter would be treated as aliens. Only those who had kept their family registry in Japan through such arrangements as marriage and adoption would be allowed to retain Japanese nationality. Those who automatically lost their Japanese nationality on April 28 but hoped to gain it back would do so through a regular naturalization process under the terms of the new Nationality Law (Law No. 147) enacted on May 4, 1950.[80] The avenue to naturalization was not entirely closed, but the eligibility rule was so rigid that only a limited number of Koreans could qualify.

On the day the San Francisco Peace Treaty went into effect (April 28, 1952), the Japanese government enacted two separate laws concerning the status of aliens in Japan: the Immigration Control Law and the Alien Registration Law. The Immigration Control Law of 1952 regulated the entry of foreigners into Japan, the Ministry of Justice's issue of visas and passports, and the deportation of certain undesirable aliens. Like the Nationality Law of 1950, this new immigration law was not applicable to most Koreans in Japan, as they had already established residence without having been issued passports. To provide a provisional ruling for the Koreans' status in Japan, the government issued a separate supplementary law "the Disposition of the Law and Orders Related to the Ministry of Foreign Affairs by the Acceptance of the Potsdam Declaration" (Law No. 126). At least this law allowed temporary residency to those who had entered Japan before September 1, 1945, and established their residence since then and that of their descendants born from that date until April 28, 1952. A child born after April 28, 1952, to such parents was required to obtain separate legal permission to reside in Japan at the time the parents applied for birth registration. This permission was valid only for a period of three years and was renewable subject to approval by the Ministry of Justice.[81]

The new Alien Registration Law (Law No. 125), which was substantially the same as the SCAP-enacted Alien Registration Law of 1947, required these foreign residents to apply for registration with the local government official within ninety days from their date of entry into Japan. As Koreans in Japan were placed on the government checklist, registrants were issued a Certificate of Alien Registration, which they were required to carry at all times (excluding children under the age of fourteen), and to present it to police officers and other public officials upon request.

The following secret memorandum of a conversation between the U.S. Defense Department staff and Japanese Ambassador Araki Eikichi on the occasion of the latter's visit to the Defense Department on August 20, 1952, clearly illustrates the solidarity of postwar U.S.-Japanese accord on the disposition of Korean residents in Japan.

Secretary [of Defense Robert] Lovett mentioned that the North Koreans are a particularly primitive and barbaric type of people, and he asked Ambassador Araki whether Japan had difficulties with the North Koreans when they held Korea. Ambassador Araki replied in the affirmative, indicating that all Koreans are the same.[82]

As the Cold War advanced in Asia, Japan was reappointed as the region's junior leader, and the idea of Pan-Asianism was restored. A tacit agreement betraying the constitutional language emerged between the occupiers and the occupied on the postwar status of minorities residing in Japan. Thus, Japan was allowed to preserve—and resume under the Cold War sanction of the United States—its presumption of superiority over other Asians. Also, Japan's racist wartime ideology, which had propelled atrocities against Asian soldiers and civilians alike, escaped scrutiny and condemnation.

Kiyose Ichirō, deputy chief of the Japanese defense counsel, offers a clue as to how the Japanese justified their own racism while deploring that of the West toward them in his eloquent opening statement at the Tokyo War Crimes Trial. Japan's militarism and Pan-Asianism were countermeasures against white racism, he explained. He went on to say that Japan's purposes were consistent with those advocated by Woodrow Wilson after World War I (i.e., independence, the abolition of racial discrimination, and democracy). He claimed that these were "universally subscribed to and cherished by the entire Japanese nation since the opening of Japan in 1853."[83] Pan-Asianism did not imply world conquest but respected the independence of every country, he continued, and he defended the ideology of the New Order as a way of abolishing racial discrimination between the white West and Asia. The New Order was never intended to be a racial plot against whites; it was instead a response to racial discrimination by whites. In lawyerly fashion Kiyose was able to shift the blame to his opponent. He concluded: "Whether the tragedy of modern wars might be due to racial prejudice or unequal distribution of natural resources or more misunderstanding between governments or the cupidity and covetousness of the favored or the less happy peoples, the cause must be ferreted out in the interests of humanity."[84]

Kiyose's search for the cause of modern wars was intended to serve the "interests of humanity." And the cause, as far as Kiyose was concerned, was planted squarely at the doorstep of the West. Kiyose could hardly admit that Japan had done anything wrong. Japan failed to meet the challenge of eliminating its racism on its own terms, while this neglect was a driving force in bringing the United States and Japan into consensus as powers in Asia. The form of racism inflicted upon the minorities during the Occupation was substantive and harsh in comparison to SCAP's treatment of the Japanese. While the politics of race between the United States and Japan was expressed mainly in terms of mutual images, the racism against these Asian minorities was implemented through a series of measures and laws that severely affected their political, socioeconomic, and cultural status in Japan. For these other Asians, racism was not merely an ambivalent image but a very real practice, spawning violent consequences. Japan's failure to confront its own racism against these Asians was not only an irony of the Occupation but a tragic mistake.

CHAPTER 4

Japanese Overseas Emigration

In the early years of the Occupation, the Japanese dream of creating a cosmopolitan region in Manchukuo was already a thing of the past. Instead, Japanese revised their prewar view that the great European capitals—Paris, London, Berlin—were the cosmopolitan centers of the world into one that equated Americanism with cosmopolitanism. This was a rebirth of the Japanese dream to become integrated into the Western world. Thus, emigration to the United States was now the most tempting path toward achieving this dream. The obstacles that kept this dream from becoming true, however, proved too intractable of many Japanese.

In matters of emigration and immigration, race has historically been a major consideration. Many countries have used eugenics theories to prevent the immigration of undesirable racial stocks for fear of weakening the biological quality of the mainstream population. Even when immigration is permitted, even in limited numbers, the old melting-pot idea in American life frequently restricts those newly immigrated who do not blend with the Caucasian races both physically and culturally. In the case of Japanese immigrants, even after they had established residence in American society, they continued to face exclusion in the antialien land law (ban on ownership of land) and the naturalization law (ban on acquisition of U.S. citizenship), in both cases because of race.

As we have seen, largely due to Cold War strategic considerations the United States moved to amend the Japanese exclusion clause of the 1924 Immigration Act and passed the McCarran-Walter Act of 1952, which allowed the Japanese (and other Asians) the privileges of naturalization as well as a token immigration quota. In doing so, American society invented a new concept of sociocultural assimilation that did not require a total biological blending. However, the implicit message of the annual immigration quota of a mere 185 persons was that America did not welcome an influx of Japanese immigrants. This harked back to the "gentleman's agreement" at the turn of the twentieth century, which required Japan's self-regulation in the name of mutual friendship.

Although the United States recognized Japan's ability to assimilate into Western civilization, the limited quota for Japanese immigrants was of course a blow to the Japanese dream of joining American society. Yet the Japanese were not particularly disheartened by these limitations because, after living with GIs during the Occupation, they had learned about rejection from the white community. In the name of mutual friendship, they pledged that they would not attempt to emigrate to the United States or any other region dominated by white emigrants, such as Canada and Australia.

Far from giving up their goal, Japanese emigration activists began an effort to turn their cosmopolitan dream into Western reality. They focused on undeveloped regions shunned and uninhabited by the whites as targets for Japan's new emigration. With American approval, they invented a new self-image as the most advanced colored race and declared their new mission to be the creation of a new civilization in undeveloped areas as surrogates for the whites. The new image of Japanese immigration overseas again reflected Japan's traditional dual identity—their cultural desirability or assimilability (a positive image as an advanced and democratic nation) and their racial undesirability or unassimilability (a negative image as individuals with a non-white physical appearance and skin color).

Based on such images, just as the Americans found a special niche for Japanese emigrants within American society, the Japanese tried to find those convenient vacuums in the racial cartography of the world where they would pose no threat to the West while they pursued their version of the cosmopolitan dream. The U.S.-Japanese accord on Japanese overseas expansion was to work hand in hand toward the advancement of world civilization in spirit only, while separate geographic spheres were maintained in order to preclude any physical interactions between Americans and Japanese.

The postwar dream of overseas emigration became a beacon of hope to Japanese living through the grim uncertainty of the Occupation years. There was no knowing how long the Occupation would continue[1] or even where their country was heading. In 1947 and 1948 the nation experienced a severe depression. Japanese industrial production lagged far behind capacity. Budget deficits were increasing while the inflation rate spiraled upward out of control. Living standards declined even below wartime levels. Most Japanese survived at a bare subsistence level. In addition, the Japanese were starving both culturally and intellectually. A country without sovereignty under the Occupation, Japan was not permitted to maintain diplomatic relations overseas or send people abroad. They lived without much contact with the world, except for the limited access allowed by SCAP. It was difficult to get books and journals from abroad because of censorship. Everything written by foreigners, including news by foreign correspondents in Japan as well as news from abroad, was censored and did not appear in its original form.[2]

The Japanese reached out for contact with the Western world. Because of the material hardships, they became more fascinated with the seeming affluence of the West. The great hit songs of these hard years, for example, reflect this popular yearning. In a 1947 blockbuster song, "Tōkyō Bugi [Tokyo Boogie]," Kasagi Shizuko sang about a provocative dance invigorated by a spirit of freedom and energy: "This Tokyo boogie is echoing all across the seas / The boogie dance is the world's dance. . . . / When you dance the boogie / the whole world is united as one/because the rhythm is the same / And the melody the same."[3]

The summer of 1947 brought the "Hawaiian boom" to Japan and Aloha (or Hawaiian) shirts became trendy, especially among young urban males. Hawaii had no lingering association with Pearl Harbor. Rather, it represented a romantic sentiment, almost a nostalgia, for the Pacific crossroads of East and West. In the summer of 1948 the entire nation hummed to the buoyant melody of another great hit song "Akogare no Hawai kōro [The dream voyage to Hawaii]" by Oka Haruo. The song tells of a ship's cheerful departure to Hawaii on a clear day, carrying passengers filled with hopes and dreams. In the following year 1949, a similar song "Amerika gayoi no shiroi fune [A white ship to America]" became another great hit. The lyrics tell of two young lovers on a hilltop watching a great white Pacific ocean liner leaving for the United States. The lovers talk about Hawaii as a place of dreams and watch the ship as if it were carrying on board their bright future to America.[4]

But the Japanese government looked beyond such popular romantic concepts toward a much more pragmatic aspect of expansion overseas. As soon as the war ended, the aforementioned Japanese Foreign Ministry's Executive Research Committee on Problems Concerning a Peace Treaty tried to secure the principle of racial equality between the Japanese and Westerners in the terms for peace. The motivation was not merely to restore national status. The committee regarded it as a crucial affirmation of the rights of Japanese emigrants to live and do business in the economically advanced regions populated by the whites, without racial discrimination.

A classical Malthusian concern proved to be an important incentive for their search for living space abroad. In fact, upon Japan's defeat about six million repatriates—demobilized soldiers as well as civilians—surged into Japan from its colonies. In addition, a total of 550,000 former colonial subjects residing in Japan—Koreans, Formosans, Chinese, and other Asians—opted to remain rather than return to their native countries.[5] Unless emigration overseas resumed as a population outlet, the country, stripped of its colonial empire, was physically incapable of supporting a suddenly increasing population.

Japan's own "baby boom" also added pressure to the population problem. With the return of large numbers of men, Japanese couples resumed having the children that had been postponed by the war. The National Eugenics Law, effective as of July 1941, prohibited birth control and encouraged large families. Most postwar families continued without any contraceptive methods or instruction in family planning. The "baby boom" peaked from 1947 to 1949, when the Japanese produced 7,500,000 babies—a number almost equal to the total population of Australia—more than 10 percent of the 1945 population. In 1947 the birth rate reached a peak of 34.8 per thousand—the highest ever recorded—compared to 31.7 during the war. At the same time, the death rate declined dramatically because the Occupation's public health program reduced deaths from tuberculosis and other respiratory diseases. It plummeted to 14.8 per thousand in 1947 and 12 per thousand in 1948, marking the lowest death rate in the history of Japan.[6]

The sharp population increase also seemed to upset the balance between population and industrial capacity. Because of the scarcity of raw materials and the limitation on overseas markets, it was unlikely that agricultural yield and industrial output could be increased to sustain a larger population. Therefore, gaining access to lands overseas for surplus population as well as to overseas trade markets became a vital issue for the nation's survival. Yet the idea of Japanese emigration to the Western nations on any massive scale was improbable because of Oriental exclusion policies. Emigration to neighboring Asian nations was even less likely.

The situation facing Germany and Italy was totally different from that of Japan despite the fact that they were also former Axis nations. Regarding overpopulation as a cause of poverty and deteriorating living standard for both Germany and Italy, the Western nations adopted overseas immigration as one solution and coordinated their efforts. Both the Yalta and Potsdam conferences had addressed the postwar disposition of refugees and surplus populations. According to the Allies' population survey in the summer of 1945, about eight million people in Germany, Austria, and Italy had been displaced from their homes in the conquered parts of Europe under the Nazis' forced labor recruitment policy. In addition, there were also the Jewish refugees, the victims of Nazi persecution who had survived the concentration camps. Anti-Communists had also fled before the Soviet advance across Poland and into Germany in 1944 and 1945.

The United States acted promptly in accordance with the United Nations. On December 22, 1945, President Truman announced a new program for the admission of 40,000 displaced Europeans a year into the United States. On the same day, he also authorized the resumption of German immigration to the United States, scheduled to begin at the end of 1945.[7] Under the leadership of the United Nations, a series of international emigration programs also began. Through the United Nations, the European nations discussed international cooperation to deal with the supply and demand of skilled human resources for mutual benefit across national boundaries. The recipient nations involved in these international discussions were the United States, Canada, Australia, and several nations in Latin America—those that historically had received European immigrants and opposed nonwhite immigrants.

Unlike other race-related issues, the Japanese were outspoken about the harm of the Oriental exclusion policy. As we have seen, Kiyose Ichirō, deputy chief of the Japanese defense counsel, argued at the Tokyo War Crimes Trial that Western racism was responsible for Japan's desperate military preparations before the fall of 1941. He stated plainly that the Japanese went to Manchuria because both Canada and the United States restricted Japanese immigrants and denied Japan room to expand. In Kiyose's argument, Japan's "advance" in Asia was self-defense by a country of small area with meager natural resources and a large population, when their emigration was restricted by most of the Western powers, many of which had found their own outlets in imperialist ventures.[8] When the newspaper *Yomiuri* interviewed Roger Baldwin, director of the American Civil Liberties Union, who visited Japan and Korea for a survey of civil liberties in these nations, the interview touched upon U.S. immigration laws. Although the portion referring to American racism was censored by SCAP and did not appear in print, in the precensored galley proofs Baldwin agreed that these laws should be abolished in the near future.[9]

The demand for a change in the Oriental exclusion policy was also shared by Japanese individuals. On July 20, 1947, shortly before the Foreign Ministry's Executive Research Committee submitted its final draft to SCAP, a member of the Japan Communist Party in Osaka, Yamada Hideo, gave MacArthur his personal agenda for the reconstruction of a peaceful Japan, including new rules on emigration and immigration.[10] Yamada listed twenty-five stipulations for a socialist revolution and the creation of a government "of the people, by the people, and for the people." In this list he included the right to free emigration overseas. He demanded fair treatment and free emigration side by side with other socialist ideals. For example, item nineteen says: "In order to maintain the people's healthy and peaceful life, the Japanese government will demand that every nation in the world allow Japan freedom of transportation [kōtsū], commerce, and emigration." Item twenty continues: "We the Japanese insist that any people [jinmin] of the world will not discriminate against us but treat us with equality and fairness." In conclusion, he declared that a new Japan would stand for peace and equality for all the people in the world.

It was the Overseas Emigration Association (Kaigai Ijū Kyōkai), a nongovernmental organization, which led in the promotion of overseas emigration for Japan. The perception of Japan as an overcrowded country with no natural resources prompted the organization's ardent demand for emigration. In addition, the people who rallied around the organization focused on emigration as a way to expand Japan's economic activities abroad and as a step toward the building of a nonmilitant mercantile world power.

These activists shared the traditional notion of overseas expansion as a source of national strength. Since the late nineteenth century, advocates of Japan's overseas emigration had argued that emigration and colonization were the means through which the European powers had acquired wealth, power, and prestige, and that Japan should follow suit. As Kiyose's defense argument indicates, the prewar rhetoric of Japan's overseas expansion often referred to the ideas of emigration and colonization interchangeably for overseas settlement, thus blurring the demarcation between a civilian enterprise and militant aggression. These postwar activists attempted to exonerate themselves of any imperialist ambitions. Along the line of the new rhetoric of democracy and cosmopolitanism, they advocated Japan's overseas emigration solely as a way to engage in commercial, financial, and industrial activities abroad and contribute to the construction of a better world community.

In the prewar period, such Japanese ambitions seemed to Americans to be a direct challenge to Western superiority, the historical notion of the yellow peril—a fear that Western civilization would be overrun and conquered by the yellow race. More specifically, they feared that an influx of Japanese immigrants would endanger the preservation of the Caucasian race on American soil. Such notions suggest a fatalistic belief that the two races could not share the same living space and that the expansion of the one's living space would lead to the other's eventual extinction. The Japanese emigration activists in the early postwar period totally discounted such race-related concerns. In their vision, Japanese cultural assimilability into Western civilization was the key to successful coexistence.

In the fall of 1947 a group of private citizens, mainly from business and finance, convened to discuss the issue. Thirty of the people who gathered at the first meeting had been associated with prewar emigration groups such as Rikkōkai (a Christian organization which in the Meiji period provided financial aid to Japanese students in the United States), Manchurian development organizations, and so on.[11] The group originally selected as their leader Reverend Kagawa Toyohiko, a world-renowned Christian social activist and pacifist, who before World War II had been involved in various projects to promote U.S.-Japanese friendship.

SCAP learned about the newly organized movement for overseas emigration while it was still in the preparation stage, and unofficially advised Kagawa to resign as its head. If he accepted the position, SCAP warned, he would be purged.[12] SCAP considered popular interest in overseas emigration to be a remnant of Japan's imperialistic expansionism—a manifestation of its racial ambitions—and sought to discourage anything that might draw attention to the issue of going abroad or making contact with the outside world. Discussions in the press of Japanese emigration remained taboo because of the inevitable references to America's own exclusion policies.

Travel overseas was strictly prohibited. Until the early half of 1948, the Japanese Foreign Ministry's record showed that besides those who served as witnesses and defense lawyers at the war trials held abroad, only a handful of people had been authorized by SCAP to leave Japan. In April 1946, Uemura Tamaki, a Christian activist who had attended both Wellesley College and the University of Edinburgh, was allowed to go to the Women's Conference for the North American Presbyterian Church. In October of the same year, three students from Jōchi (Sophia) University received a special invitation from the Vatican to study at Pontifical University in Italy. In April 1947, Morimizu Shuntarō, chief of the Japan Agricultural Research Institute, left Japan as a SCAP counselor to attend the International Food Conference held in India. In January 1948, Hase Shin'ichi, an expert on communication technology, went to Geneva to attend the International Wireless Communications Conference.[13] These travelers were very much the exception, hardly constituting a precedent for Japan's resumption of overseas activities.

SCAP censorship also prohibited the mention of Japanese contact with the outside world. Between November 1947 and June 1948, more than four articles in the newspaper *Yomiuri* were suppressed by SCAP because they reported the plans of various Japanese to go abroad, mostly to the United States. The stories about several Japanese-American entrepreneurs visiting Japan from Los Angeles and Hawaii with plans to introduce Japanese popular culture, including a sumo exhibition match, to American audiences were also omitted.[14]

SCAP had some reason to suspect a revival of militant expansionism enmeshed with the ambition for world conquest. A letter from a Japanese which arrived at MacArthur's office in March 1946, for example, informed SCAP of the survival of many who had been active in wartime expansion. During the war, the writer's school, the former Takushoku (immigration and colonization) University, had cooperated with militarists in training students to become colonial agents in China, Manchuria, and the South Sea. Though the university temporarily changed its name after the war to Kōryō University, the writer insisted that the main theme of the teaching remained the same—overseas invasion and aggression—and the school continued to be a hotbed of dangerous expansionists. Since the students at this university all seemed anxious to resume Japan's aggression with the help of militarists, the writer asked SCAP to crack down immediately on the university—otherwise, "the same teaching under the guise of a new name would continue to produce men with vicious ambitions."[15]

Those in the emigration movement recognized the importance of projecting a constructive image to the world and therefore worked to eliminate any militaristic (not to mention racial) connotations. Members of the emigration movement subsequently moved the first meeting to the Ginza Christian Church, hoping to emphasize their peaceful and pro-Western intentions.

On October 25, 1947—about three months after the Foreign Ministry completely abandoned the peace treaty draft containing the request of free emigration for Japan—the Overseas Emigration Association (Kaigai Ijū

Kyōkai) was officially established.[16] On October 31, twenty-eight members and six temporary members gathered at the Japan Industrial Club (Nihon Kōgyō Kurabu) for the first assembly. Matsuoka Komakichi, a leading member of the prewar labor movement, now a member of the postwar Japan Socialist Party as well as a member of the Diet since 1946, was elected president. Aware of Western opposition to their immigration, Japanese activists nonetheless were optimistic that Japan's transformation into a civilized, democratic, and peace-loving nation would prompt the West to drop its anti-Japanese racism and welcome Japanese immigrants. Just as Japan's prewar overseas expansion involved the rhetoric of a national mission to the world, Japan's postwar emigration movement emphasized an altruistic desire for the development of world industries.

At the first meeting, the members issued a basic agenda and Matsuoka Komakichi gave his inaugural address.[17] In sum, he portrayed Japan's new emigration as a welcome service to the world community. The organization focused on economic concerns. Overseas emigration played a crucial role because, in a land with no natural resources, it stabilized society by easing population pressures. More importantly, Japan's emigration activity was presented as altruistic because Japan would send its skilled immigrants to areas in need of development. They would go only where there was a demand for their skills. Cultural differences would not be a problem. With the enactment of the new constitution, Japan was stepping forward as a democratic, peaceful, and cultural nation (*bunka kokka*) like the leading Western countries. Therefore, as the Japanese became more cosmopolitan (a euphemism for "Westernized") in their identity and were perceived as such, they would find assimilation in the world much easier.[18]

Although Matsuoka did not mention the issue of race in his speech, he seemed to assume that Japan's sincere effort at cultural assimilation into Western civilization would be the fundamental solution to Western racism. The association resolved to help prepare the Japanese people for overseas emigration until SCAP approved a plan. To achieve these goals, the association began to provide the public with accurate information on immigration abroad. It also assumed the responsibility of educating future emigration applicants in becoming Westernized, or cosmopolitan, enough to qualify as immigrants (*ijū-sha ni fusawashii kokusai-jin*). In his inauguration address, Matsuoka explained that the reason for the prewar anti-Japanese racism lay in the fact that most Japanese immigrants were lower-class unskilled laborers who lacked intelligence and sophistication. The prewar world had judged

Japan's standard of civilization by the behavior of its immigrants—Matsuo-ka cautioned—so new Japan should not repeat the mistake of sending abroad hordes of ill-prepared Japanese unable to adjust to a higher standard of living.

The major difference between the approach of the association and that of the Ministry of Foreign Affairs was the absence from the agenda of the principle of racial equality with Western nations. The association never touched on the issue of Western racial bars against Japanese and other Asian immigrants as an obstacle. Rather, in the association's view, it was not American racism but the deplorably low quality of Japanese immigrants that was most responsible for the passage of the Japanese exclusion clause. They were, in effect, blaming the victim. The Japanese, unable to adjust to a superior American culture, caused their own exclusion.

The association's reticence about American racism may, however, have been simply a rhetorical tactic to placate SCAP. The Japanese had by then learned to accept the unwritten racial rules under the Occupation. They knew that any criticism of American, or Western, racism against the Japanese was taboo. The association perhaps opted to avoid the topic altogether in an effort to continue its campaign in the Occupation. Either way, the new Japanese immigrants would not demand racial equality. The association pledged to make Japan's new immigrants do their best with superior skills and a cosmopolitan (or Westernized) mindset so that they would be welcomed in host nations. It was up to the Japanese themselves to secure a good future. Japan had to improve every aspect of its national life and culture in order to produce citizens who were well-educated, intelligent, and socially responsible enough to blend well into Western civilization. Cultural assimilation meant everything—indeed, it was seen as a panacea for all the confrontations between races.

Thus, despite their noble mission to serve the welfare of the entire world, the image of Japanese immigration presented by the association was surprisingly low-key. They did not have any superior identity to boast of to the world. The only assertiveness retained in this new outlook was the steadfast belief in the superb quality of Japanese labor and skills. Yet the association never linked this idea to their race or to the racial issue. There was no manifestation of racial pride. On the contrary, perhaps their finest virtue would be seen to be their very willingness to assimilate into a "superior" culture.

Even with the complete absence of the race issue, it was hard to miss a strange gap in the argument. Although the association encouraged would-be Japanese immigrants to improve their culture and lifestyle to the level of the Western standard, there was no recommended plan for accomplishing this assimilation into the Western communities. What did it mean for immigrants to improve their culture and lifestyle in the Western manner? What would they do with their language and religion, for example? How about the problems of retaining Japanese customs and identity? Under what arrangement was it anticipated that the "cosmopolitan" Japanese would live in the Western community? Should they live in isolated communities, or should they seek wider integration? Should intermarriage with whites be encouraged? In the association's blueprint, what would a totally assimilable cosmopolitan Japanese really look and be like? Answers to these questions—real questions certain to come up once people actually began living on foreign soil—were nonexistent.

The Japanese government itself did little about the emigration movement. The Japanese Diet at least discussed the issue of overseas emigration on several occasions and demanded that the reluctant Japanese cabinet take some kind of action despite SCAP suppression. In mid-October 1947, one Diet member, Itaya Junsuke of the Japan Liberal Party, put several questions to the Upper House Committee on Foreign Affairs (Sangi-in Gaimu Iinkai). Itaya asked: When was SCAP most likely to lift the ban on Japanese traveling abroad? Was it true that a request had come from the Pará State Government of Brazil to send five million Japanese immigrants for the development of the region? And finally, was it true that Germany had already been permitted to start overseas emigration even before the conclusion of a peace treaty? Although the rumor about the German situation was indeed true, the representative of the government committee simply replied that he had never been informed of such allegations. He did not comment on the other two questions and declined to accept further inquiries in this regard.[19]

At a meeting of the Lower House Committee on Foreign Affairs on April 1, 1948, Kikuchi Yoshirō (Democratic Liberal Party) applauded the activities of the Overseas Emigration Association under the leadership of Matsuoka Komakichi, now chairman of the Lower House, and requested that the Japanese government start active petitions for foreign nations to accept Japanese immigrants.[20] Prime Minister Ashida Hitoshi, who had been in charge of drafting the Foreign Ministry's Executive Research Committee's peace treaty plan and was now head of the coalition cabinet, was by then vigorously promoting the import of foreign capital to aid Japan's economic recovery. Fully aware both of the strategic importance of emigration for Japan and the impossibility of such a movement under the Occupation, Ashida replied in a very cautious manner. He admitted that the twin issues of emigration and immigration had been one of great concern to the government. But he added that the government's decision was to withhold any official statement on the matter "due to various circumstances, until every related problem was solved." He requested the understanding of Diet members on this matter and ended any further inquiry.[21]

Six months later, on December 14, 1948, shortly before concluding the session at the Lower House Committee on Foreign Affairs, Baba Hideo (Japan Socialist Party) raised the issue of overseas emigration again.[22] He agreed that a discussion of the issue of emigration before the conclusion of a peace treaty was inappropriate. Yet, he argued, considering the seriousness of the population problem, Japan should make clear to the world that its insistence on the right to overseas emigration was not solely a matter of self-interest. Japan wished to use its surplus population for the reconstruction of the economy of other nations, making its human resources of use to the world community. To expedite the resumption of overseas emigration, Baba insisted that the Japanese government make a serious effort to convince the world of Japan's good intentions.

Ōno Katsumi, a cabinet representative for the committee, said that he fully agreed with Baba. But he suggested that the Japanese government remained unable to make any official statement, since world sentiment against Japanese overseas emigration was still so hostile, and no favorable Western response was anticipated. Ōno asked the Diet to realize that this was why the Japanese government had taken no step toward solving the issue.[23]

Despite the government's unwillingness to make any statement, the Overseas Emigration Association began a petition drive in June 1948 to heighten public awareness of the issue. The petition drive was especially successful with college students in the Tokyo metropolitan area. By early December 1948, the association submitted the petitions to SCAP, asking for an easing of restrictions and an understanding attitude toward Japanese emigration.[24]

On May 13, 1949, Tokonami Tokuji (Democratic Party, Opposition faction) and twenty-three other Diet members brought "the Resolution on the Population Problem" to the floor. It was the first official postwar statement on the issues of emigration and immigration. Citing population pressures as a crucial issue facing the nation, the resolution proposed three remedial policies—the promotion of industry, birth control, and overseas emigration.

More importantly, the resolution emphasized the positive effect overseas expansion would have on the world's image of a new democratic Japan.[25]

Sunama Ichirō, a member of the Communist Party, criticized the remarks on the resolution, including those on the emigration plan. He claimed that prewar Japanese military and financial cliques used population problems as an excuse for imperialistic invasion, which he said was directly responsible for the rise of the anti-Japanese movement in North America. The Communist Party would strongly oppose such an emigration policy as a tool for a new imperialism, he declared. But if Japan were to become a truly democratized peace-loving nation, he added, other democratic nations of the world would surely welcome Japanese immigrants in their societies. The key to the problem of emigration, he said, lay in the nature of the Japanese nation and people, not in the racial attitudes of host nations. Sunama thus seconded the resolution, provided that the democratization of Japan be constantly promoted along with the emigration program.

After Sunama's remarks, a vote was taken and the resolution passed unanimously. Hayashi Jōji, minister of welfare, remarked that the cabinet would establish a population problem council and start an investigation into the matter. But he made no reference to the emigration problem.[26]

Six months after the passage of this resolution, on November 17, 1949, Prime Minister Yoshida made the first official postwar statement regarding emigration activities. When Matsui Michio, a member of the Diet, inquired on the floor of the Upper House about the prospect of the resumption of emigration, Yoshida answered that he, too, wished that Japanese immigrants could go and be welcomed anywhere in the world and that he was happy to hear that the United States apparently planned to set an immigration quota for Japanese immigrants. Yoshida commended the past achievements of Japanese immigrants "who are industrious and assimilate quite well in their host countries." However, considering that Australia and some other nations remained suspicious of the motivation for Japanese emigration, Japan's insistence would only intensify their fears. Therefore, concluded Yoshida, Japan's priority was to work closely with the Allies so they would understand that the immigrants had truly peaceful purposes—seeking only to contribute to their host countries' growth—and that the Japanese people were democratic, peaceful, and peace-loving. Yoshida nonetheless added that the Japanese had a long way to go. In conclusion, he recommended the postponement of a national discussion on this matter until after the signing of a peace treaty.[27]

On March 18, 1950, the Overseas Emigration Association expanded its activities by establishing the National League of Technicians for Overseas Emigration (Kaigai Tokō Gijutsu-sha Zenkoku Renmei). The league held its first meeting at Kuramae Industrial Hall (Kuramae Kōgyō Kaikan) with Tomabechi Gizō (Democratic Party, Opposition faction)—once Chief of the Cabinet Secretariat in the Katayama cabinet and a member of the Lower House—as president. The league intended to pursue a twofold goal in Japanese overseas emigration. First, Japanese technicians working abroad would be especially devoted to exploring and developing the untapped raw materials of host nations. Second, they would contribute to improving the world's image of Japan. Once these goals were combined, the league's ambitious plan for Japan's overseas emigration would pave the way toward achieving Japan's century-old dream—that Japan would some day assume an honorable international status as a civilized, or cultural, nation (*bunka-teki kokka*) and achieve an important place in the world.[28]

Throughout the year 1950, political parties in Japan (with the exception of the Japan Socialist Party) gradually spoke up about the issue of Japanese emigration. The Liberal (*Jiyū*) and National Democratic (*Minshu*) parties issued agendas on basic principles they hoped would be discussed in the peace treaty. They demanded the recognition of Japan's right to free trade, a solution to the population problem, fair economic opportunities overseas, and overseas emigration for the purpose of sustaining the nation's economic level.[29]

The Japanese public, while more and more aware of the nature of Western racism surrounding them, nonetheless continued their fascination with the outside world. In an opinion survey conducted by the National Research Center on Public Opinion (Kokuritsu Yoron Chōsa-jo) in May 1950, 3,500 people were asked what would be the best solution for Japan's problem of overpopulation; 71 percent mentioned overseas emigration, compared to 56 percent who supported birth control.[30] In the same month, the Overseas Emigration Association began petitioning Japanese Diet members, asking them to press for the Japanese right of emigration in the context of the U.S.-Japanese Security Pact. The association sent petitions to about seven hundred Diet members. There was, however, little response from them.[31]

In July 1951, Ishibashi Tanzan became chairman of the association. An exponent of Keynesian ideas, he had supported freedom of trade as a key to Japan's economic strength even before the war. In 1946–47, as Minister of Finance in the first Yoshida cabinet, he had made proposals for national economic recovery based on Keynes's theories, which sometimes resulted in criticism of SCAP's economic policies. Consequently, he was dismissed by SCAP in 1947. He was reinstated only a month before his appointment as chairman of the association. With such a high-profile figure as its chairman, the Overseas Emigration Association could keep the project of Japan's emigration in the public spotlight for some time.[32]

On November 14, 1947, Emperor Hirohito met MacArthur for the fifth time since the Occupation began. Although the topics under discussion were deleted in Japanese newspapers, the *New York Times* reported that the two-hour meeting dealt with the Japanese peace treaty and Japan's economic situation—underproduction, inflation, and overpopulation.[33] Although SCAP opposed Japanese overseas expansion, it nevertheless responded to the question by sharing the Malthusian view of the Japanese emigration activists that Japan needed to transplant its surplus population somewhere outside the country.

According to official SCAP estimates, in order to become self-supporting, Japan's industrial activity had to reach at least 1937 levels. However, in 1947 Japan's industrial production, both manufacturing and mining, stood at only 45 percent of the 1930–1934 average, when the population was less by fifteen million.[34] Under the Occupation, Japan was at least allowed to continue foreign trade. Nonetheless, as of 1948 its imports stood at 37 percent of the 1930–1934 average, while its exports stood at slightly under 26 percent. Japan had to import iron ore, cooking coal, food, and other costly items formerly obtained in its own empire. There were no assured food and raw material sources or markets. Nor was there any income from its former overseas investments. Japan's trade revival was further obstructed by the unwillingness of many of Japan's former enemies to admit Japanese traders to their territories or to permit the establishment of Japanese trade offices.[35]

By early 1948, SCAP received a preliminary study of Japan's natural resources prepared by Edward Ackerman, a University of Chicago geographer. Ackerman recommended that Japan stabilize its population through birth control, not overseas emigration, a suggestion that disturbed MacArthur's conservative supporters both inside and outside Japan. Angry letters of protest descended on him from the American Catholic Women's Club of Tokyo and Yokohama. The Roman Catholic voters in the United States were a sensitive issue for MacArthur, who was rumored to be considering a presidential campaign, which would depend heavily on a large bloc of conservative voters.[36]

American Catholic organizations took the initiative in supporting overseas emigration plans for Japan, primarily because of their opposition to birth control and not especially because of their desire to fight anti-Japanese racism itself. In June 1948, Cardinal Francis Spellman visited Tokyo on a tour of the Pacific and the Far East and met Emperor Hirohito for the first time. After the half-hour meeting when correspondents asked if there had been a discussion of birth control, Cardinal Spellman answered that it was hard to understand how these eighty million Japanese were able to live in such a small island nation and added: "It is only reasonable and natural to expect that some provision will be made whereby they may be enabled to do so and to raise their families." He said that the Catholic Church had been attempting to help international refugees and displaced persons resettle in safe places in cooperation with various agencies. In this connection, he said he knew "a lot of empty places" to absorb the surplus population in the world. However, he cautiously added that he had no recommendation regarding lands to which the Japanese might be permitted to go.[37]

In spite of Cold War strategy, a West still fearful of the yellow peril opposed Japanese emigration. Canada and Australia especially regarded Japan's overseas expansion as a direct threat. Since the mid-nineteenth century, when the early gold rush in Britain's Pacific coast colonies induced a migration of Chinese laborers, both Canada and Australia had adopted immigration policies that totally excluded nonwhites. White Canada and white Australia both wanted to preserve systems very much like those in the United Kingdom, and to do so meant the complete exclusion of Asians and Africans.[38]

Influential Catholic figures in the United States, such as the Reverend Edmund Walsh, S.J., vice president of Georgetown University, held discussions in search of an ideal destination for the surplus Japanese population. Since their primary objective did not lie in the antiracism crusade, they did not direct their criticism toward the Oriental exclusion policies of the Western nations at all. On the contrary, they understood the anti-Japanese sensitivity completely and looked for a region with few or no Western inhabitants where a large Japanese influx would not be likely to cause any racial protest. Their choice was New Guinea, the world's second largest island after Greenland, with an area almost twice that of the total area of Japan proper. New Guinea was sparsely settled by Westerners and was inhabited by people who retained many elements of a Stone Age culture. Before the Pacific War, about six thousand Japanese settlers also lived there. The island had mineral resources such as copper, silver, manganese, and known deposits of oil and natural gas near the coast.[39]

This was not the first time that Dutch New Guinea had received the attention of the Christian world as a place to absorb Japan's surplus population. On the eve of the Pacific War, the internationally revered Christian activist Kagawa Toyohiko, who was nominated as a leader of Japan's postwar emigration movement, insisted that Dutch New Guinea be ceded to Japan as the new Lebensraum. In a last-minute attempt to avert war, Kagawa believed that Japan's militarists would be appeased if the United States showed sympathy for Japan's need for more territory and resources for its overpopulated nation. Kagawa's proposal was seriously considered by E. Stanley Jones, Kagawa's friend from the Princeton School of Theology and a prominent liberal Christian with substantial experience in Asia. Jones, though contemptuous of Western and Japanese imperialism, felt that such a territorial concession would be the only way to get Japan to withdraw from China and drop out of the Axis alliance. He spent much of the fall of 1941 lobbying American officials to consider this plan.[40]

After World War II, in which New Guinea had been a battleground for fierce fighting between Japan and the Allied nations, it was split in two, with the entire eastern half administered by Australia under a United Nations trusteeship as Papua New Guinea and the western half under Dutch control. New Guinea seemed the only rational place to absorb the undesirable Japanese surplus population without stirring up racial anxieties in the Western community, but Australia vigorously opposed the plan. In fact, Borneo and other undeveloped regions in Africa, South America, Australia, and North America were also under consideration for the same reason. Although one official at SCAP in Tokyo admitted that New Guinea should not be flooded with Japanese, he nonetheless suggested that it could be colonized by five million Japanese and other "Orientals" and thus bring great advantages to the world. During his sojourn in Tokyo in 1947, Robert McCormick of the *Chicago Tribune* declared that Japan should be granted New Guinea for migration purposes. William Teeling, Conservative member of a British parliamentary delegation that visited Japan late in 1947, also supported the idea as the only realistic approach to the population problem.[41]

American policymakers preferred, however, to increase Japan's industrial and economic capacity as a way of sustaining the ever-growing population at home, rather than launching a massive emigration to New Guinea. A desirable solution now seemed to allow Japan to supply manufactured goods to the industrially less-developed countries of Southeast Asia, while obtaining from them the raw materials for Japan. As Philip Taylor, a political scientist and former Occupation official, said at a discussion held at the State Department in October 1949, "We have got to get Japan back into, I am afraid, the old [Great East Asian] co-prosperity sphere."[42]

It was against this background, one that allowed Japan's old Pan-Asian market to revive, that Japan's reentry into the family of nations gradually began. The UN's Economic Commission for Asia and the Far East (ECAFE) had initiated a study of the trade agreement between ECAFE countries and occupied Japan, including an exchange of human resources. In late March 1949, ECAFE received a letter from the Government of Pakistan, an independent nation since August 15, 1947, requesting expert assistance in various fields—manufacturing, seismology, metallurgy, and commercial banking. In all these fields, the Pakistan government specifically preferred Japanese technicians. In mid-April, Cloyce Huston, acting chief of SCAP's Diplomatic Section, replied favorably to the Executive Secretary of ECAFE. Beginning on August 1, 1949, SCAP gave official approval for Japanese technicians to serve in foreign countries (most of which were developing nations in Asia).[43]

By late November 1949, SCAP had permitted about sixty Japanese technicians and experts in various fields to go abroad, mostly in the non-Western world, to help local industries: two electrical engineers to Egypt, two experts on locomotives to Thailand, two experts on communication cables and eighteen engineers and other experts in light industries to India, two electrical engineers to Pakistan, one agricultural expert on linen to northern Borneo, ten textile engineers to Burma, one ceramic engineer to Ceylon, fifteen medical experts and three other technicians to Mexico, three technicians on spinning machines to Paraguay.[44] Sixty Japanese technicians per year hardly constituted a resurgence of overseas emigration, or a sound solution to Japan's population problem. Nonetheless, these technicians officially sponsored by SCAP to go to the industrially less-developed nations for technical assistance almost perfectly coincided with the Japanese hope for a new image as a nation willing to help less-developed nations in their development and reconstruction. The fact that there was no reference to racial identity or quality attached to the image was also important: only that way was their reentry into the postwar world possible.

As the U.S. government gave its cautious approval for Japanese overseas emigration, American society also sensed a growing need to overhaul its rationale for Japanese exclusion. According to the conventional logic of exclusion, the Japanese and other Asians were unassimilable in American society because they could not merge with other white races in the melting pot and therefore become part of the mythical American race. In the postwar period, such a biological determinant gave way to a sociocultural adaptability, allowing the Japanese immigrants rhetorical room for assimilation into American democracy. However, American society was not ready to throw open the door to the Japanese and other nonwhite immigrants; America kept its strict national quota system, which predominantly favored immigrants from Europe. The slight shift in emphasis on Japanese assimilability into American society simply marked another tacit American consensus on the same balance of acceptance and rejection of the Japanese race, i.e., the Japanese cultural construct (or image) for tolerance and their physical construct (actual interactions) for exclusion.

America's immediate post–World War II opposition to Japanese emigration appeared in the debate over admitting Hawaii to statehood. Since 1935, when Congress first concerned itself with Hawaiian statehood, the strategic importance of Hawaii had continued to grow, and the postwar U.S. position in the Pacific immediately rekindled the Hawaiian statehood debate.[45] On January 24, 1946, a House Territory Subcommittee declared in a report that the Territory of Hawaii met the necessary requirements for statehood. The report was then submitted to Chairman Hugh Peterson, representative from Georgia, with the recommendation that Hawaii be admitted as the forty-ninth state. Three days before this report was issued, President Truman urged Congress to admit the islands to statehood.

The Hawaiians often stressed racial harmony as their strongest attribute—a peaceful pattern somewhat comparable to that of Brazil. In the words of Roy Vitousek, chairman of the Territorial Republican Central Committee, Hawaii "has been the one community in the world where people of all racial ancestries live together harmoniously and congenially without any feeling as to the superiority or inferiority of these of any racial groups."[46] According to the report of January 24, 1945, submitted by the House Territorial Subcommittee, the racial diversity of Hawaii—Caucasians, Hawaiians, part-Hawaiians, Japanese, Chinese, Koreans, Puerto Ricans, and Filipinos—existed at the time Hawaii was annexed to the United States as a territory and this mixture, therefore, was not regarded as an obstacle to statehood.[47] Although the subcommittee of the House Committee on Territories recommended immediate consideration of statehood legislation, the Senate rejected the statehood bills in 1947, primarily because of a fear of racial mixing.

The major obstacle facing Hawaii was the presence of the Japanese immigrants, three-quarters of whom were U.S. citizens, who constituted 37.3 percent of the total population of 500,000. During the war, despite the fact that the Japanese-American workforce, comprising one third of the island's labor force, was indispensable to the economy and the war effort, 1,440 Japanese aliens and American citizens of Japanese ancestry were taken into custody, 981 of whom were sent to relocation or alien detention centers on the mainland.[48] To the Americans on the mainland, the lingering fear of an invasion of Japanese and other colored races into the mainland by way of Hawaii remained the greatest stumbling block to Hawaiian statehood.[49]

The debate on Japanese immigration to mainland United States was once again sharpened by the Judd bill. American wariness regarding acceptance of the Japanese, or any Asian people, as a desirable component of American society became evident in the national debate over this bill, which aimed at providing naturalization to all immigrants having a legal right to permanent residence, and making immigration quotas available to Asian and Pacific peoples. In securing passage of the Judd bill, Congressman Walter Judd and other proponents of the bill reassured the public that the measure, though a token of new friendship, was carefully designed to prevent a flood of Japanese immigrants into American society. Reflecting the invidious image of the unwanted Japanese immigrants, the Judd bill provided a perfect example of America's reluctant compromise, perhaps out of its best intention, with Japanese emigration overseas.

The Judd bill, introduced in the same form as the previous H.R. 199 on March 1, 1949, made the Japanese its principal beneficiaries. In the Census of 1940, of 90,000 persons who remained ineligible for citizenship because of race, Japanese aliens represented 96.26 percent of the total, while Koreans accounted for 3.57 percent and the remaining 0.17 percent by representatives of other national groups in the Pacific and the Far East.[50] The bill would also increase the annual immigration quota for Japan from the minimum 100 to

185 because of the increase in the number of naturalized Japanese persons residing in the United States.

Judd assured the American public that under this proposed bill fewer than one thousand immigrants per year of "Asian races and cultures" were expected to come to the United States. Since this was 1/1,500th of 1 percent of the population of the United States, "that could not conceivably constitute any danger to the United States, whether economically, culturally, socially, politically, or in any other respect," Judd reassured the American public.[51]

The Judd bill also guaranteed the preservation of the white majority in the United States. According to the 1940 U.S. Census, the Japanese alien group had dropped sharply from 1930 to 1940. The birth rate among persons of Japanese ancestry was lower than that of the general population, while the death rate among Japanese-Americans exceeded the birth rate. Under the ongoing law the median age of Japanese aliens ineligible for citizenship was 49.7, compared with a median age of 29.0 for the general U.S. population. The largest number of Japanese aliens was in the 50-to-54 age group, and about 61 percent of foreign-born Japanese males were fifty years of age or older, compared with 29 percent of the females.[52]

This demographic pattern showed that the primary target of the bill was this "soon-to-disappear" block of population and as such constituted no threat for the existing components of American society, argued Judd. He insisted that the United States needed to treat these people with justice by awarding them the privilege of U.S. citizenship. Besides, with their small number, they would be extinct sooner or later, posing no threat in any way. Judd continued: "It seems to me a matter of justice and a matter of good sense . . . from the standpoint of making clear to the world that we believe in the things we talk about . . . to take those people in, or at least give them the opportunity to become naturalized, like any other persons who are here legally."[53]

Judd had also changed some wording in the bill. Originally, Section 1 had read: "The right of becoming a naturalized citizen of the United States shall not be denied or abridged because of race." In the revised bill, Judd changed the word "right" to "privilege." At the hearings, he explained the reason: "[It is because] we believe it is a privilege rather than a right for persons to become eligible to citizenship."[54] Sen. Howard McGrath of Rhode Island, who later served as Truman's attorney general from 1949 to 1952, was disturbed by this definition of citizenship; he argued that while the concept of right was all-inclusive, the concept of privilege was limited in scope. A privilege was granted and might be taken away, he argued. The word "privilege" implied that the measure was not intended to improve the status of Asians in the United States. Judd replied that he did not want to argue about that point. Instead, he repeated once again that "we are granting that privilege."[55]

Americans had been very concerned about the assimilability of the Japanese. Since interracial marriage was out of the question in the high tide of nativism in the 1920s, immigration opponents argued that the Japanese, because of their heredity, would not make valuable and loyal citizens. But the Japanese-American community made a desperate attempt at acceptance without intermarriage. Kiichi KANZAKI, general secretary of the Japanese Association of America, San Francisco, and Kiyo Sue INUI, assistant professor of political science and Far Eastern history at Southern California University, both claimed that by virtue of length of residence, character education, Christian religious training, and other cultural and sociological conditions in American society, the Japanese immigrants were successfully being Americanized.

Japanese immigrants were even changing physically, they said, with exposure to American society, especially American-born Japanese children. Just as European immigrants changed in terms of height, weight, the cephalic index (a taxonomic measure of the human skull), and hair color as they adjusted to new American customs, lifestyles, and modes of thought, Japanese immigrants were going through similar transformations. Their hair color, formerly jet black in Japan, was becoming brownish, and their skin color was losing its dark pigment and becoming fairer. When compared with Japanese children in Japan, the stature and weight of American-born Japanese children showed a marked increase as well. Even the facial expressions of the latter changed, because of their free and easy mode of living in America. Kanzaki and Inui thus concluded that even without biological racial amalgamation through an intermixture of blood with the white population, Japanese immigrants were subject to the law of racial evolution and therefore both were confident that they could be absorbed without difficulty into the American scene.[56]

After World War II, however, the intellectual current changed in favor of Japanese social and cultural assimilation. American social scientists increasingly denounced scientific racism (biological racialism) as an absurd concept and moved to establish "ethnicity" as a central paradigm of the reinterpretation of the immigrants. Instead of discussing blood, skin color, hair type, shape of the nose or head, and so forth, they focused on distinctive lifestyles and sociocultural traits as an objective mode of group identification within the framework of American social structure.

The implicit message was that assimilation should be color-blind, that it could take place for those historically kept outside the melting pot. While racial (color) distinctions were invidious and even derogatory in the historic context of superiority and inferiority, new ethnic (sociocultural) distinctions need not be. With the introduction of the concept of ethnicity, some groups formerly defined in derogatory racial terms were given a chance to destigmatize their position by simply redefining their status and identity in new ethnic terms. For example, "Negroes" became "Afro-Americans," an ethnic group referring to ancestral origin, like other white ethnic groups. By eliminating skin color as a means of classification, social scientists sought to point out that the problem of their status was not inherently different from that of white ethnic groups and could be solved and improved along with them.[57] It is important to note, however, that this new rhetoric did not attempt to dissolve the color line itself but merely upheld the possibility of assimilation not only inside but also outside the melting pot. In a sense, the concept of ethnicity institutionalized separate-but-equal relations. The case of the Japanese Americans as a new ethnic group was no exception.

In "A Discussion of the Degree of Assimilation Among Persons of Japanese Ancestry in the United States," an eighty-seven-page report submitted to the Senate hearings as a supplement to the Judd bill, Elmer R. Smith, a professor of anthropology at the University of Utah, demonstrated how total assimilation was possible for the Japanese without biological mixing with the whites. He defined "assimilation," differentiating it from "acculturation." "Has assimilation taken place only when the immigrant has become entirely indistinguishable from that mythical creation of the Sunday supplements, the 'Average American'? . . . Is one who retains in toto his homeland culture, but who has transferred political allegiance to this country, assimilated?" Smith asked.

According to Smith, Americanization included the totality of American life, not only social institutions such as churches, schools, and participation in economic life, but individual contacts as well. Categories such as length of residence and its location, labor force and employment, relief and unemployment, education, religion, crime rates, mental illness rates, war records to determine loyalty and political activity, and use of language—they all determined a person or group's adaptation to American society. He claimed that in the case of Japanese-Americans, social assimilation was sufficient to make them desirable citizens.

But Smith was cautious about raising the prospect of biological assimilation for the Japanese. He acknowledged that interracial marriage "threw some light upon the more general problem of assimilation," and, without expressing his own opinion, he observed that the negative attitude of the United States would mean that marriages between the Caucasoid and Mongoloid races would not be numerous in the immediate future.[58] Besides, since the Japanese had already been successfully assimilated into American society without disturbing the biological harmony among whites, argued Smith, they would and could continue to do so—to carry on a separate existence yet constitute an integral part of American society. Smith's assimilation thesis thus assured the public that the desirable form of coexistence between Japanese and whites could be in the realm of social function only, and never on biological and racial terms. To sum up, Japanese immigrants became Americanized in the English language, Christian faith, democratic creeds and norms, group customs (e.g., celebrating American holidays), dress, foods, sports, and entertainment. However, their total biological assimilation remained both impossible and undesirable despite their new status as a "model" ethnic minority. Thus, this slightly more inclusive mood toward the Japanese did not generate any leniency toward interracial marriage.

Since immigration regulations were directly related to marriage customs, objections to the Judd bill began to come in from other Asian-Americans, especially from the Chinese community. Chinese throughout the nation were deeply concerned about the negative effects of this bill on their already established "rights." Historically, since the mid-nineteenth century, they had always suffered from an uneven ratio of males and females, and according to the sixteenth Census Report (1940), the ratio of unmarried Chinese males to unmarried Chinese females was approximately four to one. Since marriage to white women was virtually impossible, it was essential for Chinese-American men to "get a wife from China." But Chinese protests against the Judd bill went unheeded on Capitol Hill.[59]

When the Judd bill reached the Senate in 1949, the Judiciary Committee decided to postpone all immigration measures until the subcommittee reported its findings. The question of terminating the Asian exclusion policies involved the larger problem of reevaluating the overall immigration policy of the United States. The basic principles of the Judd bill were approved in the final report delivered in 1950, to be incorporated into an omnibus immigration bill that was the forerunner of the McCarran-Walter Act of 1952.[60]

In the spring of 1951, between March 6 and April 9, the Senate and House Judiciary Committees held joint hearings on the three omnibus bills presented by Sen. Pat McCarran and Representatives Francis Walter and Emanual Cellar, chairman of the House Judiciary Committee. The committees discussed at length sections of the omnibus bills dealing with the exclusion of subversives, but also paid a good deal of attention to those sections dealing with Asian immigration.

All the witnesses approved of the decision to end the policy of Oriental exclusion primarily from the strategic point of view. The compromise between the new ideals and ongoing racism embodied in the Judd bill remained unchallenged. According to Walter Judd, William Sebald, U.S. ambassador in Japan, was said to have confirmed that this new measure would "electrify the people of Asia" at a time when the Communists were threatening them and that "from the standpoint of the touch-and-go situation in Japan, it would have the greatest effect."[61] Mike Masaoka, the national legislative director of the Japanese-American Citizens League, also endorsed the bills in his testimony, speaking of the need to keep the friendship of the Japanese in the "coming trying days."[62]

National opinion, however, was divided over the bills' continuous use of racial quotas for Asia. While some applauded this as a major improvement from all-out Oriental exclusion, others criticized it as preserving racist practice against Asian peoples. Major organizations of Asian-Americans, such as the Chinese-American Citizens League, the Filipino Federation of America, and the Korean National Association, made compromises and endorsed the principle of racial quotas in the bills. Will Maslow, general counsel of the American Jewish Congress, Simon Rifkind of the Synagogue Council of America, Read Lewis, executive director for the Common Council for American Unity, among others, opposed the use of racial quotas. They claimed such an approach would harm American prestige in Asia, and instead demanded equal treatment between European and Asian immigrants as a necessary step toward perfecting an immigration policy.[63]

In January 1952, four months after the San Francisco Peace Treaty, the two Congressional Committees reported favorably on the McCarran-Walter bill. Full congressional discussion of the McCarran-Walter bill began in April 1952 and continued through the spring until a decision was reached in late June. Despite opposition to the use of racial quotas for Asians, Congress passed the McCarran-Walter bill by overwhelming majorities. On June 25, President Truman returned the bill to Congress accompanied by a strong veto message, calling the measure excessively restrictive and discriminatory. Although the antirestrictionists responded by praising the veto message, on June 26 the House overrode the president's veto by a decisive margin of 278 to 113. The following day, on June 27, the Senate passed the McCarran-Walter bill, in a roll-call vote, by a margin of 57 to 26.[64]

The Soviet Union lost no time in attacking the quota system in the McCarran-Walter Act. Radio Moscow programs beamed to various parts of Asia called attention to it in a manner similar to Japan's wartime propaganda on the Oriental exclusion laws. A program aired in Korean on July 5, 1952, for example, compared the act to the Nazis' theory of racial superiority. The law, Radio Moscow said, was only one of many things that showed the contempt of American ruling circles for the Asian people.

Reacting swiftly to Moscow propaganda, the U.S. President's Commission on Immigration and Naturalization concluded that the national origins system caused more harm than good to U.S. foreign relations with "the nonwhite people of the world who constitute between two-thirds and three-fourth of the world's population." This presidential commission, composed of seven men, held hearings in major cities of the United States during the fall of 1952. In its report submitted in January 1953 the commission recommended a sweeping revision of the immigration laws, including the elimination of the national origins and racial quota system. No legislative action resulted until the following decade.[65]

The Japanese government, fully aware that unrestricted Japanese immigration was out of the question, gracefully accepted the spirit of the McCarran-Walter Act.[66] The Japanese public also understood the bleak reality that America's amity toward Japan was merely a by-product of its anti-Communist sentiment, and not genuinely founded on an improved feeling toward their race. The McCarran-Walter Act proved to them that American friendship was simply based on strategic calculations and as such would easily fade, or even become reversed, should U.S.-Soviet relations improve and anti-Communist sentiments subside.[67] The Japanese media printed only brief accounts of the act, referring to the embarrassingly small annual immigration quota of 185 in a matter-of-fact tone with no apparent criticism.[68]

Meanwhile, regardless of the racial hardship, Japanese proponents of overseas emigration continued their persistent crusade. As they became aware of American strategic interests, they even made efforts to include a redefinition of the benefits that Japanese emigration could bring to U.S. Cold

War strategy. Since Dulles's first mission to Japan in June 1950, the Overseas Emigration Association had worked aggressively to have the issue of Japanese emigration included in the peace treaty talks. During the second Dulles mission in January 1951, the association expressed its hope that the United States would cooperate with Japan in resuming Japanese overseas emigration because of their strategic interests in the Pacific that bound the two nations ever closer to each other.[69] The nominal immigration quota under the proposed McCarran-Walter bill shattered the association's ambition for emigration to the United States or any other Western nation. Instead, it worked to convince Dulles of the benefits of a plan of massive Japanese emigration to Dutch New Guinea.

On the occasion of Dulles's third mission to Japan in April 1951, the association asked him to consider how America could benefit from that plan. Focusing on the strategic importance of Southeast Asia, the association argued that the development of this region's natural resources under the joint cooperation of Japan and the United States would not only stabilize the region's economy but prevent "fifth column activities under a Communist leadership." They emphasized that these goals would be possible only if the United States permitted Japan to send emigrants to Southeast Asia. In his reply dated May 15, 1951, Dulles is said to have expressed his deep interest in their arguments.[70]

Although the Japanese emigration activists were disappointed in the McCarran-Walter Act, they did not openly accuse the United States of continuing racism against the Japanese. To do so would have ruptured the sensitive diplomatic relations between the two nations. Rather, in the hope of bolstering their movement, they carefully altered their ideological overtures to make them acceptable to Americans, trying both to anticipate and avoid adverse racial reactions. The Overseas Emigration Association, for example, acquiesced in the undesirability of Japanese emigrants in the white community. Yet at the same time, the association worked to invent a skewed racial rhetoric as a rationale for their overseas expansion. They argued that the Japanese—as the most advanced colored race possessed of the white race's intellectual capacity and the colored race's physical durability, especially in the harsh climate—would become the purveyors of technology and developers in the tropical climate zone. The rhetoric attempted to maximize the permitted versatility of the Japanese dual racial identity, while it discarded any hint of demand for equality with the whites.

Such arguments were founded on a revived interest in human climatology and physiology, which often provided the Western nations with a scientific measurement of success regarding their colonial enterprises in the tropical and subtropical zones. As early as May 1949, under the auspices of the Club of Friends of Cherry Blossoms (Ōyū Kai), a private organization, a secret report on the Japanese population problem was published by a group of university professors and officials from the Population Planning Committee of the Ministry of Welfare, calling themselves the Committee on the Overseas Population Movement (Kaigai Jinkō Idō Taisaku Kenkyūkai). The report aimed to prove that new postwar Japanese immigrants—peace-loving, democratic, hard-working, and highly-skilled—were the best developers of the so-called backward and undeveloped nations of Asia, including the South Pacific, and Central and South America.

For that purpose, this secret report cited two wartime works, *Nihon-jin to nettai eisei* (The Japanese and Tropical Hygiene), published in 1942 by Ogura Seitarō and Katō Michio, and *Nettai seikatsu mondai* (Problems of Life in a Tropical Climate), a work by Kuno Yasu published in 1943. Both works hypothesized that the Japanese, retaining larger amounts of melanin and a larger number of sweat glands than those of the white race, had a superior resistance to the tropical sun and heat-related fatigue. They also claimed that the higher birth rate for the Japanese in Hawaii and in other South Pacific islands than that in Japan proper reflected a higher degree of Japanese adaptability to a hot environment; otherwise, fertility rates would be lower. In conclusion, the report warranted that with such advantageous racial traits, the Japanese would be best fit to develop such regions as Malaya, Indochina, Siam, Burma, India, New Guinea, and Central and South America.[71]

Toriya Torao—deputy president of the Overseas Emigration Association, and the main architect of the proposal submitted to the Dulles mission—was largely responsible for reviving these racial arguments from prewar propaganda and bringing them into the spotlight. As early as August 1948, in an article entitled "Minshu-teki imin no seikaku [Characteristics of democratic immigration]," Toriya wrote that the Japanese were the only people who could settle down anywhere in the world. With their superb physiological adaptability to various climates, the new Japanese émigrés would be able to develop any region as a service to the welfare of the entire world.[72]

The Overseas Emigration Association presented Toriya's arguments to the Dulles mission, claiming that the Japanese were equal to whites in terms of intellectual capacity, and especially in the knowledge of science, but were even superior in terms of physical adaptability to a tropical climate. The Indonesians, Malayans, and other peoples living adjacent to New Guinea lacked these versatile racial qualities and were thus inadequate as colonizers. Therefore, Japanese immigrants would do the best job in developing New Guinea, the argument concluded.[73]

The association's newly defined Japanese racial quality soon established itself as an authoritative driving force for ardent sympathizers with Japanese overseas emigration. The business journal *Keizai Jīpu* (Economic Jeep) dedicated its February 1951 issue exclusively to the theme of overseas emigration and the peace treaty, and also recommended these underdeveloped regions as the best destinations for Japanese expansion. The United States was not even mentioned as a possibility. The journal conducted interviews with people in intellectual, business, and political circles, asking for their opinions. All expressed optimism that after the peace treaty, once Japan was again a member of the world community (*sekai kokka*), the situation would improve.

In regard to the nature of new Japanese emigration, the majority argued that it should not serve merely as an outlet for the surplus population of Japan. Emigrants should be skilled in agriculture or industry and bring benefits to their recipient countries. Interviewees were also asked to name the countries they would choose as possible recipients of new Japanese emigrants. Almost everyone named Brazil, Argentina, New Guinea, Borneo, or other parts of Latin America or the South Pacific. This time, very few named the United States. As one interviewee quipped: "Why bother going where we're not wanted?"[74]

According to a poll conducted by *Asahi* in October 1951, to the question of what would be the best way to solve the overpopulation problem, 28 percent of the people answered overseas emigration, while 24 percent mentioned birth control, and 14 percent said a combination of both. More men than women—40 percent of the men—and more people engaged in commerce and industry—40 percent of them—supported the idea of overseas emigration. Compared to the poll conducted two years before, when birth control had received the highest percentage as the measure to solve Japan's population problem, more people now preferred the role of overseas emigration. To the question "When overseas emigration becomes possible, would you like to go overseas?" 25 percent of those polled answered "yes." Again, more men than women answered positively, and the majority who answered "yes" were in their twenties.

When those who expressed interest in overseas emigration were asked to name the place they wanted to emigrate to most, Brazil received the highest response (21 percent). The United States and Hawaii came in second, at 18 percent. Then followed the South Pacific regions, including the Philippines, Indonesia, Burma, and New Guinea, with 16 percent, and Central and South America (excluding Brazil) received 11 percent. Manchuria still attracted 8 percent of the people, while China and Taiwan received 7 and 2 percent, respectively. Both Canada and Australia received 1 percent each, and the remaining 15 percent said "anywhere would do."[75] In all, places in the South Pacific and Central and South America—including Brazil—attracted as many as 48 percent of those who said they were interested in overseas emigration.

Brazil loomed larger than the United States as a destination for Japanese emigration. Emigration to Brazil began in 1908 and grew steadily due to demand from the coffee plantations. In the prewar period, as the United States became increasingly inaccessible to Japanese immigrants, Brazil became an alternate destination, replacing the former as the country outside of Asia that received the largest number of Japanese emigrants. From 1923 on, the Japanese government encouraged emigrants to Brazil by subsidizing travel expenses. But in Brazil, too, anti-Japanese sentiment developed, and the 1934 Brazilian constitution placed loose limits on immigration. By 1940, Brazil was the country with the third largest number of Japanese immigrants (202,514), after Manchuria (819,614) and China (365,412), followed by the United States and Hawaii (197,508).[76] With such a background, Brazil loomed as a plausible destination for postwar Japanese emigration.

An invitation from the Brazilian president, Getúlio Dornelles Vargas, triggered an expectation among the Japanese that the Amazon Valley could be a new paradise for Japanese immigrants. President Vargas, who had held absolute authority as president from 1930 to 1945, was ousted from power in 1945 but reelected in 1951, remembered that prewar Japanese settlers had quite successfully raised jute and black peppers along the Lower Amazon. In late September 1951, shortly after the San Francisco Peace Conference, Vargas approved a plan to settle five thousand Japanese families in Brazil to produce jute for export to the world market. Despite the still strong anti-Japanese sentiment in the country, the Brazilian Immigration and Colonization Council gave preliminary approval to the plan in November 1951.[77]

Many Japanese interpreted the Brazilian invitation as a sign of Brazilian respect for Japanese industriousness. Diet member Tawara Haruji (Japan Socialist Party, Right faction) spoke to the Lower House on December 20,

1952, reiterating his belief that only the Japanese had the capacity to develop the backward regions of the world. The Japanese had turned the arid countryside of Fresno and the Imperial Valley in California into lettuce and orange fields. They had turned coffee and jute plantations in Brazil, and cotton plantations in Argentina, Paraguay, and Peru—all places where the white race had had to abandon colonization efforts—into mainstays of each nation's economy. Tawara even went so far as to say that the Japanese were model immigrants, unlike the Southern European immigrants, who were mostly "hooligans." Therefore, he continued, the world had good reason to welcome Japanese immigrants with open arms.[78]

The Japanese public learned more about the rosy picture of life in Brazil from prewar Japanese emigrants. For example, Miyasaka Kunito, a successful prewar emigrant to Brazil and chair of the São Paolo Chamber of Commerce, told a story in a popular journal of how racism against the Japanese was nonexistent in Brazil because the Brazilians were so easygoing, unlike their North American counterparts. He also revealed to Japanese readers another supposed advantage of Japanese settlement in Brazil: Brazilians did not exceed the Japanese in terms of intelligence (chinō) or diligence (doryoku). Therefore, once Japanese tried their best, they were welcomed in the local community and could work side by side with Brazilians. Unlike their counterparts in North America, the Japanese in Brazil did not suffer an inferiority complex from white racism, but rather enjoyed a carefree life. Miyasaka also added that male Japanese immigrants might have a good chance to court charming mulatas and morenas—dark and tawny-complected women—an advantage that could not be found in the United States.[79]

President Vargas himself held a similar view of the merit of the Japanese immigrants, though he based it on a completely opposite assessment. In a message sent to the Federal Congress of Brazil on March 15, 1953, Vargas admitted that only the Japanese could assume the task of colonizing areas where white European immigrants would refuse to go, as "the Japanese have marvelous adaptability to a climate such as that of the Amazon Valley, which the European race in general would have to reject as an unhealthy tropical climate quite unacceptable to them." Consequently, Vargas did not find it either necessary or appropriate to introduce Japanese immigrants to developed areas in the southern part of Brazil, where an abundant number of European immigrants were available.[80] To Vargas, the Japanese would merely provide cheap labor in the regions where no white Europeans wanted to go.

It was not long, however, before the Japanese realized that these regions now open for Japanese emigration would never meet their demand for living space overseas. In these regions there was a complete absence of the traditional "pull factor," an attractive socioeconomic and cultural incentive for those who aspired to a higher level of living than Japan could provide.

Wakatsuki Yasuo, professor in the Department of Agriculture at Tamagawa College, specializing in studies of Japanese emigration/immigration and colonization policies, explained that the Japanese government could in no way be selective in its choice of host nations; finding an immediate solution to the population problem was the priority. Nonetheless, he criticized the scheme to send Japanese emigrants to the barren undeveloped regions of the world as ill-planned and doomed to failure. The new slogan for Japanese emigration ("Contributing to the advancement of the world's welfare by developing undeveloped regions") was invented as a denial of postwar reality because the Japanese were not allowed to emigrate to and participate in societies of the so-called civilized Western nations.[81] The Japanese were merely voicing this new slogan as a passive adjustment to the devious ways of a Western-dominated world.

The pattern of Japanese overseas emigration showed that only those regions with a much higher standard of living than Japan's—the United States being the best example—would serve as a natural magnet for Japanese emigrants, who aspired to a better life where their advanced skills could be utilized to the maximum level, or where there was a guarantee of high business profits. In the case of the prewar emigration movement to Manchuria, for example, it never recruited a significant number of agricultural settlers, who would have been obvious primary targets within Japan's surplus population. Instead, the Japanese emigrants to Manchuria were predominantly urban-based social and economic elite such as administrators, businessmen, engineers, entrepreneurs, and other professionals and their families. In 1939, for example, only 10.3 percent of civilian Japanese were engaged in agriculture in Manchuria, while the rest were engaged in industrial and other sectors. In Japanese-occupied China, the figure was only 1 percent in 1940.[82]

For a decade or so after the conclusion of the Occupation, the Japanese Ministry of Foreign Affairs promoted the policy of "planned emigration [keikaku ijū]" to Central and South America. It established within itself the

Bureau of Emigration (Imin-kyoku), an office in charge of policy-making concerning overseas emigration, as well as diplomatic negotiations with recipient nations. Under this policy, emigrants (most of them carefully screened farmers) would settle on designated plantations in Central and South America, such as those in Bolivia, Brazil, Paraguay, and Argentina, and launch their new lives with governmental and nongovernmental subsidies.

In January 1961 the Prime Minister's Office (Sōri-fu) conducted a poll of 20,000 randomly selected adults on their awareness of overseas emigration. Although the living standard in Japan was now constantly rising, 11.8 percent of them said they had thought about possible overseas emigration for a better life, and 1.4 percent said they actually planned to emigrate. According to the survey, those with positive views on overseas emigration tended to have higher educational backgrounds and labor skills. The survey predicted a rise in the number of emigrants with special labor skills and of emigration of small and midsize companies, should the "pull factor" on the part of the recipient nations grow stronger.

The problem, the survey indicated, was the lack of attraction provided by Central and South America for those Japanese with entrepreneurship and talent. Despite early enthusiasm for its vast land in the Amazon Valley, the Japanese never regarded Brazil—one of the few nations to open the door to postwar Japanese emigrants—as a "civilized" nation. "Backward [kōshin-koku]" and "uncivilized [mikai-koku]" were the unanimous responses in regard to Brazil's image among the Japanese, while they of course considered Japan to be "civilized [bunka-koku]." At this point, the government survey raised a doubt that regions with lower, or inferior, living conditions would attract a natural flow of able Japanese emigrants. In light of the contemporary situation, however, regions with a higher standard of living than Japan's were either in Europe or in nations outside Europe where the population was largely comprised of European immigrants. Since these nations all kept their doors closed against the Japanese or any other colored races, the report conceded, it is unrealistic to expect a large natural flow of Japanese emigration in search of a higher standard of living abroad. Thus, the Japanese government predicted an early termination of the emigration program for Brazil and other Central and South American regions and added that it had no further plans to pursue any large-scale overseas emigration program.[83] Instead, the government worked to raise the standard of living at home so it would generate growing demands for a labor force by domestic industries, and the domestic market itself could then absorb the excess human resources. Henceforth, Japan's rapid domestic economic growth accounted for a sharp decline in emigration overseas.

The postwar world order into which Japan was allowed to enter was being reconstructed under American leadership, and any confrontation with the expansion of American racism meant the end of Japan's crusade. Therefore, it was not altogether illogical of the Japanese emigration movement to avoid any contact with Western racism and to become collaborators with the United States in overseas expansion by cultivating a new racial ideology for their raison d'être in the niche of America's racism. However, the newly established amity was viable only as long as Japanese expansion remained outside the Western sphere of influence, as the two had originally agreed upon. Worse, the reality was that there was no place for Japanese expansion anywhere in the world anyway. Japan's conciliatory racial creed—the creator of a new civilization as a proxy for the whites (which was vigorously propagated by emigration activists)—actually did very little to lead the Japanese toward a goal of cosmopolitanism.

In separate American and Japanese discussions of new Japanese emigration overseas, no underlying argument took into account issues arising from possible interracial coexistence in a shared community. The only unspoken agreement they upheld in the name of friendship was the mutual avoidance of contact, which they understood would inevitably trigger a racial confrontation. A few decades later, when the Japanese economy had recovered fully and became competitive with the industrial nations of the West, the undeveloped regions of the world could no longer contain Japan's rising ambitions and the Japanese naturally turned to the West for expansion. This was a breach of the "gentleman's agreement" made during the Occupation at a time when neither Americans nor Japanese had yet solved the riddle of interracial coexistence. It was at that point that the smoldering embers of racism burst into flame.

ADDENDUM: SCAP AND INTERMARRIAGE

As early as September 15, 1945, SCAP issued Circular no. 70, GHQ-AFPAC, regarding the marriage of military personnel in occupied territory. Besides the fact that the law of many states in the United States prohibited miscegenation, an American serviceman could not take his Japanese wife and half-Japanese dependents home because the 1924 Immigration Act barred them from becoming citizens or permanent residents. On December 2, 1945, SCAP issued a subsequent announcement to recommend "that the attention of all personnel contemplating marriage with aliens be invited to Par 3, AFPAC Cir 70, especially to that part concerning the exclusion from immigration to the U.S. of persons not having a preponderance of White, African, or Chinese blood."[84]

No Armed Forces approval was granted a serviceman to marry a Japanese at the American consulate—the only registration legally recognized by Japan or the United States. On May 31, 1946, SCAP ruled that American personnel married in Japan must abide by the Japanese civil code to establish the legality of the marriage. It ordered the Japanese to arrange a "mutually satisfactory mechanical procedure for registration of the marriages of American citizens."[85] Following this order, many couples were married by Shinto or Buddhist priests, or by a Japanese Christian pastor who did not know that it was against military rules to perform weddings without a consulate registration.[86]

The U.S. government took a cautious limited action. On June 28, 1947, President Truman signed a bill as Public Law No. 126, which allowed racially ineligible alien brides to enter the United States and join their husbands. Consequently, if the marriage had been performed between July 23 and August 21, 1947, the Japanese bride was allowed into the United States on a non-quota basis. On August 22, a day after this thirty-day amnesty expired, the Associated Press reported that a total of 823 marriages had taken place in occupied Japan between American men and Japanese women during that period. Of the Americans involved, 597 were Nisei, 211 were white, and 15 were black. A large number of the non-Nisei were soldiers who became civilians in order to stay with their wives in Japan.

After that special measure, the consulate marriage mill shut down. The American chief consul announced that he would continue properly marrying authorized Americans and Japanese, but warned that future brides would not be allowed to accompany their husbands to the United States.[87]

A memorandum, "Marriage of American Citizens in Japan," issued by the Diplomatic Section of SCAP on August 10, 1949, defined interracial marriage as follows: If one party to the marriage was "an alien who is 50% or more of the Japanese race, both parties to the marriage must sign in the presence of two American witnesses [a statement entitled 'Declaration Concerning Marriage to Aliens of Japanese Race']." Such declaration of the spouse's racial identity automatically disqualified her entry into the United

States and nullified the newlyweds' life together, thus discouraging the attempt at marriage altogether.[88]

In the spring of 1949, when Cecil White, a congressman from the state of California, petitioned for SCAP's approval of a marriage between one of his constituents, a Japanese-American civilian employee of the Army in Japan, and a Japanese woman, SCAP denied his request despite the fact that it was essentially to be a marriage between two people of the same race. The letter from SCAP plainly stated the rationale: "The admissibility of alien spouses . . . [and children] poses serious problems to the parties to the marriage and to the military service." The policy in the Far Eastern Command on the marriage of United States citizens to Japanese nationals conformed to the immigration laws of the United States. Therefore, until such time as laws were enacted to authorize Japanese spouses of U.S. military personnel and Department of the Army civilian employees to enter the United States for purposes of residence or citizenship, no planning was possible for eventual residence of the family in the United States. SCAP thus disapproved any marriage that was not considered to have a reasonable chance of success.[89]

CHAPTER 5

The Problem of Miscegenation

On June 28, 1946, ten months after American troops landed in Japan, Japanese radio announced that a child of mixed Japanese and American parentage had been born that morning. The announcer called the baby a symbol of love and friendship between Japan and the United States: "a rainbow across the Pacific." SCAP headquarters immediately issued an order to fire the announcer for condoning fraternization. In a comment that SCAP considered sarcastic, he called the baby "the first Occupation present."[1] After that, the presence of mixed-blood children—most of them illegitimate—became a taboo subject, avoided by both the Japanese government and SCAP. In the spring of 1952, when the Occupation drew to a close and the first generation of mixed-race children came of school age, both Japan and the United States were faced with an unprecedented racial debate.

The problem of mixed-blood children is often considered an apolitical, aberrant issue in the Occupation, a consequence of the amorous rendezvous of American GIs and Japanese women. However, when the two peoples simultaneously demonstrated both their abhorrence toward the hybrid offsprings and desire for their exclusion from their societies, they found yet another occasion for diplomatic collaboration in tolerating mutual racism. Their mutual hatred of miscegenation drew them closer.

Owing to a common perception that racial purity was essential to a wholesome nation—the preservation of the pure white American race and of the pure Japanese race—interracial marriages and their offspring posed almost identical problems for Americans and Japanese. Both countries looked upon mixed marriage as a social evil, a threat to public health, safety, morals, and the general welfare. Post–World War II studies usually discredited claims that certain races, especially blacks, were biologically inferior, and that the progeny of racially divergent couples were likely to be inferior. Nevertheless, the negative social effects on mixed-race children remained a strong justification for opposition to intermarriage.

In the United States, while in the Southern states miscegenation statutes were aimed principally at the black population, in other parts of the country marriage between whites and Asians was particularly frowned upon. Asians had to be isolated in order to preserve biological harmony among the whites. The laws of Montana and Nebraska specifically banned Japanese from marrying whites, charging the violator with a misdemeanor in the case of Montana and, in the case of Nebraska, up to six months in prison and/or a $100 fine.[2]

It was only in October 1948 that the Supreme Court of California, in *Perez v. Lippold*, ruled unconstitutional the California statute, in Section 60 of the Civil Code, which read: "All marriages of white persons with negroes [*sic*], Mongolians, members of the Malay race, or mulattoes are illegal and void."[3] Even after that groundbreaking decision, about thirty states still had similar statutes against racially mixed marriages.[4] In 1951 the *Duke Bar Journal* put forward several items to consider with regard to the constitutionality of miscegenation. For example, under many state segregation laws the white parent would be barred by law from associating with his or her child in restaurants, theaters, and other public places. The child would be shunned by other whites, and the white parent would not be accepted in the family of his or her "colored" spouse. Thus, a gap would develop not only in public places but also in the home. Such adverse effects could produce "problem progeny," and cause serious long-term social problems.[5]

In Japan the duality of Japanese racial identity—the belief that they were the embodiment of better elements from both white and colored races—might have led to the tolerance of mixed-blood children. However, Japanese racism was an abstract idea, not a physiologically measurable reality, and it did not allow the Japanese to willingly incorporate these half-Japanese, half-American children. The public was concerned about the negative impact of the addition of this new racial category. On the basis of varied "scientific" research, hybridization with whites, blacks, and other Asians was believed to produce racial groups inferior to the pure Japanese. After all, in the Japanese myth of "dualistic racial attributes," biological purity was the source of Japanese uniqueness. Hybridization, even with the "superior" white race, could only be harmful to such Japanese racial quality. Despite the national enthusiasm for assimilating American culture, physical and biological acquisition of American racial traits was not welcome.

It was only with the Cold War that an attempt was made at bi-national co-operation toward a solution. Moreover, such a solution based on diplomatic interests aimed at nothing more than a swift erasure of the problem: a massive American adoption plan for the children (which of course would have removed the problem from Japan). The plan never became more than a propaganda effort, since the anti-Oriental immigration policy of the United States blocked the entry of these half-Japanese children.

The Japanese perception of the racially mixed children reflected their view of the racial hierarchy of the world. Prejudice against Americans, both white and black, and against other Asians, combined with a view of their own "unique" racial characteristics, was, in turn, a mirror image of America's own racial perceptions. Had the two peoples joined voices in an attempt to overcome and understand this persistent and parallel nature of racism, an evolving discourse on the rightful place for these half-American and half-Japanese children in each society might have taken place. But when preservation of mutual racism was the compelling force for promoting the U.S.-Japan friendship, why change tunes? Nothing changed beneath the conventional diplomatic protocol, and these children were quickly pushed into a pariah group. The mutual abandonment of these children again demonstrates the consensual toleration of shared racism under the veneer of U.S.-Japanese friendship.

During the Occupation, there was no official discussion concerning the problem of interracial babies. In 1947, when the Institute of Population Problems of the Japanese Ministry of Welfare proposed taking a census of the babies born of American fathers and Japanese mothers, Col. Crawford Sams, the chief of the Public Health and Welfare Section of SCAP, prohibited them from officially gathering statistics because it would be unwise to "probe so serious a wound."[6] By mid-1948, estimates of the number of these babies—"Occupation babies" or "half-half babies," as the American media called them—ranged from 1,000 to 4,000.

SCAP threw the blame for the problem on the lewd elements in the Japanese environment, which "made good clean American boys go morally wrong," and left the situation unattended. It became the job of shabby public or semiprivate orphanages to keep the abandoned mixed-race babies along with Japanese orphans. When an American journalist published the first article on this problem in the June 19, 1948, issue of the *Saturday Evening Post*, charging that the owners of two orphanages had been arrested for starving more than one hundred babies, many of them "Occupation babies," he was immediately ousted from Japan by SCAP's order.[7]

Combined with the governmental and military discouragement of interracial marriage, American military law freed a soldier or officer of responsibility to his child or its mother unless he wished to admit paternity. Moreover, children born in or out of wedlock were Americans only if their American fathers admitted paternity and registered the birth with the American Consulate.[8] Under such policies, the mother, an enemy alien, could not take her case to court to prove paternity.

Colonel Sams instructed that the babies be treated as Japanese. He had been aware of the historical problem of so-called Eurasian minorities in Asia. In countries long occupied by Western nations, the Eurasian population, fathered by European military and civilian administrators and mothered by the indigenous population, had grown into a problematic minority living in a political and social limbo between the native populations and the Western settlers. The Anglo-Indians, the Dutch-Indonesians, and other Eurasians of British, French, Dutch, and American paternity had almost always identified themselves with the "superior" country from which their fathers came, and demanded the special privileges of their white fathers, thus creating a disturbance to Western prestige and social disorder for these Asian nations.[9]

Sams wanted to avoid the creation of a problematic racial minority in Japan that would later demand the same privileges enjoyed by Americans. He wanted the babies to be thoroughly assimilated into Japanese society. Besides, Sams believed that it would be much easier for the babies to integrate into Japanese society than into American society because, according to wartime American propaganda, the Japanese were not a race but a "hodgepodge mixture of Chinese, Koreans, Malayans, and others." Sams also discouraged plans by some GI wives to make contributions to the orphanages. Giving these babies special American treatment, such as clothing, drugs, and foods that were luxuries beyond the ordinary Japanese means, would automatically brand them as outsiders. It would cause the Japanese to regard them as foreigners and refuse to absorb them into Japanese society, claimed Sams. Therefore, he supported the work of LARA (Licensed Agencies for Relief of Asia), which supplied milk, food, and clothing to institutions "without reference to race, color, or religion."[10]

In contrast, Japanese welfare agencies as well as Japanese people regarded abandoned racially mixed babies as a problem that the Occupation authorities or "the foreigners' religion" should bear responsibility for. They sent many of them to Christian institutions, mostly Catholic orphanages. By mid-1948, Our Lady of Lourdes Home in Yokohama, built especially for such babies, had 130 children.

Another notable orphanage for racially mixed babies was the Elizabeth Sanders Home, established on January 31, 1948, by Sawada Miki, a high-profile international philanthropist and granddaughter of Iwasaki Yatarō, a founder of the Mitsubishi industrial and financial empire.[11] According to Sawada's autobiography, her encounter with the mixed-blood babies was accidental. She had never seen a GI baby until February 1947, when she witnessed the corpse of a newly born baby—perhaps half-black and half-Japanese—naked, wrapped in a cloth, and left on a luggage rack of a train. She became convinced that she had to save these babies. With reluctant permission from SCAP, she purchased back her father's estate at Oiso overlooking the Pacific Ocean, which had been confiscated by SCAP, and with moral and financial support from friends in the United States, France, and England, began the construction of her own private orphanage in affiliation with the Episcopal Church.

Like the Sisters at the Our Lady of Lourdes Home, Sawada wanted to make the mixed-race children bilingual, educate them about both Japan and the United States, eventually "send them back" to the United States, and, in her words, "let them serve as a future link of the two nations." Sawada believed that their best hope lay in anonymity in a segregated environment. She felt segregation was the best way to protect the physically different children.[12]

Aware of the censors' views, the Japanese press printed few stories on mixed-race babies during the Occupation. Between 1948 and early 1950 there were only three articles on the babies published in major Japanese newspapers. All three approached the problem of GI children as a "peculiar social phenomenon in defeated Japan, which every Japanese rather wanted to ignore." They praised the Sanders Home for extending Christian charity to unfortunate babies ostracized by the Japanese because of their different physical appearance. Even *Akahata*, the official newspaper of the Japan Communist Party, printed an article on the Sanders Home praising Sawada's charitable efforts on behalf of the "Orphans of Destiny [*shukumei no koji*]." The article described the extensive Western-style facilities of the Sanders Home, told of Sawada's hope to raise these children to be respectable Japanese who sincerely loved peace, and encouraged readers to understand, love, and welcome these children into Japanese society. The article did not explicitly speak out against racial discrimination, but instead emphasized the potential significance of the babies as a hopeful tie binding Japan and the United States.[13]

After SCAP's censorship policy was lifted in 1949, the Japanese press began to discuss the issue of the so-called GI babies, pessimistically suggesting that these children with blue eyes, curly hair, and white skin or black skin, were the seeds of a new social problem. An editorial in *Asahi* argued that just as it was too late to blame lewd Japanese women and irresponsible American GIs, neither could Japanese society blame the children themselves. The only way to prevent these children from becoming a social cancer, the editorial suggested, was to ask American society to adopt as many children as possible and to assimilate the rest into Japanese society and raise them to be law-abiding citizens of Japan.[14]

As SCAP's ban against an official census still continued, confusing statistics overwhelmed the nation with fear. Sawada of the Elizabeth Sanders Home was convinced that there were about 200,000 babies fathered by American soldiers in Japan. Takada Masami, chief of the Children's Bureau of the Welfare Ministry, estimated the figure at around 150,000.[15] It was not until the spring of 1952 that the Children's Bureau conducted the first official census on the number of mixed-blood children. It circulated a questionnaire to 5,443 obstetricians and 38,872 midwives through each Prefectural Government, excluding those working at hospitals run by the U.S. military, asking them to report on the number of mixed-blood babies they recalled delivering since the beginning of the Occupation. About 77 percent of them returned the questionnaires, from which the ministry drew a preliminary figure with considerable margin for error. The final count was 5,002, a figure far below earlier estimates. In August 1952 the Ministry of Welfare issued another set of statistics. There were 5,013 mixed-blood children in Japan. Of them, 2,635 were male and 2,378 were female. There were 4,205 half-whites, 714 half-blacks, and 94 of unknown race.[16] A year later, another official report came out, from the Division of Health and Welfare Statistics, which showed a lower figure than the census taken the previous year. As of February 1953, it stated, there were 3,490 mixed-blood children—1,783 males and 1,707 females.[17]

The Japanese public feared that the actual numbers of these children were much higher. The differences in skin color and physical appearance—and intellect—of the mixed-race babies constituted a major threat to the wholesome integrity of Japanese society. Besides, genetic and social degeneration caused by the infusion of white and black "bloods" into the Japanese race became a major topic of public discussion.

On January 31, 1953, Furuya Yoshio, a medical doctor and president of the National Public Health Institute (Kokuritsu Kōshū Eisei-in), gave a widely publicized lecture on the social and biological impact of racial hybridization on Japanese society. A "biology of miscegenation [konketsu seibutsu-gaku]," as in the case of a half-Japanese half-American child, would result in weaknesses in the immune system as well as in intelligence, due to a "disharmony of genes [idenshi no fu-chōwa]." Worse, Furuya cautioned, unlike the other types of "mixed-blood [konketsu]" children, of Japanese and Chinese or Korean parentage, the children of Japanese-white or Japanese-black parentage would grow up to pass on their non-Japanese physical features to their descendants for generations. Those with distinctive non-Japanese looks would become an isolated alien element in society, grow hostile to society's harmonious conformity, and even become the springboard for a hotbed of destructive sociopolitical movements. The combination of the biological and sociological effects of miscegenation, concluded Furuya, would leave a scar on Japanese society for many generations.[18]

Another scientific expert also explained the mixed-blood children's racial influence on Japan from both the eugenics and social cost perspectives. Since genes for black skin were dominant over those for yellow skin, three out of four half-black Japanese children would turn out to have prominent black racial traits. Many mothers of half-black children hoped that their children's black features would not be passed on to their grandchildren, and that their "black blood" would be diluted through several generations. In fact, it would take "thousands of years" before their black color completely disappeared from the Japanese race. Until then, these descendants would create a half-black community, posing a great threat to society because they would be inclined to arm themselves with their own hatred—fueled by an inferiority complex—toward the mainstream of society.[19]

The task facing Japan was to find a way to assimilate this "inferior" racial group into society. The absence of their American fathers made their situation different from other minority groups. These half-American children, living either at orphanages or with their mothers and relatives, with or without Japanese stepfathers, did not constitute an independent community. In a sense, they were the most helpless minority group. Yet because of their paternal link to the United States, they were also potentially the most powerful. The debates on their assimilation into Japanese society was never as heated as had been those on the forced assimilation of other Asians during Japan's colonialism. Rather than making an effort at absorbing these half-American children into society, the general mood was to hope that the U.S. government would help adopt them into American families and raise them as U.S. citizens.

A growing number of Japanese understood that discrimination toward Japanese-American children reflected a sense of vengeance against the United States for its treatment of the Japanese since the war, combined with a contempt for Japanese women who had affairs with Americans.[20] But the Japanese view of these Japanese-American children had another dimension. The Japanese feeling of their inferiority to white Americans combined with the feeling of condescension toward black Americans explained their different attitude toward half-white and half-black children. An associate professor at Teacher's College of Tokyo pointed out in 1953 that Japanese attitudes toward Korean and Chinese peoples and mixed-blood children were a sad result of the racial hierarchy that existed in the minds of the Japanese. Even fifth-grade Japanese children "know" that the white race is superior to the Japanese, but that the Japanese is superior to the black race—thus, he lamented, the same crooked perception determines how they treat half-white and half-black children.[21]

Shimizu Ikutarō, a leading social critic known for his acerbic comments, also acknowledged, in *Chūō kōron*, that the Japanese had a hierarchical race consciousness. Separate from the sense of Japanese superiority, the Japanese had a sense of unconditional awe toward the white race (*hakushoku-jinshu*). Prewar pro-American and pro-Western intellectuals could not escape from this sense of inferiority. Although many Westerners interpreted Japanese racism as a simple form of discrimination against outsiders, it had a structure far more complex than the conventional Anglo-Saxon supremacy that the Western world knows, Shimizu argued. Using an allegory of military ranks, Shimizu explained how racial hierarchy had dominated the dynamics of U.S.-Japanese relations since the war's end. The Japanese had stood as a junior officer (*kashikan*) between the general—the white race—and the common soldier (*heisotsu*), or Asian races. For a brief period after the Pacific War, the Japanese came close to realizing the "truth" that they were, after all, the "common soldier" in the world—just one branch of the Asian race. But soon the Japanese received American help in restoring their old pride in the junior officer position, merely because that pride was "very convenient for the new American Far Eastern policies." Among all Asian races, Shimizu quipped, Japan proved to be best qualified to serve the United States in the role of junior officer.[22]

Seki Kazuo, an expert on educational psychology, suggested a more sympathetic view of mixed-race children, based on a better understanding of the Japanese sense of racial inferiority. Seki argued that the Japanese had something in common with these half-Japanese half-American children—a suffering from a similar sense of non-belonging. These mixed-blood children were unable to belong to Japan's mainstream, and the Japanese were unable to belong to the world's mainstream because of their nonwhiteness. Seki called the Japanese man a "marginal man [shūhen-jin]" who suffered great insecurity in the world. He explained: "Among all the colored races, the Japanese are closer to the white race [Ware ware wa yūshoku-jinshu no naka demo haku-jin no hō ni chikai]. Having successfully imported Western cultures, we came to assume that we were on the level of the white at least mentally [ishiki no ue de wa haku-jin nami]. Of course, though, we never became white." This sense of insecurity eventually drove the Japanese into the tragic war, in which they desperately tried to reach equal footing with the whites and exacted great sacrifices of their fellow colored races. The Japanese, he thought, should be able to understand the feelings of these children about their uncertain identity and show tolerance toward their integration into society.[23]

Kitabayashi Tōma, a writer, pointed out that the root of the Japanese problem with half-white children was not a fear of racial degeneration but the inexplicable Japanese sense of inferiority toward the white race, which often made them self-deprecatory and hypocritically humble toward them. This inferiority complex, and the accompanying repressed animosity, he argued, could be a factor that explained the vengeful treatment of helpless half-white children. Owing to such a national psychology, no matter how hard the half-whites tried to assimilate into Japanese society, they would only face greater persecution. However, Kitabayashi continued, when these half-white children grow up, acquire U.S. citizenship, and are transformed into "the white man," the Japanese would no longer be able to continue their discrimination and would instead let these half-whites take on the role of condescending, superior white men.[24] Furuya Yoshio, president of the National Public Health Institute, expressed his fear that the half-white Japanese would some day form a privileged group in Japan and would be disdainful of the mainstream. Maki Ken'ichi, president of the Elizabeth Sanders Home, agreed, contending that they might grow up arrogant because the Japanese admire their physical appearance.[25]

Many Japanese women were eager to identify themselves with whites through sexual relationships—surely a sign of the Japanese sense of inferiority. One article in the popular journal Ushio sarcastically explained the psychology of these "Madame Butterflies." These women had expected to gain a higher status by having children by the occupiers and ended up harming not only themselves but the nation. However, he added, since quite a few respectable Japanese intellectuals also foolishly insisted that Japan would be better off by becoming "annexed" to the United States, how can we criticize these ignorant Japanese women? All of Japan had succumbed to the common mental state of being the conquered people.[26]

Shimizu Ikutarō followed up on the above point by describing a pitiful scene at a medical inspection, where prostitutes catering to Japanese clients looked ashamed and miserable, while "panpan" women were quite boastful and even proud of their liaisons with the Americans. The latter were also proud of their half-American children. Shimizu argued that the problem of mixed-blood children would not have existed if the Occupation army had consisted of Chinese soldiers, not white soldiers. He suspected that no Japanese women would have wanted to flirt with Chinese soldiers. But many Japanese women had been rushed into friendships with the "Western [Seiyō-no] soldiers" after the defeat because these soldiers were the powerful, well-dressed victors—and white. Again, who could blame these women?[27]

On May 5, 1952, a special committee on the problems of mixed-blood children in Japanese society was formed under the direction of Furuya Yoshio, then chief of the Public Health Division of the Ministry of Welfare. In the prewar period Furuya, as head of a research department in the Ministry of Health and Welfare conducting eugenics studies on the maintenance of Japanese racial characteristics, cautioned against miscegenation between the Japanese and native peoples in the colonies.[28] The postwar committee, consisting of experts from the fields of eugenics, racial physiology (minzoku seibutsu-gaku), racial psychology (minzoku shinri-gaku), racial sociology (minzoku shakai-gaku), and social biology, launched an investigation of the effects of miscegenation. They collected data on the physiological character of the children, especially in relation to eugenics, and laid the groundwork for future plans which included special educational projects.[29]

In gauging the effect of the race mixture, the committee took a keen interest in its intellectual dimension and made a meticulous attempt to measure IQ levels. IQ tests were especially important because, as the rhetoric of the Japanese emigration movement went, the myth of high Japanese intelligence levels had survived the defeat. The perspective of the genetic superiority of the white race had also influenced the Western view of the effect of miscegenation on IQ levels. For example, P. A. Witty, an American psychologist, conducted studies on mulattoes in the mid-1930s and concluded that the more white blood in the mixture the higher the mental capacity.[30] The Japanese, however, did not believe that the mix with the white race would raise the IQ of that child to a higher level than the pure Japanese. On the contrary, according to conventional wisdom, they believed that racial mixture with the "superior whites" would lower not only the intellectual but also the spiritual (seishin-sei) level of these half-Japanese, half-white children compared to that of pure Japanese children.

They based their belief on some widely publicized prewar research by a Japanese scholar on the intellectual superiority of the Japanese. Between 1937 and 1938, Tanaka Kan'ichi had administered an IQ test on a total of five thousand children, ages six to fifteen, from various racial groups living in Los Angeles, San Francisco, and Honolulu.

The Japanese made the top score, ranging from 49.49 percent to 49.92, while white Americans stood at 44.05, trailing Chinese, Korean, British, and Russian Jewish children. Southern Europeans, Mexicans, Hawaiians, and black Americans were at the bottom of the list.[31] On another occasion, he used a separate test to compare IQ levels among Asian races and again claimed that Japanese children made the highest score of 49.48, followed by the Chinese in the central region (44.06), Taiwanese (42.92), the Chinese in the northern region (41.46), Manchurians (41.08), and Koreans (39.76).[32]

Various other tests administered in North America by white scholars before World War II generally supported the view that the "Mongolid," not just Japanese, were as intelligent as the "Europid." The IQs of Mongolid children in North America were found to be about the same as those of Europids. Though in some cases their bilingual backgrounds depressed their scores in verbal tests, they often surpassed the Europid in nonverbal tests. A 1926 test by Peter Sandiford of the University of Toronto on 276 Japanese and 224 Chinese children in Vancouver, using the Pintner-Paterson "Scale of Performance Tests," showed that the Japanese "form the cleverest racial group resident in British Columbia, with the Chinese forming a more doubtful second." Sandiford subsequently concluded that the "presence of so many clever, industrious and frugal aliens constitutes a political and economic problem of the greatest importance."[33]

A 1921–1923 investigation of Japanese children, made under the direction of American psychologist Lewis M. Terman, using the complete Stanford-Binet and the Army Beta, concluded that no significant differences were found in the mental capacity of Japanese children compared with white American children. The research staff defined the term "American" to designate "the conglomerate of races, mainly northern-European in origin and Anglo-Saxon in tradition which two or three centuries of more or less geographical and cultural isolation have served to fuse into a rather distinct national type." Neither the Binet nor Stanford Achievement scores justified any final conclusion as to racial differences in variability, although boys were superior to girls in general mental capacity among both American and Japanese students. Also, among both Japanese and American populations there was a tendency for children of parents engaged in professional occupations to surpass those whose parents were manual laborers.[34] Thus, supported by this prewar scientific research, Japanese confidence in their own mental capacity influenced their postwar criticism of miscegenation as detrimental.

In late August 1952, new data came out in Japan as a result of a four-year joint research project. Research on the anthropological features of mixed-blood children was conducted jointly by the Microbic Institute at Nihon University and the department of physiology at the University of Tokyo, while research on their IQ levels and temperament was separately conducted by the department of psychology at Nihon University and the Central Counseling Center for Children. The report was made from a limited sample—267 mixed-blood children (66 of them "Negrasians") living at various institutions including the Elizabeth Sanders Home—and was thus of highly questionable value. Nonetheless, it set the tone for the scientific interpretation of mixed-blood children as a specific racial group in Japanese society.

The children were labeled as the nation's first "Eurasian race." The "white-mix [shiro-kon]" tended to be more pink and white in skin color in comparison to the Japanese; therefore, they were closer to the white race, while losing their Japanese traits. The "black-mix [kuro-kon]," on the other hand, tended toward a dark skin tone. Eye colors were darker in both cases.[35]

The IQ and temperament tests, conducted on children under age five, attempted to prove that temperament depended upon race. Although the research recorded the presence of some remarkable children, aged three and above, who had a superb ability to memorize and process information, the average IQ resulted in a lower level than that of pure Japanese children. The report remained cautious, avoiding the linkage of their inferiority to a hereditary effect of miscegenation, instead ascribing it to environmental factors such as the social backgrounds of their mothers and an absence of close communication with adults at the orphanages. But the report treated temperament as an innate trait and concluded that the children were highly emotional, egotistical, and hypersensitive. Under certain social circumstances such a temperament might direct them to rebel against or withdraw from society, thus becoming antisocial. Therefore, the report advised that good supervision was necessary for their healthy growth.[36]

Confusing results continued to come from various research institutes. In September 1951 the staff at the Central Counseling Center for Children tested ten mixed-blood children living in Yokohama for their mental development index, using the IQ test. The average score for these children, seven of them half-black, was higher than that of mixed-blood children at other orphanages. The top score, attained by a half-black child, was higher than the index among sixty-three pure Japanese (*junketsu*) raised at normal Japanese homes in the city of Kawasaki. The research concluded that mental development among mixed-blood children, especially half-black, was more advanced than that among average Japanese. Another study by a professor at Nihon University showed that 5 percent of the Japanese had some mental defect (*chinō ijō*), compared with 30 percent of the mixed-blood children at a certain orphanage.[37]

An official report, issued in June 1954 by the Institute of Population Problems, Ministry of Welfare, confirmed the view that lower intelligence would result from miscegenation. The report, entitled *Konketsu oyobi imin ni yoru Nihon-minzoku taii no eikyō ni tsuite* (The Anthropometric Influences of Emigration and Blood Mixture on the Japanese Race), was the result of a major research project on the anthropometric effects of biological and environmental changes on the Japanese race in order to predict the future of the Japanese race (*Nihon-minzoku*) in physiological terms. Two separate investigative reports, one on mixed-blood Japanese children and another on Japanese emigrants to North America, were issued to compare which was a better way to improve the anthropometric aspects of the Japanese—through genetic changes, through miscegenation, or through environmental changes.

Meiji intellectuals had discussed racial improvement in the same way. In the last decades of the nineteenth century, some scholars and politicians came out with an astonishing theory that for the survival of the Japanese race in competition with the superior Westerners, they needed interracial marriage to draw superior Western blood into their veins. Opponents claimed that miscegenation between the Japanese and Europeans would not only invite promiscuity but produce new diseases. Worse, it would lead to the eventual disappearance of the Japanese race and the subsequent disappearance of Japan as a nation. The Japanese should remain Japanese, racially speaking; yet they could improve their racial quality and catch up with Westerners by various social reforms. By 1910, popular sentiment favored the theory that the Japanese could continue their racial improvement through environmental improvement only. By improving political, economic, social, and cultural institutions, the Japanese could achieve the level of Western civilization while biologically and physiologically remaining the yellow race.[38]

Since emigration to North America (a place with better socioeconomic conditions than Japan) had long been considered to have a positive effect on Japanese physical improvement, the 1954 report attempted to reevaluate this theory by comparing the Nisei, who had benefited from such environmental advantages, with their Japanese counterparts living in Japan. On the other hand, the report maintained a doubtful tone on the positive effects of genetic improvement through miscegenation.

As for mixed-blood children born in Japan (during and after the Occupation), the 1954 report investigated the racial characteristics of 267 "hybrids" (201 white American-Japanese and 66 black-Japanese), all of them under six years of age, living in the vicinity of Tokyo and Kanagawa Prefecture. It drew on the children's height, weight, measurement of various parts of the body, blood type, fingerprints, color of skin, color and type of hair, color of eyes, Mongolian folds (the epicanthic fold of the upper eyelids unique to the Mongoloid race), stature and weight, to clarify quantitative differences in physical appearances, and attempted to determine prominent racial traits in these "hybrids," as compared to the pure Japanese, especially the children's characteristic mentality and deformities.

Though the 1954 report admitted that environmental factors, rather than heredity, played a vital role in mental development, it nonetheless referred to several works to support the view that hybridization lowered the mental capacity of mixed-blood people. In the work on mixed-blood children of Ainu and Japanese, Tanaka Kan'ichi, the scholar who had conducted research on IQs among children of different racial and national backgrounds in North America in the 1930s, as well as on IQs among mixed-race children of the

Japanese and Ainu, concluded that the act of hybridization itself produced a few extremely superior and a few inferior offspring, compared to average "Japanese natives." Although it acknowledged the fair value of Tanaka's theory, the Welfare Ministry's own research, using Binet's mental test, nonetheless favored a hypothesis that racial hybrids, both half-white and half-black, resulted in a somewhat lower mental capacity than that of average Japanese natives.[39] Therefore, the racial mix had only negative effects on the wholesale racial quality of the Japanese.

In contrast to Tanaka's work, the 1954 report recommended the improvement of Japanese physical quality through environmental control alone. Research was conducted on 534 Nisei born in the United States to Japanese parents born in Japan, to prove their physical superiority because of better environmental conditions. According to the data, the Nisei exceeded native Japanese adults living in Japan in average height, weight, circumference of upper arms, leg length, and other measurements. The report stated that these differences had been caused by better nutrition and exercise, in contrast to the sedentary habits of daily life in Japan, which curbed the growth of native Japanese.[40]

As for intelligence, the report quoted various prewar data on Japanese children in North America and Hawaii, including similar studies by Tanaka Kan'ichi, which had claimed their IQ tended to be higher than that of white Americans. In terms of temperament (as well as lower crime rates), Nisei proved to be far superior to any other racial group (*minzoku*). Moreover, they had IQs even slightly higher than that of native Japanese, presumably due to better nutrition. The report therefore concluded that environmental changes alone would suffice to improve Japanese physical build. Although such characteristics as skin color, hair color, and blood type would not be altered, improving environmental conditions was still to be preferred over racial mixing. In conclusion, the report claimed that the Japanese had a hereditary "gift" of becoming a race with both intellectual and physical superiority (*taiiku chiiku tomo ni yūshū na minzoku taru tenpu no soshitsu o motte iru*). To achieve this goal, the improvement of nutrition and other environmental conditions in Japan should be a priority.[41]

The report harshly criticized genetic changes through miscegenation as likely to lower the quality of the pure Japanese. Although it cautiously stated that poor environmental factors surrounding the mixed-blood children might account for a lower IQ, it nonetheless emphasized the children's "hereditary physical defects,"[42] and did not even suggest that a good environment would help improve the innate inferiority resulting from miscegenation. In sum, the report implied that whether in Japan or North America, only by remaining pure of blood could the Japanese improve and excel through constant environmental development.

Although the Japanese public generally preferred to prevent racial mixing with whites because of what was perceived to be the intellectual deficiencies of half-Japanese children, some actually saw such racial blending as contributing to the physical improvement of the Japanese. The supposed physical inferiority of the Japanese in comparison with the white race became a subject of serious medical debate (as it had during the Occupation), especially as the average height and weight in school children had not overcome the effects of wartime malnutrition. In 1952 a medical professor at the Japan College of Medicine (Nihon Ika Daigaku) introduced the Japanese public to a theory that, in France and Britain, a stout physique with a long torso and short legs (characteristics also of the Japanese race) tended to appear predominantly among children from poorer families. Nevertheless, he claimed that such physical disadvantages should not be regarded as the destiny of the Japanese race. Instead, he suggested that Japanese authorities should contemplate a new socioeconomic policy to improve living standards as well as dietary patterns for the general Japanese population so that Japanese youth in the future would have longer legs and would be taller like European people of the upper classes. He even added that physical improvement of this kind would some day lead the Japanese to excel in those international athletic competitions where height mattered.[43]

The Japanese public pursued the subject of their physical improvement with passion. In the summer of 1952, Japan sent a total of 112 athletes to compete in the Helsinki Olympics—the nation's first Olympic participation in sixteen years—and won only one gold medal in wrestling, as well as three silver medals in swimming, and two bronze medals. This unsatisfactory performance made some Japanese deplore that their body size and type left them unable to compete successfully against white and black athletes. The Japanese lacked the long legs and tall stature so helpful in running races, especially short distances, and the height and powerful build that had such obvious advantages in certain competitions.[44] In the summer of 1953, when Itō Kinuko won third place at the Miss Universe Pageant held in the United States, her slender proportions and small head—the so-called *hattō-shin*, the length of a head measuring exactly one-eighth of the whole body height—

gave the Japanese something to celebrate and helped deflate the myth that a perfectly proportioned body was a Western monopoly.[45]

In this sociocultural climate, some Japanese expected that racial mixing with whites would create a new type of Japanese able to participate in new fields of endeavor. Ōya Sōichi, a conservative social commentator, was among those who supported the theory of a favorable racial mixture to bolster Japan's image overseas. In terms of facial and physical features, many half-white children seemed to embody the advantages of both races, especially half-white girls, many of whom were quite pretty, Ōya argued, espousing a typical formula of sexism and racism.

In such fields as the arts and sports these children might represent Japan better than would the pure Japanese. Traditionally, a Japanese opera singer lacked vocal power owing to a diminutive physical build, and a Japanese ballerina would never be world-class because of her poor physique. However, a Japanese citizen of mixed blood might some day become a Broadway musical star, Ōya continued, thanks to his or her well-proportioned figure as well as an ability to sing and dance, which he believed to be a genetic endowment within the white and black races. Likewise, a half-black half-Japanese athlete might win dozens of gold medals for Japan at the Olympics because of his inherited qualities from the black race, which, Ōya believed, had exceptional athletic talent. If racial mixing successfully combined the physical advantages of the white or black race with the Japanese style of mental training, these mixed-blood children would surely become leading figures in the fields of art, entertainment, and sports. Thus, concluded Ōya, the mixed-blood children—both half-white and half-black—would make a great contribution to Japanese society.[46]

Japan had another set of half-Japanese offspring to deal with. In this case, because it was a matter of the children born of intermarriage between Japanese settlers and native peoples in Japan's former colonies, the Japanese sense of superiority over all other Asian races created a different sort of problem. During the war, intermarriage between the Japanese and the peoples of their colonies was officially discouraged. It would not only produce generally "inferior" mixed-blood children but would also destroy the spiritual solidarity of the Japanese race. Despite, or because of, this official admonition against intermarriage, in Southeast Asia alone an estimated 70,000 to 100,000 illegitimate children were fathered and abandoned by Japanese soldiers at the end of the war.[47]

Despite demands from these former Japanese colonies for governmental intervention or compensation, these children never received as much attention from either the Japanese government or the public as did the half-American children. On the contrary, many Japanese experts claimed that they posed no problem in Southeast Asian societies at all. One essay discussing the problem of half-American children in Japan compared it to the situation of half-Japanese children in Southeast Asia and argued that the latter were more welcome because of local admiration for the Japanese race. The writer claimed that the children were a "romantic product of Japanese men and local women celebrating a victorious alliance of the colored race [*kangeki-teki na yūshoku-jinshu dōshi no shōri-kan kara umareta jōkō*]"—so why complain?[48]

Between March and July 1952, Fujiwara Michiko, Diet member from the Socialist Party–Left faction, traveled to Indonesia, Thailand, Burma, the Philippines, and several other nations in Southeast Asia to interview the mothers of these children who hoped to trace their putative Japanese fathers. Although many of these women expressed a hope that their half-Japanese children might be sent to Japan for better educational opportunities, Fujiwara reported, they were having fewer problems in raising their half-Japanese children in Southeast Asia than those women raising half-American children in Japan. It is because, she explained, a "mix with Japanese blood" made their children superior beings in their communities and the mothers are well respected.[49] Sawada of the Elizabeth Sanders Home agreed, saying that women in Southeast Asia did not complain about Japanese men because their society preferred this racial mix. In fact, Sawada continued, in Africa mixed-race children are treated as precious treasures.[50]

An article that appeared in *Asahi* in February 1953 reinforced the self-serving myth of a superior and welcome Japanese mixture in Asia. It reported that all half-Japanese children in Sumatra and Java were smart, healthy, well-built, and cute, thanks to Japanese blood. Their mothers, their relatives, and neighbors were so proud of these half-Japanese children that they could not possibly be discriminated against. Unlike the situation in Japan, where the Japanese and American governments were confused about responsibility for the children, it seemed unlikely that these women in Southeast Asia would ever accuse Japanese men or claim that the Japanese government was responsible for them, the newspaper article reported.[51]

As for half-black children, quite a few critics raised serious concerns that, unlike half-white children, they would suffer much more severely because of their "different outlooks."[52] Hirabayashi Taiko, a leading female proletarian writer since the prewar period known for her concern for basic social problems, contributed an essay in *Asahi* encouraging the nation to assume a positive attitude toward these half-black children. Without hesitation she acknowledged that Japanese inferiority to the white race derived from the former's lack of physical attractiveness. But just as the Japanese would be offended if they were looked down on only for that reason, the black race, although "bizarre" in physical appearance, should react the same way, since they too have superior talents in a spiritual (nonphysical) ways, Hirabayashi argued.

Since the Japanese are themselves a conglomerate of various races of Asia and not a "pure" race, she was convinced that the participation of these children in Japanese society should pose no problem, and that two or three generations into the future their black skin color would vanish into the Japanese yellow skin color, only to enrich the Japanese racial stock. Quoting a discussion with American novelist Richard Wright in France, who spoke approvingly of marriages between Japanese women and black GIs, Hirabayashi again emphasized that the Japanese should proudly raise and educate the offspring of these unions.[53]

The importance of education for these half-black children was much discussed, perhaps even more so than for the half-white children. Advocates claimed that only the cultivation of better knowledge, will power, and personality through good education would help these half-black children to overcome discrimination and become respectable Japanese. A political cartoon by Yokoyama Taizō entitled "Mixed-Race Children Problem," appearing in the June 1952 *Shōsetsu Shinchō*, shows a half-black boy graduating as an honor student with the highest scores from elementary school through college. He enters the Japanese Ministry of Foreign Affairs with the highest recommendation and receives an unusually rapid promotion toward a diplomatic position. In the last scene he is shown working alone and smiling inside a small Japanese Embassy building in a jungle.[54]

In arriving at a national decision about an educational program for these children, debates took place over which policy—benevolent separation or integration—would be better. One issue was the questioning of their presumed lower mental capacity. In December 1952, Fujiwara Michiko made an inquiry to a governmental representative at the Upper House Committee on Welfare: "I have heard that these mixed-blood children are, in many cases, sort of idiotic. I suspect one reason for the high rate of idiocy among them is their mothers, who are prostitutes and, again, idiotic in very many cases." These children would in the future very likely constitute a serious social problem on a large scale, Fujiwara claimed, and she demanded that the government take an active role in dealing with this question.[55] Many educational experts responded that the difference in mental capacity and emotional development between these children and other "general" children (*ippan jidō*) required segregated educational facilities.[56]

In the spring of 1952 the local PTA of the City of Oiso attracted nationwide attention when its parents objected to the entry into the local public school of the children from the Elizabeth Sanders Home—seventeen of them in all, three of them half-black. The PTA based its opposition on rumors that these children had been idiotic from birth, emotionally insecure, and were violent and prone to throw fits, especially in the case of "black children." Some feared that they carried venereal diseases inherited from their mothers. When the city's board of education offered to build a separate classroom for them, Sawada opted for building her own school on the site of the Sanders Home.[57]

Sawada of the Elizabeth Sanders Home remained the foremost advocate of the separation policy, which she believed would protect the children's "mental and physical handicaps" from the hostile outside world. Only in a shielded world would they learn to gain self-esteem and become strong and secure. Then, when they became mature enough to accept their "destiny" (*shukumei*) and face future obstacles, Sawada was convinced, they would be ready to go outside into the real world, possibly to the United States.[58]

Sawada's segregation plan raised some doubts among experts on education. In a newspaper interview, Takeshita Seiki, chief of the Nursery Section of the Children's Bureau at the Ministry of Welfare, argued that these children should become accustomed to various forms of discrimination from an early stage of life so that by the time they reached adolescence they would be immune to discriminatory treatment and cope with it better. Takeshita supported the basic governmental principle of treating these children as equal members of society, as long as they had Japanese nationality, and also supported an integrated school system which, he said, would expedite their assimilation into Japanese society. Takeshita, however, added his personal view that these children would be better off in American society.[59]

On August 14, 1952, the Ministry of Welfare convened the Central Committee on Child Welfare (Chūō Jidō Shingi-kai) to officially discuss whether segregated or integrated education would facilitate the healthy development of these children. The committee established a special subcommittee, with twenty members, representing academics, governmental agencies, and various institutions in charge of the welfare of mixed-blood children.[60] In early September 1952, before any suggestion came from the committee, the Ministry of Welfare announced a plan to build segregated educational facilities designed exclusively for mixed-blood children. The spokesman explained that enrolling them in the integrated school environment with other Japanese students would be too abrupt a change and a cruel measure for these children.[61]

Students and parents for their part, however, expressed a degree of ambivalence about accepting the mixed-blood children as their "equal fellows." In September 1952 the Teacher's Union of Yokosuka, a city with a large U.S. naval base, conducted a survey of 482 students in both elementary and junior high schools in the city to ascertain their willingness to accept these "different" children. Ninety-three percent said that they had seen mixed-blood children. Of those, 46 percent of male students and 57 percent of female students said that they felt pity (*kawaisō*) for them. Seventy percent of the entire student group answered that if they saw these children being teased or bullied, they would stop the act, while 7.5 percent said it could not be helped (*ijime rarete mo shōga nai*). To a question of whether they would play with these children, 64 percent answered yes, while 28 percent answered they were not sure; 8 percent said they would not play with them.

A separate survey of 635 members of PTAs, conducted by the Teacher's Union, showed much lower acceptance levels among the adults. Although 65 percent supported a completely equal educational environment for these children, 19 percent supported a separate educational facility for them. Sixteen percent, or 101 parents, even went so far as to advocate a sort of asylum or internment camp (*shūyō-jo*) where these children could be educated.[62]

In Kisarazu, Chiba Prefecture, where there was a large U.S. military base, the Teacher's Union took similar opinion polls of 150 students in the city's elementary and junior high schools. The result showed less friendly attitudes. Of 150 students, 132 said that they had seen mixed-blood children before and knew how they looked. Sixty-seven percent of them said that they were not sure whether they liked them or not, while 29 percent said they would not make friends with them. Only 4 percent of the students said that they did not mind making friends with them.[63]

The Japanese government, wary both at national and local levels because of the inevitable repercussions on U.S.-Japanese relations, issued a cautiously worded "enlightened" policy toward this problem and supported the school integration program. On October 16, 1952, the Tokyo Municipal Government convened a special meeting, inviting representatives from the departments of education, welfare, and health as well as from the institutions that housed mixed-blood children in the metropolitan area. By then, there were seventy-seven mixed-blood children in these institutions, fifteen of whom (eleven half-white and four half-black) would become six years old by the following spring. The officials estimated that outside these orphanages there were more than eight hundred mixed-blood children who lived with their mothers or relatives. Although several PTAs continued their opposition to integrated schooling based on fear that the presence of these children would destroy an otherwise peaceful environment at school, the meeting concluded with the Tokyo Municipal Government's requesting the cooperation of schools and PTAs in integrating the mixed-blood children into normal schools. On November 13, 1952, the Kanagawa Prefectural Government, too, announced that as a principle the mixed-blood children should attend public schools on an integrated basis.[64]

Two weeks later, on November 26, when the Japanese Ministry of Welfare convened the Central Committee on Child Welfare, the committee officially proposed for the first time since its first meeting in August 1952 that the Japanese government support integrated public education for mixed-blood children as long as they held Japanese nationality.[65] Japan had long adopted the rule of jus sanguinis through the father, which stipulated that a child is a Japanese national only when the father is a Japanese national at the time of the child's birth. However, according to Article 2 of the Nationality Law of May 4, 1950 (Law No. 147), a child is a Japanese national under the following circumstances: when the father is unknown or has no nationality, but the mother is a Japanese national; or when a child is born in Japan with both parents unknown or having no nationality. Under the nationality law and family registry (koseki) system, an illegitimate child, as long as he was born in Japan to a Japanese mother, could acquire Japanese nationality through proper registration—that is, if his Japanese mother compiled a separate family registry of her own and entered her child into it as a Japanese national.[66]

According to the Japanese government's estimate, 20 to 30 percent of mixed-blood children, many of them illegitimate with putative American fathers, were not registered with the Vital Statistics authorities in the family registry system and thus lacked Japanese nationality. The government encouraged local governments to find such cases where the mothers neglected to register the births of their children and to make arrangements to register their status with Vital Statistics authorities. On December 19, 1952, the Ministry of Education officially requested the Ministry of Justice to investigate the status of such children without Japanese nationality as part of the governmental campaign in support of integrated schooling.[67]

The Japanese press showed unanimous support for the integration plan. In early 1953 major newspapers and journals printed stories about successful integration plans for mixed-blood children. The Suginami Ninth Elementary School, Tokyo, was to admit three mixed-blood children from the orphanage in the school district in the spring. At the height of vigorous opposition by the PTA, some parents threatened to transfer their children to other schools where there were no mixed-blood children. However, the school principal and teachers convinced the parents of the importance of "racial equality [*jinshu byōdō shugi*]" and the PTA eventually accepted the plan. Some parents even asked to have their own children "share the same desk, sit side by side with poor half-black children," one newspaper reported.[68]

The Japanese Ministry of Education set out to prepare special guidelines for the treatment of mixed-blood children in regular schools. The basic policy was to treat them as Japanese as long as they had Japanese nationality. The long-term goal of their education was to prepare them for obtaining vocational skills so that they would become self-supporting. In February 1953, two months before Japan's new school year began, the Section of Primary Education at the Ministry of Education issued a twenty-four-page mimeographed reference booklet. Entitled *Konketsuji no shūgaku ni tsuite shidō-jō ryūi subeki ten* (Checkpoints for Instructing Mixed-Blood Children in School), the pamphlet instructed teachers and other people in educational fields on how to deter racial discrimination in the minds of children as well as their parents, and to nurture in them a sense of equality in relation to the mixed-blood children.[69] The pamphlet emphasized the importance of the PTA's cooperation for the children's successful integration, especially since adults were much more biased while children were relatively free of racial prejudice. The pamphlet first suggested that local boards of education work closely with PTAs and welfare committees (*minsei iin*) to find out the exact number of mixed-blood children in each community who had reached school age. In case some of them were not entered in the family registry, each local board of education should with "compassionate attitudes" encourage such mothers or other guardians to enter their children in their family registries so that they would receive automatic acceptance in the public schools upon their becoming Japanese citizens.[70]

The next step was for teachers and counselors to convince mothers and guardians of mixed-blood children that their children would not be bullied or ostracized. Teachers should always act as their "sincere sympathizers." Teachers who had mixed-blood children in their classrooms should learn about their family background in detail so they could give better assistance if trouble should arise. If the teachers could not get information from the mothers, they should turn to neighbors. The pamphlet advised local boards of education and schools to ask teachers, members of PTAs, and people in local communities to abandon exclusionist attitudes toward these children altogether and instead become "understanding and sympathetic." Yet, the pamphlet cautioned, they should not be overprotective of the mixed-blood children because that would amount to reverse discrimination against the rest of the students.[71]

The pamphlet also gave detailed instruction on pragmatic problems, such as class assignment and seating arrangements for the mixed-blood children, which might arise because of the commonly perceived discomfort of being physically close to those with different skin color and physical features. The authorities predicted opposition from parents of children who were assigned to the same classroom or activity group with mixed-blood children. They also anticipated some form of protest from children and their parents who were assigned to share a desk with mixed-blood children. The pamphlet recommended against physically isolating the mixed-blood children in any way—by seating them alone, or with another mixed-blood child, or even at a corner or a rear seat, away from the rest of the students. Assign them to any class and desk at random based on a color-blind policy, the pamphlet recommended. But, it also instructed, teachers should contact the parents of those children who were assigned the same desk as a mixed-blood child and ask for their understanding.[72]

Once the school year began, a new set of statistics came out on the total number of mixed-blood children entering school. In the spring of 1953, only 396 children entered school, 77 of them from orphanages. Of them, 345 were enrolled in public education (263 schools in total), and 51 in private education (14 schools in total). Of those 345 children enrolled in public school, 279 were half-white and 66 half-black. Of those enrolled in private schools, 43 were half-white and 8 were half-black. By the end of the academic year, 31 more children became enrolled in school, increasing the total of mixed-blood schoolchildren to 427.[73]

Considering the fact that less than four hundred children were involved, governmental instruction was extraodinarily meticulous and even paternalistic. The basic principle of integrated education for these mixed-race children was not the same as the idea of Japanization in the colonial period, when Japanese customs and culture were prescribed. There was some hesitation to impose the Japanese way on these children. Rather, the Japanese government and press together presented the idea of integrated education for these mixed-blood children as an occasion for Japan to learn about the meaning of racial equality and tolerance. The Japanese press often printed sentimental human interest stories with photos celebrating integrated education as a symbol of U.S.-Japanese friendship.

Half a century before, when the first Japanese immigration controversy occurred in San Francisco, American parents were vehemently opposed to the idea of Japanese students studying in the same classroom, especially sitting close to their own children—Japanese boys sitting near white girls in particular—and demanded their segregation. For the sake of U.S.-Japanese friendship, however, President Theodore Roosevelt intervened and ordered the San Francisco Board of Education to reintegrate these ninety-three Japanese children into white schools. Some fifty years later, the Japanese government adopted a similar measure toward its own half-American children, again for diplomatic reasons, thereby transforming the issue from a racial one into a political one, just as Theodore Roosevelt had done.

When Cold War strategic considerations entered the scenario, the U.S. government finally moved to resolve the problem through a massive overseas adoption plan—literally the physical removal of the children from Japan. From the American point of view, the presence of thousands of half-American illegitimate children was now a problem wherever the U.S. military was stationed, specifically in West Germany, whose society was confronted with the presence of "mullatoes" fathered by black American soldiers.[74]

The U.S. government was highly concerned that half-American children might become a source of anti-Americanism abroad. Thus, in Japan, the U.S. government abandoned its original idea that these children ought to be assimilated into Japanese society and launched a new plan to adopt these children, thereby removing the problem from Japan. The immigration barrier, however, made American adoption of half-Japanese children impossible. Prior to the U.S. government's acknowledgment of these babies' existence, some personnel of the U.S. Armed Services and the Foreign Service, together with several private American organizations in Japan, had unofficially initiated various schemes to care for these children, including adoption by members of the Occupation.[75] Getting permission for half-Japanese adopted children to enter the United States was extremely difficult because of the racial exclusion provision of the immigration laws. Under section 13(c) of the Immigration Act of 1924, an alien child who was at least one-half Japanese, or one-half any other race that was ineligible for citizenship, was defined as ineligible for citizenship, and thus inadmissible to the United States.

Before the enactment of the McCarran-Walter Act of 1952, in order to get U.S. entry permission for half-Japanese adopted children, a waiving of the racial exclusion provision was required, usually through passage of an individual bill by Congress for each adopted child, a process usually taking four months to two years. In October 1951 alone, six separate bills were favorably introduced in Congress, asking for the special entry of such children as non-quota immigrants.[76]

Between September 30 and October 29, 1952, at the Congressional hearings to study the effects of the McCarran-Walter Act, the question of obtaining visas for "Japanese-American war orphans" was raised by Rosalind Bates, chair of the Southern California Women Lawyers, and the Reverend Sung Tack Whang, pastor of the Korea Gospel Church in Los Angeles. (By then, owing to the Korean War, the problem of GI babies had also spread to Korea.) Bates claimed that "in order to solve the problem of new minorities being created in various countries, . . . our immigration laws should be amended to allow the adopting parents to give their nationality to the adoptee." James Finucane, associate secretary of the National Council for the Prevention of War, also insisted on adoption by U.S. citizens. "American soldiers have fathered children in almost every quarter of the globe," he stated, estimating the total number of such babies all over the world as somewhere between 150,000 and 300,000. He recommended the formation of a United States Commission to examine the records of every one of these cases, and, where the evidence supplied by the mother or an admission by the father warranted belief in American paternity, the child should be granted American citizenship as an American responsibility.[77]

While the U.S. occupation of Japan was still in effect, some American Christian groups had organized a movement to solve the problem of mixed-blood children. The Reverend Verent J. Mills, overseas director of the Christian Children's Fund of Richmond, Virginia, with headquarters in Hong Kong, proposed a mass adoption of mixed-blood babies by American families as a "means to shoulder the American responsibility." He also planned a special school fund to provide the children with a bilingual education, which would prepare them for jobs with foreign trading companies, either in Japan or the United States.[78]

Under the McCarran-Walter Act, however, because of the small immigration quota of 185 it allocated to Japan, there was no provision for accommodating any proposals for the mass adoption of half-Japanese children. In June 1953, in the Tokyo area alone, the American Consulate had two thousand applicants for the annual slot of 185; the average waiting period for an adopted child to be screened for eligibility for emigration was ten to twelve years.[79]

When it became clear that the mass overseas adoption of the half-Japanese, half-American children was caught between humanitarian propaganda and the harsh reality of anti-Oriental immigration policy, a semiofficial American organization emerged in Tokyo to serve as a liaison between the U.S. and Japanese governments on how to resolve the problem of the mixed-blood children. This was the American Joint Committee for Assisting Japanese-American Orphans, established on October 2, 1952, and representing such American organizations in Japan as the American Chamber of Commerce, the American Legion Post No. 1, the Christian Children's Fund, Inc., the Inter-Board Missionary Field Committee, the Tokyo Union Church, and Veterans of Foreign Wars of the United States, Tokyo Post No. 9450. The American Joint Committee did not, in fact, have much of a task, since it regarded mixed-blood children as Japanese nationals and primarily the responsibility of the Japanese government. The committee basically supported the Japanese government's decision to integrate these children into Japanese school life as Japanese citizens.[80]

The committee did, however, have a delicate but much needed role (at least from the U.S. perspective) to play in the U.S.-Japanese alliance. It provided a public relations balm for the Japanese people, serving as a smokescreen to hide America's actual lack of interest or resources in resolving the issue of mixed-blood children in Japan. Its widely publicized existence, if not its activities, reassured the Japanese public that Americans felt some responsibility about the issue. The committee even withheld publicity on its existence until the legalization of its status under Japanese law, so it would not give the Japanese an impression of American intervention.[81] The committee routinely informed the State Department of its activities through the American Embassy in Tokyo. In the first few years, the State Department classified the committee's official documents as restricted.

The committee voted in early January 1953 to instruct the Japanese on how to deal properly with these children. It also proposed to aid the Japanese government in a program of public information and education against racial prejudice, using lecturers, PTAs, the press, and movies, "so that existing feelings against these children might be removed, and so that these children may be received by the general public as full-fledged Japanese citizens."[82]

A Japanese film studio was preparing for the late February release of the movie *Yassa Mossa*, featuring the mixed-blood children at the Elizabeth Sanders Home. The film was based on a novel of the same title by Shishi Bunroku, which also appeared as a series in a newspaper. The movie describes with humor the hectic lives of people involved in a private orphanage for mixed-blood children. The characters include some American soldiers—both black and white—and their Japanese prostitutes, their offspring at the orphanage, a feminist activist, a philanthropist, and a Japanese businessman who tries to milk a huge profit out of the presence of the U.S. military base. The American GIs are depicted as sincere, naive, and lovable men. The committee members saw this movie as a heartwarming comedy, likely to enlighten the public. They considered giving the Japanese public "proper guidance" on this film "in a way that would improve the general attitude toward these children."[83]

On January 29, 1953, when the American Joint Committee officially announced its purpose and activities to the Japanese public, it made headline news in the major newspapers in Japan, both Japanese and English. Despite anti-American sentiment and calls for Japan's independent action, the Japanese public showed substantial interest in the committee and several experts turned to it for advice on a better solution to racial issues related to the mixed-blood children.[84]

The International Orphans Relief Society, organized in Japan on November 11, 1952, also expressed interest in cooperating with the committee in solving this "difficult but worthwhile subject." The society's membership included such dignitaries as the former Prince Kuni and the former Princess Higashikuni, a daughter of Emperor Meiji, and greatly enhanced the status of the American Joint Committee in Japanese eyes.[85]

At their fourth meeting on December 17, 1952, the committee had suggested working toward improving U.S. immigration procedures to accommodate the adoption of the children. In February 1953 the American Joint Committee decided to solicit the help of influential figures in the United States. On the committee's list were impressive names such as former First

Lady Eleanor Roosevelt, Mrs. John D. Rockefeller III, James Michener (author of the 1954 best-selling interracial romance *Sayonara*, which also became an immensely successful Hollywood film starring Marlon Brando) and Pearl Buck (who had by then just started a project in Bucks County, Pennsylvania, to house Eurasian orphans).[86] Within a few months, the American Joint Committee began to receive enthusiastic replies from these people. Eleanor Roosevelt informed Herbert Gallop, the committee's chairman, that she looked forward to discussing problems with the committee when she visited Japan in the near future.[87]

Meanwhile, the Department of State continued to believe that a mass adoption plan would be the best and quickest solution. In a letter to Dean Rusk, president of the Rockefeller Foundation, Robert McClurkin, deputy director at the Office of Northeast Asian Affairs, explained: The problem of mixed-blood children in Japan "has the seeds of becoming a potential irritant if, at some future time, American-Japanese relations should not be as harmonious as they are now." He said that the State Department would give sympathetic consideration to the matter if the Rockefeller Foundation successfully pushed Congress to enact bills permitting the admission of these "biracial children" into the United States either for or after adoption.[88]

When the American Joint Committee learned, on March 25, 1953, that a bill had been introduced in the U.S. Congress to permit more orphans to enter the United States, the committee abandoned its early support for their integration into Japanese society and passed a motion in support of the bill. The bill, House Joint Resolution 228, originally introduced by Congressman Francis Walter on March 19, would permit five hundred children under six years of age to enter from any country if they were adopted by United States citizens who were either serving abroad in the Armed Forces of the United States or employed abroad by the United States government. The American Joint Committee decided to inform the chairman of the House Judiciary Committee that they supported the legislation, and to request that the bill, instead of limiting the age of such orphans to six years, include all children born after May 1946.[89]

When Eleanor Roosevelt accepted an invitation from the American Joint Committee on U.S.-Japanese Intellectual Exchange (Nichi-Bei Chi-teki Kōryū Iinkai) and visited Japan for five weeks from late May to June 1953 as part of her world tour, the committee made arrangements for her to attend their meeting. The Japanese press highlighted the former first lady's involvement with the problem of mixed-blood children in Japan. On May 27, Mrs.

Roosevelt attended the committee's meeting along with representatives from the Veterans of Foreign Wars of the United States, Tokyo Post No. 9450, and the American Chamber of Commerce, as well as Tokonami Keiko, manager of the orphanage in Tokyo. Mrs. Roosevelt mentioned several instances when she had been asked to act on behalf of the immigration by mixed-blood children into the United States. After a general exchange of views, Gallop issued a public statement that the committee expected the social and political influence of Mrs. Roosevelt to expedite a solution to the problem.[90]

At this juncture, however, the massive adoption of some thousand half-Japanese children by American families, considered the most efficacious solution to the problem, seemed unlikely. Though childless couples in the United States were eager to adopt European war orphans, there was no such demand for half-Japanese children. There was even less interest in half-Japanese, half-black American children. Nonetheless, while the committee's exchange of communication with the Japanese Ministry of Welfare continued to promote the adoption program, the idea of assimilating the children into Japanese society had not been dismissed. Following a preliminary meeting on June 12, 1953, initiated by Dazai Hirokuni, chief of the Children's Bureau of the Welfare Ministry, Gallop invited Dazai to a luncheon meeting at the American Club on June 15, 1953, to discuss the Welfare Ministry's views on an assimilation policy versus an adoption program. Concerning an assimilation policy, Dazai stated that the Japanese public should be educated about the equal rights of these children, and that the Japanese government would try to guarantee them equal treatment in every respect. Dazai continued that the Welfare Department planned to assist them in acquiring special vocational skills to become self-supportive and self-reliant. At the same time, he suggested to Gallop that material and spiritual support from their putative fathers would be a great help for these children and that the ministry welcomed the committee's cooperation as an intergovernmental liaison in such matters. Within two weeks after Dazai's visit, on June 25, 1953, the Japanese government officially recognized the American Joint Committee for starting direct negotiations between the two governments.[91]

Sawada Miki, for her part, never believed the Japanese would accept these mixed-blood children and continued her own crusade toward American adoption. In late 1952 she made a much-publicized fund-raising trip to the United States. American reporters followed her with sensational questions about the mixed-blood children and possible consequences of a rise in anti-

Americanism in Japan. In turn, she gave a speech on the urgent need for Americans to adopt these children and free Japan of the burden. She met prominent Americans through her prewar connections as well as those of her husband Sawada Renzō, now ambassador extraordinary and plenipotentiary to the United Nations. Texas made her an honorary citizen for her humanitarian contribution to U.S.-Japanese friendship. She made a special effort to reach the black American community and to ask their help in adopting half-black children. She paid courtesy visits to prominent black American public figures such as Rev. Mordecai Johnson, president of Howard University, Roy Wilkins of the NAACP, Hubert T. Delany, justice of the Domestic Relations Court of the City of New York, and others.[92]

Pearl Buck cultivated a friendship with Sawada and actively publicized the need for Americans to bring these children to the United States. Calling the children a "burden on a small country already very low economically" and a "constant reminder of Japan's national disgrace" (permanent stationing of U.S. military troops on its own soil), she argued that there would be little hope for them in Japan unless the United States was responsible "to at least half the extent." Her article soon caught the attention of Sen. John F. Kennedy, who referred it to Thurston Morton, assistant secretary of the State Department. Morton replied quickly and favorably. He informed Senator Kennedy that although the U.S. government had not yet dealt with this matter officially, there did exist an American Joint Committee, created expressly to assist these children.[93]

Once the U.S. government gave official approval for American assistance to these children, hoping thereby to counteract the negative American image overseas, it avoided any reference to racism. Any official statements about the ways in which the problems related to the mixed-race children were racist problems might seem anti-American and provide fuel for the Communists. The U.S. government was also suspicious when individuals who had no affiliation with the American Joint Committee spoke for mixed-blood children. Sawada Miki, thus, soon fell under such suspicion. According to a confidential letter dated October 1, 1953, from James B. Pilcher, American consul general in Tokyo, to the Office of Northeast Asian Affairs, Department of State, Sawada "greatly exaggerated the GI baby problem" during her 1952 visit to the United States. In view of her previous activities, often taken in defiance of SCAP policies, Pilcher questioned whether it was appropriate for her to travel around the United States and solicit funds for the children, a cause the American Embassy in Tokyo saw as "charged with political overtones."

Pilcher insisted upon Sawada's security clearance before she was allowed to be involved in "the proper resolvement of the GI baby problem in Japan." In a confidential reply, Franklin Hawley, the officer in charge of Japanese affairs at the State Department, implied that such suspicion was unwarranted as Sawada had been warmly welcomed in the United States. Nonetheless, he promised to keep a close watch on her activities in the United States before determining whether any action should be taken against her.[94]

The American public had now come around to consider the "save the half-American children" campaign as a positive Cold War measure. An editorial in the *Washington Post* on July 1, 1953, insisted that the United States had an obligation as well as an opportunity to show a "humanitarian interest" in these children, for "advancing their care and education in these societies" was "in the Nation's long-range interest" in winning the Cold War.[95]

Rep. Frances Bolton fully endorsed this editorial on the congressional floor. She mentioned the Kremlin's program of sending "home" to the Soviet Union some 29,000 children fathered by Russian soldiers in East Berlin. Among this large number, there were 467 half-black, half-German children allegedly fathered by black American soldiers. Bolton claimed that the action of the Soviet Union showed its zeal to recruit and raise children as totalitarians and atheists from the earliest possible age. In contrast, the half-American children, left fatherless in foreign nations without proper assistance from the United States, "will quite certainly be a group of rootless, discontented young people who will be fertile soil for any and all 'isms.'" In order to keep them from becoming anti-American or Communist tools, Bolton urged Congress to get actively involved in helping these youngsters to win public acceptance in their own society. Then, she argued, they would be a "segment of America's participation in the future of the world."

While, for the similar growing problem of the half-black, half-white children in West Germany, Bolton advocated American assistance in their assimilation into German society, in Japan's case (she argued) because of severe population pressures, the Japanese were unwilling to accept these children. She therefore demanded the amendment of the immigration laws and the speeding up of American adoption procedures.[96]

In the summer of 1953 the American campaign resulted in the enactment of two separate laws: the Admission of Orphans Adopted by United States Citizens, and the Refugee Relief Act of 1953, which authorized the issuance of special nonquota immigrant visas to up to four thousand eligible orphans from all over the world. By mid-August 1953, American religious organizations announced plans to find homes in the United States for approximately four hundred Japanese-American orphans arriving under the Refugee Act. The American Joint Committee was fully involved in this process, supplying information on its progress to the State Department. In 1954 the committee increased its membership to include Catholic and Jewish groups as well as women's clubs and charity organizations, and continued registering orphans on the waiting list of the American Embassy for adoption and entrance into the United States.[97]

The Japanese government regarded the new movement as continuing evidence of American good will toward Japan, but it was aware that the emigration of regular emigrants as well as the wives of American GIs or mixed-blood children to the United States would remain strictly limited. In late August 1953, Japan's Ministry of Welfare issued a statement that the mixed-blood children who stayed in Japan, rather than being adopted by American families in the United States, would receive special care and attention from various governmental agencies so that they would grow up to be respectable citizens of Japan.[98]

Although some frustrated Japanese criticized the immigration policy of the United States and demanded a more "humanitarian American measure" in adopting mixed-blood children, others called for Japan to take action on its own. The latter argued that because American society was racist in nature, these half-Japanese children would never be fully integrated into society and equal with white Americans. Japanese society should assume the sole task of assimilating them, and overcome its own racism independently.

Kanzaki Kiyoshi, a leftist critic and president of the Council of Juvenile Culture at the Ministry of Education, warned in early 1953 that these mixed-blood children should not be made pawns in political games between Japan and the United States. America's interest in aiding Japan with the problem of mixed-blood children, he said, was not based on humanitarian concerns but directly connected to the importance of Japan in anti-Communist strategy. Moreover, he added that America's growing friendliness toward the Japanese did not mean the disappearance of their wartime racism. He warned that the fundamental problem of racism still remained unsolved, but that it was easily camouflaged by friendly gestures based on diplomatic calculation. Rather than expecting American assistance, the Japanese should learn to accept mixed-blood children as full members of their society. Through such efforts, Kanzaki claimed, the Japanese would eventually become truly generous and open-minded cosmopolitan citizens (*sekai-teki kokumin*), not merely rhetorically but also substantively.[99]

The presence of mixed-blood children compelled some Japanese to confront Japan's own historic racist attitudes. In response to the government's plan of integrating the mixed-blood children into regular schools, some critics demanded that the government adopt the same standard toward the *burakumin* and other Asian peoples in Japanese society. A letter to a readers' column in the newspaper *Tokyo* criticized the narrow-mindedness of the Japanese, which had caused a similar kind of persecution against the *burakumin*—these people with the same skin color—because of the special type of hereditary occupation they engaged in, and against the Koreans, because they were Japan's former colonial subjects. The letterwriter advocated equal treatment for all these people, regardless of background.[100]

In an editorial in *Shakai taimusu* (Social Times), Suga Tadamichi, president of the Committee for Protection of Children in Japan, argued that the nature of discrimination toward the mixed-blood children was the same as every other form of discrimination. Although a discriminatory feeling toward a specific group of people is not innate, people grow up with such a feeling, take it for granted, and behave as if they had been born with it. That is, social conditions often determine the level of prejudice, Suga argued. In rural areas, he continued, where feudal attitudes persist, hateful prejudice against "different people" is rampant. In towns with foreign military bases, the local people are often trapped in a colonial mentality and an inexplicable sense of debt toward the white and half-white people emerges, Suga pointed out. He suggested that people should try to delve into the roots of these discriminatory feelings toward specific groups and find out how irrational such unfair views actually were.[101]

In the March 1953 *Fujin kōron* (Women's Review), Horie Tadao presented the Marxist viewpoint on the nature of discrimination. Racial differences do not lead human beings to fatal confrontations against each other. Neither does alleged innate racial superiority and inferiority induce a power relationship between the oppressor and the oppressed. Horie claimed that since the age of imperialism, the class struggle had constantly pressured oppressed groups of people into a disadvantageous position and transformed such unequal relations into categorical discrimination based on the pseudoscientific concept of race. Horie thus argued that the Negro problem in the United States was in essence an economic issue, in which blacks as a group had been exploited as cheap labor.[102]

An executive official at the Division of Culture and Education, Teacher's Union of Japan (Nikkyōso), expressed his hope that the new educational opportunities provided for the mixed-blood children would pave the way to establishing a cosmopolitan environment in Japanese schools, where students could capture a true sense of the world. The Teachers' Union of Yokohama agreed on this point. It advocated equal treatment for these children based on the principle of racial equality as expressed in the new Japanese constitution.[103]

One newspaper editor encouraged the Japanese people to raise these mixed-blood children by themselves. Once Japanese adults were determined to do so with the pride of an independent first-rate nation, children would understand the point and cooperate with them willingly. Then the Japanese would no longer have to listen to America's paternalistic instructions or slavishly wait for its aid to arrive. He concluded: "Give them Japanese foods—natto or misoshiru—and let them play with a kite or hanetsuki [Japanese badminton-like game] or go enjoy watching kamishibai [picture-story shows] with other children. Just let them be a member of this country—the effort of assimilating them into Japanese will itself prove that the Japanese are the people worth self-governing a first-rate civil nation."[104]

Another discussion, which appeared in Jidō shinri, criticized the plan of "sending back" the mixed-blood children to the United States, claiming that this would be tantamount to dumping them amid white racism. Despite official preachments on democracy, one participant pointed out, American society segregates black people. Half-black children would be adopted by black Americans and, once sent "back" to the United States, would very likely be absorbed into black society, remaining forever segregated from white society and persecuted by it. Since Japanese people are also colored, the author argued, the Japanese might have a better chance of successfully merging these half-black children into the mainstream. By establishing a new principle of racial relations, the Japanese might enter a new phase of history as well.[105]

The Ministry of Education added its voice to the clamor with the publication of Konketsuji shidō kiroku (The Record of Instruction on Mixed-Blood Children). Volume 3 of this series, published in April 1956, reported a total of nineteen case studies on individual children since 1953, with special attention to the children's temperament, sensitivity toward discrimination, family conditions, and relations with other children, which the report said were taken care of by educators successfully.

In this volume there was also a special essay on the sociological analysis of minority groups, with an emphasis on the importance of the abolition of ethnic and racial discrimination in Japanese society. Koga Yukiyoshi, a renowned sociopsychologist who had studied in the United States, Britain, and Germany between 1921 and 1924, criticized the heavy emphasis on the physiological and biological aspects of mixed-blood children as their primary problem. Instead, he called for research focusing on group psychology to prevent the creation of ostracized minorities. In a society like Japan, where a "sense of superiority and inferiority and exclusionistic attitude are intensified by the feudalistic class system," mixed-blood children did not have a bright future unless some fundamental basis for collective social psychology was adopted.

Koga also criticized the still widespread pseudoscientific research in Japan which, based on unreliable methods and dubious hypotheses, produced misleading data on the negative characteristics of mixed-blood children. The latest scientific investigation abroad proved that what was formerly considered genetic was largely a product of culture, he explained. Thus, it was the socioeconomic background of black Americans that tended to lower their educational performance, not innate intellectual inferiority. Race, Koga argued, was not a biological fact. Rather, the concept of "race" is a human invention existing only in the cultural sphere. Thus, racial difference exists only as a matter of one's faith. Disciplines in the humanities and social sciences should all collaborate to investigate how and why such a concept of differences emerged and what it signifies in human activities, Koga insisted.

In understanding the case of the mixed-blood children in Japan, Koga proposed new research toward a better understanding of the cause and nature of "prejudice [*henken*]" and "discrimination [*sabetsu*]" in general. According to his thesis, prejudice is a complex cultural construct, and discrimination exists in the form of actual practice in society. He advocated that Japanese society first abolish any form of different treatment based on race, thereby working to remove discriminatory practices. Only by securing such a pattern of fair practice in Japanese society, Koga argued, could the Japanese move on to create a new sociocultural environment in which prejudice would be reduced.[106]

Beyond the discussion in print, there was also an attempt to present the nature of racism through popular films. When a left-wing Japanese film director portrayed the problem of mixed-blood children as a tragic by-product of the American military occupation of Japan, it created a controversy in both Japan and the United States, but for different reasons. The movie *Konketsuji* (Mixed-blood Children), produced by an independent Japanese film company, was released two months after *Yassa Mossa*. Lacking the humor of *Yassa Mossa*, *Konketsuji* dealt with social problems arising from the presence of U.S. military bases in Japan. The film depicts the life of mixed-blood children at an orphanage near a U.S. military camp. Henry and Tommy, half-black half-Japanese children, are the victims of the American military control of Japan. The two children often wonder why their skin color differs from the others. They want to become white, so Tommy is disappointed when he finds out he is going to be adopted by a black American couple. Henry runs away when a half-white girl refuses to play with him. Yet they learn from a Japanese teacher at the orphanage about the "equality of people despite skin color" and determine to be strong.

One Japanese movie critic criticized the film's attempt to portray the United States as the sole offender in the complicated issue of mixed-blood children. The tragedy of these children is racism in general, not the American military occupation of Japan, the critic pointed out. The film's overemphasis on American control simply exploited the issue of mixed-blood children for the sake of criticizing U.S. policy toward Japan and side-stepped the fundamental problem of Japanese lack of compassion. The critic disparaged the film's superficial treatment of Japanese reaction to these physically different children. One scene of the film showed a charitable woman kissing a half-black half-Japanese child and later secretly wiping her lips. In another scene at a school's physical examination for entering pupils, the camera captures the cruelty of children and their parents scrutinizing the mixed-blood children. After such moments, the film utterly fails to zero in on the nature of racism, the critic lamented. In this sense, *Konketsuji* ends up merely documenting the facts of racial discrimination, taking no social responsibility for its solution.[107]

The American side, meanwhile, never understood or even attempted to understand Japan's arguments concerning race and racism, whether social or biological. When news of the film *Konketsuji* reached the United States, Americans were furious—not with the issue of Japanese racism but with the film's critical portrayal of the U.S. military base. The fact that the U.S. Army had provided soldiers and trucks for extras and props, and allowed the filmmakers full access to restricted military areas, emerged as a highly controversial aspect of the congressional debate. On June 11, 1953, Congressman

Thomas Pelly of Washington declared the movie to be part of a larger anti-American conspiracy. "This is not only an insult to our soldiers and our flag, it is most disturbing to the mothers, sweethearts, wives, and families of these soldiers," he argued. He demanded a full investigation on how Sekigawa Hideo, a movie director with a long history of Communist activities, was allowed to take his anti-American script into United States Army properties and shoot the film. Pelly also alerted Congress that the media had already widely criticized the film's portrayal of Japanese discrimination as "violently anti-American." The *Tokyo Evening News*, an English newspaper, printed a full-column lead editorial and went so far as to say that this movie was "in all its loathsomeness, the sinister and cynical workings of the Communist mind." The *Seattle Times* introduced the picture as especially controversial when it portrayed "American soldiers trying to get rid of illegitimate babies, grabbing Japanese girls to rape them, and a married officer going through a bigamous marriage with a shy Japanese maiden."[108] *U.S. News and World Report* criticized the film's treatment of black Americans as anti-American because the only American in the film who emerges with humanitarian credit was "a Negro officer who adopts a Negro-Japanese baby." The article suspected that "his role in the picture is to talk about the Negro problem in the American South, a favorite topic of discussion among Communists in Japan as elsewhere."[109]

Some American diplomatic experts, who had noticed the peculiarity of Japanese dualistic racial identity and advocated its shrewd manipulation in soliciting Japan's friendship, were not so alert to the cause and mechanism of Japan's racism itself. American official analysis never went beyond treating it merely as a primitive psychological phenomenon among people with a peculiar history. On March 12, 1953, Robert Murphy, U.S. ambassador to Japan, wrote to the Department of State, giving his impression of Japanese attitudes to the problem of mixed-blood children. Regarded as one of the most ubiquitous U.S. diplomats between 1940 and 1970, Murphy had served as political adviser to the U.S. Occupation government in Germany until 1949, then as ambassador to Belgium where he worked to implement the Marshall Plan. As U.S. ambassador to Japan, he had to deal with Japanese left-wing forces as well as the maintenance of U.S. military control over the Bonin Islands, the improvement of Japanese–South Korean relations, and the Korean truce talks. While he acknowledged the extensive publicity given to the issue in the United States, he nonetheless tried to assure the State Department that the problem in Japan was not as acute as it was in Britain, with an estimated 70,000 illegitimate babies, or in West Germany, with 94,000 such babies fathered by American GIs.[110]

Murphy went on to explain that the primary reason for Japan's focus on these children was Japan's "ethnic [*sic*] homogeneity." He wrote: "Racial differences accentuate the problem here in a country where there is remarkable ethnic homogeneity and where the people have never before had occasion to cope with a problem of this kind." Otherwise, he continued, "the problem in Japan is not an acute one from a public relations point of view." Murphy concluded that the nature of the issue would not harm U.S.-Japanese relations or create a race problem in Japan. As long as the United States went along with the proposal to make it possible for persons in the United States to adopt these biracial children, "most of the unwanted bi-racial children could be placed with American families in a very short time," and it would bring a quick end to the whole matter in both Japan and the United States.[111]

The American Joint Committee also displayed a naive perception of the nature of Japanese racism, underestimating the complexities underlying the racism of both nations. When the committee first supported Japan's assimilation plan, it assessed the problem as one of unfamiliarity, which would vanish as soon as the Japanese people became accustomed to the presence of these children. The report pointed to several international seaports such as Yokohama and Kobe, where the citizens had long been accustomed to the presence of a variety of peoples. Mixed-blood children were not persecuted in these areas simply because local people were used to their different physical characteristics. But that was not the case in other large cities and in rural areas where local people were not accustomed to seeing non-Japanese features.[112] The American Joint Committee thus predicted optimistically that discrimination would easily fade away once the Japanese became used to physical differences. The committee seemed oblivious to the historical evidence in American society, which, after a couple of centuries, was still not comfortable with the presence of blacks.

James Michener, in a March 1954 *Reader's Digest* article, "The Facts about GI Babies," explained Japanese discrimination against mixed-blood children. His article, replete with misinformation, summarized the standard American understanding of Japanese racism, which had not changed since the prewar period. Michener told of a boy, one of the first GI babies born in Japan. At age six, living at an orphanage in Tokyo, he was "a robust boy with light sandy hair, blue eyes and a marvelous complexion." Despite being such an adorable kid—with Michener taking it for granted that Caucasian features were the only acceptable universal standard of charm—things would surely be rough for him in Japan. He explained that Japan's history made its people exclusive and narrow-minded: "The Japanese believe that their race is unique and pure, unsullied by outside blood for at least 6,000 years. Custom keeps this foolish belief alive, although educated Japanese know that the Japanese are actually a combination of North Asian, Chinese, Korean, Malayan and other races. But because the main additions to the Japanese blood stream ended some thousand years ago, the myth of an unsullied race has developed." Proud of this myth, Japanese people were obsessed with "race pollution." This incurable custom, combined with other traditions such as the feudalistic and authoritative family system, would make life miserable for the racially mixed boy. Michener urged America to get involved in solving the problem by adopting the children.[113]

In spite of well-publicized binational collaboration, the actual pace and scale of Washington's actions in resolving the problem by massive American adoption did not meet expectations. Even after Congress opened the door to Japanese brides in 1952 under the McCarran-Walter Act, GIs found that within their military units there were obstacles to marriage with Japanese women. Chaplains usually counseled against intermarriage, and unit commanders blocked the marriage by changes in assignment, transfer, and other forms of pressure.[114] Yet the Japanese continued to hope that America would adopt these children. Takasaki Setsuko, chief of the Woman and Juvenile Section at the Department of Labor, predicted that the adoption plan would be the best solution because she believed these children would be stigmatized from birth and could not survive in Japan.[115] An executive at the Elizabeth Sanders Home agreed that a society that had never been able to solve the problem of *burakumin* and Korean peoples would not be likely to accept these children with understanding and love. Rather than expecting a society lacking in humanity to become generous enough to accept people with black skin as equals, he said, Japan would rather send these children back to American society, where there are millions of their "fellows."[116]

In pressing for mass adoption in America, the Japanese believed that American society was more tolerant than their own. At a meeting of the Japanese Lower House Committee on Education, held on February 28, 1953, Tanaka Hisao (Reform Party), committee member, again expressed doubts that mixed-blood children could be successfully integrated into the Japanese public schools. He said that in a society with a mongrelized population such as America, miscegenation was never a problem anyway. According to Tanaka, in the United States different races had mixed and coexisted from the beginning of the nation and "the race mix would not pose any problem." In contrast, he continued, "We, the 'Yamato race,' have been consolidated together through a strength of a pure blood and have a social situation quite different from American society. Therefore, an emergence of mixed-blood elements within the society would create a tragedy for Japan."[117] He thus justified shifting the burden to America.

Regardless of the rhetoric on both sides, the adoption plan for mixed-blood children never operated effectively. By January 1955 the American Joint Committee had sent a total of only fifteen children to the United States under the provisions of the 1953 Refugee Relief Act. Through joint cooperation with the National Catholic Welfare Conference, the American Joint Committee arranged for these fifteen Japanese-American orphans—five girls and ten boys (ranging from two to eight years old) from Our Lady of Lourdes baby home at Yokohama—to enter the United States for adoptions by American families.[118] Congressman Francis Walter, cosponsor of the Mc-Carran-Walter Act, had put forth various private bills and by early 1956 had admitted about 350 Japanese orphans (both mixed-blood and pure-blood) into the United States for adoption by United States citizens.[119]

The number of mixed-blood children enrolled in Japanese schools increased slightly each year. By 1956 there were 1,280 mixed-blood children studying in Japanese schools nationwide, both public (1,139 schools) and private (141 schools), excluding those enrolled in American schools inside U.S. military bases. The oldest group, some 451 children, was in the third grade. There were 402 mixed-blood children in the second grade and 427 about to finish the first grade. Forty-eight percent of these children were in Kanagawa and Tokyo prefectures.[120]

The ideal of a new Japan—a democratic and cosmopolitan nation as a creator of a new civilization—did not engender tolerance for these children. Japan's mission and expansion overseas were widely discussed among postwar intellectuals, but any nonideological issues, such as interracial fraternization and racially mixed offspring, were absent from their vision of interaction with the outside world.

Strict social opposition to interracial sexual liaisons continued in the United States as well. Even in 1967, after the passage of the Civil Rights Act of 1965, sixteen states still forbade marriage between white and black.[121] Mississippi classed miscegenation as incestuous fornication. Missouri put intermarriage in the same class with incest and "marriage with imbeciles." The definition of the white race remained strict. In Georgia the term *white* legally included only persons of "white or Caucasian race who have no ascertainable trace of Negro, African, West Indian, Asiatic Indian, Mongolian, Japanese or Chinese blood in their veins." Virginia law provided a similar definition, though persons who had one-sixteenth or less of American Indian blood, and no other non-Caucasian blood, would still be considered "white."[122]

As for the impact of these half-American, half-Japanese children on U.S.-Japanese relations, there could have been valuable binational research projects on such subjects as integrated education for minority students, the status of and opportunity for minority groups in each society, and larger projects on the biological and social effects of miscegenation. A scholarly exchange of opinion on race issues would have benefited both societies, compelling them to confront their mutual racist thinking and to deal with it. No such initiative, let alone progress, occurred. Instead, total silence prevailed on the issue of racism per se. Each nation believed that its own prejudices were philosophical and crucial to its national ideology, whereas the racial bias of the other was simple, primitive, even superstitious prejudice. They did not see how similar the two racisms were and so ruined a momentous opportunity for mutual understanding.

The Aftermath—
The Lesson of the Occupation

"The first international conference of colored peoples in the history of mankind," as President Achmed Sukarno of Indonesia described it, began on April 18, 1955, at Bandung in Indonesia.[1] Organized by the governments of Indonesia, Burma, Ceylon, India, and Pakistan, the conference represented half the world's population and seemed to usher in a new era in which the non-Western world was determined to win equality with the West.

The conference offered Japan the first opportunity in the postwar era to attend an international political conference. Japan publicized its role as a peaceful mediator between the West and Asia. As it turned out, its primary mission at the Bandung Conference was to be there as a Western proxy and to appease the West's fear of the rise of Asian antiwhite racism. The U.S. delegation specifically expected Japan to suppress the growing anti-Western sentiment among Asian nations. As in the immediate postwar period, U.S. policymakers in the 1950s planned to preserve the racial and ideological status quo in Asia. The U.S. government feared that the Communists would support anticolonial resolutions, win over Asian and African leaders, and thus "ensnare the relatively inexperienced Asian diplomats into supporting resolutions seemingly in favor of goodness, beauty and truth."[2] At the same time, the U.S. government also feared Asia's growing defiance of the West, which Western politicians labeled "reverse racism" against their former colonial masters.

When the opening date for the Bandung Conference drew near, Secretary of State Dulles had several conversations with British ambassador Sir Roger Makins and Lebanese ambassador Charles Malik on the anti-Western nature of the Pan-Asian movement. Dulles was concerned about what he called "racialism in the opposite direction" and was afraid that it would affect the "whole concept of human brotherhood, of equality among men, the fundamental concepts of the United Nations." He admitted that the West had frequently shown a sense of superiority but pointed out that it had brought good as well as bad (Christianity and material progress for instance) and that it would be tragic if "the Asians should select only the bad things in the record of the West, such as racialism, to imitate."[3]

On January 28, 1955, Secretary of State Dulles met with Iguchi Sadao, ambassador of Japan, for a discussion of Japan's attendance at the Bandung Conference. Dulles pointed out the possibility that the Communists might press for anticolonial resolutions under the doctrine of "Asia for the Asians." Such scenarios would cause difficulties for "our friends the French and British," as well as endanger the ties between Asian countries and the United States. He expected the Japanese delegation to "include people who understand that this is one world and that to exclude U.S. influence and ties from any continental area can only result in dominance by the Soviet Union."[4] Accordingly, the Hatoyama cabinet appointed Takasaki Tatsunosuke, director of the Economic Planning Agency (Keizai Shingi-chō), and Fujiyama Aiichirō, head of the Japanese Chamber of Commerce and Industry (Nihon Shōkō Kaigisho), and later minister of foreign affairs, as chief members of the Japanese delegation. Kase Toshikazu, a veteran pro-Western diplomat since the prewar period, served as Japan's ambassador extraordinary and plenipotentiary.

Throughout the Bandung Conference, the Japanese delegation maintained a low profile, while Chou En-lai, Jawaharlal Nehru, and Gamal Abdel Nasser projected strong images as able new leaders of the third world.[5] According to several accounts by Japanese insiders, however, the Japanese delegation worked behind the scenes to repair the rift between pro-Soviet and pro-U.S. nations of Asia, each of which condemned the new colonialism of the superpowers. In the final stage of the conference, twelve representatives held a secret meeting in order to prepare a closing declaration—the conference's official statement. Kase later wrote in his memoirs that at this final secret meeting he successfully bridged the ideological gap between the anti-Western camp, led by Chou En-lai and Nehru, and the anti-Communist nations, and reconfirmed a sense of solidarity among the Asian and African nations. Kase believed it was the effort of the Japanese delegation which led the Bandung Conference to a nonideological, middle-of-the road consensus that condemned "colonialism in all of its manifestations."[6]

On the final day, April 24, 1955, the conference adopted a ten-point declaration on the promotion of world peace and cooperation, incorporating the more generic principles of the UN charter, including the recognition of the equality of all races and of all nations large and small.[7] Thus the conference concluded, overcoming the ideological schism among the participating nations and censuring both continuing Western colonialism and Soviet policies in eastern Europe and Central Asia.

Japan perhaps helped to instill pro-Western sentiment at the conference. The U.S. government was relieved that the Bandung Conference did not form an "exclusive grouping of the colored races" directed against the West.[8] At the same time, Japan as a United States proxy also patronized the young Asian nations by posing as their big brother. It stood above the other Asian nations, nurturing their sense of belonging to one Asian civilization, and coordinating their rapport with the West. But Japan at Bandung played up the liberator role while avoiding reference to its colonial past in Asia, adopting the guise of its recent Westernized identity. Kase commented on the heated anticolonial sentiment at Bandung, which he said was the essential force that drew these young nations to the leadership of Japan. He said: "These delegates from Asia and Africa expressed gratitude to Japan, who expelled the imperialistic powers from Asia, and showed great hospitality to the Japanese delegate. In sum, they highly appreciated the past role of Japan in promoting their national liberation [*minzoku kaihō*]" (i.e., from the West).[9] In Kase's view, at Bandung Japan's Pan-Asianism was peacefully revived with a blessing from the West—testimony to the validity of Japan's racial duality.

Throughout the U.S. occupation, Japan successfully maintained the same racial identity as in the prewar period, quickly stabilized its relations with the United States, and reintegrated itself into the world system. But caught between Asia's decolonization movement and the West's continuing desire to dominate the region, Japan's attitudes and actions within the complicated world politics of race and ideology still remained full of contradictions.

The dualism of Japan's identity served to solidify its position in the Western community as a junior regional representative—a permanent "associate" member of the circle of Western nations. Yet the Americans could not truly consider Japan an ally during the Cold War. The Japanese failed to see their own racism and this made it difficult for them to understand the new movement in Asia, or to overhaul their racist practices at home. There was no way for Japan to assert itself as a trustworthy ally of Asia. The Japanese were paying the price of quick national recovery built upon the racist ideology and practice they had preserved in the Occupation.

In 1956, a year after the Bandung Conference, Japan was admitted to the United Nations. Although Japan had applied for membership in the international organization immediately after gaining independence in 1952, the Soviet Union had blocked it because of its opposition to the San Francisco Peace Treaty. Now came another opportunity to play a role on the international scene.

Japan's earlier attempt to gain membership in the United Nations demonstrates its ongoing diplomatic tactics in garnering world recognition. The Japanese Association of International Law set up a study group to prepare for UN membership, insisting that such a step would contribute to Japan's cultural development. Japan had been one of the leading powers of the League of Nations because of its political and military capacity, not because of its social and cultural advancement. This time, the group suggested, Japan should try to improve its cultural standards to a level appropriate for UN membership. Yet the report did not hesitate to recognize a leadership role for Japan in Asia and proposed that it strive for a solution to problems in neighboring countries.[10]

When membership in the United Nations was finally approved in December 1956, following the Soviet-Japanese Joint Declaration of the previous year, Japan proudly declared its mission to serve as a bridge between the East and the West, but with a healthy self-identity as an Asian nation. In an acceptance speech to the UN membership at the General Assembly, Shigemitsu Mamoru, deputy prime minister and foreign minister of Japan, explained how the dualism of Japan's position should ideally allow it to serve as a peaceful mediator between the West and Asia. Shigemitsu spoke of the inseparability of Japan from other Asian nations, whose overall growth and development remained a great concern for Japan. He expressed sympathy for the rising nationalism in Asian and Arabic regions (*Ajia-Arabia chiiki*), which he called a natural course of human evolution. He also called for UN assistance in the economic development of Asia, which would be indispensable for creating peace and progress amid political turbulence.[11]

In 1957 the Japanese Ministry of Foreign Affairs began publishing basic principles of Japanese diplomacy in its annual *Gaikō seisho—waga gaikō no kinkyō* (Diplomatic Blue Book—Recent situations in our diplomacy). In its first issue it declared Japan's determination to make strenuous efforts to secure world peace as a member of the world community (*sekai no rekkoku ni gosuru waga kuni*). In the service of that goal, Japan would base its diplomacy on the following three principles: respect for the United Nations as a central organization; cooperation with other free, democratic nations; and, finally, strong identity as a member of Asia (*Ajia no ichi-in to shite no tachiba no kenji*).[12]

For a short while, Japan exercised its tradition of racial diplomacy, representing the colored races as their champion, especially in the criticism of apartheid. The Western nations, burdened by their own racial issues at home, adopted a more conservative approach to the question of apartheid in South Africa. In the UN General Assembly, in 1959, the South African delegate protested against intervention by countries with their own racist practices at home. Only Denmark, Iceland, Ireland, Norway, and Sweden, among Western nations, supported the motion to place apartheid on the UN agenda.

The United States, despite Truman's early decision and its leadership in the United Nations, was opposed to challenging apartheid. The U.S. delegate pointed out that South Africa was not the only country with discriminatory practices. With Christians, Jews, Moslems, Hungarian patriots, and Tibetan nationalists persecuted in other regions, the U.S. delegate argued, the demand for adoption of a radical measure against apartheid was unreasonable. President Eisenhower even privately argued that South African segregationists were only concerned "that their sweet little girls are not required to sit in school alongside some big overgrown Negroes."[13]

At first Japan took a different approach to apartheid from its Western allies. At a UN special political committee meeting in 1960, the Japanese delegate referred to Japan's traditional stance against racial discrimination, and criticized the South African government for apartheid.[14] Japan also responded to the Congo crisis, which was triggered by the European decision to withdraw from colonial occupation and the subsequent intervention of the United Nations. Kosaka Zentarō, minister of foreign affairs, made a speech at the fifteenth General Assembly in September 1960, supporting the UN role in aiding newly independent nations in Africa by mediating between them and their former colonists. Kosaka declared: "The Japanese delegate would like to draw the General Assembly's attention to the principle of racial equality, which Japan has proclaimed since the Versailles Peace Conference. Implementing the principle of racial equality is among the objectives of the United Nations, as declared in the UN Charter. It is the core principle which enables all human beings to shake hands with one another as common members of the world community. . . . Only upon this principle can we build a relationship of equality and mutual respect between a newly independent state and its former colonists."[15]

Ironically, after a brief period in which Japan adopted the "racial justice" approach to remote and abstract issues in Africa (but not in Asia for its anticolonial movement), Japan was placed by the South African government in the "honorary whites" category in acknowledgment of its ability to make capital and technological investment as a first world member. In April 1964, Japan became a member of the OECD (Organization for Economic Cooperation and Development), an elite club of advanced Western nations—merely a decade after the Japanese government had issued its famous declaration on the "end of the 'postwar' period [*mohaya sengo de wa nai*]" and the completion of recovery from their defeat. The Japanese Ministry of Foreign Affairs interpreted the new cooperative relations with North America and Western Europe at the OECD preferable as an enhancement of Japan's international status politically as well as economically. The ministry stated that Japan's membership at the OECD meant full Western recognition of Japan as a world power (*sekai no yūryoku koku*). As Prime Minister Satō Eisaku said on the National Diet floor in January 1965, Japan was determined to make a full commitment to its responsibilities as a nation with rising international status.[16]

The 1964 Tokyo Olympics, the first Olympics ever to be held in Asia, also proved to be a great success. Coupled with the opening of the world's fastest "bullet train," the Olympics instilled a sense of great national pride in Japan's status as a leading industrialized nation (*senshin koku*)—a postwar term equivalent to the prewar term "civilized nation." The year 1965 marked the beginning of the long era of foreign trade profits for Japan. Three years later, when Kawabata Yasunari won the Nobel Prize in literature, Japan's GNP was the third highest in the world, just after the United States and the Soviet Union. American, European, and Japanese economic hegemony over the third world was a group picture that gradually came into focus.

About this time, the Japanese people began to express some confidence that their national capacity was comparable to that of the "Westerners [*Seiyō-jin*]." Shortly after the end of the Occupation, various opinion polls had shown that many Japanese believed they were inferior to Westerners (*Seiyō-jin ni kurabete ototte iru*). In 1951, 47 percent of those interviewed expressed a belief in Japanese inferiority to Westerners, 28 percent believed the Japanese to be superior to Westerners, and only 14 percent believed they were equal. In the 1960s the ratio of opinions gradually reversed and, by 1968, 47 percent of those interviewed supported a view of Japanese superiority to Westerners while only 11 percent believed the Japanese to be inferior, and 12 percent felt they were equal.[17]

This regained confidence did not produce anti-Western sentiment. On the contrary, throughout the 1960s the psychological attachment to the

Western nations persisted. The popularity of the United States declined primarily because of the extremely controversial U.S.-Japan Security Treaty of 1960, which was basically a renewal of the 1951 security pact. Even though the new treaty retracted the old clause which had allowed U.S. forces to intervene in Japan's internal affairs, as well as the clause that gave the United States the right to approve other countries' bases in Japan, such amendments were not enough: throughout Japan there was a storm of protest against the renewal of the treaty itself since the treaty not only reflected a fear of Japan's rearmament and but continued to make Japan subservient to U.S. military activity. Yet three to four out of ten people almost always mentioned the United States as their favorite nation. Switzerland and France consistently captured 20 to 30 percent in these polls. The Germans continued to attract Japanese respect as a "superior people [*sugurete iru*]," side by side with the Americans. In contrast, the Japanese showed a much lower level of acceptance and respect for non-Western nations. The Soviet Union remained the least popular, or the most hated, nation in the 1960s, but the People's Republic of China and North and South Korea were never far behind it.[18] Not only diplomatically and strategically but psychologically too, Japan's self-identification and sense of affinity remained with the West, not Asia.

Nonetheless, the West's implicit exclusion of Japan on racial grounds compelled it to see the unfathomable gap between them as "the West versus Japan." For example, a 1963 book discussing the effect of cultural relations on U.S. foreign policy explained: "Japan occupies a unique place in the foreign relations of the United States." The book describes Japan as a nation that, despite its geographical distance from western Europe and North America, forced itself through a developmental process that was Western in character and achieved a level of education, science, technology, and industry "comparable to that of most of the Western prototypes." However, "historically and racially it sometimes seems similar to the economically underdeveloped countries." Therefore Japan cannot be classified as Western, Communist, or underdeveloped.[19]

Race and proximity seem to be the two issues that lie deepest. The U.S. government was never sure of Japan's sincerity as an ally and was always suspicious of Japan's bias in favor of the People's Republic of China because of their racial tie. These fears implied a lingering trace of the "yellow peril." In 1895, Wilhelm II, the Kaiser of Germany, encouraged racial confrontation between whites and Asians in order to build up a solid German-

Russian alliance in the Far East, which he characterized as "taking a stand in the defense of the Cross and the old Christian European culture against the inroads of the Mongols and Buddhism." More than half a century later, Japan's "alliance behavior" with the West caused much suspicion in a similar scenario. Even America's foremost Japanologist, Edward Seidensticker, was not certain whether Japan's racial identity would lead eventually to a betrayal of its American friends. Seidensticker hoped that in the case of Japan, race did not count, because their "most unmixed dislike" was directed toward the Koreans, who were of the same Asian race. Thus he expected that political proximity would be of first importance to Japan in choosing alliances.[20]

By virtue of its surging economic power alone, Japan was never allowed to become an integral part of the first world. Instead, the Japanese worker became likened to an "economic animal [*ekonomikku animaru*]"—a dehumanizing label applied in the late 1960s that ridiculed the supposedly "fanatic" Japanese obsession to increase the nation's GNP through sheer hard work and labor. Other offensive terms emerged, such as "Yellow Yankee," "economic invader," "economic parasite," and so on. By the early 1970s these had practically become household phrases around the world. In 1979 another derogatory expression leaked from a classified European Community document and upset the Japanese. The EC document derided the Japanese for being a horde of predatory workaholics in a densely packed island nation, toiling like animals and content to live in shacks that were no better than a rabbit hutch (*usagi goya*). After all was said and done, the economic power and material progress which had transformed the Japanese into "honorary whites" among nonwhites served at the same time to characterize them as uncivilized when compared to white Westerners.[21]

In the post-Occupation period, the racial ostracism of Japan from the first world became clear again in the immigration issue. For a while, the Japanese were eager to export their skilled laborers and advanced technology to undeveloped regions, in order to help develop the world as a whole and at the same time to ease Japan's population pressures. This ideal scheme, however, never functioned as planned because no region would accept major Japanese migration. Meanwhile, between 1946 and 1952, Europe experienced a net emigration of 3.3 million people. The largest proportion came from Britain and Italy to the United States, Australia, and Canada. In 1954 the United Nations, under the auspices of the Population Bureau, convened the *Congrès mondial de la Population* in Rome to discuss the population problem on the European continent.[22]

Upon gaining UN membership, the Japanese delegate explained Japan's population problem to the General Assembly, and the subsequent need for overseas expansion, which Japan promised to proceed with in strict accordance with UN principles. In his speech accepting UN membership, on December 18, 1956, Japan's foreign minister, Shigemitsu Mamoru, spoke about Japan's difficulties in maintaining a large population in a small territory with no natural resources. Japan, he said, wished to contribute to the basic UN mission of developing undeveloped resources and enriching the worldwide standard of living. He therefore urged a strong UN role in encouraging peaceful and smooth exchanges of people, work forces, and products across national boundaries (*kokkyō o koete hito to mono no kōryū o enkatsuni sen*).

However, Shigemitsu was cautious not to refer to Western opposition to Japanese immigration into their sphere. Instead, he first solicited UN cooperation in removing Western barriers against Japanese trade. Under Article 35 of GATT (General Agreement on Tariffs and Trade), to which Japan won membership in 1955, the European nations retained the right to withhold most-favored-nation status from Japan because of their fear that Japan's cheap labor would threaten their economies. Shigemitsu added that although Japan could most likely improve living conditions without shipping its surplus population elsewhere, the United Nations could nonetheless help Japan increase both domestic industrial output and foreign trade volume.[23]

At the twelfth United Nations General Assembly, on September 19, 1957, Japan's foreign minister Fujiyama Aiichirō elaborated on Japan's need for overseas expansion. After expressing Japan's determination to contribute to world peace as a UN member as well as an Asian nation, Fujiyama requested that the United Nations use its various agencies to coordinate the appropriate exchange of human resources, capital, and technology necessary to accommodate the supply and demand between nations. Furthermore, Fujiyama added, Japan hoped that world restrictions on emigration and immigration would be relaxed.[24]

The United Nations, however, offered no help for Japanese overseas expansion, and the U.S. immigration policy remained equally discouraging. The strict national quota of 185 immigrants per year determined by the McCarran-Walter Act left Japan no illusions about expansion into the United States. In terms of American immigration, Japan was clearly considered a third world nation. In contrast, America during this period opened its doors wide for quota immigrants and refugees from not only the first world but the second world as well. Between 1951 and 1955, a total of 611,299 immigrants entered the United States from all quota areas in the world.[25] A total of 406,026 displaced persons and refugees were admitted to the United States between 1948 and 1955, of which 99.3 percent were from Europe.

In an effort to alleviate mutual embarrassment over the U.S. immigration policy, the U.S. and Japanese governments made an unusual joint effort between 1953 and 1956 to admit nonquota Japanese emigrants under the terms of the Refugee Relief Act of 1953. The act defined a "refugee" as any person who was out of his usual place of abode and unable to return thereto because of persecution, fear of persecution, natural calamity, or military operations. The U.S. Embassy in Tokyo and the Japanese government together recruited those Japanese who had suffered from natural disasters such as floods and earthquakes, and repatriates suffering from poverty. They even discussed recruiting people whose lands were confiscated for use by the U.S. Army in Japan and designating them as refugees eligible for entry into the United States. Both the American and Japanese sides lobbied in Washington, D.C., with help from Mike Masaoka, a leading figure at the Japanese American Civil Liberty Union, to loosen the definition of "refugees" so as to allow more Japanese into the category.[26]

Only after the Japanese consulate in California found a labor shortage on the West Coast and succeeded in enlisting several orchard growers as their American sponsors did the U.S. government reach a compromise and allow the Japanese entry under the 1953 Refugee Relief Act. In May 1955 the first group of fifty-six flood refugees from Wakayama Prefecture entered the United States and began to work as farmhands in their sponsors' orchards. Except for GI brides, mixed-blood children, and Japanese-Americans who returned to the United States after having spent wartime in Japan, these fifty-six farmhands were postwar Japan's first bona fide emigrants to the United States. Until 1956, when the act expired, a total of 2,268 Japanese entered the United States as refugees and worked at the two orchards in California.[27]

The success of Japanese farmhands in California and the local need for their labor prompted another program, begun in 1956, to bring more Japanese agricultural laborers to the same state for a three-year duration. According to an official statement issued by the Information and Culture Bureau at the Japanese Ministry of Foreign Affairs, those who settled in California were welcomed not only by their sponsors but also by their neighbors, for their industriousness and skills. While already building good reputations and friendships, the statement said, they were taking courses in English and history offered by nonprofit organizations and preparing to become naturalized citizens of the United States, thus serving as a new link between the two nations.[28]

The reality, however, was not as rosy as the government's interpretation. Although working conditions were in no way comfortable, relatively high pay, combined with the positive image of "going to America," attracted many applicants among rural youths in Japan. Yet Japanese laborers were needed simply as a supplement to the migrant workforce from Mexico. Worse, as in the prewar years, these Japanese farmers soon met opposition from organized laborers who claimed that they took away jobs and lowered wages and the standard of living. By 1964, when opposition from the American labor union caused cancellation of the program, a total of 4,331 Japanese had worked in California as seasonal agricultural laborers—temporary farmhands, the only job opportunity in America open to Japanese.[29]

By 1965 the U.S. Congress had finally put an end to national origin quotas by passing the Hart-Celler Act. The law removed discrimination against Asians and southern and eastern Europeans and instead set the total number admitted at 170,000 from the Eastern hemisphere and 120,000 from the Western hemisphere. It also contained certain preference criteria such as occupational skills and humanitarian reasons, and the law adopted a "first-come, first-served" principle, regardless of race, ethnicity, or nationality. With a similar amendment in the immigration laws of Canada and Australia, emigration to these nations quickly increased.

Shortly before that, in 1963, the Japanese government had allowed unrestricted overseas business travel and, in 1964, sightseeing tours. However, the opening of the United States to Japanese emigration, technically up to twenty thousand persons per year under the 1965 Immigration Act, did not capture Japanese enthusiasm. Japan's interest in expanding into the United States arose in a different form.

In 1970, upon request by Prime Minister Satō Eisaku, the Council of Emigration (Ijū Shingikai) was convened to discuss basic government policy concerning overseas emigration. In the council's report, the newly emerging availability of the United States as a recipient for Japanese emigration hardly received any notice. Instead, the council discussed a new vision of Japanese overseas growth (*kaigai hatten*) in terms of studies abroad and often temporary work at Japanese-owned overseas companies. Throughout the 1970s, the combination of vigorous economic growth at home and the liberal immigration policy of the United States produced an increase in this new type of travel to the United States. The numbers of businessmen, investors with sufficient capital to start small businesses, and tourists going to the United States were all on the rise.[30]

In this context, for the first time since the war's end, the eagerness to expand economically into advanced industrial nations grew. Japan no longer needed to export its surplus population because its domestic industries required a massive labor force for production. Japan now discovered that it could expand overseas by exporting "businesses and industries" instead of labor. In 1971 the Ministry of Foreign Affairs issued a booklet, *Waga kokumin no kaigai hatten* (Overseas Development of Our People), claiming that overseas emigration of superior industries was a technical contribution not just to underdeveloped regions but also to advanced industrial states.[31]

Japanese industrial products—electric appliances, automobiles, and so on—at last fulfilled the dream that the Japanese emigrants could never attain. These goods made their way into Western communities and were welcomed, contributing to their culture and becoming an integral part of it. The Japanese thus achieved the goal of presenting themselves in the Western societies via their products of "superior" quality. These products were "colorless" and "faceless," with no association of the images of an "undesirable" Asian race. Significantly, nowhere in the advertisements was there a sign of the producers' membership in the yellow race. Here was the answer to the original search for cosmopolitanism begun during the U.S. occupation—the rationale for Japan's overseas expansion, its ticket to the Western world.

There was still no solution for the problem of the mixed-blood children. As the diplomatic momentum surrounding the issue dissipated, the national debate on miscegenation became almost completely suspended.

As hope for the U.S. adoption plan waned, Brazil began to seem the best place for the children. Keimei Gakuin in Tokyo, a private orphanage for mixed-blood children, concerned about the intensity of racial discrimination in Japanese society, planned to send the children as immigrants to Brazil, which they understood to be a paradise for racially mixed people. The orphanage board launched preliminary negotiations with organizations of Japanese-Brazilians in Brazil, planning future immigration activities in detail. Sawada Miki, losing hope for further U.S. aid, purchased three hundred hectares of virgin forest in Pará, Brazil, and started to offer the children at her orphanage courses in Brazilian geography and Portuguese. Takasaki Setsuko, chief of the Woman and Juvenile Section at the Department of Labor, expressed her excitement at imagining that ten years hence these children, now branded as "children of fate," would be actively developing the lands of Brazil as welcome immigrants.[32]

Brazil, of course, was never the promised land that would absorb these children. Some Japanese immigrants in Brazil protested the plan, arguing that these mixed-blood children—representative of the stigma of Japan's defeat in the war—should be quarantined within the Japanese islands at all costs. One doctor in São Paolo wrote to Sawada that rather than send them to Brazil, she should press the Japanese authorities to solve the problem domestically.[33] Nor did the plan necessarily appeal to Sawada's children. One seventeen-year-old boy, the first half-black baby to arrive at the Elizabeth Sanders Home, refused to join the Amazon-bound team, confronting Sawada with the question of why he and the other boys had to go and live in the barbaric jungle. According to Sawada's autobiography, the emigration plan to Brazil was especially conceived for the half-black children like him because she "knew" that, because of their skin color, they would never be part of Japanese society. However, Sawada reluctantly granted the boy's wish to stay in Japan. Later she allowed him to pursue a career as a jazz drummer because, she said, like any black person his ancestral blood (*senzo no chi*) drove him toward the rhythms of such music.[34]

Although between 1952 and 1965 approximately 47,700 Japanese had emigrated to Brazil, the emigration of mixed-blood children to Brazil did not take place until August 1965, when six boys from the Elizabeth Sanders Home, all eighteen years of age and recent junior high school graduates, arrived at the pimento plantation developed on the land purchased by six Japanese settlers who had made a contract with the Elizabeth Sanders Home. With help from other Japanese communities in the region, these six Japanese boys arrived in Pará in 1963, cut down and burned the forests, made open land for planting pimentos, and built a village for the eventual arrival of the children from the Elizabeth Sanders Home. Sawada and the Japanese planters were optimistic, thanks to material supplies from private Japanese emigration companies and favorable offers from the Brazilian government (such as a tax exemption). Sawada expected that within the next ten years her agency would send its junior high school graduates every year to the pimento plantation. When the last of the 140 children left Japan, Sawada said, she would join them on the plantation and spend the rest of her life there with them.[35]

Not much was known about the mixed-blood children after the mid-1950s in spite of the intense publicity they had received early on. Since the Japanese government did not require the specification of racial identity when a child was registered in the family registry, no systematic demographical record was available on these children. Nor was any figure available for the mixed-blood children adopted by U.S. citizens, since the U.S. Department of State did not differentiate pure-blood from mixed-blood children in issuing passports. In 1957 rumors circulated that the mixed-blood babies had been sold on the black market for adoption in the United States for thirty dollars each. Both American and Japanese agencies investigated the whereabouts of the 785 mixed-blood babies adopted by 674 American families, three Canadian families, and one French family between 1952 and 1955, only to discover that at least 50 percent of the adopting families could not be found.[36] The only reliable data on the condition of the mixed-blood children still in Japan was kept by the Japanese Ministry of Education, which monitored the integration procedure over a decade. As of 1959, records showed a total of 2,401 mixed-blood children nationwide, attending 1,105 elementary schools and 209 junior high schools.[37]

Despite such an unusual pattern of existence in both Japan and the United States, their number continued to rise during the next decade because of the increase of American GIs stationed in Japan during the Vietnam War. In 1968 the Japanese press estimated their number to be between 20,000 and 25,000, one-sixth of whom were black-Japanese. By the mid-1970s, the International Social Service declared that there were between 10,000 and 50,000, with a growing concentration in Okinawa. As for those who migrated to the United States, a total of 618 U.S. passports were issued to adopted Japanese orphans, both pure-blood and mixed-blood, from June 1957 through the end of 1958 alone. Sawada Miki later claimed that by the early 1980s she had arranged eight hundred adoptions by foreign, mostly American, families. Various researchers concluded that the total number of mixed-blood children adopted by American families was "considerably well over 1,000."[38]

For those who stayed in Japan, there was a phenomenon called "*konket-suji būmu* [the mixed-blood children boom]" in the 1960s. In 1959 the movie *Kiku to Isamu* (Kiku and Isamu), about a half-black Japanese brother and sister living with their grandmother in a small village in Japan, became a commercial hit.[39] The film's great popularity perhaps reflected a slight shift toward a willingness to accept mixed-blood children. The two half-black children who played Kiku and Isamu briefly enjoyed the spotlight as child stars. When Japan's entertainment industry began to actively recruit half-white and half-black Japanese teenagers as pop singers and musicians, and fashion models, the Japanese public responded with enthusiasm, since their "exotic" features corresponded to Japan's new ideal of cosmopolitanism. Ultimately, this trend turned out to be no more than superficial sensationalism, confined to the commercial realm, and it produced no fundamental change in social or legal perceptions of race.

In 1971, when nine of the Elizabeth Sanders Home "alumni," most in their twenties, were arrested for stealing more than twelve million yen in the Tokyo metropolitan area, the Japanese media publicized the incident as the sorry but inevitable result of their racial background. Sawada also confessed her disappointment in them in her autobiography, saying "no matter how much education and religion one pours onto them with care and affection, it seems their 'innate' bitterness will never vanish."[40] In reporting the crime, the Japanese press called these adults "konketsuji"—the mixed-blood children—as if they remained permanently juvenile.[41]

In 1975, Sawada's plantation in Brazil finally closed down due to bankruptcy. During its fourteen years of operation, Sawada had sent a total of twenty-eight children from her orphanage, all of whom now had successful jobs outside the plantation. Sawada said the closure symbolized the completion of her mission.[42] After this, reports of mixed-blood children almost completely disappeared from the Japanese media. There was no follow-up investigation on those born during the Occupation and now reaching their thirties (for example, of the pattern of their assimilation into Japanese society, including their education, occupations, marriages, where they lived, as well as what happened to their offspring). Their presence forever receded into a public memory of the Occupation as a brief anomaly of the defeated nation's racial humiliation.[43]

The status of racial and ethnic minorities in Japanese society, at least, gradually improved. Since the 1960s, Koreans, Chinese, Ainu people, and other groups began to organize a fight for their rights, which postwar democratization had not recognized, challenging the notion of the Japanese as a pure homogeneous race—a source of their dualistic identity. Their civil rights movement reached its peak in the 1970s.

In 1964 the Ainu successfully won the local government's consent to resume their traditional bear festival, which had been banned since 1955. In the

1970s they traveled to the People's Republic of China, the United States, and Canada, met the indigenous people in each nation, and exchanged ideas about the preservation of minority history and culture. In 1984, Hokkaidō Utari Kyōkai, the independent Ainu organization which since 1961 had promoted assimilation, urged the Japanese government to adopt a new law guaranteeing them a constitutional right to exist as a distinctive ethnic group and to retain their own culture as a legitimate part of Japan's heritage.[44]

Descendants of former Chinese and Korean subjects residing in Japan (or second or third generation Chinese and Korean immigrants with permanent residency) continued the legal battle for their political, socioeconomic, and cultural inclusion in the interpretation of the Japanese constitution—a fight to resolve their entangled postwar status. In 1974 a high school graduate born in Japan to parents who were former colonial subjects from Korea won a court case against the Hitachi corporation, which had discriminated against him in employment based on his ethnic and national origin. In 1976 a college graduate born to former colonial subjects from Korea who were permanent residents of Japan successfully petitioned the Supreme Court to allow him to practice law in Japan without first applying for citizenship. Two years later he became postwar Japan's first "non-Japanese" lawyer. After these precedents, a series of reforms was gradually introduced to eliminate discrimination in employment based on ethnicity and nationality (*minzoku sabetsu*).[45]

The government's attitude remained negative and even hostile toward the civil rights movement. Worse, in 1986, Prime Minister Nakasone Yasuo boasted of Japan's racial and ethnic homogeneity as a source of its strength. Nakasone stated to the Lower House:

> In Japanese society, I believe there is no single minority group who suffers from so-called discrimination [*iwayuru sabetsu*], as long as they have Japanese nationality. I also believe I am right in reporting so to the United Nations. . . . [In the long history of Japan] there has been a substantial level of miscegenation taking place among the Ainu, Japanese and other people migrating from the continent. For example, I can tell you that I must have much Ainu blood in myself since I am rather hairy, having bushy eye-brows and thick beard [for a Japanese].[46]

By making this inappropriate and thoughtless joke about the physical characteristics of the Ainu people, which in itself was a common as well as crude slur against them, Nakasone not only belittled minorities but also refused to admit the fact of their presence and their rights as a minority group in Japan.

In the mid-1980s the racial dimension of U.S.-Japanese relations suddenly erupted and people on each side alleged racism by the other. As we have seen, since the end of World War II the racial issue had been quietly submerged between the two nations. Yet almost all the problems from the prewar period remained lurking beneath the surface—mutual issues such as immigration, miscegenation, and, above all, a racial ideology that accounted for each one's raison d'être in the world. When Japan emerged as an economic superpower and seemed to threaten Western dominance, the Japanese developed greater confidence vis-à-vis the West while the West saw a potential crisis brewing. The unspoken agreement to suppress racial matters quickly disintegrated and all the buried concerns erupted at once, making racial friction unavoidable. The question of postwar Japan's racial identity in the world was suddenly answered.

The racial friction began with the sudden boom in the domestic Japanese economy, which allowed Japanese firms to invest aggressively in the United States, especially in the real estate market, and in the takeover of prominent American corporations. The American mass media did not hide their revulsion at the thought of an ultimate Japanization of their society. The American and European mass media openly expressed their alarm at the possibility of Japanese economic domination of the entire world market. Caricatured less-than-human images featuring hordes of ugly and belligerent little Japanese businessmen assaulting helpless big Westerners in their own countries became widespread all over the world. The Japanese, assertive of their national strength more than at any time before, quickly pointed to an American double standard which allowed more British and Dutch investment than Japanese, and blamed American racism.[47]

Many Japanese, including politicians and prominent critics, found the source of American anti-Japanese sentiment in American bitterness about the decline of their own society and economy. Pundits openly attributed Japan's economic success to the superior quality of the Japanese and the Japanese effort to keep their racial homogeneity. When Prime Minister Nakasone made international headlines with a remark that the African-American and Puerto Rican population lowered the intellectual level of American society, Americans responded furiously, regarding such a remark as due to the racial arrogance of the Japanese.[48]

These confrontations were not surprising; the U.S. occupation of Japan had, after all, consciously preserved prewar race relations. In the post–Cold War environment, the United States no longer had a strategic need to support Japan's dualistic racial identity. In fact, since the end of the Cold War, the question of a racial division between the United States and Japan has emerged repeatedly as a cause of disharmony. In the summer of 1993, when Samuel P. Huntington published a controversial article in *Foreign Affairs* called "The Clash of Civilizations?" he claimed that Japan existed along the "fault lines of civilization" and reminded the reader of Japan's dubious dualistic racial identity that made the Japanese unfit allies in America's campaign to spread its values. Huntington predicted a world in the twenty-first century where culture would be the dominant source of international conflict. He rarely points to the concept of race as part of the cultural divisiveness. The traditional racial lines of the white, yellow, and black, however, coincide with the lines of his cartography for "West" and "non-West" civilizations. According to Huntington, Japan's post–Cold War development is a challenge, or even a threat, to the West; the United States cannot share the kind of political bond with Japan that exists between the United States and Europe. Although in the final analysis Huntington supports promoting and maintaining cooperative relations with Japan, as well as with Russia, he does not offer insight into what he calls the "unbridgeable" gap between the Japanese and Americans, one caused by culture and race. In Huntington's opinion, Japan remains the West's latent and inevitable nemesis.[49]

What is remarkable about the recent revival of racial rhetoric between the United States and Japan is the idiosyncratic adoption of the archaic white-versus-yellow color scheme, which is far from the contemporary complexity of racial reality in both nations. Since the 1960s, American society has been confronted with its own civil rights movement and has begun to move toward closing the gap—political, economic, social, and cultural—between whites and nonwhites. A multiracial and multiethnic society has gradually become a new norm for the United States, at least in principle. American society can no longer consider itself a white man's nation, not in ideological consensus nor in demographic fact. Nonetheless, when Americans cry out that Japan presents a threatening challenge, the old paradigm of white supremacy rises to the surface and Asian minorities—as well as other minorities—feel the repercussions.

The Japanese, too, have reached a historic juncture in reexamining their own racial practices and ideology. In the late 1980s, Japan began to face a new flood of foreign workers from South and Southeast Asia, the Middle East, and Northern Africa, many of them day laborers and "sweat shop" workers. Japanese society had to reconcile the economy's growing demand for a diversified labor force and deep-seated sentiments against nonwhites.[50] There is a growing chorus of concern over the conduct of Japanese corporations in the United States, which often discriminate against minorities, especially blacks and Hispanics—those whom Japan's Prime Minister Nakasone Yasuhiro openly called intellectually inferior in 1986.[51] These new conditions make it increasingly hypocritical of the Japanese to criticize American racism.

The U.S. occupation of Japan did not fundamentally alter race relations between whites and Asians in the international framework. It projected the basic structure of Western civilization onto the Japanese, who in turn accepted it for the sake of retaining their own dualistic racial identity. The recent exchange of hostile racial rhetoric on both sides of the Pacific may not be so much a clash of racist expression as an outlet for the suppressed mutual guilt accumulated over the half-century since the Occupation. The postwar collaboration was built on a shared racist view of the world, in which both nations assumed a duty to lead the "inferior non-West" nations, a concept in which Japan was an "honorary Western nation." They also shared similar principles on such issues as racial and ethnic minorities in domestic society, emigration and immigration, and miscegenation. Both nations have so successfully exploited the legacy of their mutual racism that they feel almost compelled to call each other hypocritical and racist. But there is no admission of guilt on either side.

The racial hierarchy that characterized U.S.-Japanese relations throughout the twentieth century is actually beginning to lose ground. Japan's own racial dualism is also likely to lose both its meaning and efficacy, as the non-Western world continues its vigorous modernization (Westernization) and dualistic identity becomes more or less a common phenomenon among the non-Western peoples. Edward Said, in *Culture and Imperialism*, criticized Japan for its total lack of international cultural power, despite its international economic power. Quoting Masao MIYOSHI, Said pointed out the impoverishment of Japan's cultural dependence on the West.[52] This self-effacement on Japan's part may continue, insofar as Japan's century-old ideology of dualistic racial identity (which was further reinforced by the U.S. occupation) maintains itself. For a breakthrough, Japan first needs to realize that its success in today's world is built on the dilemma of its own racial rhetoric, of power relations between the presumed superior and inferior peoples. It is not a task for a single nation. What is needed is a true international discourse.

In the history of U.S.-Japanese relations, the race factor orchestrated the psychological responses of both nations and generated the dynamics of their cooperation. A U.S.-Japanese discourse on race has never occurred; it has not been encouraged or even suggested. The legacy of the U.S. occupation of Japan still challenges both Japanese and Americans today.[53] These two nations, both world leaders, joined by a mutual racism, are now faced with the task of overcoming the past in order to explore a new highway leading into the twenty-first century. One hopes that this new partnership will be based not on a hierarchy of superior and inferior peoples, but on the true principle of equality—and therefore on true friendship.

A NOTE ON THE SOURCE CITATIONS

The major libraries and archives used for this work are Columbia University, C. Van Starr East Asian Library, New York; the Gordon W. Prange Collection, McKeldin Library, University of Maryland, College Park; MacArthur Memorial Archives, Norfolk, Va.; the National Archives, Washington, D.C.; Nihon Gaimu-shō Gaikō Shiryō-kan (Japanese Foreign Ministry Archives), Tokyo; Nihon Kokuritsu Kokkai Toshokan (the Japan National Diet Library), Tokyo; Nihon Kokuritsu Kyōiku Kenkyūjo (the National Institute for Educational Research of Japan), Tokyo; Nihon Kokusai Kyōryoku Jigyōdan Toshokan (Japan International Cooperation Agency [JICA] Library), Tokyo; Shōchiku Ōtani Toshokan, Tokyo.

Each note has complete information on the source(s), both primary and secondary, Japanese and English. In the case of a primary source, the specific location of the repository is provided in addition to its full citation of a series, file number or name, subgroup, record group, repository, and so on. In special cases, an additional explanation on the nature of the source or its archival collections is also provided.

Since the original research for this book was completed, most records from both the downtown National Archives building in Washington, D.C., as well as accessed records at the Washington National Records Center in Suitland, Maryland, have been relocated at the new National Archives building in College Park, Maryland. It should now be noted that, in order to track down the archival materials formerly housed at Suitland and downtown D.C. buildings to this new location, a record group (RG) number and a box number is no longer sufficient. (Also note that records may be reboxed in the future with different numbering.) Series or subgroup information, in addition to the RG and the box number, is crucial to relocate specific sources at College Park. Therefore, in the following section of this book, each note containing archival materials from the Suitland and other branches of the National Archives has been given a full citation with as much information as possible pertinent to its depository nature, so as to facilitate the relocation process.

As for the Japanese sources, some crucial titles and names of publishing organizations are given English translation. If the English translation is provided in the main text, there is not necessarily a repetition in the note. Also, in Japanese, both "Nippon" and "Nihon" stand for the same English word *Japan*, and these two words are thus loosely interchangeable, except for certain proper nouns which specify the use as well as the pronunciation (e.g., Nippon Hōsō Kyōkai [NHK], Nippon Electric Co. [NEC], Nihon Gakushi-in [Japan Academy], Nihon Ginkō [Bank of Japan]).

NOTES

INTRODUCTION: RACE IN U.S.–JAPANESE RELATIONS

1. John Dower, *War Without Mercy: Race and Power in the Pacific War* (Pantheon, 1987), 301–302.

2. Akira IRIYE, *Power and Culture: The Japanese-American War, 1941–1945* (Harvard University Press, 1981), 265–68.

3. For Japanese analysis of the trade dispute in the mid-1980s, with discussion on the racial and cultural dimensions, see the following reports: Nihon Zaigai Kigyō Kyōkai (The Association for Overseas Japanese Firms), *Tai-Bei tōshi masatsu—sono hassei no kanō-sei to taisho-saku* (Conflicts arising from investments in the U.S.—The causes and remedies), Kaigai Chokusetsu Tōshi Enkatsu-ka Iinkai hōkoku-sho (Report by the Committee on Improving Problems Pertinent to Overseas Direct Investment) (April 1987); Nihon Keizai Chōsa Kyōgi-kai (Japan Economic Research and Consultation Association), *Senshin-koku ni okeru tōshi masatsu to Nihon no taiō—kyōzon kyōei to kōken e no michi o motomete* (Conflicts arising from Japan's direct investments in the advanced industrial nations—What Japan can do to avoid the conflicts and seek mutually beneficial coexistence) (May 1992).

Nō to Ieru Nippon, by Ishiwara Shintarō and Morita Akio (Kōbun Sha, 1989) a bestseller in Japan and also translated into English with the title *The Japan That Can Say No* (Simon and Schuster, 1991), perhaps offers the best glimpse on the revived white peril in Japan. The book attacks America's attitude of white supremacy, which discriminates especially against the Japanese, and extols Japan's superiority to the United States. The book posits that this superior quality of Japan increases America's insecurity and makes the nation more racist. Also see the follow-up volumes *Soredemo Nō to Ieru Nippon* (The Japan that can still say no), ed. Ishiwara Shintarō, Watabe Shōichi, and Ogawa Kazuhisa (Kōbun Sha, 1990), and *Danko Nō to Ieru Nippon* (The Japan that says no with determination), ed. Ishiwara Shintarō and Etō Jun (Kōbun Sha, 1991).

For graphic images of contemporary "trade wars" as harbored by Americans and Europeans, see John Dower, *Japan in War and Peace: Selected Essays* (New Press, 1993), ch. 9 ("Graphic Others/Graphic Selves: Cartoons in War and Peace").

4. For correlations between "race" and "racism," see the following works by Michael Banton: *The Race Concept* (with Jonathan Harwood; Praeger, 1975); *Racial Theories* (Cambridge University Press, 1987); *Discrimination* (Open University Press, 1994). Other useful studies include Pierre L. van den Berghe, *Race and Racism: A Comparative Perspective*, 2d ed. (Wiley, 1978); John Rex, *Race Relations in Sociological Theory*, 2d ed. (Routledge and Kegan Paul, 1983); Donald Horowitz, *Ethnic Groups in Conflict* (University of California Press, 1985); and Thomas Sowell, *Race and Culture: A World View* (Banz, 1994).

For an up-to-date theorization of the dynamics of "race" as a conceptual force in the modern world, see David Theo Goldberg, *Racist Culture: Philosophy and the Politics of Meaning* (Blackwell, 1993), esp. 84.

5. In the early 1980s, when the author was a graduate student in Japan, there was a subtle reluctance among Japanese scholars of American history, especially those in their fifties and over, to discuss American racism toward the Japanese. One renowned Americanist called such a Japanese attempt rather insensitive and provocative and claimed that as a Japanese who had spent the late 1950s in New York City as a graduate student of American history, he never encountered even a small trace of racism. In the mid-1980s, when the author came to study at Columbia University, there was a similar hesitancy to discuss the race factor in U.S.-Japanese relations, especially among political scientists. In a class discussion, one famed political scientist of Japanese diplomacy dismissed the factor of race and racism in U.S.-Japanese relations as too elusive and irrational to be included in analysis.

6. UNESCO, "Text of the Statement of 1950," *The Race Concept: Results of an Inquiry*, 98–103 (appendix) (UNESCO, 1952).

7. Franz Boas, *The Mind of Primitive Man* (Macmillan, 1911) and *Race, Language, and Culture* (Macmillan, 1940); Ruth Benedict, *Pattern of Culture* (Houghton Mifflin, 1934); Margaret Mead, *Sex and Temperament in Three Primitive Societies* (New American Library, 1950).

For the recent literature on cultural relativism, see Clifford Geertz, *The Interpretation of Culture* (Basic Books, 1973) and *Local Knowledge* (Basic Books, 1983); Melford Spiro, *Oedipus in the Trobriands* (University of Chicago Press, 1982) and "Cultural Relativism and the Future of Anthropology," *Cultural Anthropology* 1 (August 1986): 259–86; Howard Stein, "Cultural Relativism as the Central Organizing Resistance in Cultural Anthropology," *Journal of Psychoanalytic Anthropology* 9 (Spring 1986): 157–75, and *The Dream of Culture* (Psyche Press, 1994).

8. Iriye's analysis of mutual racism appears in *Pacific Estrangement: Japanese and American Expansion, 1897–1911* (Harvard University Press, 1972) and Akira IRIYE, ed., *Mutual Images: Essays in American-Japanese Relations* (Harvard University Press, 1975).

With an aim to promote improved understanding of the structure of international community, Iriye's cultural approach encouraged the development of new perspectives on the nature of conflict so that new means for conflict resolution could arise and new methods of cooperation within the international community could emerge. Iriye's intercultural approach helped to change the conventional analysis of international relations from a focus on military strategy, national security, and economic interests—as defined by governments and their agents—to the study of cultural interactions transcending national boundaries. Cultural approaches to the history of international relations continue to lure scholars to challenge the analysis of culture beyond the definitions set by Geertz, Foucault, Derrida, and others. As for Iriye's theorization of cultural approach, see Akira IRIYE, "Culture and Power: International Relations as Intercultural Relations," *Diplomatic History* 3 (Spring 1979): 115–28, and "Culture," *Journal of American History* (June 1990): 99–107.

9. It is interesting to note that even Ruth Benedict, while claiming that real "racial differences" occurred only in "nonessentials such as texture of head hair, amount of body hair, shape of the nose or head, or color of the eyes and the skin," nonetheless admitted that race was a scientific "fact." In other words, racism was the dogma but race is a fact. See Ruth Benedict, *Race: Science and Politics* (Modern Age Books, 1940), 12; and Ruth Benedict and Gene Weltfish, *The Races of Mankind* (Public Affairs Committee, 1943), 5, cited in Peggy Pascoe, "Miscegenation Law, Court Cases, and Ideologies of 'Race' in Twentieth-Century America," *Journal of American History* (June 1996): 54–55.

10. For the exclusionary nature of the melting pot rhetoric, see Thomas Dyer, *Theodore Roosevelt and the Idea of Race* (Louisiana State University Press, 1980). For debates on Japanese racial unassimilability, see the following works: H. A. Mills, *The Japanese Problem in the United States* (Macmillan, 1915), 27; Kiichi KANZAKI, "Is the Japanese Menace in America a Reality?" *The Annals of the American Academy of Political and Social Science* (hereafter, *The Annals*) 93 (January 1921): 88–97, in a Special Issue entitled "Present Day Immigration with Special Reference to the Japanese," ed. Carl Kelsey; and Kiyo Sue INUI, "California's Japanese Situation," *The Annals* 93 (January 1921): 97–104. For opposing points of view to the two latter citations, see the following in the same volume of *The Annals*: James Phelan, "Why California Objects to the Japanese Invasion," 16–17; V. S. McClatchy, "Japanese in the Melting-Pot: Can They Assimilate and Make Good Citizens?" 29–34; and Lothrop Stoddard, "The Japanese Question in California," 42–47. For an argument on the Japanese physical and biological assimilation in America similar to that espoused in his article, see Kanzaki's testimony at congressional hearings in U.S. House Committee on Immigration and Naturalization, *Hearings on Japanese Immigration*, 66th Cong., 2d sess., 1920, 681–702.

11. Since Gordon Allport, Thomas Pettigrew, and other scholars established the new term "institutional discrimination" in the 1960s, it has gained wide recognition

among social scientists as a great conceptual advance. Institutional racism is a discriminatory practice in institutions or entire societies, independent of racist beliefs. The assertion is that a company, school, agency, or government is racist regardless of the beliefs of its members, if the system produces any inequalities between racially defined groups. Any "race-blind" policy would thereby be labeled racist if it does not eliminate any differences between racial groups. The deliberate nonrecognition of race would also erode the capacity to recognize racism. Quite paradoxically, antiracism became a form of racism, as the recent debate on the affirmative action program suggests. For this intriguing argument, see, for example, Pierre L. van den Berghe, *The Ethnic Phenomenon* (Praeger, 1987).

12. At an international and interdisciplinary scholarly conference on the topic of racism, convened in Hong Kong, November 1994, Frank Dikötter, coorganizer of the conference, was alarmed that the formation of racial discourse in the modern world had been reduced to a uniquely "Western" phenomenon and that similar systematic discriminatory exclusions in East Asia required a serious investigation in order to reduce all forms of racial discrimination on an international scale. See the proceedings of the conference, Barry Sautman, ed., *Racial Identities in East Asia* (Division of Social Science, the Hong Kong University of Science and Technology, 1995), especially Dikötter, "Racial Identities in East Asia," 4–5.

The Han people—the majority ethnic group in China who trace their origins back to the mythical Yellow Emperor—used the concept of Sinocentrism to distinguish themselves from the barbarians of the four quarters of the world. The neo-Confucianists of Korea in the seventeenth century invented a self-centered Sinocentrism, claiming to be the legitimate descendant of Chinese civilization, with all its cultural pride and disdain for others. Bok-Hee Chun, "The Social Darwinist Racism of Progressive Korean Intelligentsia in the late 19th Century," in Sautman, ed. *Racial Identities in East Asia*, 173–76.

The Japanese too, emulating the ancient Chinese view of a Sinocentric world, placed themselves in the center of the universe as opposed to peripheral "others." During the years of isolation, a growing sense of nationalism evolved in Japan, based on a renewed notion of the country's divine origin and its superiority to China. Ronald Toby, *State and Diplomacy in Early Modern Japan: Asia in the Development of the Tokugawa Bakufu* (Stanford University Press, 1984).

13. In Japan, too, there has been a growing interest in the modern formation of Japan's racial identity and ideology, along with numerous case studies on racial and ethnic minorities. For a comprehensive survey of the origin and development of the myth of modern Japan as a racially homogeneous nation, see Oguma Eiji, *Tan-itsu minzoku shinwa no kigen* (Shin'yō Sha, 1995). Relying on numerous original arguments from the late nineteenth century through the postwar period, Oguma claims that the fact that the Japanese colonial empire was growing to become a multiethnic

and racial empire prompted Japanese leaders to legitimize their reign on the theory that they were a superior race; thus, the need for an ideology on racial distinctions.

14. One of the oldest records of an antimiscegenation law and its operation is found in the biblical account of the "trespass against God" by certain Israelites who had taken unto themselves "strange wives" from among other tribes (C. D. Shokes, "Serbonian Bog of Miscegenation," *Rocky Mountain Law Review* 21, no. 4 [June 1949]: 425). In the history of the United States, the court in the state of Georgia approved in dicta in *Scott v. state of Georgia* (1869) the spirit of an antimiscegenation statute in the following comments: "The amalgamation of the races is not only unnatural, but is always productive of deplorable results. . . . Such connections, never elevate the inferior race to the position of the superior, but they bring down the superior to that of the inferior. They are productive of evil, and evil only, without any corresponding good" (*Scott v. State*, 39 Ga. 312, 324 [1869]). For one of the most recent studies of miscegenation law, see Peggy Pascoe, "Miscegenation Law, Court Cases, and Ideologies of 'Race' in Twentiety-Century America," 44–69. Also, see Eugene Marias, "A Brief Survey of Some Problems in Miscegenation," *Southern California Law Review* 20, no. 1 (December 1946): 80–90; and also *Scott v. State*, 39 Ga. 321, 324 (1869).

The following, written when California's Alien Land Laws were being debated in 1913 and widely quoted afterwards in numerous magazine and newspaper articles, stands as a historical illustration of white resistance to marriage with a Japanese: "Near my home is an eighty-acre tract of as fine land as there is in California. On that land lives a Japanese. With that Japanese lives a white woman. In that woman's arms is a baby. What is that baby? It isn't a Japanese. It isn't white. I'll tell you what it is. It is the germ of the mightiest problem that ever faced this state; a problem that will make the black problem of the South look white." Quoted in H. A. Mills, *The Japanese Problem in the United States*, 274.

15. Dower, *War Without Mercy*, 275–77. Also see Oguma, *Tan-itsu minzoku shinwa no kigen*, esp. ch. 13 ("Kōmin-ka tai yūsei-gaku").

16. Michael Hunt, *Ideology and U.S. Foreign Policy* (Yale University Press, 1987), esp. ch. 3 ("The Hierarchy of Race").

17. Hunt, ibid., 79–80. James D. Richardson, ed., *Messages and Papers of the Presidents, 1789–1908*, vol. 11 (Bureau of National Literature and Art, 1909), 1165–67. See also Thomas Dyer, *Theodore Roosevelt and the Idea of Race*, 135–37.

18. Komiya Akira, "Jūkyū-seiki jinrui-gaku to kindai Nihon—Adachi Buntarō o chūshin to shite," *Tōkyō Joshi Daigaku Hikaku Bunka Kenkyūjo kiyō* 53 (January 1, 1992): 23.

19. For the Iwakura mission's view, see Kume Kunitake, *Tokumei zenken taishi Bei-Ō kairan jikki*, ed. Tanaka Akira, vol. 5 (Iwanami Bunko, 1982), ch. 89 ("Yōroppa-shū seizoku sōron"), 146–60, and ch. 96 ("Arabiya-kai kōtei no ki"), 271–75. In the same volume, see also Tanaka Akira's editorial note ("Iwakura shisetsu-dan to Yōroppa to

Ajia"), 353–80, for an analysis of the mission's comparative observations on the West and Asia.

In relation to the mission's distrust of innate racial superiority and inferiority, Tanaka points out in his separate analysis ("Iwakura shisetsu-dan to Amerika Igirisu," 411–33) in *Tokumei zenken taishi Bei-Ō kairan jikki*, vol. 2, that the mission never considered the black American's poor living conditions as resulting from their racial inferiority. Rather, the report analyzes: "It is obvious that skin color has no bearing on one's intellect [*hifu no iro wa chishiki ni kankei naki kotomo mata akikeshi*]" (my translation). Therefore, those ambitious blacks who saw the importance of education strove to learn and work harder and became great intellectuals, for whom uneducated whites were no match (ibid., 419).

20. The Japanese acquiesced in these policies with remarkable resiliency, perhaps because they too, as a result of their historical experience, were accomplished followers of the manipulation of racial images, both conceptual and visual. In the late nineteenth century, as their Westernization process rapidly moved on, the Japanese people increasingly portrayed themselves in popular images as looking more Caucasian. Perhaps the spearhead of this trend was the 1888 engraving of Emperor Mutsuhito, or the Meiji emperor, by the Italian artist Edoardo Chiossone, which was distributed throughout the country to be worshipped as a sacred symbol of national unity and progress. In this famous imperial image, there was no trace of Japan in sight—his clothes, furniture, and interior decoration were all Western. His imperial visage, too, had thicker eyebrows, double eyelids, and rounder and bigger pupils—making him look somewhat Caucasian. Most likely, Chiossone "Westernized" Mutsuhito's facial features in his engraving, either on his own initiative or by governmental request. This Westernized visage of the emperor became the official royal image of modern Japan, deeply embedded in people's minds as a proud symbol of Japan's successful enlightenment. Henceforth, Japanese tended to portray themselves as closer to whites than to other Asians in physical characteristics. Inoue Naoki, *Mikado no shōzō* (Shōgakkan, 1986), ch. 12 ("Tsukurareta goshin'ei"), 424–47.

21. British sociologist Ronald Dore commented on the differing "conceptual map" of Japanese and Westerners, which bears similarity to this work's argument on Japan's dualistic identity. According to Dore, while Europeans and North Americans divided the world into white Caucasians and the rest, the Japanese tended to split the twentieth-century globe into three parts: the Confucian-Mongolian world, "into which the Japanese merged and where they felt no more alien than an Englishman in Sicily"; the white world, "of which they wanted to be honorary members, but in which they never expected to feel at home"; and the rest of the world's underclass, "starting with alien Asia and extending to the more barbaric shores of Africa." Dore also implies that "Asia," as a meaningful social category to Europeans, is not much so to Japanese. The above comments are quoted in Christopher Thorne, *The Issue of*

War: States, Societies, and the Far Eastern Conflict of 1941–1945 (Oxford University Press, 1985), 158.

22. California's 1920 Alien Land Law was passed with even tighter restrictions than the 1913 measure. As nationwide exclusionist sentiment supported the passage of the 1921 Immigration Acts—the country's first attempt to regulate immigrants on a quota basis—the anti-Japanese movement culminated in the 1922 U.S. Supreme Court decision in the Ozawa case which ruled against Japanese eligibility for citizenship because of race. Ozawa Takao, the petitioner, had arrived in California as a student in 1894 and after attending the University of California for three years moved to Honolulu. After his first application for citizenship was denied, he challenged the decision in the U.S. District Court for the Territory of Hawaii in 1916. Well-educated, "Americanized," and Christian, he seemed to have no obstacle in gaining citizenship. Six years later, the case went before the Supreme Court, with George Wickersham, a former U.S. Attorney General, as Ozawa's counsel. The Supreme Court, however, held that Ozawa Takao was not entitled to naturalization because Japanese were neither "free white persons" nor "aliens of African nativity," as the time-honored naturalization act stipulated. In the same term, the Court also denied citizenship to Japanese veterans who had served with American forces during World War I.

Two years later, the same formula was incorporated into a clause in the 1924 Immigration Act to prohibit the admission of "aliens ineligible for citizenship." Since the previous 1917 and 1921 Immigration Acts had already excluded all other Asian peoples, the sole purpose of this wording was to single out the Japanese. This section of the Immigration Act thus came to be known as the "Japanese exclusion clause," which served as a final declaration in the U.S. legal code that Japanese were undesirable. The Consulate General of Japan, *Documental History of Law Cases Affecting Japanese in the United Sates, 1916–1924*, vol. 1, *Naturalization Cases and Cases Affecting Constitutional and Treaty Rights*, part 1, "Naturalization Cases," ch. 1 ("The Ozawa Case"), reprinted by Arno Press, 1978.

23. Standard Japanese works on Japan's response to the 1924 Immigration Act include Hirakawa Sukehiro, "Uchimura Kanzo and America—Some Reflections on the Psychological Structure of Anti-Americanism [the original text is in English]," *Tōkyō Daigaku Kyōyō Gakka kiyō* 6 (1973): 1–19; and Minowa Kimitada, "Tokutomi Sohō no rekishi-zō to Nichi-Bei sensō no genri-teki kaishi," in Haga Tōru et al., eds., *Seiyō no shōgeki to Nihon* (Kōza hikaku bungaku, vol. 5 in the series) (Tōkyō Daigaku Shuppankai, 1973).

24. Ben-Ami Shillony, *Politics and Culture in Wartime Japan* (Oxford University Press, 1981), 140–41. See also the following contemporary arguments on the wisdom of Japan's coexitence with the West published during the war: Kamikawa Hikomatsu, "The New Order in the Pacific," *Nippon Hyoron* (August 1940), cited in Joyce Lebra, ed., *Japan's Greater East Asia Co-Prosperity Sphere in World War II: Selected Readings and Documents* (Oxford University Press, 1975), 46–47; Arita Hachirō, "The

Greater East Asian Sphere of Common Prosperity," *Contemporary Japan* 10, no.1 (January 1941), cited in Lebra, ibid., 73–77; Rōyama Masamichi, *Tōa to sekai—shinchitsujo e no ronsaku* (Kaizō Sha, 1941); Ōtaka Masajirō, *Dai-Tōa no rekishi to kensetsu* (Kibundō Shobō, 1943).

Japan's wartime strategy to rally support for Pan-Asianism from the Western nations also included a plan to utilize some ten thousand Jewish residents in Manchuria and Shanghai, through whom the Japanese government hoped to establish a favorable financial tie with the West for the postwar period (David Kranzler, "Japanese Policy Toward the Jews, 1938–1941," *Japanese Interpreter* 11, no. 4 [Spring 1977]: 493–527). Japan's wartime propaganda effort even went so far as to encourage Australia to abandon its "White Australia" policy and find its proper place in Japan's New Order. Japan's wartime broadcasts beamed toward Australia claimed that Japan considered good relations with Australia to be crucial for Japan's economic growth in the postwar period (L. D. Meo, *Japan's Radio War on Australia, 1941–1945* [Melbourne University Press, 1968], chs. 5, 6, and 9).

1. THE INTERNATIONAL FRAMEWORK FOR POSTWAR JAPANESE-AMERICAN RACISM

1. Alexander DeConde, *Ethnicity, Race, and American Foreign Policy: A History* (Northeastern University Press, 1992), 128.

2. Christopher Thorne, *The Issue of War* (Oxford University Press, 1985), 147, 203–206. For a historical survey of the role of racism in forming imperialism and colonialism, see Paul Gordon Lauren, *Power and Prejudice: The Politics and Diplomacy of Racial Discrimination* (Westview, 1988). See also Edward Said, *Culture and Imperialism* (Knopf, 1993), 7–11.

3. See, for example, Gary R. Hess, *The United States' Emergence as a Southeast Asian Power, 1940–1950* (Columbia University Press, 1987); J. Pluvier, *South-East Asia from Colonialism to Independence* (Oxford University Press, 1974).

4. Lindsay Parrot, "Asiatic Uprising Laid to Tokyo Plot," *New York Times*, November 11, 1945, sec. 1, p. 6. As for the political fixtures under the leadership of Burma's Aung San, who received secret military training under the Japanese, see *Burma Under the Japanese* (Macmillan, 1954), by U Nu, who became the first prime minister of Burma after postwar independence. Ba Maw's *Breakthrough in Burma: Memoirs of a Revolution, 1939–1946* (Yale University Press, 1968) and U Maung Maung's *The Burmese Nationalist Movements, 1940–1948* (University of Hawaii, 1990) provide insights into the dynamics of Burmese-Japanese interactions in the Burmese independence movement.

5. Anne O'Hare McCormick, "The Stormy Passage Toward a Free Asia," *New York Times*, February 18, 1946, sec. 1, p. 20.

6. Robert Trumbull, "The West Loses 'Face' in the East," *New York Times*, December 1, 1946, sec. 6, p. 12.

7. Ōnuma Yasuaki, *Tōkyō saiban kara sengo sekinin no shisō e* (Yūshindō Kōbun Sha, 1985), 56–57; Chihiro HOSOYA, Nisuke ANDO, Yasuaki ONUMA, and Richard Minear, eds., *The Tokyo War Crimes Trial: An International Symposium* (Kodansha International, 1986), 155.

8. "The Major Evils of the Tokyo Trials," 1–2, 20–21. This material is available in a microfilm form in National Archives Microfilm Publications, International Prosecution Section Staff Historical Files Relating to Cases Tried Before the International Military Tribunal for the Far East, 1945–1948, M 1699 (Entry 341) RG 331, roll #2.

9. *International Military Tribunal for the Far East: The Tokyo War Crimes Trial. The Complete Transcripts of the Proceedings, 1946–1948* (hereafter cited as *IMTFE*) (Garland, 1981), 27–28.

10. Ford Wilkins, "Close-Up Report on the Japanese," *New York Times*, March 4, 1945, sec. 6, p. 10; "Wainwright Urges Occupation to 1965; Studies Beatings of Himself and Others Revealed by General in Broadcast," *New York Times*, September 18, 1945, sec. 1, p. 3; "In the Matter of Japanese War Crimes at Macassar Camp, Celebes," Affidavit (Doc. no. 5503, MD/JAG/FS/JC/76 AMBM/GC, Exhibit no. 1804A), 2. RG 238 National Archives Collection of World War II War Crimes Records, Records of the IMTFE, Court Exhibits, 1946–48, #1795 to 1819, box 209, PI-180, E-14, HM 1991.

11. PWC-111, CAC-80, "Japan: Occupation and Military Government: Composition of Forces to Occupy Japan," March 13, 1944, in State Department, *Foreign Relations of the United States* (hereafter cited as *FRUS*) (1944): 5:1202–1205.

12. Memorandum for the President, "National Composition of Forces to Occupy Japan Proper in the Post-Defeat Period (Top Secret)," August 13, 1945 (MacArthur Memorial Archives, Norfolk, Va. [hereafter, MacArthur Archives], box 75, RG 5, SCAP General Files, folder 4).

13. At the Tokyo War Crimes Trial, several Japanese witnesses confessed that the Japanese military did promote some specific racial policies against the white race. According to Yamazaki Shigeru, the deputy chief at the Prisoner of War Control Bureau in Tokyo between January 1942 and February 1943, Prime Minister Tōjō Hideki instructed the commanders of POW camps to use white prisoners of war for menial labor and work details. The idea was to degrade and humiliate the whites and to impress the local people with the superiority of the Japanese over the white peoples. Yamazaki also stated that Gen. Uemura Mikio, the chief of the Prisoner of War Control Bureau, ordered the white prisoners to perform heavy labor, including "coolie labor" such as loading and unloading cargoes into and from hulls of ships, with a similar objective to lower white prestige in Asia. "Direct Examination, IPS Doc. No. 2846 (identified by the witness Shigeru YAMAZAKI)," ORDER no. 154, National Archives Microfilm Publications, M1663, RG 311, Roll #42, pp. 1-3; National Archives, Washington, D.C.

14. Akira IRIYE, *Power and Culture* (Harvard University, 1981), 224–25, 260, and 265.

15. "Japanese Eager to Resume Old Relations with Britain," *New York Times*, October 21, 1945.

16. "Memorandum to the Imperial Japanese Government from General Headquarters Supreme Commander for the Allied Powers: 'Transfer of Custody of Diplomatic and Consular Property and Archives,' (25 October 1945)" and "Cessation of Communication between Japanese Government and Its Former Diplomatic and Consular Representatives Abroad; AG 091.1 GS (10 December 1945)," in *Documents Concerning the Allied Occupation and Control of Japan*, vol. 2, *Political, Military, and Cultural*, compiled by the Division of Special Records, Foreign Office, Japanese Government (March 1949), 40–44.

17. Watanabe Akio, "Kōwa mondai to Nihon no sentaku," in Watanabe Akio and Miyazato Seigen, eds., *San Furanshisuko kōwa* (Tōkyō Daigaku Shuppankai, 1986), 20–21.

18. "Heiwa Jōyaku Mondai Kenkyū Kanji-kai no ken (On the Research Committee on Problems Concerning a Peace Treaty) (Classified)," November 21, 1945, Japanese Foreign Ministry Archives, Tokyo (hereafter cited as JFMA) (microfilm, reel #B'0008, flash #1, 0006–7). The result of the talk was recorded as a series entitled "Heiwa jōyaku mondai kenkyū shiryō (Reference Material on Problems on a Peace Treaty) (Classified)," January 31, 1946 (JFMA microfilm, reel #B'0008, flash #1, 0008ff.).

19. "Heiwa jōyaku teiketsu mondai kihon hōshin (Basic Principles Regarding Some Problems in Concluding a Peace Treaty) (Classified)," January 31, 1946 (JFMA microfilm, reel #B'0008, flash #1, 0008–0010).

20. "Heiwa jōyaku no naiyō ni kansuru gensoku-teki hōshin, kenkyū shian (Basic Principles Regarding the Terms of a Peace Treaty) (Classified)," January 31, 1946 (JFMA microfilm, reel #B'0008, flash #1, 0025–0026); "Keizai jōkō ni kansuru shomondai—imin mondai to heiwa jōyaku (Problems Regarding Provisions on Economic Conditions—Problems of Immigration and a Peace Treaty) (Classified)," January 31, 1946 (JFMA microfilm, reel #B'0008, flash #1, 0117–0123).

21. Watanabe, "Kōwa mondai to Nihon no . . . ," 25.

22. "Keizai jōkō ni kansuru shomondai—imin mondai to heiwa jōyaku (Problems Regarding Provisions on Economic Conditions—Problems of Immigration and a Peace Treaty) (Classified)," January 31, 1946 (JFMA microfilm, reel #B'0008, flash #1, 0120).

23. "Kokuseki mondai to heiwa jōyaku (The Problem of Nationality and a Peace Treaty) (Classified)," January 31, 1946 (JFMA microfilm, reel #B'0008, flash #1, 0073–0092).

24. For a detailed analysis of the problem of dual citizenship for the Japanese in the United States, see Raymond L. Buell, "Some Legal Aspects of the Japanese Question," *American Journal of International Law* 17 (January 1923): 29–49.

25. H. W. V. Temperley, *A History of the Peace Conference of Paris*, vol. II, *The Settlement with Germany* (Henry Frowde, Hodder and Stoughton, 1920).

26. "Kokuseki mondai to heiwa jōyaku," January 31, 1946 (JFMA microwilm, reel #B'0008, flash #1, 0076–0084).

27. "Heiwa Jōyaku Mondai Kenkyū Kanji-kai—Jōyaku-kyoku Hōki-ka, Tazuke," (The Executive Committee on Problems on a Peace Treaty—by Tazuke, Legal Section, the Treaty Division)," February 1, 1946 (JFMA microfilm, reel #B'0008, flash #1, 0128–0137).

28. "Heiwa jōyaku mondai kenkyū shiryō—shian dai-ichi-ji an (Research Reference to Problems Concerning a Peace Treaty—Tentative Plan No. 1)," February 21, 1946 (JFMA microfilm, reel #B'0008, flash #1, 0138–0158).

29. "Bikō (Annex)," ibid., 0156–57.

30. "Heiwa Jōyaku Mondai Kenkyū Kanji-kai—dai-ichi-ji kenkyū hōkoku (tori-atsukai chūi) (The Research Committee on Problems Concerning the Peace Treaty—Research Report No. 1—Handle with Care)," May 1946 (JFMA microfilm, reel #B'0008, flash #1, 0164–0186).

31. Ibid.

32. *Sekai Heiwa-kai sōritsu shushi sho* (from Inagaki Yūjirō, June 1, 1946)," RG 331, box 235, file "19,000–19,999" ("Letters to MacArthur," the Washington National Records Center [National Archives Branch Depository], Suitland, Md.). For the collection of letters kept at the Washington National Records Center, look for the following entry: RG 331 (Allied Occupational and Occupation Headquarters, WWII), SCAP, Assistant Chief of Staff, G-2 Intelligence Division, Miscellanenous File, 1945–1951, Miscellaneous Letters to the Supreme Commander for the Allied Forces.

33. "Heiwa Jōyaku Mondai Kenkyū Kanji-kai—dai-ichi-ji kenkyū hōkoku (toriatsukai chūi)": see n. 30, above.

34. "Heiwa jōyaku ni kansuru (1) mondai no shozai to (2) Nihon no tachiba (Loci of Problems on a Peace Treaty and Japan's Stance on Them)," June 3, 1947 (JFMA microfilm, reel #B'0008, flash #1, 0245–0258).

35. "Whitney Shōshō to kaiken—oboegaki tsūdoku: toriatsukai chūi (Report on Meeting with General Whitney—His Review of the Memorandum: Handle with Care)," July 28, 1947 (JFMA microfilm, reel #B'0008, flash #3, 0033–0036).

36. Dr. Wilson Compton, "The West Looks West," an address delivered at the annual University of Washington Honors Convocation, May 15, 1946; reproduced by special request and permission by Nu Chapter of Phi Delta Kappa, University of Washington, Seattle (MacArthur Archives, box 1, RG 5, folder 3: Master File 1947).

37. "The Acting political adviser in Japan (Acheson) to secretary of state," September 27, 1945, *FRUS* (1945): 6:724.

38. Secret SWNCC report 162/2, "Reorientation of the Japanese," January 8, 1946, *FRUS* (1946): 8:105–109.

39. *To Secure These Rights: The Report of the President's Committee on Civil Rights* (U.S. Government Printing Office, 1947), 146–47. See also Alexander DeConde, *Ethnicity, Race, and American Foreign Policy*, 130–31.

40. Richard Polenberg, *One Nation Divisible: Class, Race, and Ethnicity in the United States Since 1938* (Pelican, 1980), 108–109; Donald R. McCoy and Richard T. Ruetten, *Quest and Response: Minority Rights and the Truman Administration* (University Press of Kansas, 1973), 66 and 120.

41. For the most comprehensive study of the law to repeal the Chinese exclusion acts, see Frederick Riggs, *Pressures on Congress: A Study of the Repeal of Chinese Exclusion* (Columbia University Press, 1950). As for the national debate on the issue, see U.S. House Committee on Immigration and Naturalization, *Hearings on H.R. 1882 and H.R. 2309*, 78th Cong., 1st sess., 1943. Ironically, Chiang Kai-shek's Guomindang Party, entrapped in the civil war against Mao Zedong's Communist Party, had never been as enthusiastic toward this repeal measure as the U.S. government had expected. It may be that, in the modernization process, the Chinese had never subscribed to a Western racial hierarchy as much as the Japanese. American racial politics was effective only with a nation like Japan, which even during the war could not discard its own dualistic racial identity within the conventional Western-made hierarchy.

See "The Ambassador in China (Gauss) to the Secretary of State, from Chungking, October 25, 1943, 893.9111/84 (Telegram)," and "The Ambassador in China (Gauss) to the Secretary of State, from Chungking, November 30, 1943, 151.10/1989 (Telegram)," both in *FRUS* (1943): 785–86 ("Diplomatic Papers: China"). For the cablegram sent by Mme Chiang Kai-shek to Vice President Henry Wallace and House Speaker Sam Rayburn congratulating Congress on passage of the bill, see *Congressional Record*, 89, no. 10397, daily ed. (December 3, 1943).

42. 80th Cong., 1st sess., H.R. 857, January 13, 1947 (MacArthur Archives, box 2, RG 5, folder 6).

43. Akira IRIYE, *Across the Pacific: An Inner History of American–East Asian Relations*, rev. ed. (Imprint Publications, 1992), 268. To illustrate the new yellow peril against Communist China, Iriye quotes a 1949 speech by Sen. William Knowland in his unsuccessful bid for U.S. aid to the Guomindang forces: "Those of us who represent the Pacific Coast states [have] a particular interest in this regard, [for] the waters of the Pacific Ocean wash upon our states. It was not so very many years ago that we had in the state of California . . . the only enemy [Japanese] shelling of an American submarine. . . . We want no repetition of that kind."

44. "A letter to General Douglas MacArthur from U.S. Congressman Bertrand W. Gearhart," August 6, 1947 (MacArthur Archives, box 2, RG 5, folder 6).

45. "Equality in Naturalization and Immigration: Extension of Remarks of Hon. Francis Walter of Pennsylvania in the House of Representatives," February 2, 1949, 2–8 (MacArthur Archives, box 74, RG 5, SCAP General Files, folder 6).

46. "Report [to accompany H.R. 199, Providing the Privilege of Becoming a Naturalized Citizen of the United States to All Immigrants Having a Legal Right to Permanent Residence, to Make Immigration Quotas Available to Asian and Pacific Peoples]," *House Report* No. 65, 81st Cong., 1st sess., 1949, 8–10.

47. *Congressional Record* (80th Cong., 2d sess.), "Extension of Remarks of Hon. Walter H. Judd of Minnesota in the House of Representatives," April 15, 1948 (MacArthur Archives, box 74, RG 5, SCAP General Files, folder 6, pp. 1–4).

48. Robert Divine, *American Immigration Policy, 1924–1952* (Da Capo, 1972), 155.

49. Committee for Equality in Naturalization, *Editorial Comment: The Judd Bill for Equality in Naturalization and Immigration*, June 2, 1949 (National Archives, Legislative Branch, RG 46, U.S. Senate, 81st Cong., SEN 81A-E11, H.R. 199–H.R. 559, box. 87, file H.R. 199, DOC 518). For the treatment of "skin color," see the following editorials: "Practical Statemanship," *Des Moines Tribune*, May 7, 1949; "Purge Racism," *Boston Herald*, March 3, 1949; "Chance to Remove Last Racial Barrier from Immigration Law," *Cleveland Press*, March 28, 1949; and other articles in the above file at the National Archives. See also "A Letter to Senate Judiciary Committee from James K. Foster, Rt.4, Box 23, Kirkland, Wash.," August 17, 1949 (National Archives, Legislative Branch, RG 46, box 87, file H.R. 199, DOC 518).

50. U.S. Senate Committee on the Judiciary, *Naturalization of Asian and Pacific Peoples: Hearings before a Subcommittee of the Committee on the Judiciary* (hereafter cited as *Hearings on the Naturalization of Asian and Pacific Peoples*), 81st Cong., 1st sess., on H. R. 199, July 19–20, 1949 (GPO, 1950; in mimeograph, unprinted) (National Archives, Legislative Branch, RG 46, U.S. Senate, 81st Cong., SEN 81A-E11, H.R. 199–H.R. 559, box 86). Note that this mimeographed record on the hearings on H.R. 199 was printed solely for the use of the Committee on the Judiciary and there was no publication available for the public.

51. *Hearings on the Naturalization of Asian and Pacific Peoples*, 61–64.

52. Ibid., 36–37.

53. "General of the Army Douglas MacArthur's New Year Message, January 1, 1949," *Documents Concerning the Allied Occupation and Control of Japan* 2:21–23 (see n. 16, above); and "M'Arthur to Ease Control in Japan," *New York Times*, May 3, 1949, sec. 1, p. 1. See also Robert A. Fearey, *The Occupation of Japan: Second Phase, 1948–1950*, published under the auspices of the International Secretariat, Institute of Pacific Relations (Macmillan, 1950), 11.

54. "Memorandum from George Kennan to General of the Army Douglas MacArthur, Supreme Commander for the Allied Powers, Tokyo, (Top Secret)," March 5, 1948 (MacArthur Archives, box 107, RG 5, folder 5).

55. "Memorandum of Conversation, by the Chargé in Japan (Huston), Tokyo (Top Secret)," July 16, 1949, in *FRUS* (1949): 7(pt.2): 807; "The Acting Political Adviser in Japan (Sebald) to the Director of the Office of Far Eastern Affairs (Butterworth), Tokyo (Top Secret)," July 26, 1949, in ibid., 808–12.

56. "U.S. Virtually Ends Civil Affairs Role Throughout Japan," *New York Times*, July 29, 1949, sec. 1, p. 1.

57. "Memorandum of Conversation, by the Acting Political Adviser in Japan (Sebald), Tokyo (Top Secret)," September 21, 1949, in *FRUS* (1949): 7(pt. 2): 862–64.

58. "Boston Council Bars Tokyo Diet Group," *New York Times*, January 31, 1950, sec. 1, p. 1.

59. "Snubbed Japanese Offered Amends," *New York Times*, February 1, 1950, sec. 1, p. 2; "Senators Condemn Boston on Japanese," *New York Times*, February 21, 1950, sec. 1, p. 16); "House in Ovation for Japanese," *New York Times*, February 22, 1950, sec. 1, p. 17. Also, as for the Japanese delegation's reception on Capitol Hill, see the following in the *Congressional Record*: " 'Broadcast in honor of 55 members of Japanese Diet visiting the United States,' extension of remarks of Hon. Elbert Thomas," *Congressional Record*, 81st Cong., 2d sess., Appendix, 1950, 96, pt. 17:A5980–5982. See also "Addresses by Gen. MacArthur to the Japanese delegation" (p. 1919), "Letter by Gen. MacArthur relative to reception in the United States of Japanese Diet delegation" (p. 2837), "Letter of appreciation from members of Diet" (p. 5056), all in the *Congressional Record*, 81st Cong., 2d sess., 1950, 96, pt. 17.

60. "Memorandum by the Consultant to the Secretary (Dulles) to the Secretary of State (Secret)," Washington, D.C., June 7, 1950, in *FRUS* (1950): 6:1207.

61. Ibid., 1208–1209.

62. "Editorial Note," *FRUS* (1951): 6:825–27.

63. "Memorandum of Conversation, by the Counselor of the Mission in Japan (Huston), Tokyo (Secret)," April 8, 1950, *FRUS* (1950): 6:1166–67.

64. Yoshida Shigeru, *Kaisō jū-nen*, vols. 1–3 (Tōkyō Shirakawa Shoin, 1982–83), passim, esp. ch. 18 ("San Furansisuko kaigi zengo"), in vol. 3.

65. Note that Yoshida wrote that the American leaders, in their effort to reconstruct postwar Asia, again recognized the Japanese people as "the superior race in Asia [*Ajia ni okeru mottomo sugureta minzoku*]," in Yoshida, *Kaisō jū-nen* 3:276.

66. "Memorandum by the Consultant to the Secretary (Dulles) to the Assistant Secretary of State for Far Eastern Affairs (Rusk)," Washington, D.C., October 22, 1951, *FRUS* (1951): 6:1381.

67. John Dower, "Peace and Democracy in Two Systems—External Policy and Internal Conflict," in Andrew Gordon, ed., *Postwar Japan as History* (University of California, 1993), 11–12.

68. Walter LaFeber, *America, Russia, and the Cold War, 1945–1990* 6th ed. (McGraw-Hill, 1991), 120.

69. "The British Embassy to the Department of State (Top Secret)," delivered on February 14, 1951, *FRUS* (1951): 6:154–55.

70. "The Secretary of State (Acheson) to the United States Political Adviser to SCAP (Sebald) (Secret Priority)," Washington, D.C., February 8, 1951, ibid., 6:150–51.

71. For arguments on the racialization of the three-world theory, see Carl Pletsch,

"The Three Worlds, or the Division of Social Scientific Labor, circa 1950–1975," *Comparative Studies in Society and History* 23, no. 3 (July 1981): 565–90; Peter Worsley, *The Three Worlds: Culture and World Development* (University of Chicago, 1984); Dean Tipps, "Modernization Theory and the Comparative Study of Societies: A Critical Perspective," *Comparative Studies in Society and History* 15, no. 2 (March 1973): 199–226.

72. David Theo Goldberg, *Racist Culture* (Blackwell, 1993), 163–64; Carl Pletsch, "The Three Worlds," 569–70.

73. Goldberg, *Racist Culture*, 164–65.

74. A detailed analysis is necessary to determine how much Japan's racial identity as a "colored" nation affected the Soviet view on U.S.-Japanese relations or its policy against Japan. Quite ironically, contrary to American imagining, the Soviet Union did not take an interest in exploring Japan's racial and cultural dimension with the aim of alienating it from the United States and other Western nations. The common Soviet approach to international issues was to explore the class dimension of each nation, not the cultural. For example, research by the Soviet Academy of Sciences in 1963 discussed Japanese monopolists, capitalists, workers, and "forces of democracy," as juxtaposed with the American counterparts and explained the nature of U.S.-Japanese collaboration as one between American imperialism and Japanese monopolists. B. I. Bukharov, *Obrazovanie Amerikano-Yaponskogo Voennogo Sojuza* (The foundation of U.S.-Japanese military alliance) (Eastern Literature Publisher, 1963).

75. From the year of independence through the early 1980s the Japanese government signed agreements on cultural exchange with the following nations: France (1953), Italy and Mexico (1954), Thailand (1955), India (1956), West Germany, Egypt, Iran, Pakistan (1957), Britain (1960), Brazil (1961), Yugoslavia (1968), Afganistan (1969), Belgium (1973), Australia (1974), Canada (1976), Iraq, Finland (1978), Argentina (1979), Holland (1980), Greece (1981), and Bangladesh and Spain (1982). Gaimushō Sengo Gaikō-shi Kenkyūkai, ed., *Nihon gaikō sanjū-nen—sengo no kiseki to tenbō: 1952–1982* (Sekai No Ugoki Sha, 1982), 186.

2. RACE AND CULTURE: PERSON TO PERSON

1. The Americans proved to be superb engineers of image control through which they conveyed appropriate racial and cultural relations to the Japaense. In the prewar period the U.S. government had succeeded in maneuvering public images in favor of Japan's dualistic identity in, for instance, the auspicious treatment of the Japanese in U.S. immigration policy. Various international expositions held at the turn of the century are perhaps good examples of this image control. Where the concept of Social Darwinism was manifested in the topology of exhibitions of various nations and races, the Japanese government was concerned that Japan attain a position worthy of the respect and confidence of other nations—fellowship in the family of nations. At the Columbian World Exposition of 1893–1901 in Chicago, the U.S. government allocated

the Japanese pavilion, a replica of the Phoenix Pavilion built in twentieth-century Kyoto, to a location that exactly mirrored Japan's position in the hierarchical order of civilization in the world: it stood on an artificial lake created halfway between the White City, where pavilions of leading nations of the West were located, and the Midway, where pavilions of primitive non-Western peoples densely stood. Neil Harris, "All the World a Melting Pot? Japan at American Fairs, 1876–1904," in Akira IRIYE, ed., *Mutual Images* (Harvard University Press, 1975), 27–28; Yoshimi Shun'ya, *Hakurankai no seiji-gaku: manazashi no kindai* (Chūkō Shinsho, 1992), 187–94, 209–12.

2. Sumitomo Toshio, *Senryō hiroku* (Chūkō Bunko, 1988), 63–69, 93–103; letter from Ted de Bary in Tokyo to Don Keene in Tsingtao, October 25, 1945, in Otis Cary, ed., *From a Ruined Empire: Letters—Japan, China, Korea, 1945–46; Correspondents: Donald Keene, Wm. Theodore de Bary, Otis Cary, Frank L. Turner, Sherwood R. Moran, Hisashi Kubota, Richard Beardsley, Warren Tsuneishi, and David L. Osborn* (Kodansha International, 1st paperback ed., 1984), 102. Shortly before and after August 15, there were several other coup attempts by military officers and another mass suicide by eleven ultranationalists in front of the Imperial Palace.

3. "Jūmin kokoroe," in Etō Jun, ed., *Senryō shiroku*, vol. 4, *Nihon hondo shinchū* (Kōdansha Bunko, 1989), 147–49.

4. Tsukuda Sadao, "Senryō no naka no shomin (ii)—Yokohama kara no shōgen," in Shisō No Kagaku Kenkyūkai, ed., *Kyōdō kenkyū/Nihon senryō* (Tokuma Shoten, 1972), 114–16.

5. Letter from Ted de Bary in Tokyo to Don Keene in Guam, September 24, 1945, in Cary, ed., *From a Ruined Empire*, 49; letter from Frank Turner in Tokyo to Don Keene in Tsingtao, October 29, 1945, in Cary, ibid., 124–25; Makise Kikue, "Senryō no naka no shomin (i)—kichi no mawari de no kiki-gaki," in Shisō No Kagaku Kenkyūkai, ed., *Kyōdō kenkyū/Nihon senryō*, 105.

6. "Japanese Make Friendly Moves Toward Tan Yanks," *Pittsburgh Courier*, October 13, 1945, 14.

7. For the interview with Kluckhohn and Walker, see "Nihon o kataru nyū-Kyō no Bei-shi kisha," *Asahi shimbun*, August 31, 1945, 2. For the interview with UP correspondent Hazel Barzog, see "Shiritai Nihon-josei tatakai no ato—jūgun Bei-fujin-kisha to kataru," *Asahi shimbun*, September 8, 1945, 2.

There are several discrepancies between the Japanese version of these interviews and the American correspondents' own reports as printed in the United States. For example, Kluckhohn wrote an article for the *New York Times* on his impressions of Japan in defeat: "If you ask why they attacked Pearl Harbor on December 7, 1941, they are embarrassed. If you answer 'Manila is worse,' to their queries as to why Tokyo is so severely mauled, you have attacked Oriental 'face.' . . . Toshiyuki Miyamoto, a reporter for the newspaper *Asahi*, . . . proceeded to try to interview us . . . and within a few moments a photographer and a man whom we took to be of the secret police arrived. The unidentified arrival questioned us as to the United States attitudes toward

Japan. . . . We said it was 'not so bad as Manila' as far as complete destruction went. He looked at us with pain and quickly left." Kluckhohn, "Japanese Bitter in Defeat; Angered by Raids on Tokyo," *New York Times*, September 1, 1945, sec. 1, p. 1. In the *New York Times* article, Gordon Walker was introduced as a reporter for the American Broadcasting Company.

For a slightly different view of the friendly Japanese reaction toward the Americans, see Peter Herzog, "The Yanks in Tokyo: A Front-Line View," *America*, November 3, 1945, 121–22. Herzog too regarded the friendly Japanese, including the "cute Jap kids," "puzzling," but he argued that it was a good sign of the cultural conquest of Japan by Americanism—most likely leading to a creation of a Christian Japan (in his vision through the Catholic missions).

8. *Asahi shimbun*, September 12, 1945, 2.

9. Sodei Rinjirō, *Haikei Makkāsā gensui sama—Senryō-ka no Nihon-jin no tegami* (Chūkō Bunko, paperback ed., 1991), 14–18. These letters are kept at the Washington National Records Center, Suitland, Md. Letters especially favored by MacArthur himself are kept separately at the MacArthur Memorial Archives, Norfolk, Virginia. For the collection kept at the Washington National Records Center ("hereafter cited as "Letters to MacArthur"), see ch. 1, n. 32, above.

10. Sodei Rinjirō, *Haikei Makkāsā gensui sama*, 247.

11. "Beikoku daihyō Makkāsā kakka [letter from Shiomi Kitarō, February 18, 1946]," quoted in Sodei Rinjirō, *Haikei Makkāsā gensui sama*, 29–31; "Makkāsā gensui kakka on-taishi [letter from Yagi Chōzaburō, February 15, 1946]," quoted in Sodei, ibid., 32–33; "Makkāsā gensui kakka [letter from Nagano Kōhei, February 18, 1946]," RG 331, SCAP, box 233, file 1 ("Letters to MacArthur," Washington National Records Center, Suitland, Md.).

12. *Our Job in Japan*, War Department Orientation Film, Official O.F.-15, Information and Education Division, War Department (National Archives Audio Visual Center: 111/OF/15).

13. Robert Smith, *MacArthur in Korea: The Naked Emperor* (Simon and Schuster, 1982), 228. Also see Lee Nichols, *Breakthrough on the Color Front* (Random House, 1953), 114.

14. "Even in Japan!" *Pittsburgh Courier*, November 3, 1945, 6.

15. Sodei Rinjirō, "Nihon senryō to Nikkei Nisei," in Hata Ikuhiko and Sodei Rinjirō, *Nihon senryō hishi* 2:278–79 (Asahi Shimbun Sha, 1977); see also Robert Wilson and Bill Hosokawa, *East to America: A History of the Japanese in the United States* (William Morrow, 1980), 236–43.

16. "Americans Entering Japan See Entirely Alien Land," *New York Times*, September 2, 1945, sec. 4, p. 5.

17. *Our Job in Japan* (National Archives Audio Visual Center: 111/OF/15).

18. John LaCerda, *The Conqueror Comes to Tea: Japan Under MacArthur* (Rutgers University Press, 1946), 46, 47, and 30.

19. Lucy Crockette, *Popcorn on the Ginza: An Informal Portrait of Postwar Japan* (William Sloane, 1949), 20–21, 98, and 145; Sumitomo, *Senryō hiroku*, 138–39.

20. Although it is true that there were fanatic Japanese admirers of MacArthur, the thesis on MacArthur's "presumed divinity" derived from the American side as well. For example, it was MacArthur's personal belief that no harm could come to him until his divine destiny—the reclamation of the Japanese—was accomplished. Also, it was at the Tokyo Correspondents' Club for Western reporters that a tale of MacArthur walking upon the waters started to circulate as a caricature of his pompousness, especially toward the correspondents. For Japanese attitudes toward him, see Sodei Rinjirō, *Haikei Makkāsā gansui sama*. For a brief sketch on the American side, see John LaCerda, *The Conqueror Comes to Tea*, 95–102.

21. Claude A. Buss, "Japan—Under the Occupation" (n.d., personal copy?) (MacArthur Memorial Archives, Norfolk, Va. [hereafter, MacArthur Archives], box 74, RG 5, General Files, folder 7).

22. 740.00119 PW/9–645, "Memorandum by the Acting Secretary of State to President Truman," Washington, D.C., September 5, 1945, *FRUS* (1945): 6:711; "M'Arthur Declares Japan Ended as a Great Power," *New York Times*, September 22, 1945, sec. 1, p. 1.

23. "Nimitz Cautions Us on Foe's Explanation," *New York Times*, September 14, 1945, sec. 1, p. 3; "East and West Now Face to Face in Japan," *New York Times*, September 8, 1945, sec. 4, p. 3.

24. 740.00119 EAC/12–1244, "The Secretary of State to the Ambassador in the United Kingdom (Winant)," no. 4980, Washington, D.C., January 13, 1945, *FRUS* (1945): 8:378–88.; Franklin M. Davis, Jr., *Come as a Conqueror: The United States Army's Occupation of Germany, 1945–1949* (Macmillan, 1967), 142–43.

25. "July 8 Fraternization Interview Date 6/14–19/45 Survey #349-K," in George Gallup, *Gallup Poll: Public Opinion, 1935–1971*, vol. 1, *1935–1948* (Random House, 1972), 513–14.

26. Davis, *Come as a Conqueror*, 145–46. In contrast, the British government strongly favored strict nonfraternization between Allied forces and the German population: see 740.00119 EAC/6–1245 "The Ambassador in the United Kingdom (Winant) to the Secretary of State," no. 23614, London, June 12, 1945, *FRUS* (1945) 3:520–24.

27. "Tachikawa chiku senryō ni kansuru Nihon seifu no mōshi-ire no ken" (September 7, 1945)—annex: "Tachikawa chiku shinchū Bei-kiheitai no meirei" (Central Liaison Office, no. 30), reprinted in Etō Jun, ed., *Senryō shiroku* 4:168–69; Harada Hiroshi, *MP no jīpu kara mita senryō ka no Tōkyō* (Sōshi Sha, 1994), 152–53. See also the following public announcement of this directive in the two major Japanese newspapers: "Oikosuna Shinchū-gun no kuruma," *Asahi shimbun*, September 6, 1945, 1; "Yakan gaishutsu genkin—Tachikawa no chūi," *Yomiuri shimbun*, September 6, 1945, 1. Note that the *Asahi* article omitted the "Respect America" provision from publication.

28. LaCerda, *The Conqueror Comes to Tea*, 53.

29. "General of the Army Douglas MacArthur's Announcement on 'Pro-Fraternization' Regulation, September 23, 1949," *Contemporary Japan: A Review of East Asiatic Affairs* 18 (July-September 1949): 437–39. For the descriptions of Japanese society under the antifraternization order, see John Curtis Perry, *Beneath the Eagle's Wings: Americans in Occupied Japan* (Dodd, Mead, 1980), 174–76; John Gunther, *The Riddle of MacArthur: Japan, Korea, and the Far East* (Harper, 1950), 91–92.

30. Edward Seidensticker, *Tokyo Rising: The City Since the Great Earthquake* (Harvard University Press, 1991), 189–90.

31. Takigawa Masajirō, "Tōkyō saiban zeiin muzai ron," *Bungei shunjū* 30, no. 9 (Supplement 1952): 112; Tanaka Masaaki, *Tōkyō saiban towa nani ka* (Nihon Kōgyō Shimbun, 1983), 83–84. See also *Asahi shimbun*, November 3, 1948, 1, for a diagram of the courtroom.

32. Harry Emerson Wildes, *Typhoon in Tokyo: The Occupation and Its Aftermath* (Macmillan, 1954), 287.

33. "M'Arthur Orders Tight Censorship: Foe's Attitude Hit," *New York Times*, September 16, 1945, sec. 1, p. 1. See also William Coughlin, *Conquered Press: The MacArthur Era in Japanese Journalism* (Pacific Books, 1952), 20–21; SCAPIN 33, "Press Code for Japan," dated September 19, 1945 (CIS), in General Headquarters SCAP, *SCAP Catalog of Directives to the Imperial Japanese Government, SCAPIN*; "The November 25 directive" (Washington National Records Center, Suitland, Md., GHQ-SCAP, RG 331, box 8568, file 211).

34. Takakuwa Kōkichi, *Makkāsā no shinbun ken'etsu: Keisai kinshi sakujo ni natta shinbun kiji* (Yomiuri Shimbun Sha, 1984), 20–31. See also Coughlin, *Conquered Press*, 47–48.

35. Kyoko HIRANO, *Mr. Smith Goes to Tokyo: Japanese Cinema Under the American Occupation, 1945–1952* (Smithsonian Institution Press, 1992), 44–45.

36. Etō Jun, *Tozasareta gengo kūkan* (Bunshun Bunko, paperback ed., 1994; originally published by Bungei Shunjū, 1989), 240.

37. "The Restart of the Proletarian Party," *Shinsei* (October 1945: pages not available from the galley proofs) (The Gordon W. Prange Collection, Publications and Unpublished Materials from the Allied Occupation of Japan within the East Asian Collection, McKeldin Library, University of Maryland, College Park [hereafter cited as Prange Collection]).

38. Yuasa Hachirō, "Amerika senji seikatsu no taiken" (My experience during the war in America), *Chūō kōron* 61, no. 11 (November 1, 1946): 58–59 (Prange Collection).

39. Hayashi Fumio, "Minshu-shugi-sha no denki—Furankurin" (Franklin—biography of a democrat), *Amerika bunka* 1, no. 1 (December 15, 1946): 13 (Prange Collection).

40. Sakanishi Shiho, "Amerika-jin no seikatsu" (The livelihood of the American people), *Amerika bunka* 1, no. 2 (January 15, 1947): 8–9 (Prange Collection).

41. Morito Tatsuo, "Heiwa kokka no kensetsu" (The construction of a peaceful nation), *Kaizō* 1, no. 1 (January 1946) (Prange Collection).

42. Herbert Passin, *Encounter with Japan* (Kodansha International, 1982), 124–25.

43. "Lady First," *Modan Nippon* 17, no. 3 (May 1, 1946): 57 (Prange Collection).

44. Wildes, *Typhoon in Tokyo*, 328; "Tākī aiwa," *Modan Nippon* 17, no. 6 (August 10, 1946): 37 (Prange Collection); Wada Toshiko, "Noboruga-san to no koto—kokusai kekkon monogatari," *Amerika* 1, no. 1 (June 10, 1946): 26–27 (Prange Collection); Makino Sadanosuke, "Nihon musume yo kono Bei-hei ni kikan—Bei-gun Mirutonshi no tegami," *Antoroposu* 1, no. 4 (December 1946): 2–5 (Tokushū: *Tōyō no on'na* [Special Issue: Women in the Orient]) (Prange Collection).

45. Tsuchiya Yukio, "Niji no kobako [A small rainbow box]," *Shōnen kurabu* 33, no. 5 (May 1946): 50–56 (Prange Collection). It is interesting to note that the entire May issue of *Shōnen kurabu*, in which this episode was completely banned from publication, is missing at the Japan National Diet Library in Tokyo, and thus unavailable to the public.

46. "Rising Sun," *New York Times*, December 7, 1947, sec. 6, p. 20.

47. Passin, *Encounter with Japan*, 134–35.

48. Mizuno Kon, "Kagaku-sha no mita Nihon no shōrai—kokumin no taii wa dō naru ka" (Japan's future seen from scientists' eyes—What will happen to our physical structures," *Kokumin no kagaku* 2, no. 4 (September-October 1947): 29.

49. Nosaka Akiyuki, "Amerika hijiki," in *Amerika hijiki/Hotaru no haka* (Shinchō Bunko, 1972), 27–28; see also *Amerika katarogu, Shinchū-gun, yakeato, yami-ichi, tokuju, han'ei* (Heibon Sha Karā Shinsho, 1977), 19. For similar passages by Nosaka's contemporaries, see the supplementary essay by Ozaki Hideki in *Amerika hijiki*. Asahi Shimbun Sha, ed., *"Nichi-Bei kaiwa techō" wa naze uretaka* (Asahi Bunko, 1995), gives a similar view by Nosaka's contemporaries on the Occupation and the American GIs.

50. Mizuno Kon, "Kagaku-sha no mita Nihon no shōrai," 29–32. More importantly, Mizuno advised that the Japanese also had to find out how to increase their weight in proper proportion to the increase in height. Otherwise, he argued, "even when we become 170 centimeters tall . . . our average weight still remains to be around 56 to 57 kilograms [125 pounds], and we end up with merely a lanky body type, not like the Westerners." After detailed analyses of differences in diet, lifestyles (e.g., the use of chairs as opposed to sitting on a floor), hygienic conditions (resulting in epidemics and the retention of parasitic worms in the intestinal system), and other inherited tendencies among Japanese, Americans, and Japanese-Americans, Mizuno proposed a hypothetical conclusion that if Japanese society were surrounded by the same environment as American society, Japanese body types would improve enough to look at least like Japanese-Americans. Mizuno continued that an intake of animal protein, especially milk, had brought superior results to the body development of Westerners, compared to Japan's traditional diet of fiber and cere-

als. According to Mizuno, fiber and cereals as a significant percentage of total consumption is always a symbol of poverty, and the world sees an increase in consumption of animal products as an increase in consumer wealth: thus, the need to change the Japanese dietary pattern.

51. Suzuki Yūko, "Karayuki-san 'jūgun ian-fu,' senryō-gun 'ian-fu,'" in *Iwanami kōza, kindai Nihon to shokumin-chi (5): bōchō suru teikoku no jinryū* (Iwanami Shoten, 1992), 243–45. "Yamato" is a poetic term for "Japan."

52. "Gaikoku-gun chūton-chi ni okeru ian shisetsu ni kan-suru Naimu-shō Keiho-kyoku-chō tsūchō (August 18, 1945)," cited in Suzuki Yūko, "Karayuki-san'jūgun ian-fu," 244.

53. Saitō Eizaburō, *Senryō-ka no Nippon—Sengo nijū-nen no shōgen* (Gen'nan Do, 1966), 414; Kajiyama Toshiyuki, "Yoru no GHQ," in *Shūkan Bunshun* (February 10, 1964): 58–64. See also Suzuki Yūko, "Karayuki-san'jūgun ian-fu," 244–45.

54. Lucy Crockette, *Popcorn on the Ginza*, 25.

55. Cited in "Shikarareta Nihon-jin," Kaji Ryūichi and Aragaki Hideo, *Tensei jingo*, vol. 1 (September 1945–December 1949) (Asahi Bunko, 1981), 247–48.

56. "General of the Army Douglas MacArthur's Announcement on 'Pro-Fraternization' Regulation, September 23, 1949, Documentary Material," *Contemporary Japan: A Review of East Asiatic Affairs* 18 (July-September 1949): 437–39.

57. On July 11, 1950, SCAP proclaimed that, beginning July 18, the ban on Japanese nationals in army post exchange restaurants was to be lifted. Between 5:00 P.M. and 8:00 P.M., Japanese could be the dinner guests of Occupation personnel in the Tokyo and Yokohama exchange restaurants. See "Restriction on Japanese Lifted," *New York Times*, July 12, 1950, sec. 1. p. 3.

58. *Shōwa—niman-nichi no zen kiroku*, vol. 8, *Senryō-ka no minshu-shugi* (Kōdansha, 1989), 318.

59. *Shōwa—niman-nichi no zen kiroku* 8:336. Tickets that originally cost 300 yen were sold for 1,500 to 2,000 yen, and counterfeit tickets were also circulated. Spectators enjoyed the privilege of purchasing American foods with Japanese yen on the stadium's premises. Hot dogs cost 100 yen and Coca-Cola 50 yen, at a time when a monthly subscription fee for a newspaper was 45 yen.

60. Ibid., 276–77.

61. Takakuwa, *Makkāsā no shinbun ken'etsu*, 95.

62. Office of Public Affairs, *International Educational and Technical Exchange in Fiscal Year 1950: Report of the United States Advisory Commission on Educational Exchange, June 30, 1950*, Department of State Publication 3893: International Information and Cultural Series 12 (GPO, 1950).

63. "Memorandum by Mr. Robert A. Fearey of the Office of Northeast Asian Affairs (Top Secret)," Tokyo, January 26, 1951, *FRUS* (1951): 6:811–16. See also the Japanese news article on Rockefeller's role: "Bunka no Nichi-Bei keitai e," *Asahi shimbun*, January 27, 1951, 1.

64. "Memorandum by the Prime Minister of Japan (Yoshida)," n.d. (1951), Tokyo, *FRUS* (1951): 6:835.

65. U.S. Department of State, *International Educational Exchange Program, 1948–1958*, Department of State Publication 6710: International Information and Cultural Series 60 (GPO, 1958), 60–63. Germany was the leading beneficiary of this program, exchanging with the United States a total of 11,524 people, followed by Britain (5,851), France (5,442), and Italy (2,881). Japan came in fourth, exchanging a total of 2,294 people during that eight-year period, including 1,010 college students, 258 advanced researchers, 112 teachers, 20 university lecturers, 14 practical trainees, and 215 consultants invited to the United States from Japan. From the United States, 50 university students, 56 advanced researchers, 41 teachers, 38 university lecturers, and 29 advisers went to Japan. Except for the following nations, the remaining participating nations in the program involved less than 500 people each between 1949 and 1956: the Netherlands (1,330), Norway (1,326), Austria (1,241), India (1,223), Finland (882), Greece (844), Philippines (792), Australia (777), Denmark (679), Belgium (653), Pakistan (554), Egypt (531).

66. "U.S. Propaganda Lacks Finesse, Mrs. Cowles Says," *Washington Evening Star*, May 1, 1953 (a newspaper article clipping with no page number available) (National Archives, Microfilm Publications, M 1664, roll #8). See also Fleur Cowles, "Our Propaganda in Asia," *Atlantic Monthly* (February 1953): 60–62; "The 'Mind of Asia' May Be Keener Than Our Intellectuals Think It Is," *Saturday Evening Post*, October 28, 1950, 12.

67. "*Tōkyō fairu 212*," *Eiga hyōron—shinario tokushū gō* 7, no. 9 (December 1, 1950); for the entire Japanese script, see 5–78.

68. "*Higashi wa higashi*," *Kinema jumpō* no. 37 (May 1, 1952): 60–61.

69. "*Itsu-itsu made mo* [synopsis]," *Kinema jumpō* no. 41 (July 1, 1952): 136; "*Futari no hitomi* [synopsis]," *Kinema jumpō* no. 47 (October 1, 1952): 81.

70. "Tokyo Tycoon and the Japanese Movie Front," *New York Times*, August 17, 1952, sec. 2, p. 5; "East Meets West with Varying Reactions—As American Producers Invade Nippon," *New York Times*, February 3, 1952, sec. 2, p. 5.

71. "Reference Department's WIROM 2892 June 11, From Tokyo To Secretary of State, No. 3922, June 16, 1953 (Confidential Security Information)"; "Walter S. Robertson, State Department, to Eric Johnston, President, Motion Picture Association of America (September 11, 1954)" (National Archives, Diplomatic Branch, Washington, D.C., RG 59, Department of State, Decimal File 1950–1954 [from 894.452/6–1650 to 894.522/5–1850], box 5677).

72. "Department of State, Memorandum of Conversation, Subject: Perry Centennial (Restricted Security Information)," July 2, 1953 (National Archives, Diplomatic Branch, Washington, D.C., RG 59, Department of State, Decimal File 1950–1954 [from 894.413/10–2254 to 894.451/13–2453], box 5676, file 894.424/5–550).

73. "John M. Allison, American Embassy, Tokyo, to Douglas MacArthur, Coun-

selor, Department of State (Official-Informal: Restricted)," August 20, 1953 (National Archives, Diplomatic Branch, Washington, D.C., RG 59, Department of State, Decimal File 1950–1954 [from 894.413/10–2254 to 894.451/13–2453], box 5676, file 894.424/5–550).

74. Wildes, *Typhoon in Tokyo*, 318.

75. "The Ambassador in London [Gifford] to the Secretary of State (Secret)," London, November 17, 1951, *FRUS* (1951): 6:1406–1407.

76. "[Attachment] Memorandum for General Magruder (Secret)," July 21, 1950 / "[Enclosure] Memorandum," *FRUS* (1950): 6:1253.

77. "Memorandum by the Consultant to the Secretary (Dulles) to the Assistant Secretary of State for Far Eastern Affairs (Rusk)," Washington, D.C., October 22, 1951, *FRUS* (1951): 6:1381.

78. Lindsay Parrot, "Japan Begins Adopting Ways of Sovereignty," *New York Times*, September 16, 1951, sec. 4, p. 3. See also "Signs Discriminating Against Offensive to Jap to be Removed," *New York Times*, September 11, 1951, sec. 1, p. 9.

79. As of July 1952 the Immigration Bureau of Japan reported that American and European residents in Japan numbered 137,000, or approximately 0.16 percent of the total population of Japan. Most of the Westerners lived in isolated communities apart from the general population and rarely came into daily contact with the Japanese. See "Back to the Kimono," *Time*, April 14, 1952, 31.

80. For contemporary Japanese criticism of the U.S. bases, see Inomata Kōzō, Kimura Kihachirō, and Shimizu Ikutarō, eds., *Kichi Nihon—ushinawarete iku sokoku no sugata* (Wakō Sha, 1953). In this book, eighteen essays by Japanese teachers, from elementary to high school, near U.S. bases across the nation, discuss effects—social, economic, cultural, ethical, and psychological—of the presence of American military bases on Japanese children.

81. Demaree Bess, "Those American Towns in Japan," *Saturday Evening Post*, August 23, 1952, 26–27, 94–96.

82. Ibid.; Wildes, *Typhoon in Tokyo*, 319. See also Wildes, "The War for the Mind of Japan," *The Annals of the American Academy of Political and Social Science* 294 (July 1954): 1–7, in a Special Issue entitled "America and a New Asia," ed. James Charlesworth.

83. Demaree Bess, "The Japs Have Us on the Griddle," *Saturday Evening Post*, April 4, 1953, 68.

84. "Tensei jingo," *Asahi shimbun*, September 11, 1951, 1.

85. "Dokuritsu shitara . . . (1): enryo wa iranai," *Asahi shimbun*, April 19, 1952, 3.

86. George Packard III, *Protest in Tokyo: The Security Treaty Crisis of 1960* (Princeton University Press, 1966), 25; "Riots Sweep Tokyo in May Day Surge," *New York Times*, May 2, 1952, sec. 1, p. 3; "Reds Riot in Japan; 3 Dead, 80 Injured," *New York Times*, May 31, 1952, sec. 1, p. 1.

87. U.S. Senate Committee on Armed Services and the Committee on Foreign Re-

lations, *Hearings to Conduct an Inquiry into the Military Situation in the Far East and Facts Surrounding the Relief of General of the Army Douglas MacArthur from His Assignments in That Area (part 1)*, 82d Cong., 1st sess., May 1951, 310–13.

88. "Nichiyō goraku ban (Sunday entertainment edition)," a comedy radio show popular for its pungent and witty political and social satires, on the air since October 1947, planned a skit satirizing MacArthur's disdain for the Japanese and his need for their cooperation for the concurrent rearmament plan:

A SOLEMN VOICE: The Japanese are only twelve-year-old children.

THE CROWD: You are quite right, your Highness.

A SOLEMN VOICE: But the Japanese have to rearm themselves.

A MAN: Holy cow! You mean the world's first children's army?

Since the Occupation was not yet officially terminated, the radio station self-censored the skit and never aired it. See Hayashi Tadahiko, *Kasutori jidai—renzu ga mita Shōwa nijū-nen-dai Tōkyō* [Asahi Bunko] (Asahi Shimbun Sha, 1987), 135.

89. "Story of a 'Japanese War Bride,'" *New York Times*, January 30, 1952, sec. 1, p. 22.

90. Futaba Jūzaburō, "*Futari no hitomi*" (review), *Kinema jumpō* no. 55 (January 15, 1953): 62.

91. Inui Takashi, "Konketsuji to jinshu-teki henken," *Mainichi shimbun* (evening edition), November 28, 1952, 2.

92. Ishikawa Tatsuzō, "Han-Bei kanjō wa kienai," *Chūō kōron* 68, no. 12 (November 1953): 88–89.

93. "Zadankai: kokusai rikai to kichi no kodomo [A Roundtable: International understanding and children living around the U.S. military base]," *Jidō shinri* 7, no. 7 (July 1953): 1–16, in a Special Issue entitled "Kokusai rikai to jidō [International understanding and children]."

94. Shimizu Ikutarō, Miyahara Sei'ichi, and Ueda Shōzaburō, eds., *Kichi no ko—kono jijitsu o dō kangaetara yoika* (Kōbun Sha, 1953).

95. Shimizu, Miyahara, and Ueda, eds., *Kichi no ko*, 86, 103–104.

96. Ibid., 74–76. See also "Kichi no ko o sukue," in Asahi shimbunsha, ed., *Koe*, vol. 3 (1951–1955) (Asahi Shimbun Sha, 1984), 137–38.

97. Shimizu Ikutarō, "Kanashimu-beki henken ni tsuite," *Fujin kōron* (September 1953): 44–45.

98. Shimizu, Miyahara, and Ueda, eds., *Kichi no ko*, 157, 169–70, 171–72, 174, 175.

99. Ibid., 108, 170–71.

100. "Bei-hei no kiken na itazura,"" in Asahi shimbunsha, ed., *Koe* 3:103–104.

101. "Jinken mushi no Bei-hei" and "Sensō ga tsukuru tsumi," in ibid., 3:192–94.

102. Michiko Wilson, *The Marginal World of Oe Kenzaburo: A Study in Themes and Techniques* (Sharpe, 1986), esp. ch. 3 ("Occupied Japan: Tales of a Gigolo"). Van Gessel's *The Sting of Life: Four Contemporary Japanese Novelists* (Columbia University

Press, 1989) also provides sketches of the "Third Generation of New Writers" (*dai-san-no shinjin*); see 27–31.

3. RACIAL EQUALITY, MINORITIES, AND THE JAPANESE CONSTITUTION

1. Raymond Leslie Buell, "Japanese Immigration," *World Peace Foundation Pamphlets*, vol. 7, nos. 5–6 (1924): 298–99; *Conférence de la Paix, 1919–1920, Recueil des acte de la Conférence, "Secret," Partie* 4:176–77, cited in Paul G. Lawren, "Human Rights in History: Diplomacy and Racial Equality at the Paris Peace Conference," *Diplomatic History* 2 (Summer 1978): 272.

2. Samples of Japanese-controlled radio comments on America's exclusion acts are printed in U.S. House Committee on Immigration and Naturalization, *Hearings on H.R. 1882 and H.R. 2309*, 78th Cong., 1st sess., 1943, 86. This comment was broadcast on shortwave on January 27, 1943, from Hong Kong to Chungking in Mandarin at 7:30 A.M. and recorded by the U.S. government listening post.

3. There had been criticism of immigrant exclusion since the passage of the Japanese exclusion clause in the Immigration Act of 1924. In December 1925 the Executive Committee of the Federal Council of Christ in America adopted a declaration at its annual meeting attacking the discriminatory naturalization law based on color alone. In 1931 the California Council on Oriental Relations was founded with the main purpose of removing the discriminatory exclusion clause from the 1924 Immigration Act and placing Japan, China, and others on a quota basis. In 1934, Rep. Charles Kramer of California introduced a bill to extend quotas to the Asian countries, although no action was taken on this measure. Eleanor Tupper, *Japan in American Public Opinion* (Macmillan, 1937), 219 and 227; Robert Divine, *American Immigration Policy, 1924–1952* (Da Capo, 1972), 147.

On February 19, 1943, a bill to repeal the Chinese Exclusion Acts and grant the Chinese right of entry into the United States and right of citizenship was introduced in the House of Representatives by Martin J. Kennedy (D—New York). With vocal support from President Roosevelt, the movement quickly reached the legislation level without difficulty. The president approved and signed the bill as law—the Act of December 17, 1943 (57 Stat.600). See Frederick Riggs, *Pressures on Congress: A Study of the Repeal of Chinese Exclusion* (Columbia University Press, 1950). As for the congressional debate on the bill, see U.S. House Committee on Immigration and Naturalization, *Hearings on H.R. 1882 and H.R. 2309*, 78th Cong., 1st sess., 1943.

4. For the symmetrical pattern between American and Japanese wartime support for independence for Asian nations, see Akira IRIYE, *Power and Culture* (Harvard University Press, 1981). Iriye argues that despite the Japanese and American rhetoric advocating freedom for all Asia, neither country intended to transform the traditional structure of the region: "The clash between Japan and the Anglo-American countries in the colonial areas had not yet forced either side to consider seriously the

relationship between the war and the future of the indigeneous colonial peoples" (ibid., 81).

5. Gen Ansei, *Nihon ryūgaku seishin-shi: kindai Chūgoku chishiki-jin no kiseki* (Iwanami Shoten, 1991), 102, 134.

6. Yoshimi Shun'ya, *Hakurankai no seiji-gaku: manazashi no kindai* (Chūkō Shinsho, 1992), 197–99.

7. Abe Isoo, "Ijinshu no kyōdō seikatsu wa kekkyoku ryōzon," *Chūō kōron* 9, no. 9 (August 1924): 89–94. Government officials and scholars were divided in their attitudes toward Korean immigrants who, as colonial subjects, had a legal right to settle in Japan. Although in October 1925 the government placed restrictions on Korean immigration, about 257,000 were successful in entering Japan. The number of Korean arrivals continued to climb despite the stiffened restrictions, due to increasing demand for cheap labor. See, for example, Richard H. Mitchell, *The Korean Minority in Japan* (University of California Press, 1967), 44–46.

8. Morito Tatsuo, *Henreki hachi-jū-nen* (Nihon Keizai Shimbun Sha, 1976), 179–80.

9. Suzuki Yasuzō, "Kempō Kenkyūkai no kenpō sōan kiso oyobi kenpō seitei kaigi teishō," *Aichi Daigaku Hōkei ronshū*, no. 28 (October 1959): 179–80; Takano Iwasaburō, *Kappa no he—ikō shū* (Hōsei Daigaku Shuppan-kyoku, 1961), 51–53.

10. Suzuki Yasuzō, "Kempō kaisei no konpon ronten," *Shinsei* 1, no. 2 (December 1, 1945): 23–25. See also Akira IRIYE, *Power and Culture*, 71–72.

11. Suzuki Yasuzō, "Kempo Kenkyūkai no kenpō sōan kiso oyobi kenpō seitei kaigi teishō," *Aichi Daigaku Hōkei ronshū*, no. 28 (October 1959): 179–80. Also, for the SCAP copies of the CIA's draft constitution and its members' profiles (in English), see "No. 155 Subject: Draft of Constitutional Revision by Private Group of Scholars [with Enclosure No. 1]" (Office of the United States Political Adviser, Tokyo, Japan, January 2, 1946), Alfred R. Hussey, Jr. Papers, hereafter cited as Hussey Papers (Microfilm Collection, Kensei Shiryō-shitsu, the Japan National Diet Library, Tokyo, reel #5, frames 21-D-1-1 to 21-D-1-2 and 21-D-2-1 to 21-D-2-5). The Hussey Papers is a collection of documents drafted and kept by Comm. Alfred R. Hussey who, along with Col. Inf. Charles Kades and Lt. Col. Milo Rowell, worked on the SCAP drafting of a Japanese constitution.

12. Suzuki, "Kempō Kenkyūkai no . . . ," 187–204. (A list of people who received the second draft is printed in ibid., 196.)

13. The original Japanese texts for these provisions are found in Takayanagi Kenzō, Ōtomo Ichirō, and Tanaka Hideo, eds., *Nihonkoku kenpō seitei no katei* 1:482–85 (Yūhikaku, 1972):

Danjo wa kō-teki narabi shi-teki ni kanzen ni byōdō no kenri o kyōyū su [Men and women shall be perfectly equal in public and private life].

Minzoku jinshu ni yoru sabetsu o kin su [No discrimination shall be executed by nationality or race].

Note that in his article "Kempō Kenkyūkai no . . ." (in *Aichi Daigaku Hōkei ronshū*, no. 28 [October 1959]: 200), Suzuki Yasuzo also introduced the earlier versions of his draft constitution. According to his December 11, 1945, draft version, the above #2 provision reads as:

Minzoku, jinshu ni yoru sabetsu wa mitome zu [No discrimination shall be tolerated by nationality or race].

14. Thus, there is "Ajia-jinshu" and "Ajia-minzoku" (both for the Asian race), "hakushoku-jinshu" (the white race), "yūboku-jinshu" (the nomad race), "Geru-man-minzoku" (the German race), "Yuda-shuzoku" (the Jewish race), "Marai-jin-shu" (the Malayan race), "Shina-minzoku" (the Chinese race), "Manshū-minzoku" (the Manchurian race), "Yamato-minzoku" (the Yamato race), and so on.

15. Suzuki, "Kempō Kenkyūkai no . . . ," 191.

16. *Constitution (Fundamental Law) of the Union of Soviet Socialist Republics as Amended and Supplemented by the First, Second, Third, Sixth, and Seventh Sessions of the Supreme Soviet of the USSR* (edition translated from the Russian text of the Constitution of the USSR published in 1940 by the State Publishing House of Political Literature, Moscow) (Foreign Language Publishing House, Moscow, 1944).

As for Lenin's discussion on racial and nationality problems within the Soviet Union, see L. N. Lenin, *Summing Up the Discussion on Self-Determination*, 197, cited in Roman Smal-Stocki, *The Nationality Problem of the Soviet Union and Russian Communist Imperialism* (Bruce Publishing, 1952), 66. See also Lenin, *Resolution on National Matters* and *The Cadets and the Rights of Peoples to Self-Determination*, cited in Smal-Stocki, ibid., 64.

17. Takano Iwasaburō, "Torawareta minshū," *Shinsei* 2, no. 2 (February 1946): 5–6.

18. Quoted in Suzuki, "Kenpō kaisei no konpon ronten," 24.

19. Suzuki Yasuzō, *Nihon no minshu-sugi* (Kakushin Sha, 1947), 15.

20. Imanaka Tsugumaro, *Minpon-shugi* (1919), cited in Imanaka Tsugumaro, *Shōgai to kaisō* (Hōritsu To Bunka Sha, 1982), 32.

21. Sugimori Kōjirō, *Sekai seijigaku no hitsuzen* (Chūō Kōron Sha, 1943), 125–34.

22. Sugimori Kōjirō, "Kojin to sekai" (June 15, 1946) [journal title unknown], reprinted in Sugimori, *Sekai jinken no gensoku* (Kenshin Sha, 1947), 7–17.

23. "The Acting Political Adviser in Japan (Atcheson) to the Secretary of State," October 10, 1945, *FRUS* (1945): 6:739–40.

24. Satō Tatsuo, *Nihon-koku kenpō seiritsu shi*, 1:191–211 (Yūhikaku, 1962). As for the American report on this process, see, for example, editorials in the *New York Times* for October 26 and 28, 1945.

25. For a detailed analysis, see Satō, *Nihon-koku kenpō seiritsu shi*, vol. 2 (Yūhi-

kaku, 1964), ch. 6. The following materials are also of use: *Matsumoto Jōji ni kiku* (Kenpō Chosa-kai Jimusho, 1960), cited in Tanaka Hideo, "Making the Constitution of Japan," in Robert Ward et al., eds., *Democratizing Japan* (University of Hawaii, 1987); Takayanagi, Ōtomo, and Tanaka, eds., *Nihonkoku kenpō seitei no katei* 1:50.

26. Tanaka Hideo, "Making the Constitution of Japan," 116.

27. Satō, *Nihon-koku kenpō seiritsu shi* 1:213.

28. "Reform of the Japanese Governmental System Concerning the Constitutional Reform Which the Occupation Authorities Should Insist Be Carried Out in Japan," *FRUS* (1946): 8:98–103.

29. SCAPIN 93, "Removal of Restrictions on Political, Civil, and Religious Liberties," October 4, 1945. in General Headquarters SCAP, *SCAP Catalog of Directives to the Imperial Japanese Government, SCAPIN* (hereafter cited as GHQ-SCAP, *SCAP Directives*).

30. SCAPIN 360, "Employment Policies," November 28, 1945, GHQ-SCAP, *SCAP Directives*. It was further decreed at this time that non-Japanese who elected to remain in Japan rather than accept repatriation would be "guaranteed the same rights, privileges, and opportunities in employment as are extended to Japanese nationals in comparable circumstances." Shortly thereafter, SCAP again issued instructions to "inaugurate immediately necessary mesures to prevent any person or group of persons in Japan from being discriminated against in the distribution of available supplies because of inability to work . . . or for political, religious, or economic belief." SCAPIN 404, "Relief and Welfare Plans," December 8, 1945, GHQ-SCAP, *SCAP Directives*.

31. Tanaka Hiroshi, *Zai-Nichi gaikoku-jin—hō no kabe, kokoro no kabe* (Iwanami Shinsho, 1991), 60.

32. *Gikai seido nana-jū nen-shi shiryō hen* (Ōkura-shō Insatsu-kyoku, 1960), also cited in Tanaka Hiroshi, ibid., 60; *Shūgi-in Shūgi-in Giin Senkyo Hō Kaisei-an Iinkai giroku* (Record of the 2d Diet, Lower House, Committee on the Election Law Reforms), December 5, 1945, no. 2, cited in Tanaka Hiroshi, ibid., 65.

33. Satō, *Nihon-koku kenpō seiritsu shi* 2:826–28.

34. Suzuki, "Kempō Kenkyūkai no . . . ," 204.

35. Memorandum for Chief of Staff, "Comments on Constitutional Revision Proposed by Private Group," January 11, 1946, Hussey Papers (Microfilm reel #5, frames 21-C-3-1 to 21-C-3-5).

36. The Japanese text (in "Shōsho," *Asahi shimbun*, January 1, 1946, 1) reads:

Ten'nō o motte arahitogami to shi katsu Nihon-kokumin o motte ta no min-zoku ni yūetsu seru minzoku ni shite nobe te sekai o shihai subeki unmei o yūsu to no kakū naru kan'nen ni motozuku mono ni arazu.

37. Secret report SWNCC 162/2, "Reorientation of the Japanese," January 8, 1946, *FRUS* (1946): 8:105–109.

38. "Summary Report on Meeting of the Government Section," February 4, 1946, reprinted in Takayanagi, Otomo, and Tanaka, eds., *Nihonkoku kenpō seitei no katei . . . 1:98–100.* This document is part of the Rowell Papers, a collection of documents related to SCAP planning on the draft constitution kept by Lt. Col. Milo Rowell. The entire collection (twenty-five documents in all) is reprinted in volume 1 of *Nihonkoku kenpō seitei no katei . . . .*

39. For different versions of the draft for "Chapter III on Civil Rights," see Hussey Papers (Microfilm reel #5, frames 24-G-2-1 to 3; 24-G-3-1 to 2; 24-G-4-1 to 3; 24-G-5-1 to 3; 24-G-6-1 to 3 [all n.d.]).

40. "(Draft) [as submitted to the Japanese Government by GHQ-SCAP on February 13, 1946] Constitution of Japan," the Rowell Papers, reprinted in Takayanagi, Ōtomo, and Tanaka, eds., *Nihonkoku kenpō seitei no katei . . . 1:274.*

41. The Civil Rights Committee consisted of two civilians, Harry E. Wildes and Beate Sirota, and one army officer, Lt. Col. Pieter R. Roest. In the process of drafting the racial equality clause (Article 13 in the earlier draft, later renumbered as Article 14 in the final draft), Wildes and Sirota were probably most responsible for the original proposal of the content. Regarding the influence of the CIA's draft on this article, Sirota later argued that she did not remember when she first learned about either the CIA's draft or Rowell's January 11 memorandum on his recommendation. According to her account, while working on the racial equality clause she did not refer to the CIA's draft, although Lieutenant Colonel Roest, her chief, may have told the committee members about the contents later. Sirota's accounts appeared in the interviews conducted by the Research Institute of Buraku Problem (Buraku Kenkyūkai), printed in *Buraku mondai to Nihon senryō kenkyū nyūsu*, no. 3 (November 1987) and no. 4 (December 1987).

42. *Buraku mondai to . . . , no. 3.* See also "Kenpō seitei no keika ni kan suru shō-iinkai dai-27-kai giji-roku, 8 and 34," cited in Takayanagi, Ōtomo, and Tanaka, eds., *Nihonkoku kenpō seitei no katei 2:157.*

43. During constitutional hearings at the Privy Council Committee Sessions held between April and October 1946, only one question was raised in respect to Article 14, and that was in regard to the definition of "family origin [*monchi*]." A committee member asked if the status of the imperial family was also included in this definition. State Minister Matsumoto answered that "monchi" meant "iegara," the same as family origin, and that the status of the imperial family was also a matter of family origin. No further discussion of Article 14 took place. *Sūmitsu-in kenpō kaisei-an shingi-roku 1 (April 22 to May 1, 1946), 138–140* (Washington National Records Center, Suitland, Md., GHQ-SCAP, RG 331, box 2088, folder 1—"Constitutional Hearings: Privy Council Committee Sessions, April 1946–October 1946").

44. The Japanese text of Article 42 in the February 13, 1946, MacArthur draft (in Takayanagi, Ōtomo, and Tanaka, eds., *Nihonkoku kenpō seitei no katei 1:283*) reads as follows:

Kokkai-giin no senkyo no senkyo-nin oyobi kōho-sha no shikaku wa hōritsu de kore o sadameru. Korera no shikaku no sadame o nasu ni attate wa seibetsu, jinshu, shinjō, taishoku, mata wa shakai-teki mibun ni yotte sabetsu o shite wa naranai.

[The qualifications of electors and of candidates for election to the Diet shall be determined by law, and in determining such qualifications there shall be no discrimination because of sex, race, creed, color, or social status.]

The Japanese text of Article 44 in its final form (in Takayanagi, Ōtomo, and Tanaka, eds., *Nihonkoku kenpō seitei no katei* 1:457) reads as follows:

Ryō-giin no giin oyobi sono senkyo-nin no shikaku wa hōritsu de kore o sadameru. Tadashi jinshu, shinjō, seibetsu, shakai-teki mibun, monchi, kyōiku, zaisan mata wa shūnyū ni yotte sabetsu shite wa naranai.

[The qualifications of members of both Houses and their electors shall be fixed by law. However, there shall be no discrimination because of race, creed, sex, social status, family origin, education, property, or income.]

45. The Japanese version of Article 14 in its final form (in Takayanagi, Ōtomo, and Tanaka, eds., *Nihonkoku kenpō seitei no katei* 1:447) reads as follows:

Subete kokumin wa hō no moto ni byōdō de atte jinshu, shinjō, seibetsu, shakai-teki mibun mata wa monchi ni yori, seiji-teki, keizai-teki mata wa shakai-teki kankei ni oite sabetsu sarenai.

[All of the people are equal under the law and there shall be no discrimination in political, economic, or social relations because of race, creed, sex, social status, or family origin.]

46. Not surprisingly, the value of Article 14 of the new constitution was best acclaimed in the civil rights movement organized and fought for by the minority peoples themselves. The following are collections of primary source documents on their postwar movement: Ryūkoku Daigaku Dōwa Mondai Kenkyūkai (Ryūkoku University Dowa [*burakumin*] Problem Research Association), *Dōwa mondai kenkyū shiryō* (Documents for Studies on Dowa Problems), 5 vols. (Ryūkoku Daigaku Dōwa Mondai Kenkyū Iinkai, 1984); Nikimori Hikaru, *Dokyumento Okinawa tōsō* (Document on the Okinawa Movement) (Aki Shobō, 1969); Kim Kyon-he, ed., *Zai-Nichi Chōsen-jin minzoku kyōiku yōgo tōsō shiryō-shū* (Documents on the Korean Move-

ment to Defend Their Right to Ethnic Education in Japan), vol. 1, and Uchiyama Kazuo and Cho Bok, ibid., vol. 2 (hereafter cited as *Shiryō-shū*) (Akashi Shoten, 1988).

47. I. Neary, "Tenko of an Organization: The Suiheisha in the Late 1930s," in D. W. Anthony, ed., *Proceedings of the British Association for Japanese Studies* 2, part 2 (University of Sheffield, 1977).

48. U.S. State Department, "The *Eta*: A Persecuted Group in Japan," Coordinator of Information Psychology Division, Divisional Memorandum No. 12 (February 5, 1942), 15; reprinted in *Buraku mondai to Nihon senryō kenkyū nyūsu*, no. 3 (November 1987).

49. The following is a collection of interviews with Matsumoto Jiichirō conducted by activists in the *burakumin* liberation movement: *Fukashin fukahishin: Matsumoto Jiichirō taidan shū* (The inviolable and the non-violable: A collection of interviews with Matsumoto Jiichirō) (Kaihō Shuppan Sha, 1977).

50. According to the memo, "His only request is that the Ainus be given some land for cultivation because the hunting and fishing are now so poor that the Ainus are being driven to agriculture for the first time in the history of the race." "Biographical Sketch of the Ainu Chieftain who Visited GHQ," October 23, 1947 (MacArthur Memorial Archives, Norfolk, Va. [hereafter, MacArthur Archives], box 2, RG 5, folder 6).

Newsweek printed a short article reporting the Ainu "king," the "bearded aborigine," running for the Japanese Parliament in Japan's first postwar general election. The article explained the Ainus as Japan's "own equivalent of the American Indians" and portrayed them as "the primitive remnant of the strange race" and "doomed race" with "the Stone Age civilization" destined to be "extinct in a few decades." See "The Ainu Comes Back," in *Newsweek*, February 18, 1946, 48.

51. Masuko Yoshihisa, "Maboroshi no Ainu dokuritsu-ron o ou," *Asahi jānaru*, March 3, 1989, 87–90. See also Yuko BABA, "A Study of Minority-Majority Relations: The Ainu and Japanese in Hokkaido," *Japan Interpreter* 13, no. 1 (Summer 1980): 78. According to Baba, she obtained this information in an interview with the chairman of the Hokkaidō Utari Kyōkai. When Occupation authorities requested the Ainu to consider independence as indigenous natives of Hokkaido, they declined this chance and subsequently established the Hokkaidō Ainu Kyōkai as an organization for all Hokkaido Ainu as a means of improving their social position (ibid.).

52. Miyazato Seigen, *Amerika no Okinawa seisaku* (Nirai Sha, 1986), 21–23 and 25–26. See also Clellan S. Ford, "Occupation Experiences on Okinawa," *The Annals of the American Academy of Political and Social Science* 267 (January 1950): 175–82.

53. An article in the *New York Times* for April 1, 1946, for example, portrayed the Okinawan people as good obedient colonial subjects: "The native Okinawans have proved to be a docile, tractable and fairly industrious people, above the average in intelligence. They are genuinely appreciative of the benefits conferred on them by the Americans.... The [U.S.] military government has not encouraged the idea of political independence for Okinawa or the other Ryukyu Islands, nor found it necessary

to discourage any such aspirations." "Okinawans Prove Amenable to Rule; Island's People Remain Docile," *New York Times*, April 1, 1946, sec. 1, p. 9.

For the view shared by MacArthur and George Kennan that the racially inferior Okinawans needed America's permanent military protection, see Miyazato, *Amerika no Okinawa seisaku*, 67–77.

54. "Ryūkyū-jin wa Nihon-jin dewa nai noka" (originally titled "Koe—hi-Nihon-jin no imi") *Asahi shimbun*, July 17, 1946, 2; reprinted in Asahi Shimbun Sha, ed., *Koe*, vol. 1 (Asahi Shimbun Sha, 1984), 207–208.

55. "Okinawa-jin no tachiba," *Asahi shimbun*, July 24, 1946; reprinted in *Koe* 1:208.

56. Changsoo Lee, "The Legal Status of Koreans in Japan," in Changsoo Lee and George De Vos, eds., *Koreans in Japan: Ethnic Conflict and Accommodation* (University of California Press, 1981), 136–37.

57. Richard H. Mitchell, *The Korean Minority in Japan*, 30–31.

58. GHQ-SCAP, *Summation of Non-Military Activities in Japan and Korea*, no. 1 (September-October 1945), part 1, 11.

59. SCAPIN 207, "Payment and Savings and Allotments in Korea and of Korean Laborers in Japanese Coal Miners," October 29, 1945, GHQ-SCAP, *SCAP Directives*. See also Edward W. Wagner, *The Korean Minority in Japan, 1904–1950* (Institute of Pacific Relations, 1951), 49–50.

60. SCAPIN 217, "Definition of 'United Nations,' 'Neutral Nations,' and 'Enemy Nations,'" October 31, 1945, GHQ-SCAP, *SCAP Directives*. In June 1948, Korea became identified as a "special status nation" along with Austria, Finland, Italy, Siam, and the Baltic and Balkan states dominated by the USSR. See SCAPIN 1912, "Definition of United, Neutral, Enemy, Special Status, and Undetermined Status Nations," June 12, 1948, GHQ-SCAP, *SCAP Directives*.

61. Tanaka Hiroshi, *Zai-Nichi gaikoku-jin*, 60.

62. Contemporary standard Japanese dictionaries, such as *Nihon kokugo dai-jiten* (Shōgakkan, 1985), *Shūeisha kokugo jiten* (Shūei Sha, 1993), and *Gakken kokugo dai-jiten* (Gakken, 1990), all define the term *dai-sangoku-jin* as the special label applied to the Koreans and Formosans, Japan's former colonial subjects, during the U.S. Occupation of Japan, whereas they define the word *gaijin* as specifically Euro-Americans (*Ō-Bei-jin*). *Gakken kokugo dai-jiten* specifies black people (*kokujin*) in the category of *gaijin*, along with white people (*hakujin*).

63. David Conde, "The Korean Minority in Japan," *Far Eastern Survey* 16, no. 4 (February 26, 1947): 42.

64. Changsoo Lee, "Ethnic Education and National Politics," in Lee and De Vos, *Koreans in Japan*, 163.

65. Richard H. Mitchell, *The Korean Minority in Japan*, 112–14.

66. Pak Kyon-sik, *Kaihō-go zai-Nichi Chōsen-jin undō shi* (San'ichi Shoten, 1989), 194–95.

67. For the reprints of news articles on the incident which appeared in *Kaihō*

shimbun, the newspaper published by Chōren, and *Akahata*, official newspaper of the Japan Communist Party, see Kim Kyon-he, *Shiryō-shū*, vol. 1, ch. 4 ("Shimbun no hōdō kiji").

68. Kaji Wataru, "Hitotsu no hikaku [A certain case of comparison]," *Minshu Chōsen* (June, 1948), reprinted in *Shiryō-shū* 2:27–28.

69. Chang Du-sik, "Zai-Nichi Chōsen-jin kyōiku mondai no sokumen [Aspects of educational problems for Korean children in Japan]" *Minshu Chōsen* (June 1948), reprinted in *Shiryō-shū* 2:48–50.

70. *Kanpō gōgai—Dai 2 kai Kokkai Shūgi-in kaigi-roku, dai 43 gō* (Government report, extra issue, Record of the 2d Diet, Lower House), April 28, 1948, no. 43, p. 366.

71. Ibid., 367–68, and also in Kim Kyon-he, *Shiryō-shū* 1:463–464.

72. "Chōsen-jin gakkō no jittai wa kōda—Nihon-jin kyōkan tokumei zadankai," *Yomiuri shimbun*, August 24, 1952, 3.

73. GHQ Check Sheet, File No. S-350/301, "Subject: Status of Koreans in Japan, From: DS to: DCS, SCAP (July 15 1949) (Confidential)"; GHQ Check Sheet, "Subject: Status and Treatment of Koreans in Japan, From: DS to: LS GS, G-1, ESS (FIB) (May 2, 1949) (Confidential" (both at MacArthur Archives, box 74, RG 5, SCAP General File, folder 1).

74. *Kanpō gōgai—Dai 2 kai Kokkai Shūgi-in kaigi-roku, dai 44 gō* (Government report, extra issue, Record of the 2d Diet, Lower House), May 1, 1948, no. 44, pp. 375–76.

75. Changsoo Lee, "Koreans Under SCAP: An Era of Unrest and Repression," in Lee and De Vos, eds., *Koreans in Japan*, 82.

76. "A Letter from the Prime Minister's Office, Tokio [*sic*], to General of the Army Douglas MacArthur," n.d. (MacArthur Archives, RG 5: SCAP Correspondence, Official Correspondence, 1949).

77. GHQ-SCAP Diplomatic Section, September 9, 1949, "Memorandum for: General MacArthur; From W. J. Sebald (Draft: 'My dear Mr. Prime Minister')" (MacArthur Archives, RG 5: SCAP, Correspondence, Official Correspondence, 1949).

78. Tanaka Hiroshi, *Zai-Nichi gaikoku-jin*, 66–67.

79. *FRUS* (1952–1954): 14 (pt. 2):1255 and 1259.

80. Nationality Law (Law No. 147; May 4, 1950), in *Documents Concerning the Allied Occupation and Control of Japan*, vol. 6, *On Aliens*, compiled by the Section of Special Records, Foreign Office, Japanese Government (March 1951), 245–49.

81. For the English text of the Immigration Control law and Alien Registration law, see the following: Immigration Bureau, Japanese Ministry of Justice, *Laws and Regulations for Immigration Control in Japan* (Ministry of Justice, 1952). For the survey of the legal status for Korean residents in Japan, see Changsoo Lee, "The Legal Status of Koreans in Japan," 141–42.

82. "Memorandum of Conversation, by Charles A. Sullivan, Director of the Policy Division, Office of Foreign Military Affairs, Department of Defense (Secret)," August 20, 1952, in *FRUS* (1952–1954): 14 (pt. 2):1314–16.

83. *International Military Tribunal for the Far East: The Tokyo War Crimes Trial. The Complete Transcripts of the Proceedings, 1946–1948* (hereafter cited as *IMTFE*) (Garland, 1981), 17017–17018.

84. *IMTFE*, 17019, 17020, 17103.

4. JAPANESE OVERSEAS EMIGRATION

1. When the Occupation started, there was no certainty as to the length of time that the American forces would stay in Japan. Gen. Jonathan Wainwright suggested in mid-September 1945 that a long-term, twenty-year occupation would be necessary. Australian newspapers protested that it was not long enough to assure a civilized way of life in the Pacific. Gen. Barney Giles, deputy commander of the Strategic Air Force in the Pacific, declared that Allied forces should occupy Japan for "not less than 100 years." MacArthur himself declared that the Allies must stay in Japan for "many years" and keep Japan on an "austerity basis." See "Australian Press Worries on Japan," *New York Times*, September 20, 1945, sec. 1, p. 3.

2. The Civil Censorship Detachment (CCD; see chapter 2) drew up a blacklist of foreign correspondents and news services whose translated dispatches should not appear in Japanese media. For example, Walter Lippman's column was censored frequently because of his leftist stance and did not appear in its original form in Japan. See William Coughlin, *Conquered Press* (Pacific Books, 1952), 47.

3. *Omoide no merodī—Shōwa hen* (Seibidō Shuppan, 1991), 64.

4. Ibid., 65, 71.

5. Sōrifu tōkei-kyoku (Director General of the Prime Minister's Office), *Shōwa 22 nen rinji kokusei chōsa kekka hōkoku: sono 4, shusshin chiiki oyobi kokuseki betsu jinkō no gaiyō* (Report on the result of the emergency national census in 1947: No. 4, "Surveys of populations according to the birth of place and nationality") (April 1948); Kōsēi-shō Jinkō Mondai Kenkyūjo hen (Japanese Ministry of Welfare, ed.), *Genka no jinkō mondai, jō kan* (The current population problem, vol. 1), 1949, cited in Wakatsuki Yasuo and Suzuki Jōji, *Kaigai ijū seisaku shiron* (Fukumura Shuppan, 1975), 80.

6. Denis Warner, "Japan's New Live Weapon," *United Nations World* 3, no. 6 (June 1949): 13; Richard L-G Deverall, "No Room to Live in Japan," *America*, May 28, 1949, 284; Robert Fearey, *The Occupation of Japan: Second Phase, 1948–1950*, published under the auspices of the International Secretariat, Institute of Pacific Relations (Macmillan, 1950), 158–59; The Mainichi Population Problems Research Council, *The Population of Japan*, Population Problems Series no. 1 (Mainichi Shimbun Sha, 1953), 1–4.

7. Concerning the issue of postwar German immigration to the United States, see the following works: "Displaced Persons in Europe," *Senate Report* No. 950, 80th Cong., 2d sess., 1948 (GPO, 1948), 8; *Interpreter Release* 23 (February 28, 1946): 50; and Franklin M. Davis Jr., *Come as a Conqueror: The United States Army's Occupation of Germany, 1945–1949* (Macmillan, 1967), 251.

8. *International Military Tribunal for the Far East: The Tokyo War Crimes Trial. The*

Complete Transcripts of the Proceedings, 1946–1948 (Garland, 1981), 17063. Note that American media uncompromisedly rejected Kiyose's statement as being the "self-defense" of a bandit." See "Tojo's Defense," *New York Times*, February 26,, 1947, sec. 1, p. 24.

9. The original interview article, "Shin-kenpō ichi-mon ittō" (Questions and answers for the new constitution), and the censorship instruction appear in Takakuwa Kōkichi, *Makkāsā no shinbun ken'etsu: keisai kinshi sakujo ni natta shinbun kiji* (Yomiuri Shimbun Sha, 1984), 140–41.

10. "[Letter from] Yamada Hideo [to] General MacArthur," July 28, 1947 ("Letters to MacArthur," RG 331, box 236, file 4). See also ch. 1, n. 32, above.

11. For the ideology pertinent to the prewar emigration movement, see Shimanuki Heidayū, *Saikin to-Bei-saku* (Nihon Rikkōkai, 1904) and *Rikkōkai to wa nanzoya* (Keisei Sha, 1911). See also Akira IRIYE's *Pacific Estrangement: Japanese and American Expansion, 1897–1911* (Harvard University Press, 1972), 278.

12. Mainichi Shimbun Sha Jinkō Mondai Chōsa-kai (Mainichi Population Problems Research Council), *Sengo no kaigai ijū no suii, shiryō dai 85 gō* (Postwar trends in overseas emigration, publication no. 85) (Mainichi Shimbun Sha, 1961), 4.

13. "Chikaku minkan-jin no tokō kyoka ka," *Yomiuri shimbun*, April 5, 1948, in Takakuwa, *Makkāsā no shinbun ken'etsu*, 246. See also the following document regarding SCAP policy: "Travel Documents for Japanese Nationals Traveling Abroad," AG 000.74 (April 14, 1947) GA (SCAPIN 1609), APO 500, in *Documents Concerning the Allied Occupation and Control of Japan*, vol. 2, *Political, Military, and Cultural*, compiled by the Division of Special Records, Foreign Office, Japanese Government (March 1949), 58–59.

14. "San-kashu no hō-Bei keikaku," *Yomiuri shimbun*, November, 11, 1947, 2 (suppressed), reprinted in Takakuwa, *Makkāsā no shinbun ken'etsu*, 231–32; "Ōzumō no to-Bei keikaku susumu," *Yomiuri shimbun*, April, 13, 1948 (suppressed), reprinted in Takakuwa, ibid., 249; "Bei no hakurankai de Nihon no orihime jitsuen," *Yomiuri shimbun*, April 24, 1948 (illustration suppressed and parts of article deleted), reprinted in Takakuwa, ibid., 251.

15. "[Letter from] 'A University Student' [no name] [to] General MacArthur," March 31, 1946 ("Letters to MacArthur," RG 331, box 234, file 4).

16. *Kaigai ijū: Kaigai Ijū Kyōkai geppō* (Overseas Emigration: Monthly Report of Overseas Emigration Association) 1 (January 1, 1948): 1–2 (Prange Collection).

17. Matsuoka Komakichi, "Waga kokumin no sabake guchi," *Kaigai iju*, ibid., 1.

18. The original Japanese text on the quality of past Japanese immigrants and the hoped-for future improvement reads as follows: "Jūrai waga kaigai ijū-sha no hinsei ga teiretsu de atte kyōyō o kaita tame ni uketa kutsujoku o kurikaesu koto naku sekai kakkoku ga morote o agete waga imin o kangei suru ni itaru hi no tame ni jūbun naru shiryoku o yashinatte okanakereba naranai" (*Kaigai ijū*, ibid, 2).

19. *Dai 1 kai Kokkai Sangi-in Gaimu Iinkai Kaigi-roku, dai 4 gō* (Record of the First Upper House Committee on Foreign Affairs), October 14, 1947, no. 4, p. 1.

20. *Dai 2 kai Kokkai Shūgi-in Gaimu Iin kaigi-roku, dai 4 gō* (Record of the Second Lower House Committee on Foreign Affairs), April 1, 1948, no. 4, p. 6.

21. Ibid.

22. *Dai 4 kai Kokkai Shūgi-in Gaimu Iin kaigi-roku, dai 3 gō* (Record of the Fourth Lower House Committee on Foreign Affairs), December 14, 1948, no. 3, p. 10.

23. Ibid.

24. Toriya Torao, "Sengo imin undō hatten shoshi," *Kaigai e no tobira* (Gateway to Overseas), no. 48 (October 25, 1953): 1.

25. *Kampō gōgai: Dai 5 kai Kokkai Shūgi-in kaiigi-roku, dai 27 gō* (Governmental Report, Extra Issue, Record of the 5th Diet, Lower House), May 13, 1949, no. 27, pp. 422–24.

26. Ibid., 425.

27. *Kampō gōgai: Dai 6 kai Kokkai Sangi-in kaigi-roku, dai 12 gō* (Governmental Report, Extra Issue, Record of the 6th Diet, Upper House), November 17, 1949, no. 12, pp. 122–24.

28. "Kaigai Tokō Gijutsu-sha Zenkoku Renmei sōritsu" (The founding of the National League of Technicians Dispatched Abroad), *Kaigai e no tobira*, no. 12 (April 10, 1950): 1. The agenda proclaimed its purpose to be as follows: "Our plan is to maintain close ties with the government in promoting overseas emigration of superior technicians, as well as to cooperate with the UN organizations in development plans for undeveloped areas of the world."

29. "Katayama Tetsu kōwa o katarazu," *Keizai jīpu* 3, no. 3 (February 1951): 12–13; Mihara Shin'ichi, "Kōwa kaigi to jinkō mondai," *Sekai keizai* 3, no. 11 (November 1950): 15–16.

30. Kokuritsu Yoron Chōsajo, *Jinkō mondai ni kansuru yoron chōsa* (*yoron chōsa hōkoku-sho, chōsa bangō*, A-14) (May 1950).

31. "Shū-san-ryō-in no zen giin e kasanete ikensho teishutsu," *Kaigai e no tobira*, no. 25 (June 10, 1951): 1.

32. For Ishibashi Tanzan's inauguration address, see Ishibashi, "Kaicho shunin ni saisite," *Kaigai e no tobira*, no. 26 (July 10, 1951): 1.

33. Takakuwa, *Makkāsā no shinbun ken'etsu*, 237. See also "Hirohito Sees M'Arthur," *New York Times*, November 15, 1947, sec. 1, p. 5.

34. Robert A. Fearey, *The Occupation of Japan*, 123–25 and 139–43: "Pre-war Industry Promised to Japan," *New York Times*, May 12, 1946, sec. 1, p. 23; T. A. Bisson, *The Prospect for Democracy in Japan* (McMillan, 1949), 104–105.

35. C. Hartley Grattan, "Australia and the 'Near North,'" *Far Eastern Survey* 17, no. 21 (November 3, 1948: 247. See also "Australia Rebuffs Tokyo on Plan for Improving Trade Relations," *New York Times*, September 4, 1949, sec. 1. p. 10.

36. John Curtis Perry, *Beneath the Eagle's Wings* (Dodd, Mead, 1980), 118–21; Denis Warner, "Japan's New Live Weapon," 6. Margaret Sanger, world-renowned birth control advocate, was not allowed to lecture to Japanese audiences on the issue of birth

control when she was invited to Japan by a Japanese newspaper company in early 1950. See Robert Textor, *Failure in Japan: With Keystones for Positive Policy* (John Day, 1951), 244.

37. "Hirohito Receives Spellman's Party," *New York Times*, June 10, 1948, sec. 1, p. 3.

38. Freda Hawkins, *Critical Years in Immigration: Canada and Australia Compared*, 2d ed. (McGill-Queen's University Press, 1991). For a brief history of Asian immigration to Canada and Australia, see 8–30.

39. On the Japanese side, Toriya Torao seems to have initiated the postwar argument in support of Japanese emigration to New Guinea. See his article "Sekai-renpō to imin mondai," *Kaigai e no tobira*, no. 1 (October 25, 1948): 2–6. Much of his argument was based on Japanese wartime surveys of Dutch New Guinea which indicated the island's vast natural resources, including oil reserves.

40. Robert Schildgen, *Toyohiko Kagawa: Apostle of Love and Social Justice* (Centenary Books, 1988), 222–23.

41. Denis Warner, "Japan's New Live Weapon," 14 and 16. As for the American Catholic view of Japan's overpopulation and emigration, see Richard L. G. Deverall, "No Room to Live in Japan," *America*, May 28, 1949, 284–87.

42. "Japan's Year of Decision," in Vera Micheles Dean, ed., *Foreign Policy Bulletin* (August 1, 1957), reprinted in Elizabeth and Victor A. Velen, eds., *The New Japan*, The Reference Shelf, vol. 30, no. 2 (H. W. Wilson, 1958), 118–19. See also Perry, *Beneath the Eagle's Wings*, 128.

43. "Provision of Expert Assistance to ECAFE Countries: Government of Pakistan, Ministry of Economic Affairs (Coordinating Branch) to the Executive Secretary, United Nations Economic Commission for Asia and the Far East (ECAFE)," March 25, 1949 (MacArthur Archives, box 107, RG 5, folder 2, Political Adviser to SCAP, Correspondence, July 1947–March 1951). For a reply, see "A Letter to Dr. P. S. Lokanathan, Bangkok, from Cloyce K. Huston, Acting Chief, Diplomatic Section," Tokyo, May 14, 1949 (MacArthur Archives, box 107, RG 5, folder 2). See also the following articles published in *Kaigai e no tobira*: Nagata Shū, "Gijutsu-sha ijū [Emigration opportunity for skilled engineers]," no. 4 (August 10, 1949): 1; "Kōshin-koku ni suisan gijutsu o [Let's transfer fishing technology to the underdeveloped nations]," no. 9 (January 10, 1950): 2; "Haku-koku dewa Hō-jin gijutsu-sha fusoku [Brazil suffers from the shortage of skilled Japanese engineers]," no. 15 (July 10, 1950): 2.

44. *Dai 6 kai Kokkai Shūgi-in Gaimu Iin kaigi-roku, dai 4 gō* (Record of the Sixth Lower House Committee on Foreign Affairs), November 19, 1949, no. 4, pp. 2–3. Adding to these technicians, five specialists in sexing chickens were allowed to go to Belgium.

45. *Congressional Digest* 29, no. 11 (November 1950): 270.

46. U.S. House, Subcommittee of the Committee on the Territories, *Statehood for Hawaii: Hearings Pursuant to H.R. 236—A Resolution Directing the Committee on the Territories to Conduct a Study and Investigation of Various Questions and Problems Re-*

lating to the Territories of Alaska and Hawaii, 79th Cong., 2d sess., January 7–18, 1946, 25. For a similar statement by Andrew Lind, a sociologist, who compared Hawaii's race relations to that of Brazil in a favorable light, see pp. 55–65.

47. "Hawaii Is Ready to Become 49th State, House Group Says, Urging Admittance Bill," *New York Times*, January 25, 1946, sec. 1, p. 9.

48. Robert Wilson and Bill Hosokawa, *East to America: A History of the Japanese in the United States* (William Morrow, 1980), 237.

49. For a discussion of Hawaiian statehood as a racial issue, see "Statehood Blocked by Racial Issues," *Christian Century* 67, no. 48 (November 29, 1950): 1; see also "Betraying the American Ideal," *Christian Century* 68, no. 4 (January 24, 1951): 102–103.

50. Elmer R. Smith, "A Discussion of the Degree of Assimilation Among Persons of Japanese Ancestry in the United States" (unpublished), Supplement to U.S. Senate Committee on the Judiciary, *Hearings before the Subcommittee on the Judiciary on the Naturalization of Asian and Pacific Peoples (H.R. 199)* (hereafter cited as *Hearings on the Naturalization of Asian and Pacific Peoples*), 81st Cong., 1st sess., July 19 and 20, 1949. H.R. 199 would have provided the privilege of becoming a naturalized citizen of the United States to all immigrants having a legal right to permanent residence, to make immigration quotas available to Asian and Pacific peoples, and for other purposes. Supplement printed for the Use of the Committee on the Judiciary (National Archives, Legislative Branch, RG 46, U.S. Senate, 81st Cong., SEN 81A-E11, H.R. 199–H.R. 559, box 86).

51. *Hearings on the Naturalization of Asian and Pacific Peoples*, 81st Cong., 1st sess., 1949, 10–11.

52. Elmer R. Smith, "A Discussion of the Degree of Assimilation Among Persons of Japanese Ancestry in the United States," 2–6 (appendix). See also Wilson and Hosokawa, *East to America*, 232–33.

53. *Hearings on the Naturalization of Asian and Pacific Peoples*, 81st Cong., 1st sess., 1949, 5–6.

54. *Hearings on the Naturalization of Asian and Pacific Peoples*, 15.

55. Ibid., 16.

56. See introduction, n. 10.

57. According to the 1972 Supplement in the *Oxford English Dictionary*, the term "ethnicity" was first used by the sociologist David Riesman in 1953. The term was included in Webster's *Third New International Dictionary* (1961), but not in the *Random House Dictionary of the English Language* (1966), nor in the *American Heritage Dictionary of the English Language* (1969).

For the early explorations into the meaning and significance of ethnicity in modern society, see Frederik Barth, ed., *Ethnic Groups and Boundaries* (Little, Brown, 1969), and Nathan Glazer and Daniel P. Moynihan, *Ethnicity: Theory and Experience* (Harvard University Press, 1975). In Glazer and Moynihan's *Ethnicity*, "Some Theoretical Considerations on the Nature and Trends of Change of Ethnicity" by Talcott

Parsons, and "Ethnicity and Social Change" by Daniel Bell, are especially helpful for understanding the early theoretical literature on ethnicity. More recent works include Cora Bagley Marrett and Cheryl Leggon, *Research in Race and Ethnic Relations: A Research Annual* (JAI Press, 1979); Richard D. Alba, ed., *Ethnicity and Race in the U.S.A. Toward the End of the Century* (Routledge and Kegan Paul, 1985); and Y. Y. Kim and W. Gudykunst, *Cross Cultural Adaptations* (Sage, 1988).

58. Elmer R. Smith, "A Discussion of the Degree of Assimilation Among Persons of Japanese Ancestry in the United States," 9, 43–52 (appendix).

59. "Statistics Provided by Law Offices of Chow and Sing, San Francisco, CA, to Honorable Richard Arens, Staff Director," Senate Subcommittee on Immigration and Naturalization, July 27, 1949 (National Archives, Legislative Branch, RG 46, box 87, file H.R. 199, DOC 518).

Sean H. Wong—commander of Boston Chinatown Post no. 328, American Legion—wrote to Sen. Leverett Saltonstall of Massachusetts (Republican) about "our complete and irrevocable animosity toward the Judd bill." Based on the fact that during World War II approximately twenty thousand Chinese-Americans had served in the armed forces of the United States, Wong wrote: "We were told time and again that we were fighting for the four freedoms, justice, and equality. By unfair provisions in the Judd bill, it works directly against the principles which we cherish and fought for. Why should not equal rights be granted to all American citizens?" "A Letter to Honorable Leverett Saltonstall, M.C., from Boston Chinatown Post no. 328, the American Legion," March 23, 1949 (National Archives, Legislative Branch, RG 46, box 87, file H.R. 199, DOC. 518).

For other arguments of protest, see statements in *Hearings on the Naturalization of Asian and Pacific Peoples*, 81st Cong., 1st sess., 1949, made by William Jack Chow, representing the Chinese Consolidated Benevolent Association of San Francisco, Edward Hong, representing the Chinese Consolidated Benevolent Associaton of New York, Y. C. Hong of the Chinese-American Citizens Alliance of San Francisco, and Mike Masaoka, National Legislative Director, Japanese-American Citizens' League, Anti-Discrimination Committee.

60. "The Immigration and Naturalization Systems of the United States," *Senate Report*, no. 1515, 81st Cong., 2d sess., 1950, 457–58; see also Robert Divine, *American Immigration Policy, 1924–1952* (Yale University Press, 1957), 155–56.

61. U.S. Congress, *Revision of the Immigration, Naturalization, and Nationality Laws: Joint Hearings before the Subcommittees of the Committees on the Judiciary on S.716, H.R. 2379, and H.R. 2816*, 82d Cong., 1st sess., March 6–April 9, 1951, 33 and 35.

62. Ibid., 70, 73–74.

63. Ibid., 393, 587–88, and 618–19.

64. *Congressional Record*, 82d Cong., 2d sess., 1952, 98, pt.6:8253–8268.

65. President's Commission on Immigration and Naturalization, *Whom We Shall Welcome?* (GPO, 1953), 52–53.

66. Tazuke Kei'ichi (Director of Information Division, Japanese Ministry of Foreign Affairs), "Imin wa dō naru ka," *Keizai jīpu* 3, no. 3 (February 1951): 8–10.

67. "Beikoku no shin-Nichi-kanjō to Nichi-Bei kankei no shōrai" (editorial), *Nihon keizai shimbun*, September 12, 1951, 1.

68. See, for example, the treatment of the law's passage in the *Asahi shimbun*: "Nihon-jin nen 185 mei," *Asahi shimbun*, June 28, 1952, 1.

69. "Daresu shisetsu-dan ni taisuru yōbō," *Kaigai e no tobira*, no. 21 (February 10, 1951): 1.

70. "Daresu tokushi e gokai me no ikensho teishutsu," *Kaigai e no tobira*, no. 24 (May 10, 1951): 1. For the Japanese translation of Dulles's reply, see "Beikoku kakkai tsūshin," *Kaigai e no tobira*, no. 25 (June 10, 1951): 2.

71. Kaigai Jinkō Idō Taisaku Kenkyūkai (Committee on the Overseas Population Movement), *Nihon-jin imin ni kansuru shōrai no sho-mondai—Nihon jinkō mondai no kinpaku-sei ni kangamite (hi: kin tensai)* (Problems facing the future of Japanese overseas emigration—in the light of the impending population crisis for Japan [Classified—no public circulation allowed]) (Ōyū Kurabu, May 1949), 73–77. Perhaps because of SCAP censorship, the publisher made this 125-page report available only to a closed circle of concerned people and organizations in Japan. The original mimeographed copy is deposited at Nihon Kokusai Kyōryoku Jigyō-dan (Japan International Cooperation Agency: JICA) Library, Tokyo, Japan. See also Ogura Seitarō and Katō Michio, *Nihon-jin to nettai eisei* (Hōbō Shoten, 1942); and Kuno Yasu, *Nettai seikatsu mondai* (Haku Shobō, 1943).

72. Toriya Torao, "Minshu-teki imin no seikaku," *Kaigai e no tobira*, no. 4 (August 10, 1949): 1.

Toriya was born in Yokohama in 1904. Graduating from the Yokohama Higher Institute of Technology (Yokohama Kanritsu Kōtō Kōgyō Gakkō), he worked at the Yokohama Customs House and later moved to the Ministry of Commerce and Industry. He worked at the Ministry of Industry of Manchukuo, along with Kishi Nobusuke, who later became Japan's prime minister. After being ousted from Manchukuo owing to his disagreement with the Kwantung Army, he was transferred back to the Ministry of Commerce and Industry with Kishi's help. After the outbreak of the Pacific War, he worked in Singapore in charge of industrial developments in Southeast Asia. In 1946, after being released from a British war prison, he returned to Japan and started the Japanese overseas emigration movement. For his autobiography, see Toriya Torao, *Yokohama no shūsen hiwa—kokusai kō to kaigai ijū undō* (Nihon Kōgyō Shimbun Sha, 1983).

73. "Daresu shisetsu-dan ni taisuru yōbō," *Kaigai e no tobira*, no. 21 (February 10, 1951): 1.

74. "Kakkai chimei-shi ankeito," *Keizai jīpu* 3, no. 3 (February 1951): 14–15.

75. "Jinkō mondai o dō omou ka," *Asahi shimbun*, November 4, 1951, 2.

76. "Chart on Japanese Emigrants by Country of Residence, 1940" under the entry for "Emigration" in *Kodansha Encyclopedia of Japan* (Kodansha, 1983).

77. Kon'no Toshihiko and Fujisaki Yasuo, *Imin shi (1): Nan-Bei hen* (Shinsen Sha, 1984), 187–89. See also "Burajiru imin saikai e," *Asahi shimbun*, December 30, 1951 (evening edition), 1.

78. *Dai 15 kai Kokkai Shūgi-in kaigi-roku* (Record of the 15th Diet, Lower House), December 20, 1952, no. 17, pp. 4–5.

79. Ishikawa Tatsuzō, "Nihon-jin ga moteru kuni guni," *Bungei Shunjū* 30, no. 10 (July 1952): 66–76. Compared to New Guinea, Brazil attracted much more enthusiam among the Japanese. *Chūō kōron*, Japan's leading intellectual journal, also printed the following articles: "Zai-Haku Hō-jin shakai to imin mondai [The Japanese community in Brazil and the immigration issue]," *Chūō kōron* (June 1951): 86–99; Goshō Kingo, "Burajiru imin [The emigration to Brazil]," *Chūō kōron* (October 1954): 197–205. See also Kamizuka Tsukasa, "Buraziru e imin wa dekiru ka [Is the emigration to Brazil plausible?]," *Jitsugyō no Nippon* (Business Japan) 55, no. 2 (January 15, 1952): 56–57; Nakamura Yoshinori, *Nan-Bei wa maneku—hirake yuku shin-tenchi no dōhō* (Herarudo, 1953).

80. Wakatsuki Yasuo and Suzuki Jōji, *Kaigai ijū seisaku shiron*, 117.

81. Ibid.

82. See the entry for "Emigration," in *Kodansha Encyclopedia of Japan*. See also the following: Andō Hikotarō, "Senzen no Manshū keiei ron to Nihon imin [The prewar Manchurian development plan and Japanese emigration]," *Waseda Seikei zasshi*, no. 171 (October 1961): 1–20; Wakatsuki and Suzuki, *Kaigai ijū seisaku shiron*, 67–79.

83. Ban Shōichi, "Kaigai ijū kibō-sha no bunbu to kaigai ijū o unagasu yōin (Socioeconomic backgrounds of would-be emigrants and the pull and push factors]," *Gaimu-shō chōsa geppō* (Japan Ministry of Foreign Affairs Monthly Report) 2, no. 11 (November 1961): 1–16.

84. AG 291.1 AGPD, "Marriage of Military Personnel," December 2, 1945 (Washington National Records Center, Suitland Md., GHQ-SCAP, RG 331, box 433, SCAP Adjutant General's Section, Operations Divisions, file 291-1, #1 [Secret]).

85. "Marriages to Japanese Lifted," *New York Times*, May 31, 1946, sec. 1, p. 7; see also Peter Kalischer, "Madame Butterfly's Children," *Collier's*, September 20, 1952, 16.

86. There were of course sincere demands for the ruling's amendment. In May 1947 a letter to the military paper *Stars and Stripes* requested army approval of the Japanese wives of thirteen enlisted men. "Why can't we marry Japanese girls?" the letter asked. "During our tour of duty . . . many of us have become quite fond of girls over here. Why, then, can't this democratic army drop some of its pride and let us go ahead in spite of the racial differences? We are supposed to impress the Japanese with the truth that all men are created equal, etc. Why don't we practice what we preach?"

See Lucy Crockette, *Popcorn on the Ginza: An Informal Portrait of Postwar Japan* (William Sloane, 1949), 146.

87. Kalischer, "Madame Butterfly's Children," 16; "Immigration Bureau Rept on War Brides Admitted to US to July 1," *New York Times*, September 17 1947, sec. 1, p. 22.

88. Diplomatic Section, GHQ-SCAP, Yokohama Division, "Memorandum: Marriage of American Citizens in Japan," 2 (Washington National Records Center, Suitland, Md., GHQ-SCAP, RG 331, box 643, SCAP Adjutant General's Section, Operations Division, file 291–1 #1, 1949).

89. General Headquarters, Far Eastern Command, APO 500, "A Letter to Honorable Cecil F. White" (draft), n.d. (Spring 1949?), (Washington National Records Center, Suitland, Md., GHQ-SCAP, RG 331, box 643, SCAP Adjutant General's Section, Operations Division, file 291–1, book 1, 1949).

For contemporary American observation on GI marriages with Japanese women, see the following articles: Janet W. Smith and William Worden, "They're Bringing Home Japanese Wives," *Saturday Evening Post*, January 19, 1952, 26ff.; William Worden, "Where Are Those Japanese War Brides?" *Saturday Evening Post*, November 20, 1954, 38ff.; James Michener, "Pursuit of Happiness by a GI and a Japanese," *Life*, February 21, 1955, 124ff.; Gerald Schnepp and Agnes Masako YUI, *American Journal of Sociology* 61, no. 1 (July 1955): 48–50.

5. THE PROBLEM OF MISCEGENATION

1. Peter Kalischer, "Madame Butterfly's Children," *Collier's*, September 20, 1952. See also Sawada Miki, *Kuroi hada to shiroi kokoro* (Nihon Keizai Shimbun Sha, 1963; rpt., Horupu, 1980), 155.

2. Before World War II, more than thirty states prohibited interracial marriage in one form or another. More than ten states, mostly west of the Mississippi, prohibited the marriage of a white person with a "Mongolian." There was inconsistency among the statutes in the selection and categorization of nonwhite groups. Seven of the states that prohibited marriage with a Mongolian also extended the prohibition to Malays. South Dakota extended the prohibition to Koreans as well as Mongolians. Some statutes included "mulattoes" within the prohibited group. Some statutes even defined the percentage of Negro blood required to be considered a Negro within the meaning of the statute. The Louisiana statute used the term, "a person of color," and the Nevada law spoke of the "Ethiopian." See James Browning, "Anti-Miscegenation in the United States," *The Duke Bar Journal* 1, no. 1 (March 1951): 32.

3. For the interpretation of *Perez v. Lippold* (32 Cal2d 711, 198 P2d 17 [1948]), see "Notes and Comments: Constitutionality of State Anti-Miscegenation Statutes," *Southwestern Law Journal* 5, no. 4 (Fall 1951): 452–53, and "Notes and Comments: Constitutionality of Miscegenetic Marriages," *Montana Law Review* 11 (Spring 1950): 53–55.

4. "Notes and Comments: Constitutionality of Miscegenetic Marriages," *Montana*

Law Review, ibid., 55; "Notes and Comments: Constitutionality of State Anti-Miscegenation Statutes," *Southwestern Law Review*, ibid., 453, 458.

5. James Browning, "Anti-Miscegenation Laws in the United States," 39.

6. Harry Emerson Wildes, *Typhoon in Tokyo* (Macmillan, 1954), 333.

7. The deported reporter was Darrell Berrigan, for his article "Japan's Occupation Babies," *Saturday Evening Post*, June 19, 1948, 24–25, 117. For the conflict between SCAP and the American press over the issue of mixed-race babies, see Wildes, *Typhoon in Tokyo*, 333, and Sawada Miki, *Konketsuji no haha—Elizabeth Sanders Home* (Mainichi Shimbun Sha, 1953), 31.

8. Wildes, *Typhoon in Tokyo*, 327; Darrell Berrigan, "Japan's Occupation Babies," 24 and 118; Janet Wentworth Smith and William L. Worden, "They're Bringing Home Japanese Wives," *Saturday Evening Post*, January 19, 1952, 81.

9. Kalischer, "Madame Butterfly's Children," 18. The Japanese also noticed the same trend in its Southeast Asian colonies during the war. In Indonesia, where officials found "half-breeds" a particularly difficult group to deal with, they established eight different categories for Eurasians, depending on their percentage of European blood. See John Dower, *War Without Mercy* (Pantheon, 1987), 277.

10. Berrigan, "Japan's Occupation Babies," 118.

11. Even before the war, while Sawada Miki lived in Europe with her husband Sawada Renzo, a diplomat and administrator in the Japanese Foreign Ministry, she had taken an interest in starting a home for Japanese orphans. In January 1946 she wrote to MacArthur explaining her ambition to bring up the parentless children—innocent victims of Japan's fanatic militarists and warmongers—as peace-loving and worthwhile citizens of the new Japan. In proficient English, she requested SCAP's cooperation with her project, inquiring if there were any former Japanese Army or Navy properties which SCAP could allocate to these orphans. In a brief reply, SCAP, while acknowledging its sympathy with her concern for the welfare of orphaned children in Japan, nonetheless instructed her to make contact with the Japanese government. For this communication, see the following document: GHQ United States Army Forces, Pacific CHECK SHEET, "Ltr from Miki Sawada, dtd 24 Jan 46" (Washington National Records Center, Suitland, Md., GHQ-SCAP, RG 331, box 425, SCAP Adjutant General's Section, Operations Division, Mail and Records Branch, file 091–4, #2.). See also "A letter to Mr. [*sic*] Miki Sawada," GHQ-SCAP, AG 091.41 (1 Feb 46) PH (Washington National Records Center, Suitland, Md., GHQ-SCAP, RG 331, box 425, SCAP Adjutant General's Section, Operations Division, Mail and Records Branch, file 091–4, #2).

12. Sawada, *Konketsuji no haha*, 3–19 and 213–16. See also Elizabeth Anne Hemphill, *The Least of These: Miki Sawada and Her Children* (Weatherhill, 1980), 96–97. Sawada's plans called for a hospital, school, chapel, nurses' home, job-training center, mess hall, and dormitory, in addition to the nursery.

13. "Shukumei no ko ni akarui Kurisumasu," *Tōkyō shimbun*, December 5, 1948; "Chichi naki ko no ai no su," *Nichi-Bei Weekly*, December 12, 1948; and "Unmei no koji tanpō," *Akahata*, January 29, 1950: these articles are from the newspaper clipping collection entitled "Konketsuji" [Mixed-blood children] (file no. 362.73 [1948–1953 and 1952.3–1965.12]), available at the Newspapers and Periodicals Center at the Japan National Diet Library (hereafter cited as "Konketsuji file").

14. "Tensei jingo," *Asahi shimbun*, July 11, 1952, 1.

15. Elizabeth Anne Hemphill, *The Least of These*, 95.

16. Kōsēi-shō Jidō-kyoku (Ministry of Welfare, Children's Bureau), *Josanpu san-fujin-ka-i ga shūsen irai atsukatta konketsu-jidō shussei sū* (August 31, 1952). As of April 1, 1952, the census reported, there were 1,000 children below the age of one; 1,204 between the age of one and two; 1,098 between two and three; 771 between three and four; 495 between four and five; 323 between five and six; and 111 between six and seven.

17. *Kōsei-shō Daijin Kanbō Tōkei Chōsa-bu, shakai fukushi tōkei nenpō, 1952* (Division of Health and Welfare Statistics, Welfare Minister's Secretariat, The Social Welfare Statistics, Annual Report, 1952), (2) "Iwayuru konketsuji jittai chōsa [Statistics on the So-Called Mixed-Blood Children]."

Of these 3,490 children, 86 percent were half-white, 11.5 percent half-black, and 2.8 percent undistinguishable. Forty-eight percent of the total were legitimate children, 39 percent were illegitimate, and 13 percent had fathers unknown. Some 84.3 percent of the fathers were from the United States. More than a dozen other nationalities made up the rest: Australia (3 percent), the Philippines (1 percent), United Kingdom (1 percent), Soviet Union (0.5 percent), India (0.4 percent), Italy (0.3 percent), Canada (0.2 percent), and the remainder, including France, Germany, Belgium, Spain, Portugal, Switzerland, Denmark, Indonesia, and Greece (10 percent).

18. "Konketsuji wa dō kaiketsu subeki ka—hogo yori konpon taisaku o," *Nihon keizai shimbun*, February, 2, 1953, 6.

19. "Aoi me no ichinen-sei—konketsuji no nyūgaku mondai," *Shūkan Asahi*, May 1, 1953, 10.

20. "Shasetsu—konketsuji to otona no henken," *Yomiuri shimbun*, February 19, 1953, 1.

21. Nagashima Sadao, "Jinshu no yūretsu to kokusai rikai," *Jidō shinri* (July 1953): 54.

22. Shimizu Ikutarō, "Amerika yo ganbare," *Chūō kōron* 68, no. 12 (November 1953): 30–31.

23. Seki Kazuo, "Konketsuji no mondai," *Kyōiku to igaku* (March 1954): 29–32.

24. Kitabayashi Tōma, "Tōsho—konketsuji no mondai," *Mainichi shimbun*, March 4, 1953, 3.

25. Maki Ken'ichi, "Konketsuji no mondai," *Shakai jigyō* (January 1953): 26. See also Kalischer, "Madame Butterfly's Children," 18.

26. Aoki Kei'ichi, "Konketsuji wa Nihon-jin ka," *Ushio* 3 (October 1952): 34–35.

27. Shimizu Ikutarō, "Kanashimu beki henken ni tsuite," *Fujin kōron* (September 1953): 44.

28. Furuya Yoshio, "Racial Integrity and Population Factor," originally appeared in *Nippon Hyōron* (July 1943) and was summarized in English in *Contemporary Japan* 12, no. 8 (August 1943). See also Dower, *War Without Mercy*, 275–77.

29. "Unmei no kokusai-ji to kyōiku—gakurei-ki made ato ni-nen," *Asahi shimbun*, November 20, 1951; "Konketsuji taisaku ni noridasu," *Jiji shimpō* (June 9, 1952): 3.

30. P. A. Witty, "Intra Race Testing: Negro Intelligence," *American Journal of Psychology* 1 (1936): 179–92.

31. Kōsei-shō Jinkō Mondai Kenkyūjo (Ministry of Welfare, Institute of Population Problems), *Konketsu oyobi imin ni yoru Nihon-minzoku taii no eikyō ni tsuite* (Anthropometric influences of emigration and blood mixture on the Japanese race), hereafter cited as *Konketsu oyobi imin ni yoru* . . . (Data Series no. 97, June 1, 1954), sec. 2, "Beikoku umare Nisei no taikaku seiseki to Nihon-jin to no hikaku [A comparative study of body structure and academic performances of Nisei and native Japanese]," by Ishiwara Fusao and Iidaka Toshiko, 74–77.

A separate private report by Shinagawa Fujirō quotes Tanaka's test results with somewhat different figures ("Chinō no tesuto," *Kokumin no kagaku* 2, no. 4 [September–October 1947]: 32). A combined result from the above government report and Shinagawa's report shows the following order of IQ levels among children of different origins: Japanese (49.49 to 49.92), Chinese (46.29), Koreans (46.22), British (44.72 to 44.80), Russian Jews (44.72 to 45.13) (note here that the above government report adopts the figure for "Russian Jews" as a category for Tanaka's prewar test, whereas the private report lists "Russians *and* Jews" [emphasis added]), Nordics (44.48), white Americans (44.05 to 44.14), Scandinavians (44.12), Germans (43.64 to 43.88), Eastern Europeans (42.55), Irish (41.54), Spanish (41.43), French (41.37), Canadians (40.97), Hawaiians (39.00 to 40.80), Greeks (40.71), Portuguese (40.53 to 41.54), Southern Europeans (39.30), Mexicans (37.04 to 38.04), Italians (36.79 to 37.48), American Indians (36.80), and black Americans (34.94 to 35.25). Note the variable figures for each group from different reports and publications may indicate a lack of legitimacy in Tanaka's experiments.

32. Tanaka himself also presented a somewhat conflicting summary based on the same experiment in his postwar article, "Nihon-minzoku no shōrai," *Kyōiku to igaku* 5, no. 1 (January 1957): 8. In this, Tanaka compared the Japanese average IQ (49.49) with the northern Europeans (44.48), eastern Europeans (42.55), southern Europeans (39.30), and that of Europe and North America combined (43.40).

In this article, Tanaka also argues that there is a serious correlation between a person's IQ level and the weight of his or her brain. Citing the brain's average weight as 1,356 grams for European males and 1,227 grams for European females, whereas it is 1,383 grams for Japanese males and 1,224 for Japanese females (and also given the fact that the average body weight for Japanese men and women tend to be lighter than that for Europeans), Tanaka concludes that the Japanese have a heavier—and thus superior—brain compared to Europeans. (Ibid., 8.)

33. Kwok Tsuen Yeung, "The Intelligence of Chinese Children in San Francisco and Vicinity," *Journal of Applied Psychology* 5 (1921): 267–74; Peter Sandiford and Ruby Kerr, "Intelligence of Chinese and Japanese Children," *Journal of Educational Psychology* 17, no. 6 (September 1926): 361–67.

34. Marvin L. Darsie, "The Mental Capacity of American-Born Japanese Children," *Comparative Psychology Monograms* 3, no. 15 (January 1926): 2–3 and 84–87. For a more comprehensive analysis of the intelligence test experiments in North American before World War II, see John Baker, *Race* (Oxford University Press, 1974), 490–92.

35. "Chinō daitai yaya hikui—hatsu no konketsuji chōsa naru," *Tōkyō shimbun*, August 22, 1952, 7.

36. In the prewar period, Western scientists treated temperament and characteristics, such as honesty, ambition, perseverance, trustworthiness, self-assertion, as part of distinctive racial traits. The 1921–1923 test by Marvin Darsie et. al, mentioned above, seems unique in that it concluded that in terms of moral-social traits, such as sympathy, generosity, conscientiousness, truthfulness, and school application, no significant differences appeared between the American and Japanese children, although in originality and general intelligence American children were judged superior to the Japanese. For an example of postwar Japanese research on the distinctive temperament of the mixed-blood Japanese children, see "Konketsuji wa okorippoku hijyō ni kanjō-teki ni fu-antei [Study finds mixed-blood children easily lose their temper and are emotionally unstable]," *Yomiuri shimbun*, February 10, 1953. See also *Konketsu oyobi imin ni yoru . . .* , sec. 1, "Nihon-jin to hakujin oyobi kokujin to no konketsu no chōsa [Anthropometric study of mixed-blood children between the Japanese and the white or black races]," by Ishiwara Fusao and Kubota Yoshinobu. In the comparative studies on their intelligence and temperament, the report concludes: "Compared to pure-blood Japanese children, mixed-blood children are emotionally high-strung, strong-willed, stubborn, talkative, and cry easily but are generally cheerful" (16).

37. "Aoi me no ichinen-sei," *Shūkan Asahi*, May 1, 1953, 5.

38. Takahashi Yoshio, in the book *Nihon-jinshu kairyō ron* (The improvement of the Japanese race) (1884), advocated interracial marriage as a way to adopt the physique and intellect of superior Western peoples. Quoting scientific theories by Arthur de Gobineau, Darwin, and others, he acknowledged that Western scientists unanimously discouraged miscegenation between the superior white race (*hakuseki-jinshu*) and inferior races. However, since the improvement of inferior Japanese quality was a matter of grave national consequences, on the eve of Japan's modernization program Takahashi insisted on further governmental investigation on the merits of Japanese intermarriage with the white race. Among prominent supporters of his theory was Inouye Kaoru, the minister of foreign affairs between 1885 and 1887, who

served in Japan's first Western-style cabinet, led by Prime Minister Itō Hirobumi. To further enrich the nation and strengthen the army, Inouye proposed to transform the empire and its people into one that looked Western. Fukuzawa Yukichi wrote an introduction to Takahashi's book, giving his support to the theory of racial strengthening, although he did not comment on interracial marriage.

Inoue Tetsujirō, philosopher and educator at Tokyo Imperial University, opposed the program of racial Westernization through interracial marriage in his *Naichi zakkyo ron* (Theory on mixed residence), published in 1890. To improve the Japanese race to the level of the Westerners, Inoue recommended the improvement of social conditions through better education for women, introduction of eugenics, nurturing of social morality, and other means. As a prerequisite for Japanese racial improvement, he also emphasized the importance of learning from the superior Western civilization about their philosophical, political, and legal thoughts. Only in this way, he claimed, would the Japanese become the most advanced nation in Asia.

Umino Kōtoku, a physiologist, published *Nihon-jinshu kaizō ron* (An argument on the Japanese racial reconstruction) in 1911 and argued for several racial adjustments for survival. He claimed that the quality of the race dictated superiority or inferiority, and that quality is not fatalistic; it could be improved in three ways—physical, spiritual, and social. He pointed out various policies and programs related to eugenics improvement, such as marriage, moderation in drinking, and charity. As for spiritual improvement, he emphasized the need of emperor worship to enhance patriotism. This way, as long as Japanese society remained racially as pure as American society (*sic*), Umino argued, the nation would stand firm and stable.

For the above arguments, see the following books: Takahashi Yoshio, *Nihon-jinshu kairyō ron*, ch. 5 ("Zakkon no koto" [On miscegenation]) (Jiji Shimpō Sha, 1884), 97–137; *Inoue Gaimu Kyō no ikensho* (1887), cited in Wagatsuma Hiroshi and Yoneyama Toshinao, *Henken no kōzō: Nihon-jin no jinshu-kan* (Nippon Hōsō Kyōkai, 1967), 50; Inoue Tetsujirō, "Tōzai bunka no sai o ronzu," in Samura Hachirō, ed., *Inoue Hakushi kōron shū* (Keigyō Sha, 1894). See also Kata Tetsuji, *Jinshu-Minzoku-Sensō* (Keiō Shobō, 1938), 60–61; Umino Kōtoku, *Nihon-jinshu kaizō ron* (Fuzanbō, 1911), 240–47.

39. *Konketsu oyobi imin ni yoru . . .* , sec. 1, pp. 14–19.

40. *Konketsu oyobi imin ni yoru . . .* , sec. 2, pp. 55, 68, 74.

41. Ibid., 83.

42. *Konketsu oyobi imin ni yoru . . .* , sec. 1, p. 19. Of all the children tested, there had been three cases of hernia, one case of syndactylism, three cases of idiocy, and several cases of exudation diathesis, in addition to numerous cases of eczema. The report concluded: "It is believed that deformities and diathesis have been caused through 'disharmony resulting from miscegenation' during the embryonic development" (ibid.).

43. Kida Fumio, "Ashi no mijikai Nihon-jin—jinshu-teki dewa nai higeki," *Asahi shimbun* (evening edition), July 25, 1952, 4.

44. For an argument on "crudely physical features that are advantageous or detrimental to members of certain taxa in sporting activities," see John Baker, *Race*, 421–25.

45. For episodes concerning the myth of *hattō-shin bijin* (*hattō-shin* beauty), especially in the context of postwar Japan's popular culture, see the following: Sezoku Fūzoku Kansatsu-kai, ed., *Gendai fūzoku-shi nenpyō* (Kawade Shobō, 1986), 76; Takahashi Nobuo, *Shōwa sesō ryūkō-go jiten* (Ōbun Sha, 1986), 139–40; Harada Katsumasa, *Shōwa sesō-shi* (Shōgakkan, 1989), 185–86.

46. Ōya Sōichi, "Taiheiyō-sensō o meguru chi no mondai—buchi [*sic*] burujowa ga deruka," *Shōsetsu Shinchō* 6, no. 8 (June 1952): 70–71. Ōya cited Japan's world-renowned opera singers, such as Fujiwara Yoshie and Satō Yoshiko, as living examples of how an infusion of Western blood (*achira no chi ga haitte iru*) helps one's career.

47. "Chichi kou 'sensō no otoshigo,'" *Yomiuri shimbun*, July 30, 1952, 3.

48. Aoki Kei'ichi, "Konketsuji wa Nihonjin-ka," 33.

49. "Chichi kou 'sensō no otoshigo,'" *Yomiuri shimbun*, July 30, 1952, 3.

50. "Nichi-Bei no otoshimono—sensyō-koku no ryōshiki ni uttaeru," *Bungei shunjū* (October 1952): 72–73.

51. Koyama Itoko, "Futatsu no konketsuji," *Asahi shimbun*, February 22, 1953, 6.

52. "Zadankai: kokusai rikai to kichi no kodomo [A Roundtable: International understanding and children living around the U.S. military base]," *Jidō shinri* 7, no. 7 (July 1953): 1–16. See also Kōno Hisako, "Konketsuji no shin ichinen-sei o mukaeru," *Fujin kōron* (March 1953): 140–43; Takasaki Setsuko, "Shiroi ko kuroi ko no kanashi-mi," *Bungei shunjū* 33, no. 8 (April 1955): 198–205.

53. Referring to prominent black-American figures such as Marian Anderson, one of the world's greatest contraltos, and Richard Wright, author of *Native Son* (1939) and other monumental works on American racism, Hirabayashi claimed that the Japanese should be proud of an infusion of black blood into their race and make an effort at full integration of these half-black children. Hirabayashi Taiko, "Kokujin konketsuji no mondai," *Yomiuri shimbun* (evening edition), May 5, 1953(?). This article is contained in the "Konketsuji file." (However, no such article is found in the *Yomiuri* Tokyo evening edition on the date recorded in that file. It is possible that an archivist misquoted the name and date of the newspaper for this article.) As for Richard Wright's own interest in racism in Asia, see note 1 of the Epilogue (this volume).

54. "Pūsan," *Shōsetsu Shinchō* 6, no. 8 (June 1952): 136. Readers are left uncertain as to whether this is supposed to be a happy ending or not. It may imply a hope for the blossoming of new relations between Japan and Africa under the leadership of a half-black half-Japanese person. Or it might simply suggest that the destiny of this elite Japanese man lies in a jungle—a symbol of the uncivilized—because of his racial background.

55. *Dai 15 kai Kokkai Sangi-in Kōsei Iinkai kaigi-roku, dai 8 gō* (Record of the 15th Diet, Upper House Committee on Welfare), December 9, 1952, no. 8, p. 8.

56. *Dai 15 kai Kokkai Sangi-in Monbu Iinkai kaigi-roku, dai 8 gō* (Record of the 15th Diet, Upper House Committee on Education), December 9, 1952, no. 8, pp. 7–8.

57. Elizabeth Anne Hemphill, *The Least of These*, 96–97.

58. Sawada, *Konketsuji no haha*, 213–16.

59. "Shiawase ni shitai konoko tachi; men'eki o isogu beki ka," *Sangyō keizai shimbun*, May 8, 1952, 8.

60. "Kōsei-shō ni tokubetsu iinkai," *Nihon keizai shimbun*, August 14, 1952.

61. "Konketsuji ni kyōiku shisetsu—zenkoku go-kasho ni kyōba," *Nihon keizai shimbun*, September 8, 1952, 3. The plan for segregation proposed the building of five special facilities in Yokohama, Osaka, and Hokkaido, each housing about one hundred children near or on the site of the orphanage where they lived.

62. "Aoi me no ichinen-sei," *Shūkan Asahi*, 6.

63. Kanzaki Kiyoshi, "Shiro to kuro—Nichi-Bei konketsuji no chōsa hōkoku," *Fujin kōron* (March 1953): 134.

64. "Sabetsukan o atae nai yō ni To de konketsuji no nyūgaku o neru," *Mainichi shimbun*, October 17, 1952, 4; "Zaitaku konketsuji ippan-kō e," *Asahi shimbun*, November 14, 1952, 7.

65. "Sabetsu-kan o atae nai yō ni . . . ," ibid.

66. The new Nationality Law, amended in 1984, stipulated that a child shall be a Japanese national when either the father or mother is a Japanese national, thus introducing a certain degree of legal flexibility to a growing number of cases of international marriage taking place among Japanese citizens of both sexes, cases that also affected their alien spouses and offspring. In addition, the new law reflected the Japanese government's commitment to completely abolish gender discrimination in any form. The law was promulgated on May 25, 1984, and went into effect on January 1, 1985. For a detailed analysis of this newly amended law, see the following: Hōmu-shō Minji-kyoku-nai Hōmu Kenkyūkai hen (Ministry of Justice Civil Affairs Bureau, Judicatory [sic] Research Committee, ed.), *Kaisei Kokuseki Hō Koseki Hō no kaisetsu* (Analysis of the amended nationality law and national registry law) (Kin'yū Zaisei Jijyō Kenkyūkai, 1985).

67. "Sabetsu-kan o atae nai yō ni . . . ," *Mainichi shimbun*, October 17, 1952, 4.

68. "Mukaeru konketsuji nyūgaku," *Yomiuri shimbun* (evening edition), February 24, 1953, 3.

69. Monbu-shō Shotō Chūtō Kyōiku-kyoku Shotō-kyōiku-ka (Ministry of Education, Division of Elementary and Middle Level Education, Primary Education Section), *Konketsuji no shūgaku ni tsuite shidō-jō ryūi subeki ten* (Checkpoints for instructing mixed-blood children in school), hereafter cited as *Konketsuji no shūgaku* (February 1953), p. 1. This mimeographed booklet is available for review at the library at Kokuritsu Kyōiku Kenkyūjo (the National Institute for Educational Research of Japan), Tokyo.

70. *Konketsuji no shūgaku*, 3–4.

71. Ibid., 4–13.

72. Ibid., 13–15, 20–22.

73. Monbu-shō Shotō Chūtō Kyōiku-kyoku (Ministry of Education, Division of Elementary and Middle Level Education), *Konketsuji shidō kiroku* (Record of instructions for mixed-blood children) (hereafter cited as *Konketsuji shidō kiroku*), vol. 3 (April 1956): 182. A copy of this booklet is available for review at the library of the National Institute for Educational Research of Japan.

74. The year 1946 showed the highest number of births of illegitimate children of German women and American soldiers. The number of mixed-blood births dropped between then and mid-1951 but was on the rise in districts such as Wiesbaden, Munich, and Mannheim, where large American garrisons were stationed. The West German government speculated that the problem should be discussed within NATO, and watched to see whether the French and British governments brought legal claims against American soldiers responsible for illegitimate children born in their territories.

In West Germany the presence of colored children—mulattoes, as they were called—fathered by black American soldiers, forced West German society to cope with the same problems of miscegenation as Japan faced. Since a large number of "mulattoes" were to enter school in 1952, West German society, like Japanese society, saw a serious need for pedagogical and psychological attention. Studies of public attitudes toward half-black American half-German children showed three types of prejudice emerging, almost identical to the situation in Japan. The first was social prejudice against the mothers' background—"Yankee's girls" who got involved with black men for profit. The second was ideological prejudice based on the theory that "mixed-race" people represented inferior heritage and intelligence. The third was based on resentment of the American GIs—"enemy occupation forces"—easily targeting half-black children as the visible offspring of the intruders. Another investigation found that of 603 mothers of illegitimate Afro-German children, ninety-two were prepared to give up the child to the father or adoptive parents in the United States, since they viewed America as a paradise for "colored people," and thus better for the child's welfare. See May Opitz, Katharina Oguntoye, and Dagmar Schultz, eds., *Showing Our Colors: Afro-German Women Speak Out* (University of Massachusetts Press, 1992), 81–82 and 94.

75. Lloyd Graham, "Those G.I.'s in Japan," *Christian Century* 71, no. 11 (March 17, 1954): 330–31. The McCarran-Walter Act permitted GIs to legally register their marriage with Japanese authorities and bring their wives with them to the United States.

76. The sole beneficiary of bill S. 527, for example, was Youichi (*sic*) Noboru, born October 12, 1946, in Tokyo, Japan, the offspring of a Japanese woman and a "former white, American soldier of the United States Army, whose present location is unknown." The adopting parent explained the boy's background to Sen. William Knowland, author of the special bill. An investigation revealed that the relationship be-

tween his parents was not the result of a common "pickup." The mother, now married to a Japanese man, was a fine young girl who had made only the one improper and unwise step. She had turned the child over to the adopting parents in person, hoping that they would take him with them to America. Three photographs of the child were attached to the letter as proof of "his personality, and fine, strong body," and especially "his lack of any Asiatic features"—an important prerequisite for the boy's successful integration into American society. See "Report to accompany S. 527. Senate Calender No. 800, Report No. 846," 82d Cong., 1st sess., 1951, 2.

77. U.S. House of Representatives, *Hearings before the President's Commission on Immigration and Naturalization*, 82d Cong., 2d sess., September 30–October 29, 1952 (GPO, 1952), 1215–1217 (Bates testimony). For Rev. Whang's statement on GI babies in Korea, see 1218–1220. For Finucane's statement, see 1742–1750.

78. Kalischer, "Madame Butterfly's Children," 18.

79. "A Letter from James E. Lloyd, Troop Headquarters Kobe Quartermaster Depot, to Chairman of the Board, House of Representatives," April 27, 1953 (National Archives, Legislative Branch, RG 233, 83rd Cong., 1st sess., H.J. Res. 228, 9E2/21/12/3, box 1113).

80. "From AMEMBASSY, Tokyo, to the Department of State, Washington; Subject: Organization in Japan of the American Joint Committee for Assisting Japanese-American Orphans (Restricted)," January 12, 1953, p. 2 of despatch no. 1306, Tokyo (National Archives, Diplomatic Branch, RG 59, box 5677), hereafter cited as the AJC file.

The committee also accepted the view of Japan's Ministry of Welfare that American assistance in solving the problem of mixed-blood children would only increase public prejudice against these children. Furthermore, if the committee conducted a program of financial help to Japanese women with mixed-blood children, "it is quite possible that some evil persons might even take the trouble to give birth to such children in order to qualify for that financial aid," the commitee concluded. See "Minutes of the Meeting on December 17, 1952, of the American Joint Committee for Assisting Japanese-American Orphans—Suggestions for Fundamental Policy towards Postwar Children of Mixed Japanese-American Ancestry Whose Fathers Are Not Contributing to Their Support," a report attached to "From AMEMBASSY, Tokyo, to the Department of State, Washington," January 12, 1953 (AJC file).

81. "From AMEMBASSY, Tokyo, to the Department of State, Washington," January 12, 1953, p. 3 of despatch no. 1306 (AJC file).

82. "Suggestions for Fundamental Policy Towards Postwar Children . . ." (p. 3), a report attached to "From AMEMBASSY, Tokyo, to the Department of State, Washington," January 12, 1953 (AJC file).

83. Ibid.

84. "Minutes of the Meeting on February 4, 1953, of the American Joint Committee for Assisting Japanese-American Orphans," attached to "From AMEM-

BASSY, Tokyo, to the Department of State, Washington," April 14, 1953 (AJC file). A representative from the *Mainichi* newspaper called on the committee chairman, Herbert Gallop of the American Chamber of Commerce, and asked for his permission to attend the committee's upcoming meeting. The *Fujin kōron*, a monthly journal specializing in women's issues from social, political, and cultural perspectives, proposed inviting the committee members to discuss the issue under the auspices of the Ministry of Welfare. A principal of the Shibasaki Primary School at Tachikawa, Tokyo, where ten mixed-blood children were to enter primary school, also paid a visit to the chairman of the American Joint Committee and asked for his guidance on proper education policy. Gallop expressed his support for the Japanese government's plan to educate these children and to treat them as Japanese children in regular Japanese schools.

85. Ibid. ("The International Orphans Relief Society"; AJC file).

86. "Minutes of the Meeting on February 4, 1953" (p. 2), attached to "From AMEMBASSY, Tokyo, to the Department of State, Washington," April 14, 1953 (AJC file).

87. Attached to her letter was a reply from the Department of Defense to her inquiries on the issue based on reports she had received from the committee. The Defense Department replied that although they acknowledged the existence of the problem, they lacked the funds to give any assistance. "Minutes of the Meeting on March 11, 1953, of the American Joint Committee for Assisting Japanese-American Orphans," attached to "From AMEMBASSY, Tokyo, to the Department of State, Washington," April 14, 1953 (AJC file). For Japanese press coverage on Eleanor Roosevelt's involvement, see "Konketsuji mondai Roosevelt fujin shinken ni torikumu," *Yomiuri shimbun*, May 28, 1953.

88. "A Letter from Robert J. G. McClurkin to the Honorable Dean Rusk, President, Rockefeller Foundation (Confidential)," April 3, 1953 (National Archives, Diplomatic Branch, RG 59, box 5676).

89. "Minutes of the Meeting on March 25, 1953," attached to "From AMEMBASSY, Tokyo, to the Department of State," April 14, 1953 (AJC file).

90. "Minutes of the Meeting on May 27, 1953," attached to "From AMEMBASSY, Tokyo, to the Department of State, Washington," July 16, 1953 (AJC file).

91. "Report of Conversation between Mr. Gallop and Mr. Dazai, Chief of Children's Bureau, Japanese Welfare Ministry, American Club, Tokyo, June 15, 1953," attached to "From AMEBASSY, Tokyo, to the Department of State, Washington," July 16, 1953; "Incoming Telegram of Department of State, From Tokyo to Secretary of State (July 8, 1953)" (both in AJC file).

92. Sawada, *Konketsuji no haha*, 288–93.

93. "The Mail Bag" column, *Catholic World* (January 1953), reprinted in "A Letter from Senator John F. Kennedy to Robert LaBlonde, Director, Office of International Information, State Department (February 9, 1953)"; see also "A Letter to

Hon. John F. Kennedy, U.S. Senator, from Thurston B. Morton, Assistant Secretary, February 17, 1953" (both documents at the National Archives, Diplomatic Branch, RG 59, box 5676).

94. "A Letter from James B. Pilcher, American Consul General, American Embassy, Tokyo, to Franklin Hawley, Office of Northeast Asian Affairs, Department of State (Confidential), October 1, 1953" (National Archives, Diplomatic Branch, RG 59, box 5677 [Miki SAWADA file]); "A Letter from Franklin Hawley to James Pilcher (Confidential), October 15, 1953" (National Archives, Diplomatic Branch, RG 59, box 5676 [Miki SAWADA file]).

95. Malvin Lindsay, "Nameless Babies—Cold War Pawns," reprinted in the *Congressional Record*, 83rd Cong., 1st sess., 1953, 99, pt. 6:8040.

96. *Congressional Record*, 83rd Cong., 1st sess., 1953, 99, pt. 6:8039–8040. Similar arguments can be found in U.S. House of Representatives, *Hearings before the President's Commission on Immigration and Naturalization*, 82d Cong., 2d sess., September 30–October 29, 1952: see statements by Mrs. Rosalind Bates, chair, Southern California Women Lawyers (1215–1217); see also n. 77 above for Rev. Whang's and Finucane's statements.

97. "Incoming telegram to Dept of State, control: 5340 Rec'd: August 18, 1953, 5:19am, From: Tokyo To: Secretary of State, No. 445, Aug. 18"; and "From AMEMBASSY, Tokyo, to the Department of State, Washington," March 11, 1954 (both in AJC file).

98. "Ippan-ji to kubetsu sezu—Kōsei-shō no konketsuji taisaku," *Asahi shimbun* (evening edition), August 20, 1953, 3.

99. Kanzaki Kiyoshi, "Shiro to kuro—Nichi-Bei konketsuji no chōsa hōkoku," 139.

100. "Koe—konketsuji no nyūgaku," *Tokyo shimbun*, August 25, 1952, 3.

101. Suga Tadamichi, "Konketsuji o miru me—nōson ni koi sabetsu-kan," *Shakai taimusu*, March 26, 1953, 4.

102. Horie Tadao, "Jinshu-mondai no honshitsu," *Fujin kōron* (March 1953): 43–44.

103. "Aoi me no ichinen-sei," *Shūkan Asahi*, 10.

104. Aoki Kei'ichi, "Konketsuji wa Nihon-jin ka," 37,

105. "Kokusai rikai to kichi no kodomo," *Jidō shinri* (July 1953): 13.

106. Koga Yukiyoshi, "Konketsuji no chōsa—johō," in Monbu-shō Shotō Chūtō Kyōiku-kyoku, *Konketsuji shidō kiroku*, vol. 3 (April 1956): 165–81.

107. "*Konketsuji*," *Kinema jumpō* no. 59 (March 15, 1953): 47; Shindō Kōta, "*Konketsuji*," *Kinema jumpō* no. 64 (May 15, 1953): 64.

108. *Congressional Record*, 83rd Cong., 1st sess., 1953, 99, pt. 11:A3368 (Appendix).

109. *US News and World Report*, June 26, 1953, 76.

110. The figures for these illegitimate babies appeared in "The Problem of the GIs' Illegitimate Children in Germany," a speech made by West Germany's Bundestag member Frau Dr. Rehling to the Bundestag on March 12, 1952; in Committee Print

(GPO, 1952), U.S. House of Representatives, *Hearings before the President's Commission on Immigration and Naturalization*, 82d Cong., 2d sess., September 30–October 29, 1952, 1747–48.

111. "A Letter from Robert Murphy, US Ambassador, to Robert J. G. McClurkin, Deputy Director, Office of Northeast Asian Affairs, US State Department (Confidential)," March 12, 1953 (National Archives, Diplomatic Branch, RG 59, box 5676).

112. "Suggestions for Fundamental Policy towards Postwar Children . . . ," a report attached to "Minutes of the Meeting on December 17, 1952" (AJC file).

113. James Michener, "The Facts about GI Babies," *Reader's Digest* (March 1954), 6.

114. William Burkhardt, "Institutional Barriers, Marginality, and Adaptation Among the American-Japanese Mixed Bloods in Japan," *Journal of Asian Studies* 42, no. 3 (May 1983): 526.

115. Takasaki Setsuko, "Shiroi ko kuroi ko no kanashimi," 205.

116. Maki Kei'ichi, "Konketsuji no mondai," 22–29.

117. *Dai 15 kai Kokkai Shūgi-in Monbu Iin kaigi-roku, dai 12 gō* (Record of the 15th Diet, Lower House Committee on Education), February 28, 1953, no. 12, pp. 9–10.

118. *Bulletin* (U.S. Department of State) 32, no. 812, Publication 5727 (January 17, 1955): 90.

119. Gaimu-shō Jōhō Bunka-kyoku (Ministry of Foreign Affairs, Information and Culture Bureau), *Gaimu-shō happyō shū* (Ministry of Foreign Affairs Bulletin), no. 3 (August 1956): 26; and ibid., no. 1 (October 1956): 3–5.

120. Monbu-shō Shotō Chūtō Kyōiku-kyoku, *Konketsuji shidō kiroku*, vol. 3 (April 1956): 182.

121. The sixteen states were Alabama, Arkansas, Delaware, Florida, Georgia, Kentucky, Louisiana, Maryland, Mississippi, Missouri, North Carolina, South Carolina, Oklahoma, Tennessee, Virginia, and West Virginia.

122. Philip Mason, *Patterns of Dominance* (Oxford University Press, 1970), 92–93.

EPILOGUE: THE AFTERMATH—
THE LESSON OF THE OCCUPATION

1. Sukarno's opening address at the conference is quoted in Richard Wright, *The Color Curtain: A Report on the Bandung Conference* (World, 1956), 136–40; also cited in Alexander DeConde, *A History of American Foreign Policy*, vol. 2, *Global Power (1900 to the Present)*, 3d ed. (Scribner's, 1978), 353. In this work Richard Wright provides a piercing observation on the dynamics of racisms in Asian politics at Bandung—of intra-Asian racisms and European colonial racism as well as American blacks' own racism toward Asia, which had it own imperialistic tinge.

2. "Minutes of the Meeting, Secretary's Office, Department of State (Secret)," Washington, D.C., January 7, 1955, *FRUS* (1955–1957): 21:2.

3. "Memorandum of a Conversation, Department of State (Confidential)," Washington, D.C., April 9, 1955, *FRUS* (1955–1957): 21:83.

4. "Memorandum of a Conversation, Department of State (Confidential)," Washington, D.C., January 28, 1955, *FRUS* (1955–1957): 23:14.

5. On April 18, 1955, the Bandung Conference opened and lasted for six days, discussing topics ranging from tension between the People's Republic of China and the United States to French influence in North Africa and the Dutch dispute with Indonesia over western Guinea. Twenty-nine nations in Asia and Africa participated in the conference, representing 56 percent of the world population. Of these, seventeen were UN members: Afghanistan, Burma, Egypt, Ethiopia, India, Indonesia, Iran, Iraq, Lebanon, Liberia, Pakistan, Philippines, Saudi Arabia, Syria, Thailand, Turkey, and Yemen. The twelve nations that had not joined the United Nations were Cambodia, Ceylon, Gold Coast, Japan, Jordan, Laos, Libya, Nepal, North Vietnam, Peoples' Republic of China, South Vietnam and Sudan. The National Committee for the Commemoration of the Thirtieth Anniversary of the Asian-African Conference, Jakarta, Indonesia, *Pictorial Record of the Asian-African Conference* (National Committee for the Commemoration, 1985).

6. Kase Toshikazu, *Kase Toshikazu kaisō-roku (ge)* (Yamate Shobō, 1986), 115–16.

7. Shimoda Takezō, *Nihon wa kō shite saisei shita—sengo Nihon gaikō no shōgen (jō)* (Gyōsei Mondai Kenkyūjo, 1984), 202–203.

8. "Memorandum of a Conversation between the Lebanese Ambassador (Malik) and the Secretary of State, Department of State (Secret)," Washington, D.C., May 5, 1955, *FRUS* (1955–1957): 21:97. The same memorandum also included discussion about forming a bloc of five Middle Eastern states—Turkey, Iran, Iraq, Pakistan, and Lebanon—at the conference, which reflected the contemporary sensitivity (or the lack of it) on issues of race, culture, and religion. Malik asserted the Muslim world's pro-Western commitment. According to the memorandum, the two discussed that, apart from Egypt and Syria, the Middle Eastern Muslim world was on the side of the West. This illustrated, they concurred, that Islam, when in concert with the rest of Asia, was likely to lean toward the West, whereas it felt uneasy with the West in acting on its own (ibid., 96).

9. Kase, *Kase Toshikazu kaisō-roku (ge)*, 115.

10. *Japan and the United Nations: Report of a Study Group Set Up by the Japanese Association of International Law*, prepared for the Carnegie Endowment for International Peace (Manhattan Publishing, 1958), 231–33.

11. Gaimu-shō Kokusai Kyōryoku-kyoku Dai-ichi-ka (Ministry of Foreign Affairs, Bureau of International Cooperation, 1st Division), *Kokusai Rengō dai 11 sōkai no jigyō* (Report of the 11th Session of the UN General Assembly) (July 1957): 408–11. Japanese activities at each session of the UN General Assembly are recorded and published in a series under the same title, while the names of the editorial bureau and division within the ministry changes from time to time. For consistency and clarity, this series will be cited as *Kokusai Rengō no jigyō*, with the number of the specific UN session given in the title.

12. Shimoda, *Nihon wa kō shite saisei shita*, 203.

13. Michael Hunt, *Ideology and U.S. Foreign Policy* (Yale University Press, 1987), 165.

14. *Kokusai Rengō no jigyō* (Report of the 15th Session of the UN General Assembly, vol. 1) (June 1961): 186.

15. Ibid., 292.

16. Watanabe Akio, ed., *Sengo Nihon no taigai seisaku—kokusai kankei no hen'yō to Nihon no yakuwari* (Yūhikaku Sensyo, 1985), 132–33, 353.

17. NHK Hōsō Yoron Chōsajo hen (NHK Public Opinion Research Institute, ed.), *Zusetsu sengo yoron-shi* (Pictorial history of postwar public opinions) (Nippon Hōsō Shuppan Kyōkai, 1975), 208–11.

18. Ibid., 184–87.

19. Charles A. Thomson and Walter H. C. Laves, *Cultural Relations and U.S. Foreign Policy* (Indiana University Press, 1963), 152–53, 162.

20. Edward Seidensticker, "The Image," in Herbert Passin, ed., *The United States and Japan* (Prentice-Hall, 1966), 20–21. Seidensticker argued that although the Japanese were not particularly quick to note their own feelings of inferiority and insecurity toward Occidentals, "the race issue may really lie nearer their hearts than any of the other noisy issues [between the United States and Japan]." He analyzed that "feelings about yellow against white must help account for the fact that Chinese nuclear tests brought a far less clamorous response from the Japanese than American tests and even Russian tests had brought" (ibid., 21).

Samuel Huntington, in *The Clash of Civilizations and the Remaking of World Order* (1996), expanded on this notion of ominous racial alliance between Japan and China. Huntington regards the People's Republic of China, along with the Islamic nations, as a source of serious threat that could lead to a global war of civilization against Western dominance. Then, he goes on to discuss the need of Western unity against a possible Asian alliance between Japan and China. Also note that he presents a faithful reproduction of Wilhelm II's "yellow peril" concept a century later. He claims that Russia's relations with the West might stabilize when their views toward China find a mutually satisfactory basis. He refers to the Russian abhorrence of Chinese expansionism in the following manner: "At some point, the 'yellow hordes' which have haunted Russian imagination since the Mongol invasions may again become a reality." See Samuel Huntington, *The Clash of Civilizations and the Remaking of World Order* (Simon and Schuster, 1996), 227, 237, 243, 245. (See also n. 49, below.)

21. Although "economic animal [*ekonomikku animaru*]" had become a household word by 1969, there were examples of use of the term in several popular journals as early as 1967 (e.g., Fujishima Yasusuke, "Nihon-jin wa ekonomikku animaru ka," *Shūkan Yomiuri* [February 11, 1967]). The EC document that contained the notorious slur mentioned in the main text reflected the typical European perception of a lower

standard of living more prevalent in Asia outside Japan, but to the Japanese this was simply another manifestation of their "black sheep" status among the so-called civilized Western societies. *Shōwa sesō ryūkō-go jiten* (Ōbun Sha, 1986), 237, 294–95.

In the late 1960s and early 1970s, several books by Japanese authors supporting such negative views of the Japanese race became bestsellers in Japan, and for some time the country obsessed on the topic of the national inferiority complex almost to the point of masochism. In *Sugao no Nippon* (Futam: Shobō, 1969; translated as *Japan Unmasked* [Charles E. Tuttle, 1969]), Kawasaki Ichirō, a Japanese diplomat in Argentina, stirred a national controversy when he argued that the Japanese are the ugliest and sexually the least attractive race in the world, next to the Pygmies and the Hottentots. *Kachiku-jin Yapū* (Toshi Shuppan Sha, 1970), by Numa Shōzō, is satirical science fiction (with a pornographic twist) about the Yapū, the lowest human race (i.e., the Japanese), a domestic animal tamed and breeded by the whites for their use. For Numa Shōzō's argument on how the Japanese today lived with a traumatic awareness of the white superiority, see "Jinshu-teki rettō-kan ga umi dasu mono," in *Bessatsu Ushio* 17 (Spring 1970): 248–59, in a Special Issue entitled "Nihon no shōrai [Japan's future]."

22. Okazaki Fuminori, *Kokusai ijū mondai* (Nihon Gaisei Gakkai, 1955), 101, passim.

23. For a text of the speech by Foreign Minister Shigemitsu on December 18, 1956, see *Kokusai Rengō no jigyō* (Report of the 11th Session of the UN General Assembly) (July 1957): 411.

24. For a text of the speech by Foreign Minister Fujiyama on September 19, 1957, see *Kokusai Rengō no jigyō* (Report of the 12th Session of the UN General Assembly) (May 1958): 503–504.

25. U. S. Department of Commerce, *Statistical Abstract of the United States, 1959 (80th Annual Edition)*, 92 and 95. Before the 1965 immigration law, there had been no limitation on immigration from the Western Hemisphere.

26. *Laws Applicable to Immigration and Naturalization (edition of 1953), Supplement I* (GPO, 1954). For Japanese reaction see the following articles printed in *Kaigai ijū*, formerly a monthly report of the Overseas Emigration Association (Kaigai Ijū Kyōkai), which changed publishers in February 1954 to the United Assembly of Japan Overseas Associations (Nihon Kaigai Kyōkai Rengō-kai, a forerunner of the Japan International Cooperation Agency (Kokusai Kyōryoku Jigyō-dan): "Beikoku iki imin ni akarui mitōshi [Good prospects for emigration fo America]," *Kaigai ijū*, no. 2 (March 20, 1954): 1; "Beikoku e tokō deki masu [Now you can go to America]," ibid., no. 3 (April 20, 1954): 3; "Mada tokō-sha nashi [Still no departure]," ibid., no. 8 (September 20, 1954): 2.

27. Wakatsuki Yasuo and Suzuki Jōji, *Kaigai ijū seisaku shiron* (Fukumura Shuppan, 1975), 181–84: U.S. Immigration and Naturalization Service, *Annual Report, 1977*, 43.

28. "Beikoku Nanmin-Kyūsai-Hō ni yoru ijū-sha no to-Bei ni tsuite [Report on emigration to the United States under the U.S. Refugee Act]," in *Gaimu-shō happyō shū* (Ministry of Foreign Affairs Bulletin), no. 1 (August 1956): 31–32.

29. Wakatsuki Yasuo and Suzuki Jōji, *Kaigai ijū seisaku shiron*, 800; T. K. Ishi, "Sengo no Nihon-jin no Beikoku ijū: imin no keizai shakai-gaku," *Ijū kenkyū* (March 1983): 21.

30. T. K. Ishi, ibid., 23–25.

31. Wakatsuki Yasuo and Suzuki Jōji, *Kaigai ijū seisaku shiron*, 820–21, 852–57.

32. "Konketsuji o Burajiru e," *Yomiuri shimbun* (evening edition), April 29, 1952, 3; Takasaki Setsuko, "Shiroi ko kuroi ko no kanashimi," *Bungei shunjū* 33, no. 8 (April 1955): 198–205; Sawada Miki, *Kuroi hada to shiroi kokoro*, 239–59 and 297–325.

33. "Hakkō no kora ni imin kyōiku—Burajiru nyūshoku e," *Nihon keizai shimbun*, March 23, 1955, 11.

34. Sawada, *Kuroi hada to shiroi kokoro*, 305–10.

35. "Konketsuji no o-nīsan Amazon e [Big brothers for mixed-blood children depart for Brazil]," *Kaigai ijū*, no. 194 (September 5, 1963): 1; "Genki ni yatteru: Amazon de ninki o hitori-jime—Erizabesu sandāsu hōmu enji [Children of the Elizabeth Sanders Home are doing fine, receive passionate welcome in Amazon]," ibid., no. 221 (October 20, 1965): 2.

36. "Konketsu yōshi wa urarete iru," *Yomiuri shimbun*, July 17, 1957, 9; "Konketsu yōshi no jinshin-baibai ni urazuke ka," *Yomiuri shimbun*, September 8, 1957, 11.

37. "Showa 34 nen-do konketsuji zaiseki jōkyō chōsa shūkei hyō [Statistical tables of mixed-blood children enrolled in schools in 1959]," in Monbu-shō (Ministry of Education), *Konketsuji shidō shiryō* (1960), 157–64.

38. These figures are from the following articles: Hiroshi Wagatsuma, "Mixed-Blood Children in Japan: An Exploratory Story," *Journal of Asian Affairs* 2, no. 1 (Spring 1977): 9; Roberta Levenbach, "Biracial Children in Okinawa," *Christian Century* (November 1972); and William Burkhardt, "Institutional Barriers, Marginality, and Adaptation Among the American-Japanese Mixed Bloods in Japan," *Journal of Asian Studies* 42, no. 3 (May 1983): 519. Burkhardt's article, a sociological analysis of the issue, provides a useful bibliographical list on the issue of Amerasian children in both the United States and Japan. For scholastic analyses of the issues, see Nathan O. Strong, "Patterns of Social Interaction and Psychological Accommodation Among Japan's Konketsuji Population," Ph.D. diss., Department of Anthropology, University of California, Berkeley (1978).

39. The grandmother in the film is a traditional farm woman who is determined to raise her granddaughter as a Japanese farmer, but decides that the best future for her grandson is to be adopted by a wealthy black American family and emigrate to the United States. Kiku, a spunky, sensitive, and strong-willed teenage girl, is determined to fight against all odds to grow up as a proud Japanese. The film portrays their various interactions with local people, some of whom support their endeavors with humor and wisdom, and some who do not. For the complete screenplay of *Kiku to Isamu*, see Mizuki Yōko, *Mizuki Yōko sinario shū* (Eijin Sha, 1978), 233–309; for a view of the film by Mizuki, who wrote the screenplay for this movie, see 310–12. For

her opinion on the issue of mixed-blood children in Japan, see also Mizuki Yōko, "Konketsuji o meguru hitobito [People surrounding the mixed-blood children], *Sekai*, no. 164 (August 1959): 131–33.

40. "Naniga hikō ni hashirase taka—Sandāsu Hōmu no shussin-sha tachi," *Nihon keizai shimbun*, June 7, 1971, 11; Sawada, *Kuroi hada to shiroi kokoro*, 311–16.

41. In October 1977, *Asahi* reported the success story of Takahashi Ryūji, one of the Elizabeth Sanders Home's Amazon-bound "alumni," who eventually became a flight attendant of the Varig Brazilian Airlines and married his colleague, a second-generation Japanese-Brazilian. The article referred to Mr. Takahashi, then a thirty-one-year-old man, as a "konketsuji [mixed-blood child]" because there was no Japanese expression for such a person as an adult. See "Burajiru ni habataku *konketsuji* [A *mixed-blood child* is now spreading his wings over Brazil]" (emphasis added), *Asahi shimbun*, October 23, 1977, 23.

42. "Ao enpitsu," *Asahi shimbun*, August 25, 1975, 19.

43. Ozeki Keiko, *Nihon-jin Keiko—aru konketsu shōjo no shuki* (Bunka Hōsō Shuppan Sha, 1967), an autobiography by a half-black half-Japanese woman, provides a rare view of her adolescent experiences in the 1960s. She narrates the difficulties she encountered in school and in a factory where she became employed after graduating from a junior high school, and she recounts as well her relationships with her various families, friends, dates, and mentors. She met a black American through a mutual friend, married him, and emigrated to the United States.

Almost all the other available references are from the tabloid magazines: "Seijin shita shūsen konketsuji no ai no nayami [Torment of love among the postwar mixed-blood children]," *Asahi geinō*, January 16, 1966; "Konketsu hosutesu: sono honpō na yoru no seikatsu [Mixed-blood hostesses: Their wild nightlife]," ibid., September 17, 1967; "Watashi-tachi wa Nihon-jin [We are Japanese]," *Asahi jānaru*, October 22, 1967.

For reports published in the United States, see Era Bell Thompson, "Japan's Rejected," *Ebony* 22 (September 1967), and "Happy Ending," *Ebony* 23 (July 1968); and Wagatsuma Hiroshi, "Identity Problems of Black Japanese Youth," in Robert I. Rotberg, ed., *The Mixing of Peoples: Problems of Identity and Ethnicity* (Greylock, 1978).

The best most recent account of conditions facing American and Japanese citizens of half-Japanese half-American heritage in the two countries—including both those who trace their interracial roots back to the early twentieth century and those who were born after World War II—is a documentary film, *Doubles: Japan and America's Intercultural Children* (59 min., Film Library, 1995; executive producer-director Regge Life).

44. Enomori Susumu, *Ainu no rekishi: Hokkaidō no hitobito*, vol. 2 (Sanseidō, 1987), 218–26; Yuko BABA, "A Study of Minority-Majority Relations: The Ainu and Japanese in Hokkaido," *Japan Interpreter* 13, no. 1 (Summer 1980): 60–92. For the English works on their civil rights movement, see "Ainu Rights," in "Trends and Topics" section, *Japan Quarterly* 21, no. 3 (July-September 1974): 227–31; Gary Clark Sala,

"Protest and the Ainu of Hokkaido," *Japanese Interpreter* 10, no.1 (Summer 1975): 44–65.

45. Tanaka Hiroshi, *Zai-Nichi gaikoku-jin—hō no kabe, kokoro no kabe* (Iwanami Shinsho, 1991), ch. 5.

46. *Hokkaidō shimbun*, October 22, 1986, quoted in Enomori Susumu, *Ainu no rekishi* 2:226.

47. For the Japanese analysis of the trade dispute in the mid-1980s, with discussion on its racial and cultural dimensions, see n. 3 of the introduction, above.

48. According to "Japanese Automobile and Television Assembly Plants and the Local Communities: County Demographic Correlates," the 1988 study by Japan Pacific Resource Network, a Berkeley-based international educational organization, Japanese firms tended to locate in areas with few blacks and Hispanics. Japanese corporations also showed reluctance to undertake affirmative action programs in the hiring and promotion of these minorities as well as Asian-Americans.

49. Samuel P. Huntington, "The Clash of Civilizations?" *Foreign Affairs* 72, no. 3 (Summer 1993): 22ff. Huntington raises a great doubt about Japan's identity due to its duality. Japan, argues Huntington, is the only non-Western civilization that has fully succeeded in becoming modern without also becoming Western: "Japan has established a unique position for itself as an associate member of the West: it is in the West in some respects but clearly not of the West in important dimensions." At the same time, Japan faces difficulties in creating an economic entity in East Asia comparable to the European one, because of its "cultural differences with these countries." Huntington sees Japan as a civilization without specific identity, belonging to neither the West nor the non-West—an accurate description of Japan's dualism. Huntington also argues: "People on each side allege racism on the other, but at least on the American side the antipathies are not racial but cultural. The basic values, attitudes, behavioral patterns of the two societies could hardly be more different" (ibid.).

Hirano Ken'ichirō denies Huntington's dichotomical view of the world and instead suggests the search for universalism in the age of globalization. He encourages the establishment of discourses on how to solve various frictions caused by interactions of different cultures rather than sensationalizing the clash of civilizations. Hirano encourages instead a search for a path toward a truly universal civilization—global civilization. (Also note Hirano's omission of race from the analysis.) See Hirano Ken'ichirō, "Bunmei no shōtotsu ka bunka no masatsu ka," *Hikaku bunmei* (November 1994): 21–37.

50. For the Japanese literature on the most comprehensive view of Japan's latest minority problems, see *Kōza gaikoku-jin teijū mondai* (Lecture series on the problems facing permanent aliens) (Akashi Shoten, 1996), a four-volume collection of articles discussing sociocultural problems facing permanent aliens in settling in Japan. For the English literature on the relatively comprehensive view of Japan's recent minority problems, see David Coates, Japan Pacific Resource Network, ed., *Shattering*

the Myth of the Homogeneous Society: Minority Issues and Movements in Japan, JPRN Monograph Series (JPRN, 1990).

51. For the latest view on relations between the Japanese and African-Americans, see the documentary film *Struggle and Success: The African-American Experience in Japan* (85 min., Film Library, 1993; executive producer-directorRegge Life)

52. Edward Said, *Culture and Imperialism* (Knopf, 1993), 329–30.

53. The current literature on miscegenation in America focuses on interracial sexual and marital relations in both demographic and legal constraints as well as on eugenics. For a bibliography of recent works on miscegenation, see Peggy Pascoe, "Race, Gender, and Intercultural Relations: The Case of Interracial Marriage," *Frontiers:A Journal of Women Studies* 12, no. 1 (1991): 5–18.

Paul Spickard's *Mixed Blood: Intermarriage and Ethnic Identity in Twentieth-Century America* (University of Wisconsin Press, 1989) has a chapter on intermarriage between American men and Japanese women after World War II and some observations on their mixed-blood children ("Part II. Madam Butterfly Revisited"), but his exclusive use of American sources prevents him from developing a comparative analysis of American *and* Japanese attitudes toward intermarriage and miscegenation.

INDEX

Abe Isoo, 93–94
Acheson, Dean, 46
Ackerman, Edward, 137
Afghanistan, 35
Africa, 33, 47, 201, 203, 205–206, 228n21, 270n54, 277n5
African-Americans: in American society, 145; intermarriage with Japanese, 157, 177; intermarriage with whites, 199; Japanese view of, 94, 166, 192–93, 194, 196, 217, 228n19, 270n53; in occupied Japan, 52, 55–56; in occupied Germany, 183, 272n74
Ainu people, 97, 172–73, 253nn50–51; civil rights movement in Japan, 215–16, 281n44; discrimination in Japan against, 90, 93; SCAP policy toward, 110–11, 253nn50–51
Aiso, John, 56
Allison, John, 78
American GIs, 5, 51, 186, 214; anti-fratization policy and, 60–61; marriage to Japanese women and, 159, 191, 264n89, 272n75; violent behavior by, 85–87
American Joint Committee for

Assisting Japanese-American Orphans, 185–88, 191, 197, 199
Anglo-Saxon: "elite club of," 42; influence in the world, 19; partnership, 17; race, Japanese and, 31–32; supremacy, 166
anti-Americanism, 183; in Japan, 67, 80, 84–85, 189, 196; in the Philippines, 18
ANZUS Pact (1951), 45
Araki Eikichi, 120
Asahi (newspaper): on GI babies, 164; interviews in, 53; on Japanese attitude toward Americans, 81–82; on mixed-blood children in Asia, 176; nonfraternization policy announced in, 60; on nonfraternization regulation, 66–67; on Okinawa repatriation, 111; on overpopulation, 151
Ashida Hitoshi, 24, 30, 116, 133–34
"Asia for the Asiatics." *See* slogans
assimilation: social scientists on, 144–46
Atcheson, George, Jr., 30, 32, 99–103
atomic bomb, 37, 39, 53, 77
Australia, 19, 41, 45, 47–48, 91, 124, 152, 208, 266n17; anti-Japanese sentiment

in, 20, 30, 135; immigration policy of, 127, 138–39, 211

Baba Hideo, 134
Baba Tsunego, 95
baby booms (in Japan), 126
Baldwin, Roger, 127
Bandung Conference (1955), 201–203, 277n5
Bates, Rosalind, 184
Benedict, Ruth, 4, 225n9
Berrigan, Darrell, 265n7
biology, 7; miscegenation and, 165; race and, 3–4, 144, 146, 194
black Americans. See African-Americans
Boas, Franz, 4
Bolton, Frances, 190
Bonin Islands. See Ogasawara Islands
Brazil: emigration to, 133, 151–53, 155, 263n79; mixed-blood children and, 212–13, 215
Britain, 19, 91, 266n17; attitudes toward Japan of, 41–42, 45, 79; imperialism of, 17; Japanese attitudes toward, 23; "white man's pact of," 45–46
Buck, Pearl, 187, 189
Buraku Kenkyūkai (Research Institute of Buraku Problem), 251n1
burakumin: discrimination in Japan, 107–108, 192, 198; SCAP policy toward, 108–10
Burma, 19, 35, 43, 152, 176, 201; Burmese, 18
Byrnes, James, 101

Canada, 19, 124, 127, 152, 209, 216, 266n17; immigration policy of, 211, 138
cartoons: "Blondie," 73; "Anmitsu Hime (Princess Anmitsu)," 73; "Pusan," 177, 270n54

Castle, William, 37–38
Celler, Emanuel, 34
censorship, 62–66, 164, 256n2; Civil Censorship Detachment (CCD), 63–64, 256n2; postpublication, 73; racial politics and, 49
Ceylon, 35, 140, 201
Chang Du-sik, 116
Chiang Kai-shek, 92
children: IQ tests of, 169–73, 264nn31–32; near U.S. military bases, 85–87, 179, 195; of mixed-blood in Japan, 159, 163, 168, 175–212 passim, 270n53, 272n76, 273n80, 274n84, 281n39; orphans in Japan, 161–63, 167, 185, 212–13, 265–66nn11–17, 271n61
China, 43; attitudes of, toward Japan, 41; sinocentric world concept, 226n12; U.S. immigration policy toward, 33–35, 41, 146–47
Chinese people: in Japan, 90, 215–16; Japanese attitudes toward, 92–94, 166, 168; SCAP policy toward, in Japan, 102, 112–113
Chōren (the Korean Resident League in Japan), 114–15
Chōu En-lai, 202
Christianity and Christians: church activities of (in Japan), 163; church activities of (in U.S.), 184–85; Japanese emigration and, 129–30; Roman Catholic activities, 88, 137–38, 191, 199
CIA. See Constitutional Investigation Association
climatology, 149–50
Coffe, James, 39–40
Cold War: improvement of race relations during, 33, 123; Japan's racial identity in, 12, 44–46, 121; San Francisco Peace Conference and, 43;

mixed-blood children and, 161, 190.
   See also propaganda
communism: at the Bandung Conference, 201–202; Japan Communist
   Party, 135, 163, 196, 254–55*n*67; Japanese occupation and, 38, 45, 70, 76,
   115–16; overseas adoption and, 183–
   84; propaganda of, 33, 75; second
   world of, 47; U.S. immigration
   policies and, 148, 191
Compton, Wilson, 31
Congress, U.S.: House Territorial
   Subcomitee, 141; Judd bill, 35–38;
   142–44, 261*n*59; Judiciary Committees on Immigration and Naturalization, 35, 146–47, 234*n*41; naturalization legislation and, 260*n*50,
   261*n*59; Senate Committee on
   Armed Services, 245*n*87; Senate
   Committee on Foreign Relations,
   245*n*87; Senate Committee on the
   Judiciary, 146–47, 235*n*50. *See also*
   legislation, U.S
Constitutional Investigation Association (CIA), 94–98, 103–105, 251*n*41
Cook, Milton, 40
cosmopolitanism, 22, 123, 128, 131, 133,
   192, 212, 215; cosmopolitan nation,
   199
Cowles, Fleur, 75
cultural: anthropology and anthropologists, 4; exchange, 27, 73–75;
   nation (*bunka kokka*), 131, 136;
   relativism, 4–5, 224*n*7
culture: differences between U.S. and
   Japan, 48, 282*n*49; race and, 4–5, 9,
   49–88
Culture and Imperialism (Said), 219

dai-sangoku-jin (the third national), 114
Dazai Hirokuni, 188

Delany, Hubert, 189
democratization of Japan, 32, 50–51, 54,
   62, 110
discrimination: institutional (in U.S.),
   225–26*n*11; sociological studies of (in
   Japan), 194
Dore, Ronald, 228*n*21
dualistic racial identity (Japanese),
   11–12, 16, 22, 31, 47, 51, 112, 160, 196,
   203, 218–19, 228*n*21, 237*n*1; absence of
   racism in public memory and, 49–
   50, 88; Dulles, and, 41; Huntington
   on, 282*n*49; miscegenation and, 160;
   U.S. immigration and, 124, 149
Dulles, John Foster, 40–42, 44, 149;
   Bandung Conference and, 201, 202;
   cultural exchange programs and,
   73–74; post-Occupation policies
   and, 79

education: exchange programs for, 74,
   244*n*65; for mixed-race children,
   177–83, 191–93; Koreans in Japan
   and, 114–16, 248*n*7
Eichelberger, Robert, 37, 117
Eisenhower, Dwight, 205
emigration. *See* immigration
Endō, Shūsaku, 88
eta. *See burakumin*
ethnicity, 144–45, 197; origin of term,
   260*n*57
eugenics, 7, 123, 126, 168
exclusion laws, 9, 11, 20, 33–35, 92, 127–
   28, 138, 141, 229*n*22, 234*n*41, 247*n*3.
   See also immigration; legislation

Farrington, Joseph, 34
films, 70; about World War II, 77;
   Above and Beyond, 77; *An American
   Guerrilla in the Philippines*, 77;
   Bataan, 77; cultural exchange

programs and, 75–77; *Flying Leathernecks*, 77; *Futari no hitomi* (Eyes of the Two Girls), 76; *Itsu-itsu made mo* (Forever), 76; *Japanese War Bride* (*Higashi wa higashi*), 76, 84; *Kiku to Isamu* (Kiku and Isamu), 214, 280*n*39; *Know Your Enemy—Japan*, 57; *Konketsuji* (Mixed-Blood Children), 195; *Our Job in Japan*, 55, 57; Motion Picture Association of America (MPAA), 77; *Rashomon*, 76; *Task Force*, 77; *They Were Expendable*, 76; *Thirty Seconds Over Tokyo*, 77; *Tokyo File 212*, 75, 83; *Yassa Mossa*, 186, 195. *See also* propaganda

Finucane, James, 184

fraternization (between American and Japanese): Japanese attitude toward, 52, 58; SCAP attitude toward, 21, 50, 58–63, 71–73, 159, 241*n*29

Fujiwara Michiko, 176, 177–78

Fujiyama Aiichirō, 202, 209

Furuhashi Hironoshin, 72

Furuya Yoshio, 165, 168

gaijin (whites in Japan), 61, 81–82, 114

Gallop, Herbert, 187–88

Gascoigne, Alvary, 41

Gearhart, Bertrand, 34–35

General Agreement on Tariffs and Trade (GATT), 87, 209

"gentleman's agreement," 124, 156

Germany, 23, 24, 27, 87, 244*n*65; immigration overseas of, 25–26, 126–27, 133, 256*n*7; mixed-blood children in, 183, 190, 197, 272*n*74, 275*n*110; Nazi racial theory, 148; nonfraternization policy in, 21, 59–60

Giles, Barney, 256*n*1

Great Britain. *See* Britain

Greater East Asian Co-Prosperity Sphere, 8, 11, 44, 140

hakkō ichiu. *See* slogans

Hasbrouck, Sherman V., 57

Hase Shin'ichi, 130

Hashizume Shirō, 72

Hatoyama Ichirō, 202

hattō-shin and *hattō-shin bijin*, 174–75

Hawaii: Japanese views of, 125, 152; race relations in, 141–42, 259–60*nn*46–49

Hawley, Franklin, 190

Hayashi Fumio, 64

Hayashi Jōji, 135

Herndon, Richard, 78

Higashikuni Naruhiko, 54, 99–100

Hirabayashi Taiko, 177, 270*n*53

Hirano Ken'ichirō, 282*n*49

Hirohito, Emperor: 52, 138; meeting with MacArthur, 137; renunciation of divinity, 104

Hokkaidō Ainu, Association of the, 110

Hokkaidō Utari Kyōkai, 216

Holocaust, 3, 15

"honorary whites": Japanese as, 10–11, 13, 16, 40, 206, 208; Japanese as "honorary Westerners," 44, 219

Horie Tadao, 192

Horikiri Zenjirō, 102

Hunt, Michael, 8

Huntington, Samuel, 218, 278*n*20, 282*n*49

Huston, Cloyce K., 38, 43, 140

Iguchi Sadao, 202

Ikeda Hayato, 69

Imanaka Tsugumaro, 95, 98

immigration, Japan: after World War II, 27, 218–19, 254*n*79; from Korea, 114–16, 248*n*7

immigration, U.S., 6–7; adoption

policies and, 183–91; from China, 33; from Germany, 256n7; from Japan, 10–11, 25, 123–58, 208, 237n1; improved policy of, 12; moral inconsistency and, 92. *See also* exclusion laws; legislation; naturalization laws

Imperial Rescript (1946), 104

India, 201, 244n65, 266n17; immigration to the U.S. from, 34–35; Japanese engineers emigrating to, 140; San Francisco Peace Conference and, 43–44; Tokyo War Crimes trial and, 19

Indonesia, 35, 150, 152, 162, 176, 201

Inoue Tetsujirō, 269n38

Inouye Kaoru, 268n38

International Military Tribunal for the Far East. *See* Tokyo War Crimes Trial

interracial marriage, 8, 146, 156–58. *See also* miscegenation

Inui, Kiyo Sue, 144

Iriye Akira, 2, 4, 224–25n8, 247n4

Ishibashi Tanzan, 136

Ishikawa Tatsuzō, 84–85

Itaya Junsuke, 133

Itō Kinuko, 174. *See also hattoshin bijin*

Iwabuchi Tetsuo, 95–96

Iwakura mission (1871–73), 10, 227–28n9

Iwasaki Yatarō, 163

Japan: Americanization of, 5–6; economic depression in (1947–48), 125–26; economic recovery of, 25, 87, 133–34, 140, 206; mixed-blood children in, 159, 163, 168, 175–212 passim, 270n53, 272n76, 273n84, 281n39; overseas markets and business activities of, 28–29, 126, 128, 208–209, 212; U.S. occupation of (*see under* Occupation)

Japanese: racial pride and, 17, 90, 104; racial superiority ideology of, 3, 18, 20, 21–22, 41, 104, 109, 236n65

Japanese American Citizens League (JACL), 147

Japanese American Civil Liberty Union, 210

Japanese-Americans: in Hawaii, 130, 150; in occupied Japan, 66; in the U.S., 68, 144–46, 153, 242n50; Nisei (second-generation Japanese-Americans), 6, 56, 172–73, 157

Japanese constitution, 89–122; CIA draft of, 95–96, 103–104; gender issues in; 89, 96, 105–106, 248n13, 271n66, 251–52nn44–45; MacArthur draft of, 105–106; Matsumoto draft of, 105; No War Clause of, 82, 89; "race" in, 96–97, 105–107, 248–49n13, 251–52nn44–45

Japanese Diet: constitutional debate by, 106; emigration and, 133–36, 152–53; mixed-blood children and, 177–78, 198–99; on the Korean minority issue, 119; tour of U.S. (1950), 39–40

Japanese government: Ministry of Education, 115, 181, 191, 193, 214; Ministry of Home Affairs, 69, 102; Ministry of Justice, 120, 181, 271n66; Ministry of Labor, 198, 213; Ministry of Welfare, 150, 161, 164, 171, 178, 180, 188, 191; Prime Minister's Office, 155. *See also* Ministry of Foreign Affairs

Jaranilla, Delfin, 19

Jim Crow, 33, 52, 56

Johnson, Mordecai, 189

Johnson, Olin, 40

Jones, E. Stanley, 139

Judd, Walter, 35—38, 142–44. *See also* Judd bill (*under* Congress, U.S.)

Kagawa Toyohiko, 129, 139

Kaigai Ijū Kyōkai (Overseas Emigration

Association), 128, 130–31, 134, 136–37, 149, 150

Kaigai Tokō Gijutsu-sha Zenkoku Renmei (National League of Technicians for Overseas Emigration), 136

Kaji Wataru, 116

Kanzaki Kiichi, 144

Kanzaki Kiyoshi, 191–92

Kasagi Shizuko, 76, 125

Kase Toshikazu, 23, 202–203

Katō Michio, 150

Kawabata Yasunari, 206

Kawasaki Ichirō, 279*n*21

Kempō Kenyūkai. *See* Constitutional Investigation Association (CIA)

Kennan, George, 38, 254*n*53

Kennedy, John F., 189

Kikuchi Yoshirō, 133

Kitabayashi Tōma, 167

Kiyose Ichirō, 121, 127

Kluckhohn, Frank, 52

Knowland, William, 234*n*43, 272*n*76

Koga Yukiyoshi, 194

Kojima, Nobuo, 88

Konoe Fumimaro, 99–102

Korea, 43, 47, 57: diplomatic relations with Japan, 119, 196; Japanese colonialism in, 7, 11–12;

Koreans: Japanese view of, 93, 166, 169; legal status of, in Japan, 27, 90, 215–16; SCAP policy toward, in Japan, 102–103, 112–21

Korean War, 87,

Kosaka Zentarō, 205

Kuni no ayumi (Our Nation's Progress) (textbook), 115

Kuno Yasu, 150

Kurosawa, Akira, 76

LaCerda, John, 57

legislation, Japanese: Alien Registration Law (1952), 120; Basic Law of Education (1947), 116; on immigration and alien registration, 255*n*81; Immigration Control Law (1952), 120; National Engenics Law (1941), 126; Nationality Law (1899), 26; Nationality Law (1950), 120, 180; Nationality Law (1984), 271*n*66

legislation, U.S.: Admission of Orphans Adopted by United States Citizens (1953), 190; on Chinese immigration, 33–34, 247*n*3; on Indian and Filipino immigration, 34; Civil Rights Act (1965), 42, 199; Hart-Cellar Act (1965), 211; Immigration Act (1924), 11, 25, 36, 123, 156, 184, 229*nn*22–23, 247*n*3; Immigration Act (1965), 211; Information and Educational Exchange Act (1948), 74; Judd bill, 35–38, 142–44, 261*n*59; McCarran-Walter Act (1952), 44, 123, 146–48, 184–85, 198–99, 209, 272*n*75; on miscegenation, 160, 199–200, 227*n*14, 264*n*2; on marriage to brides racially ineligible to enter the U.S., 156–58; Refugee Relief Act (1953), 190, 199, 210. *See also* Congress, U.S.; Supreme Court decisions

Lévi-Strauss, Claude, 4

Lewis, Reed, 147

Life, Regge, 281*n*43, 283*n*51

Lippman, Walter, 256*n*2

Lovett, Robert, 121

Lynch, George, 40

MacArthur, Douglas: arrival at Atsugi Air Base, 51; attitude toward Japanese, 58, 83; fraternization orders of, 60, 71; Japanese attitude toward, 53–55, 240*n*20; on Japanese constitution, 100; meets with Emperor

Hirohito, 137; on the nature of Occupation, 19, 38–39, 256*n*1; on Okinawa, 254*n*53;

MacArthur Constitution. *See* Japanese constitution

Mahan, Alfred Thayer, 9

Maki Ken'ichi, 167

Makins, Roger, 201

Malik, Charles, 201

Manchuria (also Mancbukuo), 123, 127, 129–30, 152, 154; Jews in, 229–30*n*24

Masaoka, Mike, 147, 210

Masland, John W., Jr., 110

Maslow, Will, 147

Matsui Michio, 135

Matsumoto Committee. *See* Japanese constitution

Matsumoto Jiichirō, 109–110

Matsumoto Jōji, 100

Matsuoka Komakichi, 131–32, 133

McCarran, Pat, 147

McCarthy, Joseph, 40

McClurkin, Robert, 187

McCormick, Robert, 139

McGrath, Howard, 143

Mead, Margaret, 4

Meiji constitution. *See* Japanese constitution

Mei Ju-an, 18

"melting pot," 6, 123, 141, 145

Michener, James, 187, 197–98

Miyoshi, Masao, 219

Miller, George, 40

Mills, Verent H., 184

Ministry of Foreign Affairs (Japanese government), 23–25, 29–30, 204, 206; emigration and, 154–55, 210, 212; Executive Research Committee on problems Concerning a Peace Treaty, 24–28, 30, 128; racial equality and, 89, 132. *See also* Japanese government

Minobe Tatsukichi, 101

miscegenation, 159–200; in American society, 8; eugenics and, 168, 283*n*53; in films, 84; in Japanese society, 8; *Stars and Stripes* on, 263*n*86; statutes prohibiting, 42, 160, 199–200, 227*n*14, 264*n*2; U.S. immigration and, 146

Misora Hibari, 76

Miyamoto Inosuke, 110

Miyasaka Kunito, 153

Miyoshi Masao, 219

Mizunoe Takiko, 66

Mizuno Kon, 68, 242–43*n*50

Morimizu Shuntarō, 130

Morito Tatsuo, 65, 95–96, 116–17

Morton, Thurston, 189

Murobuse Takanobu, 95–96

Murphy, Robert, 196–97

Mutsuhito, Emperor, 228*n*20

Nakasone Yasuo, 216–17, 219

Nasser, Gamal Abdel, 202

National Police Reserve (of Japan), 82

National Self-Defense Force (of Japan), 82

naturalization laws: in Japan, 118–20, 271*n*66; in United States, 26, 34, 92, 123, 142, 234–35*nn*41–50. *See also* immigration; legislation

Nehru, Jawaharlal, 202

Nepal, 35,

New Guinea, 35; Japanese emigration plan to, 138–40, 149–51, 152

New York Times: editorial on Asian attitudes (1946), 18; on Japanese people, 57; Kase Toshihiko interview in (1945), 23

New Zealand, 41, 45, 47–48

Nimitz, Chester, 59

Nisei. *See* Japanese-Americans

Norman, E. H., 103

Nosaka Akiyuki, 68
Numa Shozo, 279*n*21

O'Brien, Margaret, 76
Occupation, 219; democratization program in, 110; duration of, 124, 256*n*1; Japanese diplomatic recognition during, 49, 125; mistreatment of Japanese during, 57–58; public health program and, 126; segregation and, 22, 55–62; termination of, 42; two stages of, 16; U.S. wartime planning for, 16
Occupation forces: national and racial components of, 20–21; travel in Japan and, 72
O'Doul, Frank "Lefty," 73
Ōe, Kenzaburō, 87–88
OECD (Organization for Economic Cooperation and Development), 206
Ogasawara Islands, 196
Ogura Seitarō, 150
Okinawa (and the Okinawans): Japanese discrimination toward, 97, 111–12; SCAP policy toward, 110–11, 253*n*53; U.S. military in, 45, 57, 214. *See also* Ryūkyū and Ryūkyūans
Ōno Katsumi, 134
opinion polls. *See* public opinion
Orphans Relief Society, International, 186
Overseas Emigration Association. *See* Kaigai Ijū Kyōkai
Ōya Sōichi, 175
Ozawa Case. *See* Supreme Court decisions
Ozeki Keiko, 281*n*43

Pacific Stars and Stripes, 71
Pakistan, 35, 140, 201, 244*n*65
Pal, Radhabinod, 19
Pan-Asianism: Bandung Conference and, 201, 203; censorship and, 62; of Japan, 12, 34, 95, 99, 230*n*24; racial pride and, 17, 90; after World War II, 27, 45, 121, 140
Paris Peace Conference (1919), 11, 41, 91, 205; Versaille Treaty, 24, 27, 44, 118; the Covenant, 91
Passin, Herbert, 65
paternalism: colonial, 92; white, 19, 83
paternity policies, 162, 180
peace treaty: Dulles and, 41–42; Japanese attempt at, 30; Japanese emigration and, 151; SCAP rejection of, 30
Peace Treaty, Executive Research Committee on Problems Concerning. *See* Ministry of Foreign Affairs (Japanese government)
Pearl Harbor, 33, 53, 125, 238*n*7
Pelly, Thomas, 196
Perry, Matthew, 8–9, 77–78
Philippines (and the Filipinos), 18, 19, 34–35, 92–93, 142, 152, 176, 244*n*65, 266*n*17
physical traits: Japanese Westernization and, 144, 172–73, 228*n*20, 242*n*50; orphan adoptions and, 273*n*76; perceived U.S. superiority and, 67–68, 132, 166, 169, 177, 206–207; racism and, 5–6, 50; sporting activities and, 174–75, 270*n*44; tropical climates and, 149–51
Pilcher, James B., 189–90
Pittsburgh Courier, on black troops in Japan, 52, 56
Potsdam Declaration, 23, 25, 55, 120
President's Commission on Civil Rights, 33
President's Commission on Immigration and Naturalization, 148
propaganda: American racism and, 33; immigration laws and, 34, 150; Japa-

nese wartime, 11, 89, 92; during Occupation, 21, 70–71, 75; Tokyo War Crimes Trial as, 19; in U.S., 244n66; wartime animosity and, 2. *See also* Cold War; films; slogans

prostitution and prostitutes, 57, 60, 69–70, 86, 168

public opinion, in Japan: on overpopulation and overseas emigration, 136, 151–52; on mixed-blood children, 179; on the Japanese racial quality, 206;

public opinion, in U.S.: Gallup poll on fraternization with German girls, 59–60

race: anthropological view of, 4, 225n9; and culture, 49–88; as diplomatic tool, 16; Japanese words for, 96; mutual public memory of, 49–50; nature of, described, 2–3, 194; vs. racism, 224n4

racial equality: Japanese colonial subjects and, 27, 90, 198; Japanese constitution and, 89–122; Japanese emigration and, 131–33; Japanese peace treaty drafts and, 28–30; postwar diplomacy and, 23; UN and, 17

racial hierarchy, 9, 12, 31, 90

racism: biology and, 4, 144, 146, 194; Japanese recognition of American, 71, 81; mutual, 8, 15–16, 48, 49, 90–91; 224n8; scholarly trends on, 3–4, 224n5; after World War II, 1, 4, 7, 121–22, 217

Recreation and Amusement Association (RAA), 70. *See also* prostitution and prostitutes

Ridgeway, Matthew B., 79

Riesman, David, 260n57

Rifkind, Simon, 147

Rikkōkai, 129

Rockefeller, John D., III, 74; Mrs. Rockefeller, 187; Rockefeller Foundation, 187

Roest, Pieter R., 251n41

Roosevelt, Eleanor, 17, 187–88

Roosevelt, Franklin, 99, 247n3

Roosevelt, Theodore, 9, 38, 183

Rowell, Milo E., 103–04

Rusk, Dean, 44, 187

Russia. *See* the Soviet Union

Ryūkyū (and Ryūkyūans), 42, 90, 93. *See also* Okinawa

Said, Edward, 219

Sakanishi Shiho, 64

Saltonstall, Laverett, 261n59

Sams, Crawford, 161–62

Sandiford, Peter, 169–70

San Francisco conference (1945), 17

San Francisco Peace Conference (1951), 42, 81, 119

San Francisco Peace Treaty (1951), 1, 42–43, 81, 118–20, 204

Sanger, Margaret, 258n36

Sasaki Sōichi, 100–101

Satō Eisaku, 206, 211

Saturday Evening Post: on American-Japanese relations, 81–82; on Japanese orphanages, 161–62

Sauvy, Alfred, 46–47

Sawada Miki, 163–64, 176, 178, 188–90, 212–15, 265nn11–12

Sawada Renzō, 189, 265n11

Scalapino, Robert, 78

SCAP. *See* Supreme Commander for the Allied Powers

Seattle Times (newspaper), 196

Sebald, William, 39, 46, 71, 118, 147

Seidensticker, Edward, 61, 208, 278n20

Sekigawa Hideo, 196

Seki Kazuo, 167

Shidehara Kijūrō, 24, 100, 105

Shigemitsu Mamoru, 24, 204, 209

Shimizu Ikutarō, 166–67, 168

Shimoda Takezō, 24

Shinagawa Fujio, 267*n*31

Shishi Bunroku, 186

Sirota, Beate, 107, 251*n*41

slogans: "Asia for the Asians" slogans, 18, 44, 48, 202; emigration and, 154; *hakkō ichiu* slogan, 11

Smith, Elmer R., 145–46

Sone Eki, 119

songs: on Japanese images of overseas emigration, 125

Soviet Union, 19, 37, 43, 110, 266*n*17; constitution of, 97; propaganda by, 148, 190; Soviet-Japanese Joint Declaration (1955), 204; view of U.S.-Japanese relations, 237*n*74

Spellman, Francis (Cardinal), 138

sports activities: as fraternization, 53, 72–73; Olympic games, 206; physical traits and, 174–75, 270*n*44

State, U.S. Department of, 21: cultural exchange programs and, 75; immigration legislation and, 35, 36; on orphans in Japan, 185–87, 191; peace treaty with Japan and, 38–39; "white man's pact" of, 45; World War II films and, 77

State-War-Navy Coordinating Committee (SWNCC), 21, 101; "Reorientation of the Japanese," 32; secret reports from, 104

Suga Tadamichi, 192

Sugimori Kōjirō, 95–96, 98–99, 103

Sukarno, Achmed, 201, 276*n*1

Sunama Ichirō, 135

Sung Tack Whang, 184

Supreme Commander for the Allied Powers (SCAP), 16, 18: on attitude of Japanese, 58–59; censorship and, 66; democratization program of, 110; education in Japan and, 115; Japanese constitution and, 95–96, 99, 102–107; on Japanese overseas expansion, 137; Japanese supplications and, 54–55; Judd bill and, 37; Koreans and, 112–15, 117–19; on marriage of military personnel, 156–58; nonfraternization policy of, 50, 58–63, 159; Occupation and, 21, 49, 81; orphaned children and, 189, 265*n*11; racial equality and, 89–90; rejection of Japanese peace treaty, 30; termination of Japanese diplomatic rights and, 24; U.S. immigration and, 129–32, 134

Supreme Court decisions: of California, *Perez v. Lippold*, 160; Ozawa Takao case, 11, 229*n*22

Suzuki Yasuzō, 95–98, 103

Suzuki Yoshio, 117

Swing, Joseph M., 110

Switzerland, 23, 54. 207

Taft, Robert, 19

Taft-Katsura Agreement (1905), 92

Taisho democracy movement, 22, 95

Takada Masami, 164

Takahashi Makoto, 110

Takahashi Ryūji, 281*n*41

Takahashi Yoshio, 268*n*38

Takano Iwasaburō, 95–97

Takasaki Setsuko, 198, 212–13

Takasaki Tatsunosuke, 202

Takeshita Seiki, 178

Tanaka Hisao, 198–99

Tanaka Kan'ichi, 169, 172–73, 267–68*nn*31–32

Tawara Haruji, 152–53

Taylor, Philip, 140

teacher's union (in Japan), 179, 193

Teeling, William, 139

Terman, Lewis M., 170

Thorpe, Elliot R., 18

three-world theory (*tiers monde*), 46–48, 236–37*n*71

Tobey, Charles, 40

Tokonami Keiko, 188

Tokonami Tokuji, 134

Tokyo War Crimes Trials, 127, 231*n*9; Eurocentrism of, 18–19; Japanese defense at, 121–22; Japanese treatment of prisoners of war and, 20, 231*n*13; racial segregation at, 61

Tomabechi Gizō, 136

Toriya Torao, 150, 259*n*39, 262*n*72

Truman, Harry: on immigration, 127, 147–48; on racial equality in military, 56; on racial equality in UN charter, 17; on a peace treaty with Japan, 39

Uemura Tamaki, 129

Umino Kōtoku, 269*n*38

UNESCO, on racism, 3–4, 15, 224*n*6

United Nations (UN): Economic Commission for Asia and the Far East (ECAFE), 140; founding of, 17; human rights and, 15; international migration programs and, 127, 208–209; Japan admission to, 203–204; Japanese activities and, 277*n*11; UN charter, 15, 17, 202, 205

United States: census of, 6–7, 142–43, 146; Japanization of, 5, 217; military bases in Japan, 51–52, 78–80, 85, 245*n*80; overseas adoptions and, 183–91; post-Occupation control over Japan, 44–45; racial segregation in, 33; racial thinking and, 1–13

U.S.-Japanese Intellectual Exchange, 187

U.S.-Japan Security Treaty (1951), 43–45, 80, 82, 136, 207

Vargas, Getúlio Dornelles, 152–54

Vietnam, 82; Vietnam War, 214

Vitousek, Roy, 141

Wainwright, Jonathan M., 20, 256*n*1

Wakatsuki Yasuo, 154

Walker, Gordon, 52

Walsh, Edmund, 138

Walter, Francis, 147, 187, 199

Wang Ching-wei, 24

War Brides, 157, 264*nn*87–89

Watanabe Akio, 25

Webb, William, 19

White, Cecil, 157

"White Man's Burden," 17, 93

Whitney, Courtney, 30

Wildes, Harry E., 251*n*41

Wilkins, Roy, 189

Wilson, Woodrow, 17, 91; Japanese Wilsonianism, 23, 94, 98; Wilsonianism, 2, 43

Willoughby, Charles, 56

Witty, P. A., 169

Wong, Sean H., 261*n*59

world expositions, 93, 237*n*1

Wright, Richard, 177, 276*n*1

Yamaguchi Yoshiko (aka Li Hsiang-lan or Shirley Yamaguchi), 76, 84

yellow peril, 34, 45, 129, 138, 207, 234*n*43, 278*n*20

Yokoyama Taizo, 177

Yomiuri (newspaper): on Japanese emigration, 130; on Korean schools in Japan, 117; nonfraternization policy announced in, 60; U.S. immigration laws and, 127

Yoshida Shigeru, 43–44, 75, 109, 118, 119, 135, 236*n*65

Yukawa Hideki, 74

STUDIES OF THE EAST ASIAN INSTITUTE

SELECTED TITLES

Japan's Total Empire: Manchuria and the Culture of Wartime Imperialism by Louise Young (Berkeley: University of California Press, 1997)

Troubled Industries: Confronting Economic Change in Japan by Robert Uriu (Ithaca: Cornell University Press, 1996)

Tokugawa Confucian Education: The Kangien Academy of Hirose Tansō (1782–1856) by Marleen Kassel (Albany, N.Y.: State University of New York Press, February 1996)

The Dilemma of the Modern in Japanese Fiction by Dennis C. Washburn (New Haven: Yale University Press, 1995)

The Final Confrontation: Japan's Negotiations with the United States, 1941, edited by James W. Morley (New York: Columbia University Press, 1994)

Landownership Under Colonial Rule: Korea's Japanese Experience, 1900–1935 by Edwin H. Gragert (Honolulu: University of Hawaii Press, 1994)

Japan's Foreign Policy After the Cold War: Coping with Change, Gerald L. Curtis, ed. (Armonk, N.Y.: M. E. Sharpe, 1993)

The Writings of Kōda Aya, a Japanese Literary Daughter by Alan Tansman (New Haven: Yale University Press, 1993)

The Poetry and Poetics of Nishiwaki Junzaburō: Modernism in Translation by Hosea Hirata (Princeton: Princeton University Press, 1993)

Social Mobility in Contemporary Japan by Hiroshi Ishida (Stanford: Stanford University Press, 1993)

Sowing the Seeds of Change: Chinese Students, Japanese Teachers, 1895–1905 by Paula S. Harrell (Stanford: Stanford University Press, 1992)

Explaining Economic Policy Failure: Japan and the 1969–1971 International Monetary Crisis by Robert Angel (New York: Columbia University Press, 1991)

Suicidal Narrative in Modern Japan: The Case of Dazai Osamu by Alan Wolfe (Princeton: Princeton University Press, 1990)

Financial Politics in Contemporary Japan by Frances Rosenbluth (Ithaca: Cornell University Press, 1989)

Education in Japan by Richard Rubinger and Edward Beauchamp (New York: Garland, 1989)

Neighborhood Tokyo by Theodore C. Bestor (Stanford: Stanford University Press, 1989)

Aftermath of War: Americans and the Remaking of Japan, 1945–1952 by Howard B. Schonberger (Kent, Ohio: Kent State University Press, 1989)

Japan and the World, 1853–1952: A Bibliographic Guide to Recent Scholarship in Japanese Foreign Relations by Sadao Asada (New York: Columbia University Press, 1988)

Remaking Japan: The American Occupation as New Deal by Theodore Cohen, edited by Herbert Passin (New York: The Free Press, 1987)

The Japanese Way of Politics by Gerald L. Curtis (New York: Columbia University Press, 1988)

Urban Japanese Housewives: At Home and in the Community by Anne E. Imamura (Honolulu: University of Hawaii Press, 1987)

Japan's Modern Myths: Ideology in the Late Meiji Period by Carol Gluck (Princeton: Princeton University Press, 1985)

Japanese Culture by H. Paul Varley, 3d edn., revised (Honolulu: University of Hawaii Press, 1984)

Japan Erupts: The London Naval Conference and the Manchurian Incident, edited by James W. Morley (New York: Columbia University Press, 1984)

State and Diplomacy in Early Modern Japan by Ronald Toby (Princeton: Princeton University Press, 1983; paperback rpt., Stanford: Stanford University Press, 1991)

Private Academies of Tokugawa Japan by Richard Rubinger (Princeton: Princeton University Press, 1982)

Tanaka Giichi and Japan's China Policy by William F. Morton (Folkestone, England: Dawson, 1980; New York: St. Martin's Press, 1980)

The Fateful Choice: Japan's Advance into Southeast Asia, edited by James W. Morley (New York: Columbia University Press, 1980)

Patterns of Japanese Policymaking: Experiences from Higher Education by T. J. Pempel (Boulder, Colo.: Westview, 1978)

Contemporary Japanese Budget Politics by John Creighton Campbell (Berkeley: University of California Press, 1977)

Japanese International Negotiating Style by Michael Blaker (New York: Columbia University Press, 1977)

Insei: Abdicated Sovereigns in the Politics of Late Heian Japan by G. Cameron Hurst (New York: Columbia University Press, 1975)

Shiba Kōkan: Artist, Innovator, and Pioneer in the Westernization of Japan by Calvin L. French (Tokyo: Weatherhill, 1974)